LANDSCAPE DESIGN & REVOLUTION

in Ireland and the United States, 1688–1815

LANDSCAPE DESIGN & REVOLUTION

in Ireland and the United States, 1688–1815

Finola O'Kane

PAUL MELLON CENTRE FOR STUDIES IN BRITISH ART

DISTRIBUTED BY YALE UNIVERSITY PRESS • NEW HAVEN AND LONDON

For my father, Philip

First published in 2023 by the Paul Mellon Centre for Studies in British Art
16 Bedford Square, London, WC1B 3JA
paul-mellon-centre.ac.uk

ISBN 978-1-913107-38-3 HB
Library of Congress Control Number: 2022949509

British Library Cataloguing-in-Publication Data
A catalogue record for this book is available from the British Library

Designed by Catherine Bankhurst
Origination by DL Imaging
Printed in Wales by Gomer Press

COVER IMAGE: Benjamin H. Latrobe, 'View to the North from the Lawn at Mount Vernon',
Sketchbook II, 16 July 1797, Maryland Historical Society, Object ID 1960.108.1.2.10

FRONTISPIECE: Detail of Fig. 82. Edward Savage, 'View of Mount Vernon from the North',
*c.*1797, Courtesy of Mount Vernon Ladies' Association

Contents

Acknowledgements

Little scholarship can be accomplished without archives and their guardians. This book began in Georgetown in the gardens and library of Dumbarton Oaks, where a research fellowship and the resources and staff of that institution of Harvard University enabled me to study many of the American landscapes discussed in this book. Fellow scholars were inordinately patient with my questions and presented me with many more, while also steadying my more speculative flights. I am grateful to John Beardsley, Mirka Beneš, Lawrence Buell, Maggie Cao, Anatole Tchikine, Jan Ziolkowski and particularly Christine Ruane. Anne Burnham, Emily Cooperman, John Dixon Hunt, the late Rolf Loeber, Magda Stouthamer-Loeber, Therese O'Malley and the Dodd family made the United States a welcoming and endlessly fascinating home from home. I am also indebted to the staff of Bowdoin College Library, the Historical Society of Pennsylvania, the Huntington Library, the South Carolina Historical Society, the Gibbes Museum of Art, Georgia State Archives, the Library of Congress, the National Library of Jamaica, the Bibliothèque Nationale de France, Archives Nationales de l'Outre-mer, the National Library of Ireland, the National Archives of Ireland, the National Museums of Northern Ireland, the Irish Architectural Archive, the library of Trinity College Dublin and the British Library for their help and expertise. James Harte, Paul Ferguson, Bernie Metcalfe, Colum O'Riordan, Roberta Schwarz and Andrew Williams deserve particular thanks. The wonderful resources of the *Founders Online* website allowed me to access the founding fathers' copious correspondence and to read it sequentially, despite its originating in many

different archives, a difficult task before digitisation. Others allowed me to wander at will through their landscapes and gardens and to publish their private collections, for which I am most grateful.

Symposia convened at Dumbarton Oaks, the Huntington Library, California, Trinity College Dublin, Birkbeck and Queen Mary, University of London, the Universities of Aberdeen, Aberystwyth, Bath, Glasgow, York and the Benetton Foundation, Treviso, Italy helped develop much of what follows. Articles published in *Irish Architectural and Decorative Studies*, *Eighteenth-century Ireland/Iris an dá chultúr*, *Journal of Scottish Thought*, *Garden History* and *Studies in the History of Gardens & Designed Landscapes* tested the material. The faculty and student body of the School of Architecture, Planning and Environmental Policy, UCD, have supported my research in a myriad of ways, and I continue to be very grateful for the assistance, financial and otherwise, provided by the Humanities Institute, UCD.

The many colleagues and friends who have supported my transatlantic enquiries over the years include Paul Arnold, Toby Barnard, John Barrell, Stephen Bending, John Bonehill, Patrizia Boschiero, Turtle Bunbury, Donough Cahill, Hugh Campbell, Andrew Carpenter, Christine Casey, Liam Chambers, Claire Connolly, Mary-Ann Constantine, Sarah Cremin, Mark Crinson, Willie Cumming, Stephen Daniels, David Dickson, Sonja Dümpelmann, Tom Dunne, Georges Farhat, Jon Finch, Alison FitzGerald, the late Desmond FitzGerald, Knight of Glin, David Fleming, Anne Fuchs, Mary Gallagher, Raffaella Giannetto, Gert Gröning, Marion

Harney, Emmeline Henderson, Mari Hvattum, Kathleen James-Chakraborty, Kathleen John-Adler, Laura Johnstone, James Kelly, Merlo Kelly, Catriona Kennedy, the late Fred Krehbiel, Jay and Silvia Krehbiel, William Laffan, Mark Laird, Luigi Latini, Nigel Leask, Michael Lee, Mari Lending, Emily Mann, Samantha Martin, Victoria McCarthy, Maeve McCuskar, Ivar McGrath, Elizabeth McKellar, Jennifer Milam, the late Christopher Monkhouse, Sarah Moss, Monique Mosser, Ruth Musielak, Felicity Myrone, Louis Nelson, Simon Nugent, John Olley, Gillian O'Brien, Robert O'Byrne, Brian O'Connell, MacDara O'Connor, Ciaran O'Neill, Antoine Picon, Martin Postle, Mark Price, Brendan Rooney, Susan Roundtree, Alistair Rowan, Ellen Rowley, Catriona Ryan, David Solkin, Sarah Alyn Stacey, Roger Stalley, José Tito Rojo, Marc Treib, Michael Wall, Patrick Walsh, Stephen Whiteman, Gabriel Wick, Jan Woudstra, Nuala Zahedieh, Simonetta Zanon and most particularly Claire Burke and Conor Lucey.

Summers spent upstate amidst the Catskill mountains in the late 1980s and among the diverse company of New York State's Music Camp and Institute first inspired my interest in the United States and its landscapes. Mark Hallett of the Paul Mellon Centre for Studies in British Art provided early support and encouragement, while the manuscript's anonymous peer-reviewers presented me with thought-provoking criticism and much welcome advice. The wonderful Emily Lees, Christine Considine and Catherine Bankhurst have coaxed this book into shape. Neil, Aoibh, Ruth, Toby and Ivan have come to know many of these landscapes more than they might wish, often exploring the gardens while I mined the archives. But their enthusiasm for our travels and their own valuable perspectives often kept this project on course. Neil provided the more insightful viewpoints and created some of the illustrations. This book's completion is again due to him.

Abbreviations

BL   British Library

BNF   Bibliothèque nationale de France

Butler Plantation Papers   Historical Society of Pennsylvania, *Butler Plantation Papers; The Papers of Pierce Butler (1744–1822) and Successors from the Historical Society of Pennsylvania*, Adam Matthew Publications, 1997, 13 rolls microfilm

DIB   Dictionary of Irish Biography

Founders Online   Founders Online website: https://founders.archives.gov/documents

For Washington's and other founding gentlemen's correspondence this website has greatly eased and enabled this book's focus on long letter series between two correspondents (George Washington and Arthur Young, for example). It is operated by the National Historical Publications & Records Commission of the National Archives of the United States and brings together a vast array of sources held by different archives. The canonic source for letters not within the National Archives is often very long and has not been given as a consequence.

Lipscomb   Terry W. Lipscomb (ed.), *The Letters of Pierce Butler 1790–1794: Nation Building and Enterprise in the New American Republic*, Columbia: University of South Carolina Press, 2007

LoC   Library of Congress

Lord Dunboyne (ed.)   Paddy Butler, Lord Dunboyne (editor), *When the States were Young: A Remarkable Collection of Letters 1784–1799 Preserved in the British Library as Additional Manuscript 16603*, www.lulu.com, 2006

MVLA   Mount Vernon Ladies' Association

NAI   National Archives of Ireland

NLI   National Library of Ireland

ODNB   Oxford Dictionary of National Biography Digital Edition

OED   Oxford English Dictionary Digital Edition

PRO   Public Record Office [of Great Britain]

TCD   Trinity College Dublin

TNA   National Archives [of Great Britain]

Plantation, Improvement and Revolution

Landscape engages with how people view, represent and make the natural world.[1] The imaginative act of framing a space or object inspires questions about the position, relationship, hierarchy and iconography of the framed elements, natural, human and manmade. Framing delimits sites of interest and separates the observer from the examined environment, which is edited and abstracted by the process. Although derived from the tradition of seventeenth-century Dutch painting, landscape's influence is not limited to two dimensions. As its very human perspectives on the form and potential of the natural world are projected into real space they encourage landscaping – a way of making places that originates in the act of framing. Landscape also does not 'merely signify or symbolize power relations' but becomes an 'instrument of cultural power, perhaps even an agent of power that is independent of human relations'.[2] Its historical formation as part and parcel of European imperialism made these power relations between empires, countries, landowners, designers and those who tilled the soil apparent. In contexts where landownership was but recently won, of questionable authority or open to interpretation, such as in colonisation, landscape's ability to naturalise, conceal and aestheticise deeply rooted societal inequities was very useful.

This book starts and ends in Ireland and takes the island as its principal test site or laboratory. A sometime 'old world colony',[3] it contains pockets of space and time whose spatial and representational traditions parallel those of the Americas more closely than those of Great Britain and western Europe. As one of England's longest experiments in colonisation, many of the British empire's spatial paradigms were initially tested in Ireland and then transported and replicated elsewhere, particularly those connected to political and military governance and the appropriation and division of land. All nations are spatial constructs, and the precise placing of borders and infrastructure marks out the national territory. Ideas of space, utopian and dystopian, comparative and theoretical, inform their creation. The landscape history challenge is to understand how a nation is perceived, designed and made by a combination of political, geographical, economic and aesthetic forces. While the comparison of Ireland and America seems today somewhat ridiculous, in 1800 the population of both countries was close to five million, making their comparison in the eighteenth century both logical and useful.[4] In terms of the scale of their polity, economic activity and geopolitical reach, they were not then that dissimilar, save for their very great discrepancy in physical scale, then somewhat assuaged by the very small scale of American cities.[5]

Ireland and the United States both experienced plantation, a political and geographical initiative that did not occur in England, Scotland, Wales or western mainland Europe. Ireland was England's first island colony, and the plantations of Ireland

(Facing page) Detail of fig. 2

shared many features with parallel and future colonial activity in the Americas and the Caribbean. Terms like 'planter' and 'plantation' were first applied to Ireland in the late sixteenth century and were then applied elsewhere in the American and Caribbean colonies.[6] The early seventeenth-century design of the peninsula of Inishowen, last of the Ulster Plantation's initiatives, bears design similarities to the plantations of the new world. However, plantations in the United States and the Caribbean diverge from comparative Irish examples early in their evolution. Legal differences between Europe and America, such as those linking land purchase entitlement to headrights, the entailment of enslaved workers to the land they farmed and the overarching system of matrilineal chattel slavery, led American plantations to exhibit key structural and ideological differences early in their evolution and these had spatial consequences.[7] Little attention, in either art or architectural history, has been devoted to Ireland's role in defining and undermining plantation, with the historical geographer William Smyth a notable exception.[8] Yet American landscape history has frequently identified Ireland as the point of origin for British plantation design,[9] and Caribbean geographers have also looked to Ireland for the roots of early plantation geography and structure.[10] Colonial and enslaved landscapes continue to be reduced to a world of small enclosed and productive gardens, for a variety of disciplinary and ideological reasons.[11] Although architectural history often forgets the wider landscape setting, notable exceptions may be found in the work of Dell Upton, John Michael Vlach and Peter Martin,[12] and Ireland continues to play an important role in the postcolonial space of many disciplines, notably that of literature.[13] Research into 'the dark side of the landscape' is indebted to the interdisciplinary work of John Barrell, Denis Cosgrove, Stephen Daniels, Stephen Copley and Peter Garside,[14] and to the more art historical concerns of Malcolm Andrews, Jill Casid, Kay Dian Kriz, John Bonehill, Tim Barringer and Geoff Quilley, among others.[15]

For the fledgling seventeenth-century British empire Ireland was always a place where rebellion was likely to break out, where improvement was most urgently required and where military interventions were likely to prove necessary. The sectarian and sometime racial character of the seventeenth-century Ulster Plantation, involving vast transfers of land and power from one portion of the population to another, was further impacted by the seismic changes wrought by the English Civil War of the 1640s and the Glorious Revolution of 1688, when many key battles and sieges took place on Irish soil. Because the legal title to land continued to be in dispute between one section of the community and another, marks and emblems of ownership grew in significance, particularly in the Boyne valley, where Oliver Cromwell, William III and James II all ranged, their actions commemorated in a series of distinguished villa landscapes and an overarching river valley design of substantial scale. As ownership of land became conditional upon loyalty to the Crown of England and thence to the Protestant religion, questions surrounding the identity of the owner and the manner of their acquisition could overwhelm other design considerations. Landscape recast contested land in various victorious landscape designs, particularly in the vicinity of the twinned siege cities of Drogheda and Derry/Londonderry. Landscapes at an imperial heartland, such as Versailles or Hampton Court, have arguably no need of such contorted patterning. Drogheda and Derry/Londonderry's landscapes were designed to divert attention from a real battle site to its spatial, architectural and pictorial representations, and the more artful the removes the more cumulatively convincing the process.

Plantation slowly evolved into the ideology and nomenclature of improvement, which became the general eighteenth-century strategy for making countries more like England in manners, religion, agriculture, taste and all matters of design. The native inhabitants were to improve themselves, and the protective concepts of a yeoman farmer, common land, entailment and secure leasehold were roughly prohibited for many. This concept of 'improvement', whereby Ireland was not redistributed but 'improved', served the British empire well as it grew, and scholars such as Paul Roebuck, J. H. Andrews, B. W. Higman and Audrey Horning have clarified the particular character of Irish, American and Caribbean plantations and the relative absence of particular historical geographies from the rest of Great Britain.[16] Comparative research on the property structures and connected landscape designs of the French and British empires is rare and some of this book's ambition lies in this realm of comparative history, which is but rarely attempted and only where detailed case studies and exceptional sources exist.[17] This absence generates the need to use detailed case studies and is relevant also for Arthur Young, whose writings on Ireland, Great Britain, America and France were at pains to uncover such underlying comparable landscape structures. Young's *A Tour in Ireland, 1776–1779* established his reputation as a critical observer of entire countries and led in turn to his *Travels in France during the Years 1787, 1788, 1789* and his *Letters from His Excellency General Washington, to Arthur Young*, published in 1801.[18] In all of these publications Young attempted to dissect each country's geography as a constituency of hierarchical and nested landscapes. The physical and aesthetic boundaries between the more specific categories could vary substantially from one country to another, while omissions and additions to the hierarchy revealed much about a country's social, political and spatial design. Young also argued that countries 'figure[d] by comparison; and those ought to be esteemed the benefactors of the human race, who have most established public prosperity on the basis of private happiness'.[19] By comparing and contrasting one environment with another, change at home could be proven to be desirable and necessary. This comparative frame of mind operated at various scales simultaneously – from what clover species might suit a heavy Pennsylvania clay soil when compared to that of Kildare or wider discussions as to the ideal scale and size of a country's yeomanry and its farms. Young also focused on the individual's dwelling – whether, cabin, cottage, farmhouse or mansion. A house is always a personal, domestic space but it can also double neatly as the ideal space of the nation and as a proportioned environment for the ideal citizen.[20]

The design of the landed estate in eighteenth-century Great Britain differed from its Irish configuration in certain key aspects, particularly the consistent application of improvement and the evolution and translation of the landscape garden. Improvement was affected by the absenteeism espoused by leading practitioners, whether the manipulative Fitzwilliam magnates of Dublin or carousing French aristocrats in Paris. Arthur Young's publications were alive to such nuances and his careful analysis of why an Irish estate differed from an English one very provocative, particularly its imagery. Gradually the ideology of improvement was appropriately inflected to suit a variety of transatlantic environments, from the sea islands of the state of Georgia to the suburbs of Dublin and the streets of Philadelphia. The correspondence of George Washington and Arthur Young, one man in America and the other in Europe, sharply delineates the profound difficulties of reconfiguring the composite plantation structure of Mount Vernon into 'a well-regulated farm in the English culture'.[21] Young, whose only real job as a landscape improver was at Lord Kingston's

great model estate of Mitchelstown, Co. Cork, extracted much information from Washington on the reality of an American landed estate. Each man's misconception of the other's landscape reveals much about British and American landed estates in the 1790s.

Landscape design in Europe and its colonies is implicitly and explicitly also the design of property. In all western European countries the spatial legacy of monarchy and aristocracy is imprinted on the land. From the field subdivision of the countryside to the architrave of a doorcase, little escaped the spatial expression of the omnipresent societal hierarchy. Villa landscape is arguably the most expressive and readily identified locus of the spatial ideology adopted by the European ruling class.[22] This book explores how private estate landscape, particularly its centrepiece, the country house set in its surrounding parkland, was undermined in political environments that sought to eliminate aristocracy's entitled position and connected societal and spatial impact. How did new republics, that had overthrown such social hierarchies, translate their principles into spatial form? What landscape designs resulted from abolishing all palaces, sees and seats of power? It explores some seminal revolutionary landscapes, particularly those derived from the English Glorious Revolution of 1688, the American Revolution of 1776 and the Irish rebellion, or failed revolution, of 1798. How were the revolutionary principles of commonwealth, republicanism, liberty, equality and fraternity made manifest in the space of the nation as a whole and not only in its cities, great ports or public buildings but etched into the land itself? For most of the early modern period, landownership was synonymous with liberty because it was the only general means by which economic freedom could be attained and voting rights won. Revolutions changed the definition of land. It was no longer 'held' by grace of Crown or king, it was not an estate bound by customs, duties, legacies and liens – it became property, only property. This redefinition of land as personal individual property with no duties or responsibilities to lord, neighbours or community had an impact on how it was framed, landscaped, enjoyed and exploited.

The Glorious Revolution of 1688 attempted to constrain the power of the monarchy by advancing the authority of parliament, reviving the English Civil War's commonwealth ideals and stipulating a Protestant succession. For many Protestant Anglophone revolutionaries, it became the precursor and progenitor of the eighteenth-century revolutions, because corrupt aristocratic, landed and financial powers had stunted its manifest destiny. The American Revolution of 1776 was the first time a European colony won independence from a European empire by establishing a republic – a form of government composed of elected representatives with a written constitution. 'The republicanism with which the Founding Fathers rejected the parliamentary model of government itself was initially "commonwealth" in character, and owed much to the speculations put forward in the Cromwellian phase of the first English revolution.'[23] They instigated democratic government by the elected representatives of a society of male equals, with the divine acting through the people and for the people and with no monarchical intercession. Derived from earlier Greek, Roman and British concepts of republicanism, commonwealth and popular government, it placed great emphasis on the liberty to govern a country with no distant rule or oversight, liberty from hierarchy and aristocracy and liberty to engage in trade for one's own benefit and enjoyment. The French Revolution of 1789–1791 cemented the connection between liberty and equality, denouncing the three estates of aristocracy, clergy and peasantry and leading to a more total reconfiguration of society. The failed United Irishmen's rebellion of 1798 followed French precepts, attempting to overturn the power of bloodline and its entitled forms of precedence and hierarchy but ending ultimately in failure and union into the United Kingdom in 1800. The counter-revolutionary initiatives launched in its aftermath sought to safeguard the British polity and empire. More than 30,000 people died in the United Irishmen's rebellion, 'more than during the entire French Terror', with over 90 per cent 'from the United Irish side, illustrating the sheer scale of the suppression necessary to defeat their ideals'.[24]

This book does not contain a history of the Glorious, American and French revolutions and the United Irishmen's rebellion as a sequence of political or military events. The subsets of political revolution, the economic and financial revolution of the late seventeenth century and the agricultural and plantation revolutions of the eighteenth century are explored where and when they relate to landscape design. It assesses some of the landscape ideas that inspired revolution and the real projects that such ideas created. All sought to change existing spaces of power. First among these was the great landed estate – the building block of aristocratic power throughout Europe. Where its design intersected with that of

the farm and the plantation, it became a zone of pronounced conflict and complexity, in which ideas of improvement, equality and freedom often contradicted reality.[25] Many of the following chapters explore case studies where the characteristics of the landed estate, the plantation, the landscape garden and the farm are locked together – mostly in unresolved and contradictory ways. Some are intensely personal, describing the landscapes of individuals whose motives can be determined from the copious personal letters that document the making of most of the following landscapes. Letters have led the selection of the case studies, because little is as revealing as a private and personal letter. Many of the landscapes discussed also survive in maps, drawings, plans and images, where what is elided by the draughtsman may be as significant as what is not. The full French tradition of revolutionary landscape is not explored; only those areas that prove particularly relevant and fruitful to the United States and Ireland. Nor is the full impact and resonance of the Haitian Revolution examined except where it is of relevance to Pierce Butler's landscapes of slavery in the American South.

Revolution is fundamentally spatial, a turning movement that rotates an object in time. It does not change position but spins about an axis so that the world cannot be seen in the same way. Revolution more generally was an oscillating, transnational cultural and political movement, where the 'call to liberty'[26] took many different and often contradictory forms, among them designed landscapes of various scales. The ability of revolutionary thought to jump and leap borders while reimagining them differently was paralleled in landscape design, as the case studies are intended to demonstrate. Recent histories of the age of revolutions have evolved into more transnational and cross-cultural discussions as traditional national frameworks of analysis have broken down to give rise to histories of the revolutionary 'Atlantic world'.[27] Revolutions were founded on some ideal of freedom from oppression, reinforced by concepts of humanity's essential or inalienable rights.[28] They were often initiated by individuals, usually men, who tried to live their daily lives in revolutionary ways. These men all travelled, spiralling from suburb to countryside, from Ireland to Great Britain and then across Europe or America and this appears comparable to revolution's mental and spatial transfer more generally. Revolutionary landscapes resulted from the design experiments that such men conducted into the ideal forms that the tour, house, garden, farm, estate and nation should take, while recent discussion of 'revolutionary generations' has suggested how the individual lives and letters might be reframed to explore revolution and its ongoing legacy.[29]

Profoundly cosmopolitan, revolution depended on travel – the practice of moving from one country to another but also the movement of ideas, often in the form of personal letters, drawings and maps. This extends the reach of the study area beyond the borders of Ireland and the United States to Great Britain, France, Switzerland, Holland, Hamburg and Gibraltar. Jean-Jacques Rousseau's gardens and lifestyle profoundly affected the history and design of French gardens and those of the many Europeans who followed in his footsteps. The book re-examines seminal revolutionary landscapes and in the process uncovers forgotten or overlooked landscapes – those made by revolutionaries whose uprisings failed overall, making them rebellions, but whose ideas echoed down the centuries, often finding relevance in later times and other places. The power of landscape to direct and influence thought has been explored in publications such as Simon Schama's *Landscape and Memory*, William Mitchell's *Landscape and Power*, Ann Bermingham's *Landscape and Ideology: The English Rustic Tradition, 1740–1860* and Stephen Daniels's *Fields of Vision*.[30] This book is more empirical and concerned with how landscape informs and creates distinct designed environments. The methodology employed here is interdisciplinary, uniting the spatial skills of an architect with those of visual analysis and archival interpretation. Key sites have been used to examine the spatial ideas of each nation's founding fathers, with few founding mothers presenting themselves. In America such sites are iconic – national foundation documents writ large in landscape, and it is difficult to position the American Revolution without examining the plantation landscapes of George Washington, George Mason and Thomas Jefferson. Yet portions of them have been overlooked and the full extent of compromise in their design left somewhat unacknowledged. The identities of some key individuals in American landscape history have been simplified into 'English', such as Samuel Vaughan, who was born in Waterford and came to Mount Vernon via London and a long acquaintance with his own Jamaican plantations. Nor is Bernard M'Mahon's early identity as a United Irishman irrelevant to his authorship of America's first gardening book, and his role as radical Philadelphian purveyor of Thomas Jefferson's seeds and plants. Neither has the impact of Irish sites and landscapes, such as Belcamp, Co. Dublin, or Mitchelstown,

Co. Cork, on key American revolutionary sites been hitherto identified or explored.

When great changes are sought in society, as in any revolutionary period, new symbolic landscapes are created. Some of these document the radical societal reformation that revolutions mostly seek, although some revolutions, such as the Glorious Revolution of 1688, sought to return to a more radical past from a conservative present. The paradoxical nature of many revolutionary ideas, how they were spread, by whom and for what purpose, is a primary concern of the book. While this history has been examined and acknowledged in other disciplines, landscape and architectural history have not, generally, examined the eighteenth-century ambition to create more deliberately equal environments. The ambition often led to highly contradictory landscape interpretations of liberty and freedom, particularly in the American South or on the islands of the Caribbean. In France the revolutionary spatial tropes of the mountain and the festival have been analysed by such scholars as Mona Ozouf[31] and Lynn Hunt.[32] Others have sought to explain the impact of revolutionary thought on the evolution of architecture and urban space, notably James Leith's *Space and Revolution: Projects for Monuments, Squares and Public Buildings in France 1789–1799*,[33] while the projects of Claude Ledoux and Charles Boullée and their ambitions to form new spaces for a new republic are well known.[34] Yet the reconfiguration of landscape that led from such predominantly architectural activity has not perhaps been adequately assessed, particularly the relative weighting of country and city, capital and provincial town, mountain and plain, that both Jean-Jacques Rousseau and Arthur Young tried so hard to understand.

Revolution was expressed in how you moved through the world, how you travelled, who travelled by your side, and in what you saw, noticed and wrote about while doing so. If French revolutionaries sought to overturn the spatial structure of France, placing mountains in churches and gardens on forts, others rewrote the map of Europe and its sequence of key sites and vistas. In this they were facilitated by the picturesque tour, which, when coupled with the philosophy of improvement, acquired a revolutionary impact. Popularised by Mary Delany in the English home counties and Killarney, by the second half of the eighteenth century the landscape tour had jumped many scales of perception and practice.[35] A profoundly mobile experience, one's conception of a country, nation, people could be derived and influenced by the construction of the route and such views as were available from it. At the transatlantic scale the landscape tour became the last and most ambitious endeavour of eighteenth-century tourism. Incorporating critiques of landscape, politics, economics, agriculture, manners and society while also advancing new design paradigms, the transatlantic tour gave people new ways to imagine both the garden and the nation, and their ideal place and space in both. Significant Irish tourists of the young American republic, who left published and unpublished records of their travels, include Samuel Vaughan, Lord Edward FitzGerald, Theobald Wolfe Tone, Archibald Hamilton Rowan, Pierce Butler, Isaac Weld and Thomas Moore. Most of these men adopted the ethos of improvement – that people, places and countries could be designed into better, richer, more structured and more recognisably European versions of themselves. All projected their native landscape traditions, structures and interpretations onto the new world. Their published perceptions and misconceptions affected how Americans perceived and valued their own landscapes in turn. Revolutionary patterns are also revealed by studying their repression in periods of counter-revolution. The oppressive environment that followed the 1798 Irish rebellion sought to break its dangerous coupling of the picturesque tour with revolutionary thought yet the counter-revolutionary measures adopted in its aftermath still made use of many of the same techniques, structuring overt military and political activity in picturesque images.

Revolutionaries understood well the power of route reversal, where doing things in the wrong order encouraged and intensified the comparative landscape analysis that Arthur Young had advanced in his tour guides. Upsetting established hierarchies of countries, views, sites and landscapes often proved agreeably revolutionary. When visiting Utrecht in 1797 the Irishman Wolfe Tone remarked that the city put him 'in mind of Philadelphia' particularly 'the exterior of the houses, the footways paved with brick, the trees planted in the streets, the fountains, and even the appearance of the inhabitants'.[36] Before he had set foot on mainland Europe he had spent a year in Pennsylvania living the life of an ideal American farmer. Eager to project America onto the old world, he confounded expected order and comparisons in the process. Within Europe Switzerland held a similar power. Incorporated into the European grand tour as a key approach route to Italy, particularly for tourists of the Protestant north who wished to avoid France, the revolutionary tour decoupled Switzerland from its onward destinations and made it a

destination in itself. As Rousseau's origin and eventual fastness it gained additional potency as the locus of his spatial biography and through such publications as *Julie ou la nouvelle Heloise* and *Letters Written from the Mountain.*

Suburbia contained substantial revolutionary potential in the repressive sectarian society of eighteenth-century Dublin, then caught in a complex web of penal laws. The hidden landscapes that Catholics (and revolutionaries) were obliged to inhabit inspired a city exodus to Dublin's seaside suburbs, the mountains of Wicklow and the plains of Kildare. Two of the most significant United Irishmen arrived at rebellion from different directions – Edward FitzGerald via America, the Caribbean and Gibraltar, and Arthur O'Connor via France and Switzerland – the 'plank' that kept 'republicanism from sinking in the seas of despotism' and 'the most beautiful country in the world'.[37] They wove the landscapes of Halifax, New Orleans, Fort Arthur, Connersville, Frescati, Hamburg, Neuchâtel, Lake Geneva and the Curragh of Kildare into Irish revolutionary narratives. Some of the gardens that they toured or created, in keeping with French and American revolutionary thought, were very modest, with a pronounced emphasis on productive gardening and flowers. Such stories expand the architectural and landscape canon into landscapes of the more middling variety – suburban gardens, suburban housing estates and the smaller country houses that steer close to farmhouses save for a few important design gestures. Legacies of the revolutionary push to subvert the larger, prominent and more hierarchical structures, they suggest an alternative order of precedence. While places such as Versailles, Wilton, Badminton, Carton or Powerscourt do mostly express the more aesthetically ambitious and cohesive design ideas, landscapes made by those of less entitled privilege need to be included in the historical canon for corrective balance.

The most contradictory of revolutionary spaces was the revolutionary's plantation, and a case study from the low and shifting sea islands of Georgia explores the environment created by the Irishman and Senator Pierce Butler, one of that state's most successful planters. A supporter of the United Irishmen, Butler's lengthy correspondence with his manager Roswell King reveals a committed republican who was nevertheless one of Georgia's largest slaveholders. A distinguished resident of the historic centre of Philadelphia, before moving to a suburban villa, Butler made sure that his children never had to witness the landscapes that funded his comfortable lifestyle. Out of sight was, however, not out of mind, and designing from a distance leaves a damning paper trail of drawings, descriptions and instructions. These can be unpicked to reveal Butler's complicit role in laying out plantations of exact and precise levels of humidity, productivity, exploitation and cruelty. His absentee landscaping created a contradictory environment where the long avenues of orange trees and carefully dressed embankments beautified the enclosed acres of rice plants that were planted, tended, worked and dug by hundreds of enslaved men, women and children. Pierce Butler expresses concisely the shifting trans-imperial mentality of an ambitious eighteenth-century Irishman. Ideologically opposed to slavery on paper, he thoroughly benefited from its extraordinary material advantages in practice. The more radical aspects of his identity were concealed from his fellow planters in the American South and found voice in his letters home. His correspondence reveals the spatial consequences of absenteeism and the subsequent design character of much colonial space.

This book is another exploration of the nature and character of eighteenth-century Irish landscape design but reaches across the Atlantic to the young United States of America, a country long connected and associated with Ireland.[38] Many Irish people and places are bound to the United States, by blood, shared history, inclination and admiration. Many of the founding fathers of the United States, and their spaces, have Irish origins, more than is generally appreciated. Both countries are also inexorably bound to England, Great Britain and the United Kingdom for their historical definition, in Ireland's case for many centuries, while Ireland's engagement with other European countries, notably France, was often constructed with reference to England. These long relationships, pursued across intervening seas and oceans, encouraged the mutable individual and national landscape identities examined in this book. The process suggests how fluid and complex conceptions of identity, heritage and history can be. Ireland's oblique view of the larger protagonists, as that of a small island off the coast of Europe, but one familiar with borders, colonies, plantations, failed rebellions and long patterns of subverting empire, will hopefully enlighten the older, larger and more dominant perspectives.

THE MAINE SEA

Seale Iland

AN

Ramullen

Lough Suillie

Inche

COLRANE

White Castle

Red Castle

Lough

foile

FERGVS

NB. It is to be taken notice within
this Map, that all places marked
thus † are to be taken for Church-
lands.
Such places as resemble Lakes
and are shadowed all ouer with
small pricks, having this marke b
signifie boggs.

Greer

CHAPTER I

Plantation to Glorious Revolution

Plantation Landscapes

In the sixteenth and seventeenth centuries the British empire developed plantation landscapes on both sides of the Atlantic. Many of the families involved in American colonization, in both the Caribbean and Virginia, were simultaneously involved in the attempt to colonize Ireland,[1] and Ireland, through its substantial role in provisioning most British ships, became part of the evolving Atlantic trade triangles.[2] Early deeds of plantation landscapes on both sides of the Atlantic share similarities of execution and a pronounced brevity of detail. A property's area and position were identified legally by recourse to topographical features such as land ridges or lone standing trees, river courses and the surveyed boundaries of neighbours' lands (Fig. 1). A global design strategy for exploiting regions that were structurally and culturally unlike Europe, plantations did not happen organically, they were calculated and ingenious designs intended to control vast amounts of land. Harnessing law, architecture, landscape design and art for their overwhelming economic purposes, plantations combined agricultural innovation with elements of Europe's long and sophisticated villa tradition. Irish precedents in plantation design set the course for much of the British empire, with Irish land survey, landscape design and architectural design establishing a model for the empire's practices.[3] Plantation, when

transferred to the Americas, came to indicate 'an estate or large farm, especially in a former British colony, on which crops such as cotton, sugar and tobacco are grown' but crucially, 'with the aid of slave labour'.[4]

From the period of the twelfth-century Norman invasion, Ireland had exhibited a similar landed property structure to England with noble lords holding their land as grants bequeathed to them directly by the king. These large areas of land, usually received for successful military service, were structured into manors, with demesne portions held and farmed directly by the lord himself. Areas that resisted anglicisation produced weaker Norman landholding structures and these subsequently became the focus of the Elizabethan plantations that invariably followed failed Irish rebellions. The Laois & Offaly and Munster Plantations, in response to such upheavals, began in 1556 and 1586 respectively. The last large-scale Irish plantation was the Ulster Plantation, carried out from 1606 onwards. Plantation legislation stipulated that the plantation 'undertakers', typically military gentlemen on the winning side, build stone castles, bawns and houses, adopt English farming practices that aimed for profit and not subsistence, give preference to English or Scots tenants, and suppress native Irish culture, language and the Catholic religion. The Ulster Plantation aimed for an ordered geometrical landscape with little of the ambiguity that had progressively attached to the palimpsest of

(Facing page) Detail of fig. 3

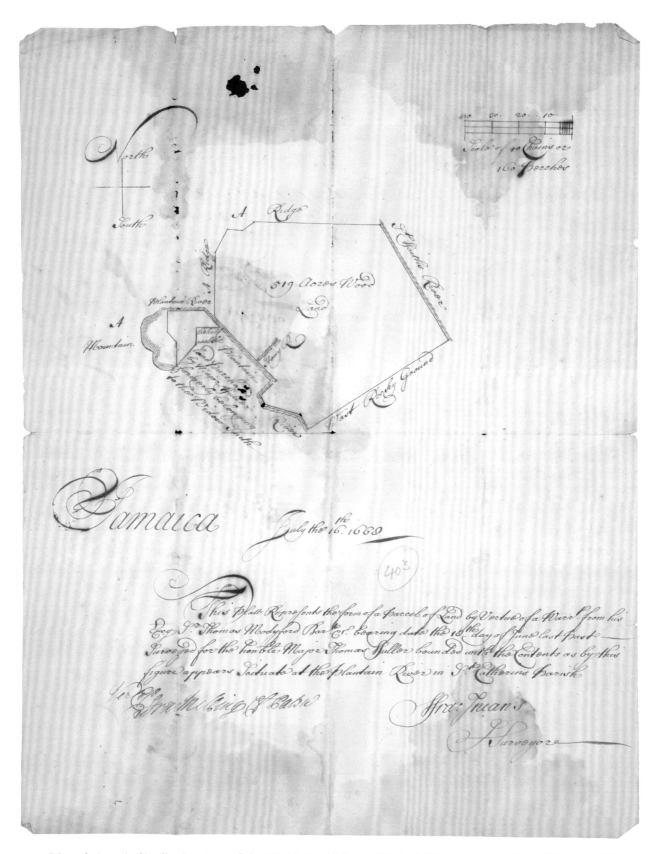

1. Map of a 'parcel of land' in Jamaica, 16 July 1668. National Library of Ireland, Westport Estate Papers, Ms 40,893/6(3)

Norman manors, old Catholic parishes and dissolved monastic foundations, together with such indigenous agricultural practices as booleying or gavelkind.[5]

Plantation required a spatial strategy, which in its initial stages involved much surveying, mapping and the redistribution of lands. The idea of plantation or 'the settling of people, usually in a conquered or dominated country, *esp.* the planting or establishing of a colony; colonization'[6] has been traced in English-language sources to a sixteenth-century English translation of an early Latin history of Ireland.[7] By 1610, when Thomas Blennerhasset published *A Direction for the Plantation of Ireland*, the strategy had matured into a large-scale systematic approach. Arguing that a 'scattered plantation'[8] would never succeed, Blennerhasset advocated a well-ordered and staged sequence of fortified towns, manors and demesnes that would eventually see 'all the land far remote … built and inhabited with good security'.[9] Fortified towns and castles spearheaded the taming of the countryside,[10] as they facilitated a plantation's nominated undertakers in 'planting a Manor under the protection of any strong built Castle'.[11] The manor's gardens, orchards and woodlands would 'beautifie' Ireland's 'desolation' while 'her inaccessible Woods' would no 'longer nourish' the 'wood kerne' or native Irish, 'but by the sweet society of a loving neighbourhood' would 'entertain humanity, even in the best fashion'.[12]

Across the early British empire laying out plantation landscape began with a compass-and-chain survey, cartographic representations of uncertain and ambiguous legal status, and the amalgamation of large blocks of land under one owner. The relative absence of infrastructure, particularly roads, led to a preference for situations close to rivers or the sea, invariably the principal arteries of communication. When starting a survey the surveyor typically stood at the corner of a pre-existing boundary line, usually that of a neighbour's property. He then used a lone standing tree or a timber post to fix the position of his next station, towards which he took a compass bearing – an angular directional measurement that positioned the second station relative to the first one. Stretching out his chain to measure the distance between the two stations, he might also carefully notch the tree for future identification. He repeated the operation from the second and subsequent stations until the field's geometry was listed in his survey notebook in columns of chain lengths and bearing angles. Stitched together, the eventual survey map lacked the overarching rigour and closing geometry of later triangulated survey methods (Fig. 1). The long diagonal measurements that accurately tie a triangulated survey together were often not taken, leaving the angular geometry prone to error. Moreover, the position of magnetic north varied over time, meaning that north itself was not fixed in a stable manner.[13] With no master benchmarks, early surveys, and the landscapes they delineated, could remain disconnected from a country's overall figure.

Sir Arthur Chichester's 1609 plantation of the Inishowen peninsula in Co. Donegal took place at the same time as the plantation development of Virginia or British Caribbean islands such as Barbados.[14] The failure of the nine years' war or rebellion by the families of O'Neill, O'Donnell, O'Cahan and others in Ulster led to the widespread confiscation or 'escheating' of their landed property to the Crown, and many of the rebellion's leading men left for the Continent in what became known as the 'Flight of the Earls'. The Gaelic chief Sir Cahir O'Doherty had been the principal landowner in Co. Donegal and in 1608 the victorious Sir Arthur Chichester applied for a grant of O'Doherty's estate, obtaining the barony/peninsula of Inishowen except for the Church lands, the offshore islands and some fishing rights.[15] This made Chichester 'the largest, single beneficiary of the plantation of the escheated counties'[16] and although counted among the initial 'wasters and destroyers' of Ulster, he became one of its most prominent 'builders and planters'.[17] Describing early seventeenth-century Ulster as 'very much waste and unpeopled', Chichester argued for populating the province with 'civil men' while chastising those Englishmen who 'endeavour the finding out of Virginia, Guiana, and other remote and unknown countries', leaving Ireland 'of our own, waste and desolate' as 'absurd folly or wilful ignorance'.[18] He advocated giving land to 'every man of note or good desert so much as he can conveniently stock and manure by himself and his tenants and followers'.[19]

Sir Josiah Bodley's seventeenth-century maps of the escheated counties of Ulster set out to map a part of Ireland that had not been mapped before, an ambition common to seventeenth-century America. These maps simplified the complex Irish system of land-division into baronies and townlands by omitting the intermediate ballybetagh land division. By including the county and parish divisions and such landmarks as churches and castles, they instigated 'a new concept in plantation cartography' whereby 'in a single operation covering six counties, the concepts of the estate survey,

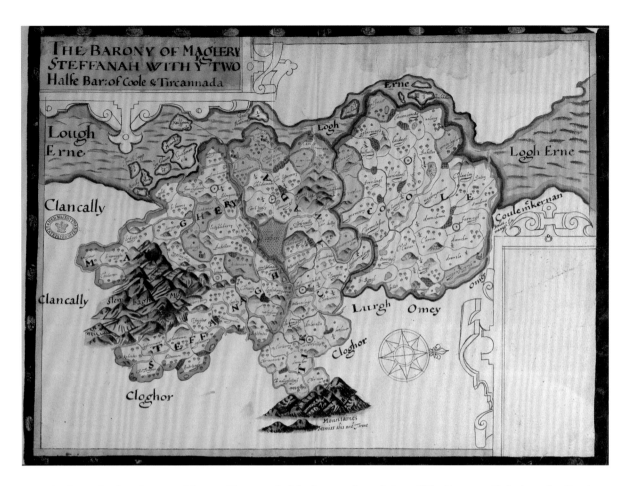

2. Sir Josias Bodley, Survey of County Fermanagh: Magherastephana. Map of 'The Barony of Maghery Steffanah with ye two halfe Bar. of Coole and Tircannada'. The National Archives, MPF 1/42

the administrative diagram and the topographical map were (it was hoped) to be brought together' (Fig. 2).[20] The exceptional nature of the Inishowen grant resulted in a 'byproduct of Chichester's mapping expedition' of 1609 – a map of the peninsula drawn by William Parsons and engraved subsequently by Wenceslas Hollar (Fig. 3).[21] The purpose of the map, and of plantation, was very clearly described in a letter of 1609: 'The use and fruit of this survey and description will not only consist in this, that his majesty shall hereby know what land he hath here, and how to distribute it to undertakers; but in this also, that it will discourage and disable the natives henceforth to rebel against the crown of England; and be a special means hereafter of preventing and suppressing rebellions in this country.' In 1609 Sir John Davies, the Irish Attorney-General, described Inishowen as a place where 'there were never any cities or towns to draw commerce or trade',

where magistrates were only recently appointed and where 'visitations of justice', namely courts, had just occurred. The peninsula was 'obscure and unknown' to the English colony, whose 'ignorance' of the native Irish 'places of retreat and fastnesses' had made the Irish 'confident in their rebellions'. The new survey would enable the English colony to 'know all the passages' favoured by the natives, to 'have penetrated every thicket and fast place' and to have 'taken notice of every notorious tree or bush'. By being 'drawn into cards [cartes] and maps' the landscape of Inishowen was 'discovered and laid open to all posterities'.[22]

Many intact plantation landscapes still exist in Inishowen. As in the seventeenth-century Caribbean or early Virginia, the peninsula had no engineered roads to speak of and most communication was by sea. All along the western bank of Lough Foyle the long rectangular plots of Hollar's map still stretch

3. Hollar Parsons Map of Inishowen, 1661 (1609 survey), Trinity College Dublin, The Long Room, OLS Papyrus Case 1 no. 1.
Reproduced courtesy Trinity College Dublin

down to the sea, their great houses positioned centrally and *en face* to the water. This side of Inishowen was almost entirely free of old manors, villages, fair greens, churches, monasteries and other elements of medieval landscape. Where old castles did exist, such as at Whitecastle and Redcastle, they were easily recalibrated into the new strip of settlement plots (Fig. 3). Plantation great houses were built out of reach of high tides but still close enough to the sea to keep an eye on maritime

traffic and trade. This was also an important defensive consideration, as the sea was the principal means of escape from any native danger coming from the interior. This sea focus reversed the standard development strategy of most country estates of the British Isles, where the sea remained an unattractive prospect until the mid-eighteenth century.[23] The last of Ulster's plantations, the Inishowen Plantation differed from the earlier ones in certain key respects. Inishowen is a peninsula that is

4. Photograph of Kilderry House. Courtesy of Claire Burke

5. Photograph from Kilderry House to the Lough Foyle. Courtesy of Claire Burke

6. Photograph of Westover House, James River, Virginia, describing a similar sectional relationship to the water as that of Inishowen's plantation houses. Author's photo, 2013

almost an island, with no dominant towns, and the plots' set-out geometry followed the coastline closely. Unlike the earlier Ulster plantations, Inishowen's plantation was spearheaded through the planting of houses and manors rather than emanating outwards from fortified towns.

Sir Arthur Chichester did not live in Inishowen or in neighbouring Derry/Londonderry, preferring to reside at Carrickfergus, Co. Antrim, and his relative Sir Thomas Chichester became the family's Inishowen undertaker. Sixteen other very substantial blocks of land were let to English undertakers/middlemen 'for terms ranging from forty to sixty-one years and for rents as little as £4 to only £70 per year'.[24] Kilderry House was built between 1706 and 1725 by the undertaker George Hart, descendant of Captain Henry Hart, sometime governor of Culmore fort and castle.[25] An interesting brick house with projecting bays, its underground tunnel concealed the shoreline connection that facilitated the loading and offloading of goods (Figs 4 and 5). Kilderry's sectional relationship to the sea and that of other Inishowen houses, such as Whitecastle, is very similar to those enjoyed by houses along the James, Rapahannock or York Rivers in Virginia or along the extensive shores of Chesapeake Bay where fast and immediate access to a river

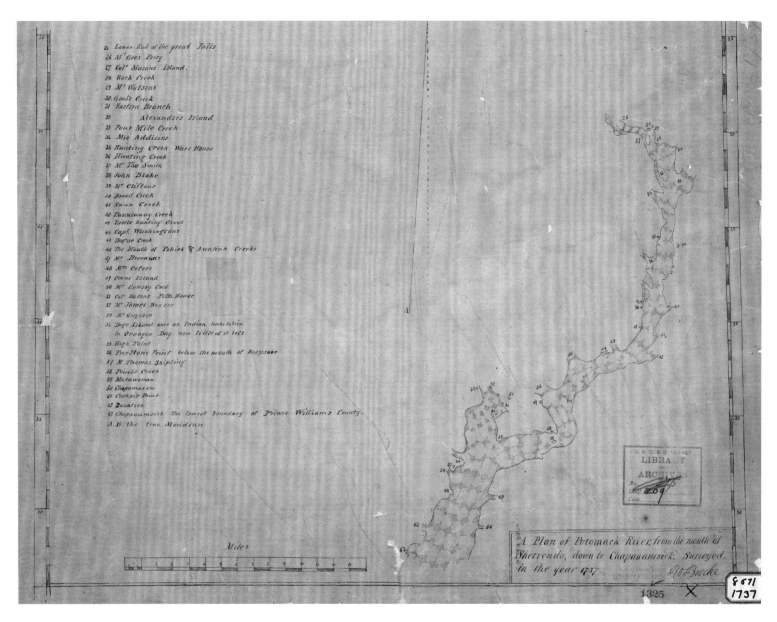

The map contains a handwritten list (partially legible):

25. Lower End of the great Falls
26. Mr Gees Ferry
27. Col Masons Island
28. Rock Creek
29. Mr Watsons
30. Goose Creek
31. Eastern Branch
32. Alexanders Island
33. Four Mile Creek
34. Mrs Addisons
35. Hunting Creek Ware House
36. Hunting Creek
37. Mr Tho Smith
38. John Blake
39. Mr Cliftons
40. Broad Creek
41. Swan Creek
42. Pascataway Creek
43. Little hunting Creek
44. Capt Washingtons
45. Dogue Creek
46. The Mouth of Pohick & Auatink Creeks
47. Mr Brenauels
48. Mrs Cofers
49. Crane Island
50. Mr Colesby Cock
51. Col Masons Fish House
52. Mr James Baxter
53. Mr Greggbys
54. Dogs Island once an Indian habitation
    in Oreogon Bay now little of it left
55. High Point
56. FreeStone Point below the mouth of Neapsewe
57. Mr Thomas Snipling
58. Powels Creek
59. Matawoman
60. Chapomaxen
61. Cockpit Point
62. Quantico
63. Chapawamsick the lowest Boundary of Prince Williams County.
A.B. the true Meridian

Miles

A Plan of Potomack River, from the mouth of Sherrendo, down to Chapawamsick, Surveyed in the year 1737.

U.S. C. & G. SURVEY LIBRARY AND ARCHIVES

1325

8571
1737

7. Robert Brooke, 'A Plan of Patomack River, from the mouth of Sherrendo, down to Chapawamsick', 1737. The map shows the positions of George Washington's plantation (44) and George Mason's 'Mr Brenauel's' near to the later Gunston Hall (47). Library of Congress, G3792.P6 1737.B7

was just as important for escape and for trading the estate's tobacco successfully. Westover House on the James River, Virginia, has just such a connection between house, landing wharf and river (Fig. 6). Chesapeake Bay, the long sea inlet of the Potomac, serving the towns of Annapolis, Georgetown and Washington DC, shares some structural similarities with that of Lough Foyle. Its plantation houses all turn towards incoming ships, and the landscape views and prospects are structured relative to each plantation's wharves, creeks and coves (Fig. 7). George Mason's house of Gunston Hall shares many structural features with Kilderry – a small compact house with modest geometric gardens, a vista towards the river and an elementary emparkment, with no boundary walls or fences (Figs 8 and 9).

8. Photograph of Gunston Hall's garden elevation and surrounding timber service buildings. Author's photo, 2013

9. *(below)* View of Gunston Hall's geometric parterre garden with view to the Potomac on the left-hand side. Author's photo, 2013

Inishowen is unusual in the extent to which the plantation figure still survives, substantially unchanged by the later improvement, enclosure and landscaping agendas of British estate design. This is the result, in part, of Chichester's fundamentally absentee presence in this portion of his estate. Residing principally in Joymount House in Carrickfergus, he was preoccupied with other concerns, such as founding the city of Belfast. Once Inishowen had been allocated to the seventeen undertakers he was happy to leave them in control. Although the undertakers' families intermarried, the incentive to amalgamate landholdings, create demesnes and parks, and adopt the improving and landscaping agendas of the eighteenth century does not appear to have occurred. David Coote's 1780 map of the plantation land of Kilderry reveals that the old rectilinear plot boundary was neither abandoned, manipulated nor elaborated over time (Fig. 10). Although it acquired some elements of parkland, walled gardens and a simple approach route, the typical estate footprint of a bounded park, delineated by wall and tree belt, is absent. The scale, ambition and design strategy of Inishowen's plantation houses continued to parallel Caribbean or Virginian examples rather than those of other Irish counties (Fig. 11) and Inishowen

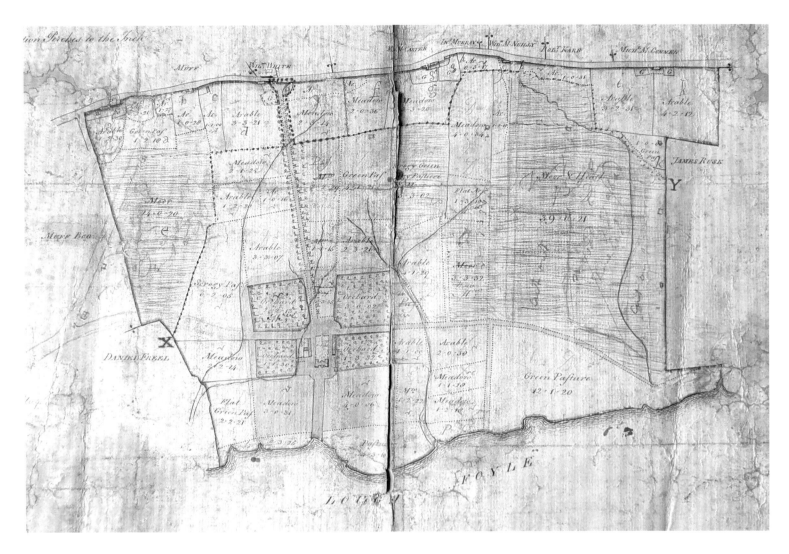

10. *(above)* Map of Kilderry House, Muff, surveyed by David Mc Cool, 1786. Private collection. Photo Claire Burke

11. *(right)* Whitecastle House, Inishowen. Photo Claire Burke

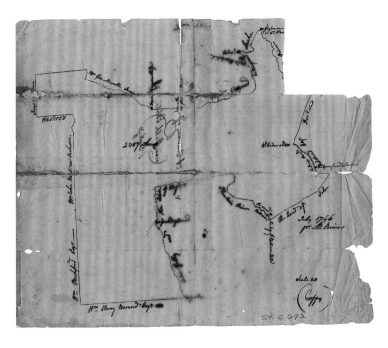

12. Michael Rivers, *A Diagram of Cocoa Walk Estate surveyed by Michael Rivers*, 1746. Note positions of 'cedar old' and 'pear tree'. National Library of Jamaica: St Catherine's 692

13. *(below)* Jonathan Barker, *A Map of Dundrum*, 1762, detail. National Archives of Ireland, Fitzwilliam Mss, 2011/2/2/4

14. *(facing page)* James Purcell, 'A Plan of a Tract of Land Situated in the Euhaws St. Luke's Parish, Beaufort District and States of South Carolina belonging to the Estate of the hon. William Middleton Esq.', 1784. South Carolina Historical Society, 32-28-06

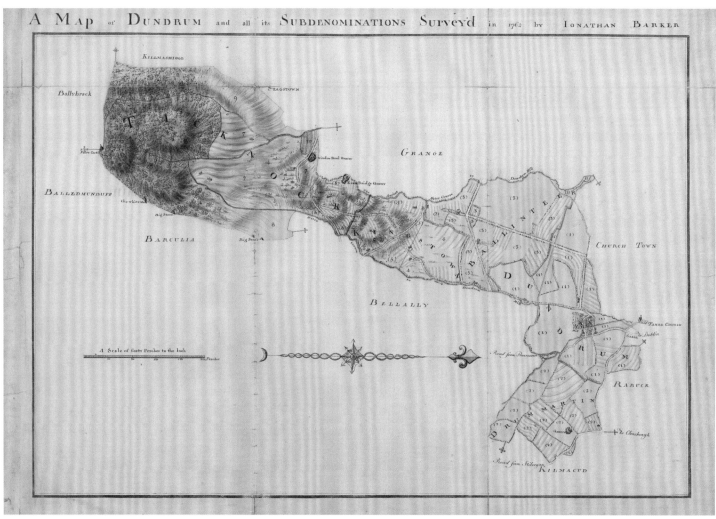

continued to be a pocket of transatlantic space whose development remained out of step with the rest of the British Isles. Other later, surprising and more substantial pockets, may be found in parts of Wicklow and Connaught, both of which spawned plantation designs as late as 1801 and 1850 respectively, and which later chapters will explore.[26]

Colonial property maps of the seventeenth and eighteenth centuries continued to be 'mostly stark and functional, compared to their English counterparts' and Irish, Caribbean and American legal land boundaries were still fixed by lone trees or standing stones well into the eighteenth century (Figs 12 and 13). Peter Benes argues that the estate map was 'unnecessary in New England where small holdings were the rule and tenancies on large properties the exception'.[27] In the southern United States, where landholdings were substantially larger, Sarah Hughes has found no evidence of 'ornate estate maps'

from the first two periods of surveying in Virginia, finding it 'curious that the first extant Virginia plat is not especially decorative' when 'Virginians at an early date were exceptionally conscious of the insignia of rank and property'.[28] American estate landscapes have been under-researched by all disciplines, and surprisingly so by archaeology, 'despite the central importance of agricultural estates and plantation slavery to the 17th-, 18th- and 19th-century histories of the much-excavated regions of the island Caribbean or the Chesapeake'.[29] Some concentrations of American demesne maps exist, notably in the South Carolina Historical Society, where the cartographic talents of James Purcell, William Diamond and others have been but lightly plumbed. One such map of the Middleton family's estate on the Sawnee River, upstream from Charleston, South Carolina, was drawn by James Purcell in 1784 (Fig. 14). The swirling outlines of the rice fields, the careful identification of

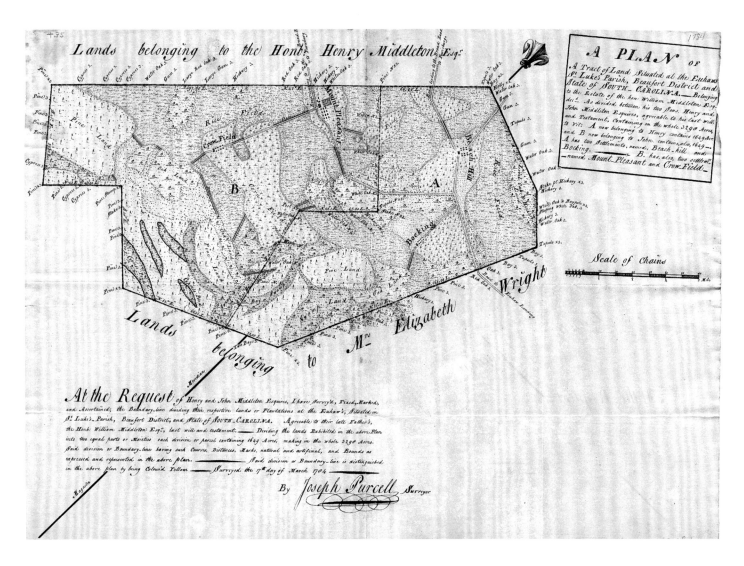

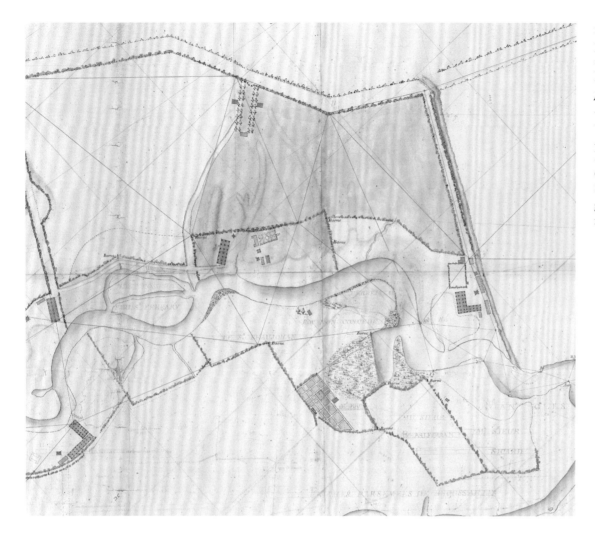

15. Detail of the Laborde plantation showing triangulated survey of Haut du Cap, Saint-Domingue on *Plan de différentes possessions à St. Domingue [sur la Rivière du Haut du Cap, près de la ville du Cap-Français], concernant Ferrary, Beaujouan, Sicard, etc.,* 1780. Bibliothèque nationale de France, département Cartes et plans, GE SH 18 PF 152 DIV 3 P 1, Source gallica.bnf.fr: http://catalogue.bnf. fr/ark:/12148/btv1b531033710

pine land and the black geometric dots of the slave quarters are far from any British landscape tradition. Yet the edge condition of tree stumps and named tree species, staking out a defined piece of territory, is familiar to Ireland.

By 1750 the compass-and-chain survey method, and its many errors and limitations, was almost only associated with colonial survey, as the complexity of most European countries' property mosaic demanded the accuracy of triangulated survey.[30] But in Ireland and British America the chain and compass survey continued with colonial surveying patterns determining the design of colonial space.[31] Walking the bounds with a compass-and-chain, taking angular bearings, drawing the single pieces of patchwork and then stitching them together, affected how landscape was perceived and thus designed. With no obligation to conform to a master, countrywide geometry and set-out, the surveyed land patches,

when sewn together, created interlocking and often contradictory puzzles. The individual plantation's design – its fields, house, cabins, mills and water courses – was then inserted into this jigsaw geometry. Irish, Caribbean and early American cartography share a similar concern for the border condition because the boundary line is the hardest and by far the most important to pin down. In contexts where ownership may have been recently won, of questionable authority or open to changing interpretation, the survey or the plat remained the most popular and necessary design drawing. This book is illustrated with many such maps and surveys – where the interior is far less defined than the edge. The technique and profession of surveying are important because the setting out of a landscape is significant for understanding the design that it generates. By connecting the final architectural decisions back through the generating decisions of plot, boundary and lease, the structure and sequence of key spatial decisions can be discerned and the necessity and desirablility of the results analysed. The legal structure of the landscape is significant for understanding the eventual form of the individual house. In many early British colonies (including Ireland) trees were often used by surveyors to legally pin down and define the exact boundaries of a patented piece of land. If such trees were cut down, or if they fell in a storm, property disputes arose as to the land's area and exact geographical position. The Virginian planter Robert Vaulx found himself in just such a predicament in 1671 when 'the beginning corner tree' of his 'pattent for six thousand acres of land in Westm[or]land County' was 'not to be found' after a storm. He petitioned the Virginia council for 'a quallified Surveyor with the ancient Inhabitants', namely established Europeans and not American Indians, to 'lay out' the land according to his patent. If the corner tree was still missing the council ordered the surveying party to 'begin opposite to Mr Tho[mas] Broughton's land according to pattent' and the wider 'neighbourhood' was 'to have notice of the time of Survey', in case of any further claimants or other legal issues.[32]

Survey methods, and their importance for compiling an accurate map record of a colony or island's changing environment, differed between empires. Triangulation, where a survey is checked using long diagonal measurements and connected into a larger triangular network of benchmarked regional measurements, was not rolled out across the British isles or its colonies until the nineteenth century.[33] In contrast, the French state employed the most avant-garde surveying techniques across its Caribbean island colonies, producing beautifully detailed eighteenth-century cadastral maps (Fig. 15). Because the state taxed land, France had legal requirements for registering land area, use and ownership that did not exist for the British Isles. Although the British parliamentary enclosure maps of the eighteenth century are somewhat similar in scale and detail to French eighteenth-century cadastral maps they only map the area to be enclosed, not the entire countryside. 'In continental European countries one of the main motives for a centrally organized mapped cadaster', as Roger Kain and Elizabeth Baigent have explained, was 'the desire to improve the efficiency with which land taxes were levied' and in many parts 'a mapped cadaster proved a vital weapon for the monarch in his battle to increase taxation.' In contrast, although the English 'propertied classes and central government also clashed over land taxation, when they reached a consensus,

it was one in which it was in no one's interest to compile a mapped cadaster' because 'a surveyed cadaster would necessarily have been in the hands of professional surveyors under the control of central government and would have removed control of the tax from the local landowners and as such was unthinkable'.[34]

Large ancestral aristocratic estates, where the property had been received directly from the Crown, often in the medieval period or earlier, were not required to register the size, exact location or boundaries of their property. This still makes it very difficult to identify property owners in the United Kingdom, and also in Ireland, where the property laws were not substantially changed by the advent of the Free State in 1922, or the republic in 1949 and the absence of consistent and entire cadastral mapping across the British empire continues to hamper landscape design analysis at a large or intermediate scale, particularly before the nineteenth-century Ordnance Survey.[35] The Irish Down Survey maps (1655–9), although very helpful for many purposes, are designed to 'record the boundaries of forfeited townlands and contain an inventory of land as cultivable, bog, mountain, or wood' for the purposes of property transfer rather than property development.[36]

The French cadastral map record exhibits far greater coverage at a large scale than any British examples and this was partly a legacy of the different approaches to infrastructure in each empire. The French state was implicitly bound up with the improvement of its colonies and infrastructural innovations were not necessarily instigated by planters but by the state itself, often from Paris.[37] France's more accurate and detailed survey methods engendered and coordinated its Caribbean colonies' many infrastructural projects because they made them automatically easier to organise, design and depict in plan,[38] with the maps produced for the ministry of the marine by the *ingenieurs du roi* revealing the owners, positions, areas, borders, building layouts, infrastructure and water engineering of many of the plantations (Fig. 16).[39] In Saint Domingue (now Haiti) the original set-out geometry of the French Crown's land grants to the *arpenteurs du roi* remained intact but was slowly subdivided over time. In the plains this geometry was slowly altered by the construction of roads, defence infrastructure and irrigation schemes. French plantation practice favoured avenues and roads planted in straight lines and the cadastral maps of Saint Domingue map such lines of street trees to an exhaustive level of detail (Fig. 16).

16. Detail from Antoine (ingénieur), *Carte topographique des environs de Léogane, dans l'île de Saint-Domingue*, 1765,
Bibliothèque nationale de France, département Cartes et plans, GE SH 18 PF 151 DIV 3 P 6,
Source gallica.bnf.fr: http://catalogue.bnf.fr/ark:/12148/cb43567051

Seventeenth-century plantation design in the Americas and Ireland took European land survey and acquisition methods, remoulding them for effective use in new environments, while other American initiatives had a character all of their own. Planters in the United States had generally amassed much more land over a shorter time interval than European gentlemen. Virginia's William Byrd I amassed almost 30,000 acres in thirty years, an area far greater than anyone could hope to acquire in most of Europe, unless the landholding pattern had been recently and dramatically altered (such as in Ireland in the seventeenth century). Western Europe, however, had no widespread scheme comparable to the Virginian headright system or 'practice of tying land acquisition to importation of people to work it' that 'originated from the grants of fifty acres of land awarded to any settler who financed his or her own passage or who paid for the transportation of another immigrant'.[40] Initially devised for indentured European servants, the Virginia council awarded headrights from 1635 onwards 'to those who imported Africans as well as Europeans, and it was members of the council who registered three-quarters of the headrights claimed for importing blacks that were used to obtain the certificates ordering the surveying of a parcel of unclaimed land, the first step in acquiring acreage granted for importing settlers'.[41] William Byrd I had 'acquired more than half' of his 30,000 acres 'using headrights, with a third of that coming from importing African slaves'.[42] This connection between the acquisition of land and the purchase of enslaved workers, where the land had not even been surveyed before the enslaved workers had been bought, grafted slavery firmly to the American great estate. By the end of the seventeenth century no great Virginian estate could be amassed without a proportional complement of enslaved workers.

Once the land required for successful planting had been amassed, the American planter generally did not attempt to compose the entire landholding into a cohesive designed estate or to draw and manage it as such. Unlike Caribbean planters who tended to concentrate on laying out and designing 'one large, integrated plantation',[43] Virginian 'planters set up multiple ancillary quarters on which the workers concentrated primarily on raising staple crops and livestock'.[44] In all American and Caribbean colonies, where little income came from rents, the plantation owner's wealth was to a great extent dependent on the sale of the one crop that had been identified

as the most profitable. In Virginia this was invariably tobacco. As Lorena Walsh has explained, a splintered plantation structure allowed planters to 'farm the best tobacco soils they owned, maintain large herds of livestock, and begin developing additional plantations that they could eventually give to their children'. Adopting a composite structure of separate plantations, sometimes euphemistically referred to as 'farms', also enabled a great planter to place 'Africans on outlying quarters' that 'served to keep them isolated from whites other than an overseer and to keep most enslaved field workers at a distance from the master's dwelling'. The central 'farm' or 'home plantation' generally contained 'most processing, craft, and manufacturing activities – which expanded during economic downturns – as well as the culture of crops (like small grains) and the raising of livestock (like sheep), to which overseers and workers were unaccustomed'.[45] The tradition of American estate mapping also differed from comparable Caribbean traditions, where elaborate maps of a planter's leading plantation were common.[46] By the eighteenth century the diverging rates of absenteeism between the United States (low), the Caribbean (high) and Ireland (medium), saw areas with high rates produce elaborate drawings for absentee owners to peruse in their 'home' environment.

Lorena Walsh has convincingly argued that the seventeenth-century 'switch among the Chesapeake elite to enslaved labor, however, surely made architectural arrangements that physically segregated domestic workers from the planter's family and guests another reason for remodeling older dwellings or for building new ones that employed architecture to enforce social hierarchy'.[47] She estimates that 'by the 1680s and 1690s, new houses were being built or old ones remodeled so that they accommodated only the white family' and this evolution clearly distinguishes the design of the American house from comparable European efforts, where servants were typically accommodated in the same building as those who employed them. The popularity of the Palladian villa as a prototype in the British Isles derived partly from its plan, which linked the central main block to its service wings internally. But the American country house, otherwise descended from European prototypes, splintered into many separate structures that had no internal connection in plan. Services such as cooking and washing, which were accommodated in the wings or basements of a typical European country house, were instead allotted distinct and separate buildings.

Entail was a legal device that ensured a landed estate was inherited by a 'fixed or prescribed line of devolution' so that it could not 'be bequeathed at pleasure by any one possessor'.[48] In Ireland and Great Britain it ensured, as it still does today in the United Kingdom, that estates could not be broken up at will by later generations. Entail was most common among the great Tidewater planters of Virginia, where the greatest concentration of wealth accumulated and where English aristocratic practices were most likely to be emulated. Lorena Walsh credits the Virginian practice 'of entailing land, and after 1705 often enslaved laborers as well, in the male line'[49] with creating Virginia's great estates, and Holly Brewer has shown that 'entail and primogeniture were feudal institutions critical to the growth and perpetuation of aristocracy and slavery in the south'.[50] The Virginian laws in 1705 'not only strengthened the grip of entails on land and allowed the entailing of slaves but limited the right to patent more than 500 acres of land to those who owned more than five slaves or servants' and furthermore, each additional slave or servant represented permission to patent 200 additional acres – up to a total of 4,000 acres. These 'acts connected the ownership of large estates with slavery' and ensured that 'entail contributed to the demand for slaves'.[51] But the Chesapeake elites did not follow British precedents in all their inheritance practices. While 'restrictive inheritance practices like entail were employed to keep wealth in the family' they did not 'force younger sons to make their own way in the world in occupations other than planting', often giving them their own plantations. Nor did they 'curtail the dowries of younger daughters', often giving or leaving to them enslaved workers that they then brought to their husband's plantations.[52] These various divergent practices from British and British Caribbean norms encouraged the more splintered character of American estate design. Because the estate was likely to be broken up between a number of children there was no need to design it as an entirely integrated holding in spatial terms.

The fact that entailment encompassed both land and enslaved people eventually helped to preference a plantation system of enslaved labour rather than one of tenants. Brewer analyses how the 'process created hierarchies' and that 'in combination with the initial headright system and continuing patronage practices by kings and governors, entail and primogeniture formed and sustained divisions between rich and poor'.[53] Yet in the aftermath of the successful American Revolution of 1776, the ideology of the young American republic required that any such hierarchies, particularly those of the aristocrat/peasant or landlord/tenant varieties, had to be refuted. That the American plantocracy might bear some resemblance to a new aristocracy was unacceptable and led to considerable efforts to conceal and repudiate any similarity. Pierce Butler, son of an Irish baronet, a substantial plantation owner and slaveholder and a great speculator in land, much of which he leased to others, wrote to his cousin in London in 1788: 'Every man here is lord of the soil he lives on, happy and independent if they are sensible of it, the earth yielding generously.' He considered the American people 'not very industrious; having no landlord to fear, they cultivate[d] enough to give them plenty for their own use'.[54] On his way to see Virginia's Natural Bridge and accompanied by Thomas Jefferson, the Marquis de Chastellux, a French nobleman, stopped at 'a little lonely house' inhabited by 'a Mr. Mac Donnel, an Irishman' and his wife, who 'had nothing rustic either in her conversation or her manner'. He generalised from their example that 'in the centre of the woods, and wholly occupied in rustic business, a Virginian never resembles a European peasant: he is always a freeman, participates in government, and has the command of a few negroes'.[55] This pithy description pinpoints how the American landed estate diverged in structure, ideology and labour practices from European models.

Entail and slavery exerted a profound impact on the form of the American plantation, and any aspirations its owner might have to improve it. Peter Martin convincingly outlines a methodology for the design of one of the largest elite Virginian plantations in his book *The Pleasure Gardens of Virginia*. Writing of Carter's Grove he explains the legal difficulties that prevented Carter Burwell from developing his newly inherited estate in 1732: 'The legacy, which came from Robert "King" Carter, one of the largest landowners in the colony, specified that Burwell had to preserve the labor force at the plantation and could not transfer any of the slaves to other tracts in order to maintain it as an important income-producing tobacco and grain plantation.' Yet Robert 'King' Carter's heir Carter Burwell's taste was for 'a landscape of woods and improved fields of wheat, barley, oats and peas' (such as George Washington was later to espouse at Mount Vernon), and he intended them to be 'naturally disposed around the house's immediate grounds' rather than a 'landscape of tobacco plants and fields dotted with slave quarters surrounding an expensive

17. Carter's Grove, Virginia. Dennis Hockman for the National Trust for Historic Preservation in the U.S.

house and overlooking a lovely river'. To do this 'he needed to abandon ideas of making the plantation a major source of tobacco income, move many of his slaves to others of his tracts, and then transform the plantation into a type of country house where rural pleasures could be pursued in a civilized setting'.[56] At Carter's Grove the entail that existed between the slaves and the land they farmed had to be broken by an act of assembly before the landscape could be redesigned and the relative proportion of tobacco plantations to mixed arable fields and groves of trees recalibrated. Even when accomplished, Carter Burwell's designed landscape was concentrated into a series of stepped terraces leading down to the river (Fig. 17). Thus the system of primogeniture entail in Britain, which both created the great landed estate and protected it from breakup, was expressly broken by republican principle in the United States and sometimes for clear design purposes.[57] Other 'remarkable alterations' made by the young republic to 'the common

law of England' included breaking primogeniture inheritance whereby 'the lands of any person dying intestate shall be divisible equally among all his children, or other representatives, in equal degree', and this breaking of entail between slaves and the land they farmed made 'slaves distributable among the next of kin, as other moveables'. It also led to the tragic breakup of enslaved families because it permitted the separate sale of individuals.[58] By breaking entail men such as Carter Burwell were free to buy and sell their lands, move their enslaved workers to other properties, sell them together or individually and design the American plantation landscape as they wished.

The villa was a fundamental design concept for European plantation and colonization. Devised initially in Italy, the prototype spread throughout Europe and thence to the Americas. It could structure large areas of very different geographical character into a familiar pattern by combining the practical demands of farming and gardening with a long and

18. Williamsburg, Virginia. Author's photo, 2013

sophisticated aesthetic tradition. This same tradition could then represent colonial landscapes in ways that addressed both the local eye of the planter and the eyes of those in power back home. The intricacies of *villegiatura* culture, as it developed in Renaissance Italy and latterly in eighteenth-century England, were born of the co-dependency of country and city. The villa-builder typically made his money in the city. By adopting the villa lifestyle, he usually left the city for defined periods of time in order to enjoy life in the country. His income could be drawn from many sources other than agriculture: rent, trade in luxurious commodities that he did not produce, state sinecures, political positions and substantial amounts of inherited wealth.[59] As James Ackerman has elucidated, 'The content of villa ideology is rooted in the contrast of country and city, in that the virtues and delights of the one are presented as the

antitheses of the vices and excesses of the other.'[60] Yet in colonial environments in the United States, and some in Ireland, urbanisation followed plantation rather than preceded it, thus 'reversing the normal dependence of the villa on the city'[61] and it also 'usurped in many respects the functions of the town'.[62] In 1710 Governor Spotswood remarked that the life he was 'likely to lead' in Virginia could not be but a 'perfect retir'd Country life' for there was 'not in the whole Collony a place that may be compar'd to a Brittish village; every one living disperst up and down at their Plantations, possessing there all food necessary for humane life (nay & luxury too) & procuring their Raiment by the returns which their Tobacco makes in Great Britain'.[63] When towns were built, the plots and thus the buildings were far more dispersed than was customary in European towns and villages (Fig. 18).

Positioning the 'Glorious Revolution': Towns, Trees and Prospects

England's Civil War of 1642–51 led to the execution of Charles I in 1649, a regicide that temporarily ended the monarchy and instituted a form of republican government. The plantation era in Ireland is often considered to have ended in 1649, when Oliver Cromwell, Protector of the Commonwealth, came to Ireland to end the Irish Catholic and royalist rebellion of 1641 and to secure the three kingdoms of England, Scotland and Ireland under parliamentary control. Over the period of 1640–60 the Catholic (typically conflated with Irish, not always accurately) share of profitable Irish land fell from 59 per cent to 8–9 per cent of the total, with most of it located in the west of Ireland.[64] Somewhat modified to a total of 20 per cent by the Acts of Settlement and Explanation in the 1660s,[65] the Catholic proportion was reduced again by the confiscations and redistributions that took place in the aftermath of the Glorious Revolution of 1688. These large-scale reconfigurations of Irish landed property required and encouraged design strategies that manipulated the memory of the most significant military events. Towns were particularly useful because they could be recast as key nodes in the new overarching web of state power. The strategy is most evident in the twin towns of Derry/Londonderry and Drogheda, where military events of international import took place. Their landscapes were explicitly twinned by the engraver John Brooks in 1746, when he published 'two Metzotinto Prints, the one the Battle of the Boyne, fought by our late illustrious glorious deliverer, King William III … the other the remarkable Siege of Derry'[66] in *Faulker's Journal* of 6 September 1746. Cast together in a commemorative and comparative embrace, the political and representational twinning of the two walled cities united urban and landscape designs of considerable ingenuity and nuance.

Unlike the newer towns of the United States, Irish towns and urban landscapes could be reconfigured for various purposes. The town of Derry/Londonderry, the destination of most ships entering the estuary of the river Foyle, is situated on the eastern neck of the Inishowen peninsula. Named Londonderry in 1613, the town became an important bridgehead for the plantation of west Ulster, its development partly funded by its corporate landowner, the City of London.[67] Because Irish plantation strategy considered building fortified towns, castles and bawns essential, they were very carefully designed, often using the most advanced military technology, with walls and bastion walks positioned so that the surrounding countryside could be carefully watched from a height. Perceived from many viewpoints as an island, and called the 'Island of Derry' in some sources, Derry/Londonderry is Ireland's youngest walled town and remains the most intact.[68] Forged from its ability to withstand many sieges, this has created an urban identity defined by walls, gates and a central diamond (Fig. 19). The Dutchman Gerald Boate singled it out as 'one of the principall fortresses of Ireland', describing it as 'very handsome, the streets being broad and well-paved, the houses some stories high' and 'inclosed with a thick and very strong stone wall'.[69] The author of the 1657 *Ireland's Natural History*, Boate defined plantation as the 'head spring of all the native commerce and trading', whether reflecting 'upon the first settlement of a plantation, to prosper it, or upon the wealth of a nation that is planted, to increase it'.[70] Indebted to 'the outlook of beleaguered European Protestantism, especially that of Hartlib and his circle',[71] his history set out to describe the entire island and its resources, particularly those that had not been plumbed economically. Written 'for the common good of Ireland, and more especially, for the benefit of the Adventurers and Planters therein' it was dedicated to the victorious Oliver Cromwell, while its author looked forward to the 'somewhat hopefull appearance of Replanting Ireland shortly, not only by the Adventurers, but happily by the calling of exiled Bohemians and other Protestants also'.[72]

A citadel almost completely surrounded by water, Derry/Londonderry's Protestant religious complex of St Columb's, with its cathedral and bishop's palace, stands at its apex (Fig. 20). This geography contributed to the slow formation of its suburbs as the military function of a glacis persisted, particularly along its western face towards Donegal and the more recalcitrant 'native' population. Many seventeenth-century Irish towns prohibited Catholics from living within their walls and while such rules were often relaxed over time they nevertheless encouraged the long ribbons of houses and cabins that stretched along the approach roads to many Irish towns and villages. Often including an 'Irishtown' precinct, such extramural developments were particularly obvious at walled towns with their clearly defined boundaries. Composed of buildings that were mostly of low architectural quality, their inhabitants enjoyed little, if any, security of tenure, due to the penal property laws

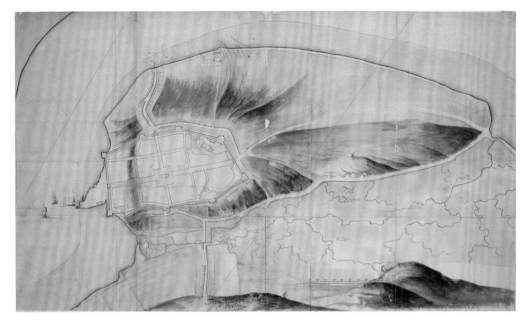

19. 'The Citty [sic] of Londonderry', Thomas Phillips, 1685. National Library of Ireland, MS 2557/34

20. *(below)* William van der Hagen, Londonderry, *c.*1730. DCSDC Heritage & Museum Collections, North is left

that the Irish and English parliaments enacted at the end of the seventeenth century. Derry/Londonderry's by-laws stringently prohibited Catholics from living within the walls long into the eighteenth century and its pointedly descriptive Catholic suburb of Bogside exemplifies the sectarian character of many Irish urban landscapes.[73] Lying at the foot of one of the town's great southwestern bastions (Fig. 19), the Bogside's low topographic position provided a neat corollary to the eastern Protestant suburb of Waterside that lay across the river Foyle, where it enjoyed many river prospects up and downstream.

The walled town of Drogheda, built on a rocky outcrop on the northern side of the river Boyne, was the scene of one of Cromwell's most defining exploits in Ireland, his siege of the town in 1649, when many of its medieval walls and castellated gateways were damaged. Its Protestant St Peter's church, like St Columb's cathedral in Derry/Londonderry, is located at the town's topographic apex while the Magdalene tower of St Mary's Dominican abbey, ruined during the course of the siege, still stands along the same ridgeline (Fig. 21). Sir Henry Tichbourne, a doyen of the Ulster Plantation, had led the

Cromwellian forces at Drogheda. Afterwards, in thanks for his military prowess, he was granted substantial areas of confiscated land and began building the villa of Beaulieu some 4.5 km east of the town in 1660. One of Ireland's earliest houses of a non-defensive nature, its south façade enjoys a close axial relationship with the Boyne River in the manner of an Inishowen or Virginian great house (Fig. 22). But its longer and principal entrance elevation was turned west to connect the villa with the town to which it owed its origin (Fig. 23) and the upper rooms enjoyed an axial prospect of the ruined Magdalene tower of St Mary's Dominican abbey. Inside the house the hall's overmantel painting by the Dutch artist William van der Hagen described the villa's spatial connection with the town by picking out the three upper gates, the ruined Magdalene tower, the cathedral's pitched roof, St Laurence's gate and a distant yet commanding prospect of Beaulieu itself (Fig. 24). The plasterwork half-roundel above the hall door, which featured helmets, pikes, shields and a miniature model of Drogheda's St Laurence's gate, made the Tichbourne family's urban and military allegiances explicit to visitors (Fig. 25).

21. Gabriele Ricciardelli, *View of Drogheda from Ballsgrove* (looking northeast), *c.*1754. Drogheda Municipal Art Collection, Highlanes Gallery

22. *(top left)* Beaulieu, Co. Louth, photograph of the south façade from the river Boyne, Author's photo, 2022

23. *(top right)* Beaulieu, Co. Louth, photograph of west entrance façade. Author's photo, 2013

24. *(bottom)* Beaulieu House, Co. Louth, William van der Hagen, overmantel view of Drogheda, Co. Louth with Beaulieu House in the background, *c.*1718. Reproduced with kind permission of Cara Konig Brock

Less than forty years after the siege of Drogheda the Glorious Revolution of 1688 consolidated and secured the thrones of England, Scotland and Ireland for a Protestant succession. William, Prince of Orange, Stadtholder of the Dutch Republic and husband of Mary, daughter of Charles I, was invited to invade England by a coterie of Whig Protestants, thereby successfully initiating the Glorious Revolution, whereby the Crowns of the three nations were made conditional upon the holder's Protestant faith. Glorious in its reinstatement of Protestant monarchical power, if somewhat less

25. Plasterwork half-roundel of military apparel and weaponry above hall door, Beaulieu House, Co. Louth. Author's photo, 2013

26. *(below)* Romeyn de Hooghe (circle of), 'Belegering van Londonderry, 1689'. Rijksmuseum, RP-P-OB-79.367

LONDONDERRI

than revolutionary in its degree of popular uprising, many of its seminal battles and sieges took place on Irish soil, also the locus, arguably, of its most long-lived political consequences. 1689 was also the year of Derry/Londonderry's significant siege when the city's western gates were shut and held by a band of Apprentice Boys against the combined Irish and royalist armies of James II and Louis XIV, neither of whom was present.[74] A 1690 engraving of the siege of Londonderry produced by the circle of Romeyn de Hooghe picked out the key protagonists from a Dutch perspective, placing the French and Irish

positions with care, noting where Mountjoy had destroyed the boom by the riverside and conflating the battle's many manouevres into one drawing (Fig. 26). Drawn from the west, de Hooghe depicted where the town's topography exhibited its steepest incline from the high southwestern walled escarpments to the low Bogside. This position remained particularly vulnerable to attack from the surrounding flat marshes and thin extramural suburbs, and generated a landscape of dugouts, redoubts and other military defence works that de Hooghe included in his drawing and that contemporary battle maps

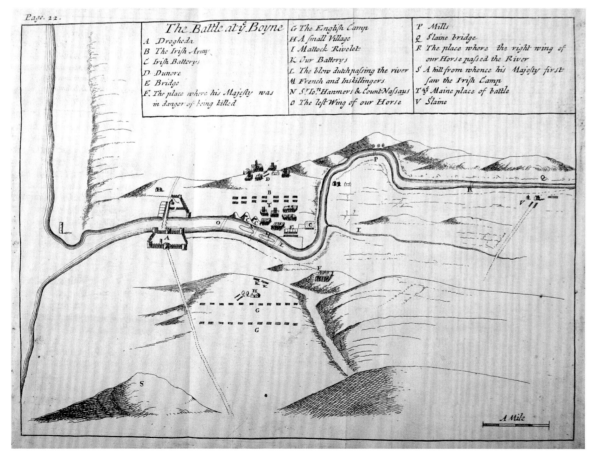

The Battle at ye Boyne

A Drogheda
B The Irish Army
C Irish Batterys
D Dunore
E Bridge
F The place where his Majesty was in danger of being killed

G The English Camp
H A small Village
I Mattock Rivelet
K Our Batterys
L The blow dutch passing the river
M French and Inskillingers
N Sr Ioh. Hanmers & Count Nassaus
O The left Wing of our Horse

P Mills
Q Slaine bridge
R The place where the right wing of our Horse passed the River
S A hill from whence his Majesty first saw the Irish Camp
T ye Maine place of battle
V Slaine

A Mile

27. *(above)* Francis Nevill, map of Londonderry, 1689. National Library of Ireland 16 H 24

28. *(left)* George Story, 'The Battle at ye Boyne', in his *An Impartial History of the Wars of Ireland* (London: Richard Chiswell, 1693), p. 22

29. 'To the Field of the Battle of the Boyne', in Extra-illustrated copy of Arthur Young, *A Tour in Ireland; with general observations on the present state of that kingdom: made in the years 1776, 1777, and 1778. and brought down to the end of 1779*, quarto edn (London: printed for T. Cadell, Strand; and J. Dodsley, 1780). National Library of Ireland, LO 10203

took care to record (Fig. 27). William van der Hagen's oil painting of *c.*1730 took the same viewpoint as de Hooghe, but, with defensive imperatives moving into memory, he crowned the town's crenellated high-level bastion walks with groves of trees rather than plumes of cannon fire (Fig. 20).[75]

Soon after the siege of Londonderry, on 12 July 1690, a little upstream of Drogheda, the battle of the Boyne was fought between James II of England (with some help from his Continental allies) and William III, both of whom were present. The battle occurred close to the town at Oldbridge, Co. Meath, where the river could be easily forded. The two armies' positions were commemorated shortly afterwards in a drawing produced by the surveyor George Story, which he subsequently published in his rather less than *Impartial History of the Wars of Ireland* with a legend keying both the landscape's geographical features and the strategic movements of the Jacobite and Williamite forces (Fig. 28). The construction in 1736 of a substantial stone obelisk close to where King William had been injured drew the battle-field and its legacies into the design of the wider Boyne valley (Fig. 29). Built by subscription, the obelisk soon became a popular print,[76] providing a frontispiece for books such as Thomas

Wright's 1748 *Louthiana or an Introduction to the Antiquities of Ireland*, and George Taylor and Andrew Skinner's 1778 *Maps of the Roads of Ireland*. Thomas Mitchell's painting of the Boyne obelisk imaginatively transposed Grinling Gibbons's equestrian statue of William III, which once stood in reality on College Green, Dublin, site of the Irish parliament, to the Boyne valley (Fig. 30).[77] Staring stoically towards the obelisk, the town of Drogheda and the distant Irish sea, William took up a position derived from the bearings that had secured his throne.

Later maps continued to displace King William's south-ward direction of travel with Mitchell's east–west vector of the Boyne valley. Matthew Wren's 1766 *Topographical Map of the County of Louth* included small drawings of the obelisk, Old Bridge Town, the ruins of Mellifont and the region's many significant churches and towers (Fig. 31). Drogheda had two small drawings, St Peter's to the north and St Mary's to the south, both ruinous in the aftermath of seventeenth-century events but each providing a convenient focus for prospects, avenues and other design axes. When Mary Delany visited Drogheda in June 1752 she described a town 'disposed with little neat gardens, old walls covered with ivy, a ruined castle, and variety of

30. Thomas Mitchell, A *View of the River Boyne with Gentlemen and Horses by a Statue to William III in the Foreground, the Boyne Obelisk beyond*, 1757. National Museums Northern Ireland

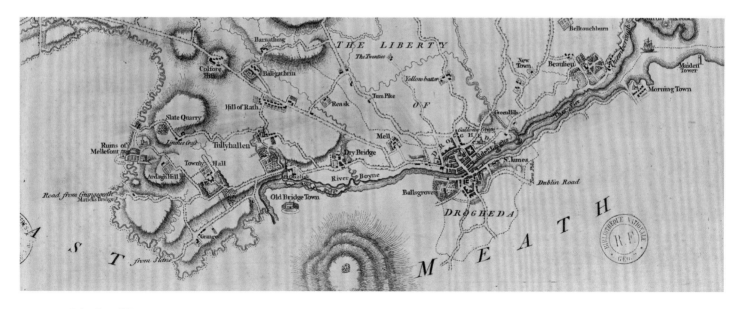

31. Matthew Wren, *A Topographical Map of the County of Louth*, 1766. Detail of the Boyne valley. Bibliothèque nationale de France, département Cartes et plans, GE DD-2987 (2658, 1), http://catalogue.bnf.fr/ark:/12148/cb41217451v

32. Gabriele Ricciardelli, *View of Drogheda looking west* (with the Boyne obelisk in the distance), *c.*1754.
Drogheda Municipal Art Collection, Highlanes Gallery

objects' that made 'a better and more pleasing show than [she could] describe; and the river, which winds and widens with a handsome bridge over one part of it, and shipping beyond that' to 'complete the scene'. She 'sallied forth' in the evening to see St Peter's, which was 'not quite finished' but which promised to be 'very handsome'.[78] Wren also carefully depicted the lineaments of Drogheda's plan and flanked it with the substantial landscaped villa plans of the houses of Ballsgrove and Beaulieu. Each villa's principal urban axis was indicated with Beaulieu's extending towards the spire of St Peter's and Ballsgrove's towards Millmount and St Mary's (Fig. 31).

When the Italian painter Gabriele Ricciardelli visited Drogheda a few years after Mary Delany he depicted the city in two pendant views, one looking northeast from the villa of Ballsgrove (Highfield) (Fig. 21) and the other looking west from the old motte and bailey site of Millmount (Fig. 32). The view from Ballsgrove flattered the city with the delicate tints of sunrise and flattened its circuit of walls, gates, Magdalene tower and St Peter's steeple into a silhouette, abstracted into attractive follies to admire from a villa's walks and lawns. In the

foreground Ricciardelli depicted a genteel *fête champêtre* admiring the city's ruins from a refined yet triumphalist perspective while two well-dressed women promenaded along the ridge walk (Fig. 21). In June 1752 Mary Delany had descended from St Peter's and had crossed the river to ascend 'Ball's walks'. Appearing as faint zigzag lines in Ricciardelli's Millmount view, they led up to the promontory villa gardens of Ballsgrove (Fig. 32):

> You wind up a very steep hill (which otherwise would be insurmountable) planted with trees – some in walks, others in groves, so that part of it looks like a thick wood – on the top is a long level walk with old trees on each side of it, and at the end a pretty, clean house and spruce garden full of flowers, which belongs to Mr Ball, who is so obliging to the town as to permit that fine walk to be a public one, and it is the Mall of Drogheda. The view from it is surprizingly beautiful.[79]

Although Drogheda had a town mall by the riverside, the prospect walks in the villa of Ballsgrove evidently also served

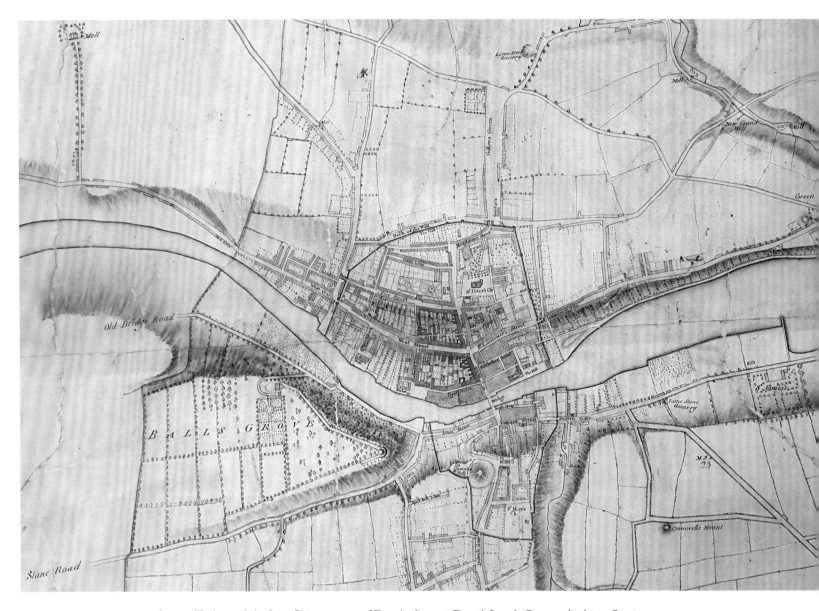

33. George Taylor and Andrew Skinner, map of Drogheda, 1778. Detail. Louth County Archives Service

as a public urban promenade. Like the wall walks of Derry/ Londonderry, they encouraged visitors to pick out the various points of aesthetic, military, civic and historical significance whilst admiring the wider prospect. At Ballsgrove's eastern prow you could stand on a circular prospect mount and look east towards Millmount and the ruined spire of St Mary's or look back and west along the axis to the house (Fig. 33). Beyond St Mary's ruined tower lay Cromwell's mount, from which he had made his assault on the town and which almost neatly aligned with Ballsgrove's mount and Millmount on

George Taylor and Andrew Skinner's 1778 map of Drogheda (Fig. 33). The heavy shading of Ballsgrove's slopes highlighted the clean lines of the tree-lined walk, hinged at its centre by a small folly building (Fig. 33).

Much of the Ballsgrove topography that Ricciardelli depicted survives today, as does the walk's alignment with St Mary's and its impressive prospect views of Drogheda's spires and ruins (Fig. 34). From these well-chosen ridges Delany remarked that you could 'on the one hand' see 'the obelisk erected in memory of the famous battle of the Boyne, on the

34. Photograph of Gabriele Ricciardelli's prospect northwards from Ballsgrove, Author's photo, 2021

35. Photograph of Gabriele Ricciardelli's prospect westward from Millmount, Author's photo, 2021

other several gentlemen's seats on the banks of the river',[80] explicitly connecting the appreciation of military and secular features. Unlike Jonathan Swift, whose 'first mortifying sight' of Drogheda 'was the ruins of several churches batter'd down by that usurper Cromwell' and who found in them damning evidence of 'the modern way of planting colonies',[81] Mary Delany was confident that the remnants of military and religious conflicts could be agreeably combined into pleasant landscapes. Gabriele Ricciardelli was not so convinced and his westward view from Millmount is rather less idyllic, and

more reflective of a battle-weary countryside (Fig. 32).[82] There the harsh lines of the barrack block offered a more ambiguous image of military achievement while the ruinous walls, sheltering thatched cabins and begging people, suggested a more troubled future. At the painting's centre Ricciardelli carefully placed a tiny distant prospect of the Boyne obelisk, its white wisp of a triangle rising above Ballsgrove's trees, but he concealed the house itself and the prospect, although bereft of the obelisk, may still be appreciated from Millmount today (Fig. 35). Two pendant views to suggest an allegory of Drogheda's

36. View of Prehen House from the river Foyle, Anon. photo

good and bad government, the city's prospects appear golden from Ballsgrove but shadowed and ambiguous from Millmount (Figs 21 and 32).

The practice of surveying, of viewing landscapes from a height while accurately noting the position of landmarks relative to one another that Mary Delany evidently practised at Drogheda was also a fundamental precursor to the accurate measured survey, confiscation and redistribution of land.[83] The Boyne valley had been parcelled out to the professional generals and soldiers who had fought there for Cromwell's army, for the Glorious Revolution, a Protestant ascendancy, and the land survey, confiscation and redistribution that followed in their wake. The prospect points were used both to survey the scene and to structure the paintings, picking out a new geometry of landownership, intended to replace and refute claims of an alternative, earlier network. Drogheda's sheer number of sacred, secular and military ruins served to evade historical accuracy and facilitated a compressed landscape design, where a mass of associations was to be skimmed over visually rather than interrogated ruin by ruin with any historical accuracy. Drogheda and Derry/Londonderry's topographical vantage points,

once so crucial for each town's defence and capitulation, were gradually converted into landscape designs. Carefully caught into the new web were the older prospect points of churches, mounts and other ruins – at Drogheda interwoven with the new master node of the Boyne obelisk. Mimicking the preference of battle paintings to document a carefully edited sequence of events, Ballsgrove's 'Mall' gave the public a viewing station from which to understand their town's urban history. Other Boyne villa landscapes, such as those of Oldbridge and Dowth, placed the Boyne obelisk in a more oblique relationship to the house, seductively linking ancient and new perspectives by accommodating neolithic mounds and barrows into their landscape designs.[84] Once the land had been mapped, bounded, drawn and apportioned, these more seductive design strategies became possible and perhaps necessary for long-term success. The substantial reconfiguration of Ireland's property footprint that these military events had created appears to have demanded such manoeuvres. Casting conquered or appropriated territory in a positive light was desirable for enticing sponsors or settlers, if not for the natives or residents.

Perceptions of Derry/Londonderry as a siege city continued, dampening suburban expansion and reinforcing the symbolic significance of its walls, bastions and trees. The citadel island topped by its cathedral spire was employed as a prospect point by villas that were built along the Foyle River, such as Prehen House, constructed in the mid-eighteenth century by the Knox family to the designs of Michael Priestley (Fig. 36). Located upstream of the town on the river Foyle's eastern bank, Prehen, like Beaulieu, turned its longer entrance façade towards the city where the cathedral spire provided the villa with a serene prospect of the Glorious Revolution's resolution. Prehen's demesne design, like that of Ballsgrove, reinforced the visual and historical connection between villa and city and the customary painting of King William at the Boyne also served to connect the two towns and their respective military events.

When the great Irish travel writer Arthur Young visited Derry/Londonderry in 1776 his first view 'at a distance of a mile or two' led him to describe it as 'the most picturesque of any place' he had yet seen in Ireland. It appeared 'to be built on an island of bold land rising from the river, which spreads into a fine bason at the foot of the town' and with 'the adjacent country hilly' *but* 'the scene want[ed] nothing but wood to make it a perfect landscape'. Young included an anonymous drawing of Derry/Londonderry taken from the north in his extra-illustrated copy of his own *A Tour in Ireland, 1776–1779* (Fig. 37).[85] The sketch closely depicted the town's upper southern quarters containing the cathedral, the bishop's palace and other ecclesiastical buildings and gardens. The prospect favoured the city's busy trading quays and although the hills rising behind the city were shown partially wooded it was evidently not enough for Young's taste, particularly the quays fronted by lines of cabins. The trees that Young found Derry/Londonderry to lack often proved useful for converting the military joys of *surveier* into a more lay appreciation of prospects and distant views.[86] The 'many new erected Manors' of the Ulster plantations had seen many useful trees planted in their gardens, orchards and woodlands to 'beautifie' Ireland's 'desolation' and to render 'her inaccessible Woods' into 'spaces made tractable'.[87] As trees became the proper accompaniment in Ireland to well-designed 'English' gardens, particularly orchards or kitchen gardens, they also reinforced the dykes and

causeways constructed in low-lying, water-logged territory, where land drainage was important for making the earth fertile, a common Irish condition and one requiring an expertise often transported to British colonies lying much further afield. Lines of trees had proved useful in Derry/Londonderry before Young's visit, with a corporation minute of February 1752 ordering 'Mr. Nat. Alexander to cut down the sycamore trees on the Mall Wall' and 'to oversee the beautifying and improving' by replanting a walk of fourteen trees, planted shortly after the siege 'as a memorial to the Thirteen Apprentice Boys who closed the Gates in 1688, the fourteenth commemorating James Morrison'.[88] Further corporation minutes directed the expenditure in 1776 of a sum 'not exceeding twenty guineas for planting trees on the Walls'[89] and in 1782 redirected the sum 'for the purpose of building steps and making other improvements to the Walls'.[90] Such clearly articulated and perennial intentions saw the geometry and positions of Derry/Londonderry's walls, walks, bastions, guns, column and trees continue to recall the

37. 'E.C.P. View of Londonderry, 1777' from extra-illustrated copy of Arthur Young's *A Tour in Ireland*. National Library of Ireland, LO 10203

power lines of an old battle and chasten anyone who might be contemplating another one. As they held their position overlooking the 'Irish' Bogside, contemporary views took care to lighten (and conceal) this triumphalism by including the Apprentice Boys' trees (Fig. 20). In such tense environments trees could translate the ambitions of 'improvement', which mostly coincided with plantation and colonization, into a more subtle and acceptable language. Quicker and easier to plant than buildings were to build, Derry/Londonderry's Apprentice Boys' trees show how military spaces, such as bastion walks, or defensive town walls, were converted to more secular and enjoyable uses.

Arthur Young planned to use his own drawing of *To the Field of the Battle of the Boyne* as an illustration for his book *A Tour in Ireland, 1776–1779* (Fig. 29) and its accompanying text revealed its almost absolute conversion from military theatre of war to picturesque prospect. Approaching 'the view of the scene from a rising ground which looks down upon it', Young found it 'exceedingly beautiful, being one of the completest landscapes' he had seen. It was located in 'a vale that lost itself in front between bold declivities, above which [were] some thick woods' where the river split 'to form an island, the point of which' was 'tufted with trees in the prettiest manner imaginable'. The obelisk stood 'on a rising ground on the banks of the river' where it was 'backed by a very bold declivity' and 'founded on a rock'. He pronounced it 'a noble pillar, and admirably placed' and he sat on 'the opposite rock' to 'indulge the emotions which with a melancholy not unpleasing' had filled his bosom. These sprang from reflecting 'on the consequences that had sprung from the victory here obtained' by William III: 'Liberty was then triumphant. May the virtues of our posterity secure that prize which the bravery of their ancestors won! Peace to the memory of the Prince to whom, whatever might be his failings, we owed that day memorable in the annals of Europe!'[91]

The landscapes discussed in this chapter document the great seventeenth- and eighteenth-century expansion of European colonization and imperialism. Design innovation was required, not at the centre, but at the edge. Setting out initially with the prosaic techniques of survey and measurement, soon reinforced by the military architecture of forts, bastions and walled towns, the conquering mind and eye then swivelled to bring more seductive design strategies into play, designing a cumulative weight of images, axes, point structures and avenues to create a web of legible state and imperial power. Landscape design at the centre of empire, in London or Paris, has no need of the contorted transfers of battle to prospect, prospect to obelisk, obelisk to villa, statue to setting, Dublin to Oldbridge, Derry/Londonderry to Drogheda. At the centre, the property footprint, secure in its past provenance and future inheritance, has no need of a political argument cast wide spatially in trees, sightlines, follies and ruins. Yet at the edge of a contested empire, as Ireland was in the late seventeenth century, minds and eyes had to be given the correct bearings, clothed in seductive landscape design. Reframing and reorienting older structures of consequence, even if ruinous, and sometimes because a ruin spoke eloquently of an opponent's defeat, made the new web of empire more powerful, visible and convincing (for some). Although necessarily more contrived and seductive in Ireland, where the competing and contradictory narratives of the recent past and its property repercussions could prove highly disruptive, the designed landscapes of the early United States held their own seeds of hypocrisy and contradiction, which later chapters will explore.

CHAPTER 2

Landscapes of Improvement

Improving the British Isles

The ideology of improvement was fundamental to British imperial expansion. Improved landscapes were designed to indicate unambiguously who owned them, how they were divided between landlord and tenant, the purpose of each piece of land, whether for tillage, grazing, forestry, hunting, leisure or aesthetic enjoyment, and how each piece of land was to be managed so as to increase the owner's profits. Improvement was thus intimately bound to novel developments in farming, both arable and dairying, and responded rapidly to innovative ideas about crop rotation, animal breeding, land reclamation and drainage infrastructure. Enclosure, or the removal, amalgamation and simplification of property boundaries, generally colluded with this process, as did the consolidation of large fortunes under the primogeniture system of inheritance that perpetuated Great Britain and Ireland's elite oligarchy of landowners. Areas of Great Britain with longer patterns of enclosure and estate amalgamation began their 'improvement' earlier, with some dating from the medieval period[1] and improvement arguably accelerated dramatically during Henry VIII's dissolution of the monasteries, when many families increased their landholdings, thus facilitating the amalgamation of the substantial core holding required for an emparked great seat. The various eighteenth-century Acts of enclosure were framed as improvements and gradually reduced the extent of common land or wasteland that lay outside estate lands. Such ambiguous areas, where the concept of property accommodated a community's rights and patterns of use, were less likely to occur in Ireland. The counties around London, England in general, the low counties of Wales and Scotland, and in Ireland the Dublin Pale and the lowland counties of Leinster, had visibly 'improved' landscapes by the early eighteenth century. The most visible feature of such improved landscapes was the gentleman's seat and its park or demesne (Fig. 38). Farmed and managed by its owner or occupant, who usually held the land in fee simple or as freehold, the remainder of the estate was leased to tenants whose rents provided much of the landowner's income. While he or she could stipulate improvements in leases and threaten annulation if the improvements did not take place, this rarely happened in practice and tenants were relatively independent, within the term of the lease, to design and manage the land as they saw fit. Many estate lands, having been improved and managed for long periods of time, were highly productive and the rents charged proportionately high.

As Paul Roebuck has shown, the principal structural differences between seventeenth-century English and Irish landscapes derived from 'the policy of letting property on very long leases – the aspect of management which more than any other provoked the difficulties of later periods'. It was 'established in the immediate aftermath of the conquest' in Ireland and 'firstly on the Chichester estates and elsewhere in Ulster'. This system was 'quite unlike that developed during the same period in most parts of England, where, under the impetus of the great contemporary rise in prices, owners, particularly of the larger estates, were rapidly changing over from very long leases and entry fines to much shorter leases and economic annual rents'. As he elucidates, 'it was this change which formed a basis

38. Aerial photograph of Carton, Co. Kildare. Ordnance Survey of Ireland

relatively frugal design gestures aligns them more with Virginia or Jamaica than with such Irish counties as Kildare, Dublin, Meath, Wexford or Carlow. These other Irish counties, unaffected by plantation, contained large estates of rich land, where Norman families could form aristocratic landscapes of great scale and design ambition.[3]

By the mid-eighteenth century most British and Irish landscape was almost entirely owned and controlled by an oligarchy of propertied gentlemen and women with the prefix 'gentle' implicitly denoting the ownership of land. Farming was central to improvement and it slowly grew in popularity as an elite occupation:

> Perhaps we might, without any great impropriety, call farming the reigning taste of the present times. There is scarce a nobleman without his farm: most of the country gentlemen are farmers; and that in a much greater extent of the word, than when all country business was left to the management of stewards … for now the master oversees all the operations of his farm, dictates the management, and delights in setting the country a staring at the novelties he introduces …The farming tribe is now made up of all ranks, from a duke to an apprentice.[4]

for the subsequent steady growth there of sound commercial farming, via a tripartite structure of owners, tenant farmers and labourers, which contrasted, and continued to contrast, so markedly with the prevailing situation within much of Irish agriculture'.[2] These itemised structural differences explain the design gap that developed between seventeenth- and eighteenth-century English and Irish landscape design. In Ireland large areas of unimproved land were controlled by middlemen who assumed the powers of the owner but never allowed control to pass into the hands of yeoman farmers or stable sub-tenants on long leases. Such middlemen's lands could never approach the scale of a great noble estate, and the Inishowen Plantation plots, for example, persisted over time, remaining unaffected by later trends in improvement, empark- ment and subdivision into smaller tenancies. Their under- takers remained tethered to agriculture, the countryside and to Inishowen and they did not become very rich. The emphasis they were obliged to place on self-sufficient farming and

The gentleman's park became the aesthetic centrepiece of the British landed estate and the powerhouse of its farming ambi- tions and its reconfiguration as the landscape garden generally harmonised and enhanced the wider structure of the landed estate. Some of the aesthetic of parkland design was derived from the separation of freehold and leasehold land, and its design inclined towards a strong figure set against the ground of the surrounding tenanted countryside (Fig. 38). The evolving landscape garden aesthetic reinforced this figure, most notably at the estate boundary wall, the tree belt, the perimeter rides and walks, and the hierarchy of lodges and approach routes. Both within and without the wall this route hierarchy served to generate many of the long- and short-distance prospects, views and vistas. Representations of the great estate positioned the great house centrally with estate portraiture depicting the most flattering view and then spiralling outwards to encom- pass other viewpoints. Although centred on the individual estate, eighteenth-century concepts of improvement reached far beyond its boundaries, encompassing landscape views, prospects, routes and towns. Estate portraiture was designed to generate, support and express this landscape structure. By the mid-eighteenth century as the landscape park evolved into the landscape garden, Capability Brown's aesthetic of lawns, clumps and modulated earth forms reached its apex. Earlier designers, in particular Charles Bridgeman and William Kent, had contributed to the formation of the pre-Brownian landscape park but Brown's ubiquity and singularity of vision subsumed all the separate components – tree belts, lawns, clumps and water features – into a powerfully cohesive aesthetic. When mid-eighteenth-century British estate landscape design moved towards a highly differentiated aesthetic from the surrounding tenanted countryside, the Brownian landscape garden gave it the vocabulary with which to do so.

Generally, the Brownian landscape garden proved to be a popular aesthetic model both at home and abroad. Its rolling lawns, lakes, sinuous tree belts and twisting circulation led many to emulate it in environments far removed from Brown's own habitat. However, once removed from its native legal, social and political context the Brownian landscape garden's capacity to achieve this could become constrained. Design transitions between tenanted and demesne land, grazed land and cropland, toned foliage belts and high stone walls were not as convincing in the Irish environment, where the unimproved surrounding countryside could curtail the charms of a long vista, and native cabins and potato lazy beds were difficult to reconcile with the lodges, drives and elegant views of the landscape garden. In England, the view and perception from within to without could be composed with relative insouciance. In Ireland, and further afield, designers could not safely assume that the view beyond would be unaffected by aesthetic and ideological discord.

Nevertheless, Brown's design vocabulary achieved widespread popularity in Ireland, if in partial or incomplete translation. Some of this was due to the physical environment, as Ireland, unlike England, has many inland lakes, and Irish demesnes were often fortunate enough to have large natural water bodies on their grounds. With limestone as the underlying bedrock throughout most of country, designed water features could be unexpectedly ephemeral – appearing and disappearing with the weather. Brown's genius for damming streams into lakes and making them appear natural was thus arguably redundant in many Irish contexts. Yet many artificial lakes were created in Ireland, particularly in such relatively flat counties as Kildare and Meath, where natural lakes are

relatively rare. Brown's impact was perhaps most evident in the lighter legacy that his aesthetic bestowed upon landscapes already possessed of great natural advantages, such as those of Ireland's lakelands and river valleys. With the hand of nature as the greater creative force, his vocabulary heightened their natural advantages and made them easier to appreciate.

Of all the landscape garden's innovations, perhaps the most innovative was its mobile aesthetic. It invited and encouraged movement. Unlike the long straight axes of canals, clipped allées and avenues that were characteristic of the baroque garden and best appreciated from a fixed and central focus point, the landscape garden demanded a twisting circumnavigation from its users. Approach routes, tree-belt rides and clumps created a designed parkland tour, implicitly to be enjoyed by carriage or on horseback, not by foot. The concept of making a tour to enjoy and appreciate a landscape predates the eighteenth century, such as when John Evelyn praised the educated traveller over someone who was merely 'making the Tour as they call it' in his 1652 publication *The State of France*.[5] One of the first instances of the use of the verb 'tour' comes from the pen of Mary Delany, who prepared 'to tour in the park' of Cornbury, Oxfordshire, with her husband in 1746.[6] As the concept of circumnavigating a defined area to better appreciate it was gradually adopted this affected the nested scales of a gentleman's park, county, tourist route and nation.[7] Designed landscapes in such tourist locales as the Wye valley or Killarney tended to express property boundaries in a less definitive fashion by extending the circuit of a tour, such as that contemplated by Mary Delany, to areas far beyond the park. It is therefore not surprising that some of the landscape garden's keenest observers were the writers of tour guides. Of these, the most influential, certainly regarding perceptions of Ireland, was undoubtedly Arthur Young.[8]

It is difficult to overstate the influence of Arthur Young's *A Tour in Ireland, 1776–1779* on perceptions of Ireland in the eighteenth century. He was 'not only the best-known agricultural reformer and publicist of his time, with an international reputation, but also a figure of importance in the political and social issues of the day'.[9] His character and writings combined the analytical and improving fervour of William Petty and Thomas Jefferson with the visual sensibility of William Gilpin, uniting aesthetic appreciation of the countryside with acutely observed description of agricultural and economic activity. Shifting between the viewpoints of agricultural improver, social commentator and landscape theorist his tours and travels managed to please and influence many by uniting English empirical theories of improvement with the roving eye of the picturesque tourist. Unlike many other early tour guides he managed to skilfully avoid a lecturing, condescending or colonial tone, and his sympathies with the actual inhabitants of a landscape were generally evident.[10] His *A Tour in Ireland, 1776–1779* was his first assessment of an entire country, and an ambitious and far-reaching work of landscape analysis. Young's tour in Ireland began on 19 June 1776 when he embarked at Holyhead. A comprehensive tour of the whole country, with very few exclusions (notably Connemara where the landscape was still too wild and uninhabited), his tour was published in 1780 and he later considered it in his autobiography 'among [his] best and most useful productions'.[11] Containing critiques of agricultural, aesthetic and economic practices, it remains one of the foremost sources for those studying the general condition of eighteenth-century Ireland. Perhaps the most influential travel writer of his own period, Young advanced comparative travel as a method for analysing countries, their modes of governance and their connected landscapes. A highly visual person, he not only described the physical, agricultural and economic characteristics of the lands through which he travelled, he also wrote about how he experienced an environment spatially, and gave his view on whether it was aesthetically pleasing or not. Thus, his publications are invaluable for reconstructing the form of Ireland's eighteenth-century designed landscape. They reveal how a travelling, educated improver perceived such landscapes and how his visual perceptions were connected to his recommendations. Not at all wary of working at a large scale, Young aimed to provide his readers with a broad-stroke analysis of the wider landscape while working at a level of detail that required the many columns, charts and tables that dot his publications.

A Tour in Ireland, 1776–1779 established Young's reputation as a critical observer of entire countries, at a scale beyond the English county studies that had occupied him for many years. In his Irish tour, he attempted to dissect the country's rural geography as a composite structure of hierarchical and nested elements that depended particularly on the landed estate and the tenanted farm. As he attempted to map his English experience onto the Irish environment, the physical and aesthetic boundaries between the more specific categories of regional

geographic landscape, gentleman's estate, gentleman's park, landscape garden and yeoman's/tenanted farm became indistinct and contradictory. In his *A Tour in Ireland*, Young distinguished carefully between parks (sometimes called 'domains') and farms. Farms, for Young, were typically substantial areas of land leased from a great landowner, such as that in Rathan, Co. Offaly (King's Co.), leased by 'the Norfolk bailiff' Mr Vancover from Lord Shelburne.[12] Descriptions of such farms invariably focused on practical farming improvements rather than on their visual assessment as designed landscapes. When describing landscape parks rather than farms, he usually gave a clear impression of their identity, using the words 'seat', 'park' or 'domain' (he did not spell it in the Irish tradition as 'demesne'). His tour remains an interesting and provocative record of an Englishman's perception and subsequent classification of Ireland's many landscapes. It is particularly valuable for his nuanced interrogation of the Irish landscape garden and of how this predominantly aesthetic paradigm became difficult to interpret in Ireland, where it was muddied both by Irish landholding patterns and by the natural form of the landscape itself.

Arthur Young completed many illustrations that he could not afford to include as plates in the final publication.[13] These are bound into his own copy of the single-volume quarto first edition published in London in 1780.[14] The quarto edition contains thirty-seven additional illustrations, including the eighteen pen-and-wash views bordered carefully in blue by Young himself (Figs 42, 46, 47, 48). Young had included illustrations in earlier books. His 1770 publication *A Six Months Tour through the North of England*[15] described his attempts to make 'a slight sketch' of the river Tees 'where it pours down the rock' and he judged the result to fall 'far short of the original'.[16] His opening image for the first volume of this work was of a bridge over a river, while the second volume was illustrated with a suite of waterfalls, a structure that he echoed in *A Tour in Ireland, 1776–1779* with a frontispiece of Powerscourt Waterfall (Fig. 39). In *The Farmer's Tour through the East of England* (1771) illustrations of ploughs, carts and farming implements predominated and this was repeated in his Irish tour, which included illustrations of a plough, a timber frame with straps, probably for restraining an animal and the illustration of a turnip drill that accompanied his description of Lord Montalt's demesne of Dundrum, despite (or because) of its being 'a place which his Lordship has ornamented in the modern stile of improvement'. Because

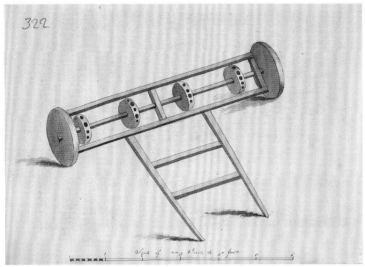

39. *(left)* Drawing of Powerscourt Waterfall for frontispiece from extra-illustrated copy of Arthur Young's *A Tour in Ireland*. National Library of Ireland, LO 10203

40. *(above)* A turnip drill from extra-illustrated copy of Arthur Young's *A Tour in Ireland*. National Library of Ireland, LO 10203

Lord Montalt 'cultivate[d] at a large scale' with some 30 or 40 acres under turnips, he had designed 'a very cheap simple drill, his own invention',[17] which Young drew and placed within his book (Fig. 40). *The Farmer's Tour through the East of England* included a chart with the characteristically pedantic 'View of the Dimensions of the Seats of the Nobility & c. throughout this Tour', and this was echoed in his Irish tour by the inclusion of measured drawings of Castletown House and Slane Castle (Fig. 41). The English tours were clear precursors to the Irish tour, and while both were illustrated with a mixture of farming implements and waterfalls, the Irish tour arguably attempted to be more picturesque and thus more attractive to a wider audience. But even in very picturesque locations he sought out experiments that fit conclusively into the improving rather than the picturesque canon. At Westport, he did depict Croagh Patrick and the islands of the bay but his descriptive focus was distracted by the walled enclosures that the Earl of Altamont was building for soil experiments.

Young disembarked at Dun Laoghaire near Dublin, as was the general practice for foreign visitors of the time. In Dublin, he was particularly impressed with the lower riverside regions of the Phoenix Park as an area where the Liffey had formed 'a variety of landscapes' rendering it 'the most beautiful environ' of the capital city. In his *A Tour in Ireland, 1776–1779* such designated 'landscapes' could exist independently of parkland, particularly in Killarney, Lough Erne, or Sligo and Ballina (but not in Galway),[18] where the naturally occurring mountains and lakes were not instances of designed improvement but had an innate beauty, invariably connected to the variety of prospects that they could afford (Fig. 42). Such places were described by Young as 'picturesque',[19] and he made a precise comparison with the painter Claude Lorraine's compositions when regarding Turk Mountain, Killarney.[20] Landscape gardens could lie adjacent to such landscapes, or contribute to them, but Young does not generally categorise discrete parks or demesnes as 'landscapes' and he did not illustrate them as such. Of the

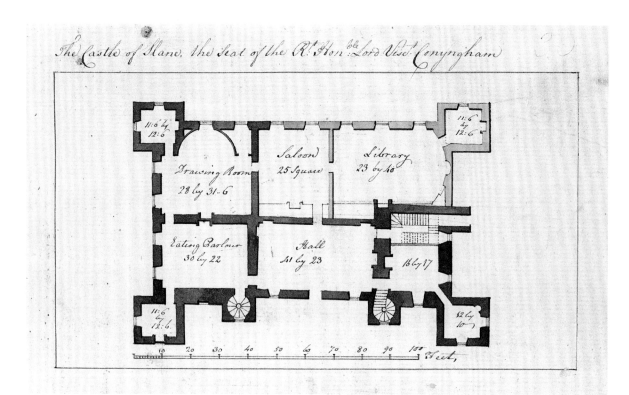

The Castle of Slane, the Seat of the Rt Honble Lord Visct Conyngham

Drawing Room
28 by 31-6

Saloon
25 Square

Library
23 by 46

Eating Parlour
30 by 22

Hall
41 by 23

16 by 17

41. Plan of Slane Castle, Co. Meath, from extra-illustrated copy of Arthur Young's *A Tour in Ireland*. National Library of Ireland, LO 10203

42. View in Killarney from extra-illustrated copy of Arthur Young's *A Tour in Ireland*. National Library of Ireland, LO 10203

drawings he considered for his tour (Fig. 43) only one is a typical view of a landscape park – that of Slane Castle, Co. Meath, and this was not in his hand and was probably modelled on an oil by Thomas Roberts (Fig. 44). Reminiscent of Jonathan Fisher and his penchant for notations, a critique of its composition ('The Prospect? of the Castle is faulty') was pencilled on to the drawing while the entrance façade was marked as 'too long' and the left-hand wood too small. Of all Irish parks, that at Carton, Co. Kildare, was one of the easiest for Young to distinguish as a landscape park that ranked 'among the finest in Ireland' consisting of 'a vast lawn, which waves over gentle hills, surrounded by plantations of great extent, and which break and divide in places, so as to give much variety' (Fig. 38).[21] He noted that 'the domain' of Luttrellstown, Co. Dublin, was 'a considerable one in extent, being above 400 acres within the wall, Irish measure'[22] and sometimes gave the exact acreage of the relevant gentleman's wider estate.[23] He generally listed the constituent parts of the landscape garden: the lawn, the undulating unadorned land forms, the water feature, the rides, the tree belts, the lawns and the circuit walk. Woodlawn, Co. Galway, a seat 'improved entirely in the modern English taste', is the Irish park most clearly identified by Young's description as one containing a landscape garden. The house stood on 'the brow [not the head] of a rising ground' looking 'over a lawn swelling into gentle inequalities; through these a small stream [had been] converted into a large river' and the 'grounds, which form the banks of this water, are pleasing and are prettily scattered with clumps and single trees, and surrounded by a margin of wood'.[24]

At Dundrum, Co. Tipperary, Young described what had been swept away by the aesthetic of the landscape garden. Lord de Montalt's 'modern stile of improvement' had swept away its old 'parterres, parapets of earth, straight walks, knots and clipt hedges' together with 'an infinite number of hedges and ditches'. He had 'filled up ponds, &c. and opened one very noble lawn around him, scattered negligently over with trees, and cleared the course of a choked up river, so that it flows at present in a winding course through the grounds'.[25] For Young landscape parks and the subset of landscape gardens that they sometimes contained were clear instances of unambiguous

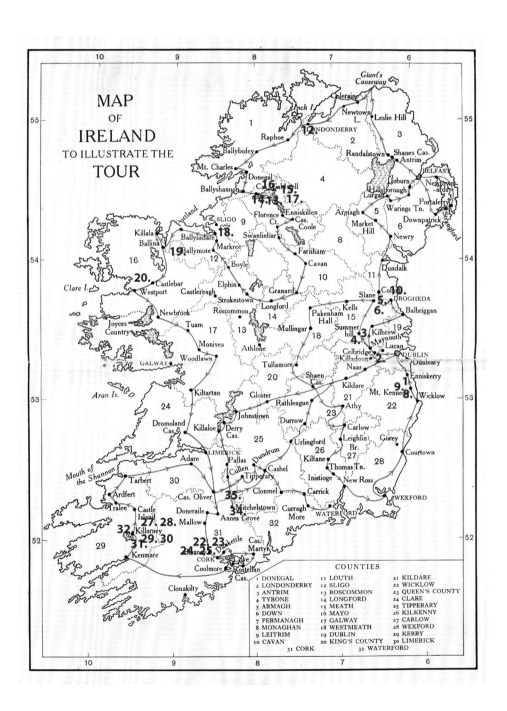

43. Map of Young's route overlaid by the author with his own numbered illustrations, from Arthur Wollaston Hutton (ed.), *Arthur Young's Tour in Ireland* (London and New York: G. Bell and Sons, 1892)

44. Estate portrait of Slane Castle, Co. Meath from extra-illustrated copy of Arthur Young's *A Tour in Ireland*. National Library of Ireland, LO 10203

practical and aesthetic improvement by an educated civil society of gentlemen, such as Speaker Foster, of Collon demesne, Co. Meath.[26] At Collon Foster had 'made the greatest improvements' Young had met anywhere in Ireland, changing 'a waste sheep-walk' with 'the cabbins and people as miserable as can be conceived' into a visibly improved landscape, complete with a demesne for demonstrating Foster's advanced landscape design and agricultural expertise. Improvement was important in eighteenth-century Ireland; it distinguished and provided

a rationale for the superior claims of one group of people over another – Protestant over Catholic, English over Irish, newcomer over native – with the dialectic complicated by many families' mixed and mutable identities.[27]

As the Irish landscape became more aesthetically and internationally interesting under the conventions of the time, Young responded by increasing the number and ambition of his views (Fig. 43). The changing nature of his illustrations reflected the changing tenor and ambition of his publications. As he became more preoccupied with the design of a nation, so the scale of his illustrations began to approach a landscape view. From the start his emphasis fell on the country rather than the city. He included no illustrations of Dublin, nor of its river valley of the Liffey with its copious portfolio of houses and demesnes. Ruined structures, beloved of the picturesque but complex to use in Ireland, are generally more absent than might be expected. But his improving mindset did extend into the urban environments on occasion and the illustrations he inserted into his own copy of *A Tour in Ireland, 1776–1779* included a suite of measured drawings of the plan and elevations of an ideal urban square, probably Blarney, Co. Cork, whose landlord's efforts at urban improvement he evidently admired (Fig. 45). Young used drawings to better understand the world and to convey the contours of the country he was trying to describe. His drawings are neither beautiful nor competent, but they are interesting. They explain much that is elided or confusing in his text. Of a consistently amateur quality, his drawings nevertheless describe a clear progression between making an image and writing the final text (Fig. 46). Young's drawings, when coupled with his influential text, explore and describe these other

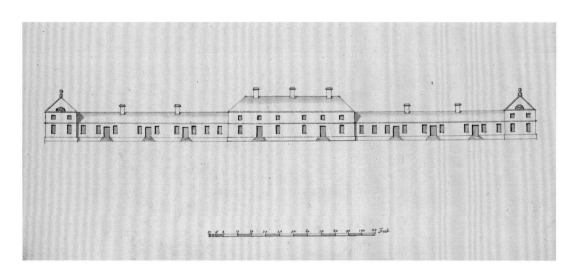

45. Drawing of Blarney, Co. Cork, from extra-illustrated copy of Arthur Young's *A Tour in Ireland*. National Library of Ireland, LO 10203

ways of understanding the world. The amateur quality brings home the role of drawing as a tool of understanding – if Young had commissioned a professional to illustrate his tour the text would not be so visual, nor would it describe Young's visual and spatial experience of Ireland so clearly.

Young attempted to do for Ireland what he never attempted for his homeland: to describe, design and improve an entire country. This ambition to encompass a whole country in one book made it more comparatively critical. Many great Irish houses discussed by Young – Rockingham, Shane's Castle and Belvedere, to name a few – were built close to great lakes. This negated the need for a man-made water feature in the grounds such as that formed by Capability Brown at Blenheim. In such situations, the boundary between the picturesque landscape (worthy of being composed into a landscape painting) and the landscape park became indistinct and the parkland's boundaries, in effect, bled out into the surrounding countryside. All of Young's most admired Irish landscapes share this watery and mutable edge condition: the harbour of Cork, the lakes of Upper and Lower Lough Erne, Lough Neagh and Lough Léin in Killarney. Young completed two particular concentrations of views for Lough Erne (four) and Killarney (five), both burgeoning tourist destinations in eighteenth-century Ireland. Each locale enjoyed the benefit of large central lakes around which the local landowners' demesnes clustered.[28]

46. View of Ballina from extra-illustrated copy of Arthur Young's *A Tour in Ireland*. National Library of Ireland, LO 10203

Using the techniques of borrowed landscape, each landscape park invariably became part of other landscapes' composition (Fig. 47). The mid-eighteenth-century landscape painter Thomas Roberts completed two pendant views of Lough Erne in 1771, one of which Young copied to make up an illustration of his own (Fig. 48). One view was painted from the demesne

47. View of Lough Erne from extra-illustrated copy of Arthur Young's *A Tour in Ireland*. National Library of Ireland, LO 10203

48. View of Lough Erne from extra-illustrated copy of Arthur Young's *A Tour in Ireland*. National Library of Ireland, LO 10203

49. Thomas Roberts, *A View of Part of Lough Erne, from Belle Isle with Elegant Figures in the Foreground and Boats on the Lough*, 1770 or 1771. Yale Center for British Art

of Roberts's patron Samuel Molyneux Madden and the other was painted from the opposing lands of Sir Ralph Gore (Fig. 49). 'The unorthodox nature' of painting pendant views of the estates of different owners 'was both unprecedented in an Irish context and practically unknown in British art'.[29] By ignoring the issue of ownership, Roberts advanced a landscape aesthetic that tried to disentangle itself from the mere expression of landed property. Although property remained a powerful sub-text, in blurring the borders between the various gentlemen's parks Roberts advanced an aesthetic that could easily be put to use in the creation of the larger national and regional tourist routes, where such limits were constricting and reductive.

For Young, because the ideal balance and hierarchy of society could be represented in landscape design, parks and gardens

became clear demonstrations of the eighteenth-century civil society that Ireland was intended to become. For Young, landscape design represented the balanced and ideal hierarchy of that society. The ideal pr oportional relationships between gentleman, yeoman tenant and cottier were replicated at the relative scales of demesne, farm and cottier holding and by great house, farmer's house and cabin. Gaps in the hierarchy were observed by Young, such as when he found 'a better yeomanry than is common in Ireland' in the county of Cavan, where the farms ranged 'from 100 to 250 acres' in size.[30] Irish absenteeism, then running at around 30 per cent,[31] compli-cated his analysis, as the benevolent landlord at the apex of the hierarchy was not where he was supposed to be. The ever-declining scale of Irish landholdings, as they were splintered by both gavelkind and the middleman, upset his classifications, with the Irish middleman providing a worrying instance of imbalance and exploitation.[32] It also made the landscape more difficult to categorise and criticise, as those in occupancy were not necessarily those who held the lease.[33] Although Young follows a descriptive hierarchy for both social and spatial relationships throughout much of his tour, he does occasionally choose not to. The nature of the tour sometimes required him to record an Ireland where such boundaries and relationships were less significant. In the great scenic enclaves of Ireland's lakes and harbours the boundaries of the individual demesnes became muted and indistinct, with Young's emphasis falling firmly on the larger scale of composite designed landscape. In this he follows the evolving practices of landscape painters and the growing fashion for touring the wider countryside and not just the gentleman's park.

'Dark and Unsatisfactory':[34] Arthur Young and Mount Vernon

The more I am acquainted with agricultural affairs the better I am pleased with them. Insomuch that I can no where find so great satisfaction, as in those innocent & useful pursuits. In indulging these feelings, I am led to reflect how much more delightful to an undebauched mind is the task of making improvements on the earth; than all the vain glory which can be acquired from ravaging it, by the most uninterrupted career of conquests.[35]

George Washington to Arthur Young,
Mount Vernon, 4 December 1788

If the great landed estate and its mid-eighteenth-century aesthetic expression in the landscape garden was difficult to translate into Ireland, the same was true of its translation into the plantation landscapes of Virginia, South Carolina and Georgia. As in Ireland, the edges of the British landscape garden were too sharp to be successfully incised into American soil, where the American Revolution had created an elite cohort of equal and untitled farmers holding their lands in freehold title, and in possession of few tenants and many enslaved people. Thomas Breen has shown how Virginia's wealthy tobacco

planters constructed a 'specific social reality' from their daily life experience of farming, which led to their championing of radical political ideology.[36] On the eve of revolution a 'republican' mentality evolved from the practical and economic rationales of plantation farming, the environmental design constraints of the local climate and topography, and the design interests and abilities of the individual planter. The American planter did not enjoy a seasonal leisured lifestyle on a typical Virginian plantation in the manner of a European villa owner. Unless he had the inclination and the wherewithal to become an absentee, which was rare in the United States, unlike the Caribbean, he lived on his plantation and his lifestyle was almost exclusively supported by his agricultural profits. The plantation's economic survival was almost wholly dependent on the produce of the estate, rendering its landscape design far more affected by the planting, harvesting and processing cycles of one crop than any comparable European estate. Once a particular crop had been fixed upon it was unlikely to change and Lorena S. Walsh finds that 'from the 1680s onwards, gain, not glory, became the planters' principal, if not sole, motive for trying alternative crops'.[37] If the principal crop was tobacco, vistas of tobacco fields had to be designed into, or more often out of, the view. Some of the classic attributes of improved landscapes – mixed arable and pastoral farming, crop rotation and the breeding of good animal and crop species – presented difficulties. This meant that improving an American estate, in the European sense of the concept, was very difficult to achieve.

The paradox for the successful eighteenth-century design of the American landed estate[38] was how to make it seem like a tenanted farm when it was not. It was held in freehold, but farming the American estate of conjoined plantations of many thousands of acres required a different model from that which prevailed in the British Isles. John Stilgoe has observed that 'in the first decades of settlement the structures, fences, and fields of the householders differed only slightly from those of men owning many hundreds and thousands of acres' but that 'by the 1750s most similarities had vanished'. An American planter such as George Washington 'worked his land with slaves and hired help and ordered his plantation about a large house he called the big house' (Fig. 50).[39] The conditions of compromise that this affected generated a design language of profound ambivalence and contradiction. Although he tried hard to emulate the British landscape tradition, the American planter was constrained both physically and ideologically. He had to

50. Photograph of the south river front of Mount Vernon. Author's photo, 2013

designs.[40] The landscape structure that evolved to express these principles was profoundly confusing to European visitors, as the design of the enormous 'farms' was relatively silent as to their scale, their relative hierarchy to other estates, and often their modes of management, working practices and population. Dissimulating in character, out of necessity, American eighteenth-century estate landscape design is a design paradigm in its own right, although difficult to frame as a positive prototype.

In the mid-eighteenth century the plantation of Mount Vernon lay seven miles south of the port of Annapolis, a small successful trading town of a few thousand inhabitants. As in Jamaica, Barbados or Donegal, the absence of a good road network had required the 1609 'Instructions' to the Virginia Company of London, advising planters 'that such places w[hi]ch you resolve to build and inhabite uppon, have a least one good outlet to the sea'.[41] The house was positioned on top of a mount, to avail of the excellent prospects of Chesapeake Bay and out into the surrounding countryside. The early history of the plantation of Mount Vernon is somewhat obscure. George Washington's father Augustine had moved his family from Westmoreland County to his Hunting Creek Plantation, 'now part of Mount Vernon, sometime in 1735, residing there until approximately 1739 when he may have moved his family to another plantation on the Rapahannock River near Fredericksburg.'[42] After his father's death in 1743 George Washington may have lived at Mount Vernon with his elder

appear a farmer rather than a landlord or an aristocrat, make his plantation appear small even if his landholding was large, practise industrial monoculture but foreground mixed farming and represent a republic of free equal commonwealthmen that were nevertheless supported by enslaved labour. Such conflicting requirements resulted in paradoxical and contradictory

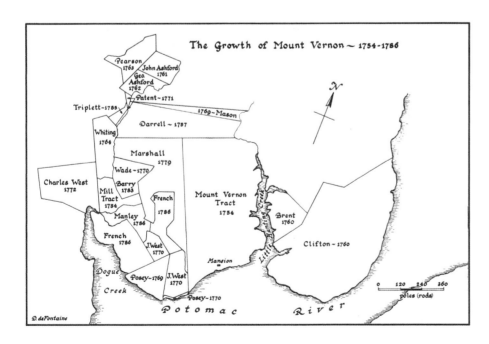

51. 'The Growth of Mount Vernon, 1754–86' by Dorothy deFontaine in *The Diaries of George Washington*, ed. Donald Jackson and Dorothy Twohig, vol. 1 (Charlottesville: University of Virginia Press, p. 240)

half-brother Lawrence, 'who had been ceded the plantation in 1740'. When Lawrence Washington died in 1752 George Washington rented Mount Vernon from Lawrence's widow, Ann, and 'finally acquired clear title to the plantation in 1761'.[43]

Nevertheless, George Washington increased the size of Mount Vernon from approximately 2,300 acres to almost 5,500 acres between 1757 and 1764, described in Dorothy de Fontaine's map (Fig. 51). The first large holding that he purchased was the Clifton estate on the other bank of Little Hunting Creek, which he surveyed himself in 1760 and subsequently redrew with his own designed alterations in 1766 (Fig. 52). The map of Mount Vernon that Washington drew in 1793 and which is now in the Huntington Library represented 'several farms within the more than 8,077 acres of the whole estate'[44]

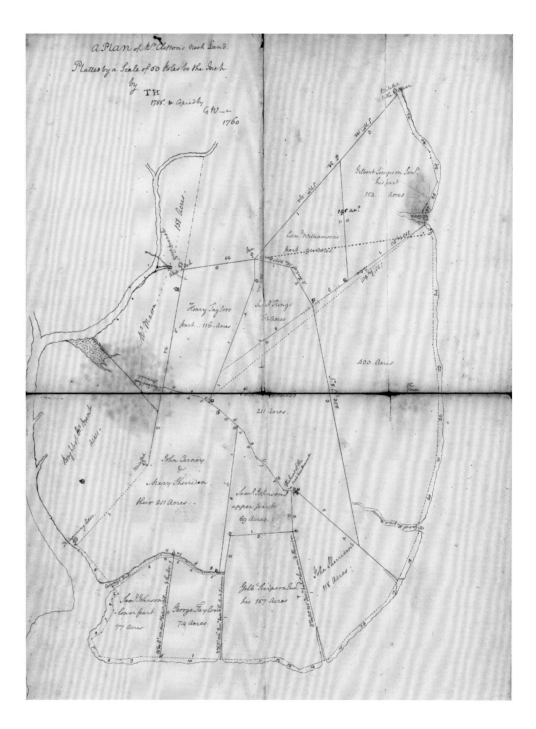

52. George Washington, *A Plan of Mr. Clifton's Neck Land. Platted by a Scale of 50 Poles to the Inch by TH 1755 & copied by GW in 1760, Old plat of the grounds in the NE part of the pasture of Mount Vernon from the summit of the hills on which the log'd cabbins are.* Library of Congress, G3882.M7B5 1755 .W3

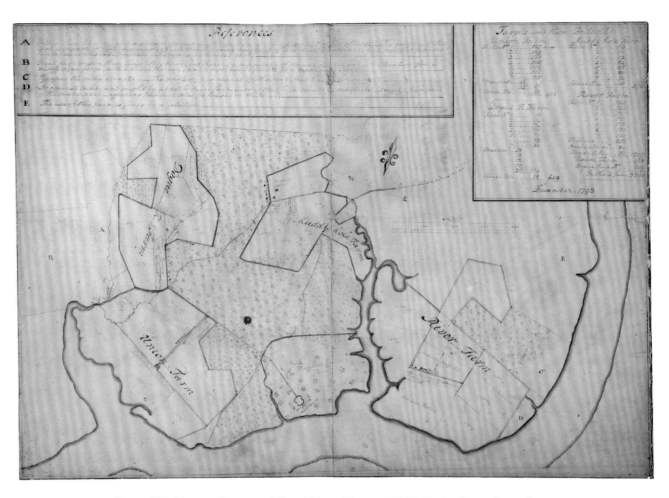

53. George Washington, *Survey and Plot of Mount Vernon and Neighboring Farms*, December 1793.
The Huntington Library, San Marino, California, Mss HM 5995FAC

but the overall area was not given on the map's legend (Fig. 53) and the composite structure made the overall boundary less legible. Later maps of Mount Vernon estimated the estate's eventual area at 7,600 acres during Washington's lifetime.[45] As Mount Vernon's footprint grew, so did the number of its enslaved workers and by 1799 their numbers reached 316.[46] The specific requirements of Virginian plantation design meant that Mount Vernon's 'Mansion Farm', its acreage left unmeasured, was much smaller than the 'demesne' or 'gentleman's park' of a comparable European estate.

George Washington compared American and English estate farming in his 1785 letter to George Fairfax of Bath with a palpable sense of urgency. American farming, or the 'course of Husbandry in this Country, & more especially in this State' was 'not only exceedingly unprofitable, but so destructive', referring to tobacco's progressive leaching of the soil. Believing

that no country had 'carried the improvement of Land & the benefits of Agriculture to greater perfection than England', Washington sought 'a thorough bred *practical* English Farmer, from a part of England where Husbandry seems to be best understood & is most advantageously practiced'. It would be difficult to 'convey to a good English Farmer a just idea of the wretched condition' of American land or 'how entirely' the American system would have to change to make the land 'productive', and he warned that if Americans did not change their system 'disappointment and continual murmurings would be the consequence'.[47] Washington was reducing his tobacco crop at Mount Vernon at the time ('I still decline the growth of Tobacco') and it was also his 'intention to raise as little Indian corn' as he could. The reduction and ultimate removal of these two plantation crops from Mount Vernon indicated how 'desirous' he was 'of entering upon a compleat course

54. Rembrandt Peale, *George Washington*, 1795. National Portrait Gallery, NPG.65.59, Smithsonian Institution; transfer from the National Gallery of Art; gift of the A.W. Mellon Educational and Charitable Trust, 1942

55. John Russell, *Arthur Young*, 1794. National Portrait Gallery, NPG 6253

of husbandry as practiced in the best Farming Counties of England'. He hoped that Fairfax would identify 'a knowing Farmer' – someone who understood 'the best course of Crops; how to plough—to sow—to mow—to hedge—to Ditch & above all, Midas like, one who can convert every thing he touches into manure'. He did not intend for Fairfax to engage a farmer personally but to 'put on foot the enquiry' and believed that his requirements 'pointed to a Farmer of the mid[d]ling class' but queried 'if one of a higher order could be had' – namely a steward who was 'not so much a farmer, as he is an Attorney or an Accomptant'. Washington knew that only a 'few of the Nobility & Gentry' of England had 'their Estates in their own hands' as he did. With most of their farms rented out, they stood 'more in need of a Collector who, at the same time that he receives the rents'[48] saw that leases were complied with and necessary repairs carried out.

George Washington and Arthur Young corresponded between 1786 and 1793 (Figs 54 and 55) and many of their letters concerned ideal estate improvements. Their correspondence began during the period between the publication of Young's comprehensive two-volume *A Tour in Ireland, 1776–1779*, published in 1780, and his *Travels in France during the Years 1787, 1788, 1789*, published in 1792. Washington had acquired a copy of the two-volume octavo Dublin edition of *A Tour in Ireland* by 1783. It had been purchased for him by William Stephens and he signed both title pages.[49] Young initiated the correspondence on 7 January 1786, having received a request for help from Mr Fairfax, who was then searching for a bailiff for Washington. Young sent Washington volumes of his published agricultural *Annals*, writing that he understood Washington's farming ambition as to 'discontinue Tobacco & maiz & wish a well-regulated farm in the English culture'.[50] He offered to supply Washington (as quoted in Washington's return of 6 August) with 'men, cattle, tools, seeds or anything else that' might 'add' to Washington's 'rural amusement'. Washington's response informed Young that the bailiff Fairfax had found for him had 'the appearance of a plain honest farmer' but had 'come over with improper ideas; for instead of preparing his mind to meet a ruinous course of cropping, exhausted lands and numberless inconveniencies … he seems to have expected that he was coming to well organized farms'.[51] Washington's letter never reached Young. Washington wrote again on 15 November 1786 to enclose a duplicate of the 6 August letter and to request 'a plan of the most complete and useful farm-yard, for farms of about 500 acres' that would include a barn and any other 'appurtenance which ought to be annexed to the yard'.[52] Effectively a request for design services, this letter set in train a complex comparative spatial analysis of British and American landscape.

Young sent Washington a barn plan on 1 February 1787,[53] publishing it subsequently in his *Annals of Agriculture* in 1791 (Fig. 56), where he noted that it was based on his own barn in Suffolk, England. He described the 'very expensive barns in Ireland, which the owners have boasted would confine a mouse', considering this 'so much the worse: there cannot be too much air all around: the sides for this reason, should be neither of brick nor stone'.[54] Young also asked Washington for 'the general arrangement of farms in your area', 'the courses of crops', the 'system' for 'connecting cattle with crops' and

'the prices of products and labour'.[55] Washington's response was to avoid the particular and to begin with the general. He 'observe[d] that there' was 'scarcely any part of America where farming' had 'been less attended to than in' Virginia where 'the cultivation of Tobacco' had 'been almost the sole object with men of landed property, and consequently a regular course of Crops' had 'never been in view'. He was 'not able to give' Young the 'the price of labour as the land is cultivated here wholly by Slaves'.[56] He did include some particulars for Young who responded with further queries about sheep and the lack of them, more volumes of his *Annals*, and a request to publish Washington's letters in future *Annals*.[57] Washington refused the last by return, citing his desire 'to glide silently and unnoticed through the remainder of life'.[58]

Many of Washington's letters gave Young a 'comprehensive view of the different parts' of the United States and sometimes revealed considerable personal opinion: 'Was I to commence my career of life a new, I shd not seek a residence north of Pennsylvania, or South of Virginia'. And he also warned Young of his possible bias 'in favor of the River on which' he lived. He positioned the 'Potowmac River' at 'the centre of the Union' lying between 'the extremes of heat and cold' watering the soil and 'run[ing] in that climate, which is most congenial to English grains, and most agreeable to Cultivators of them' and enclosed a map of America with his letter.[59] Young's letter to Washington of 18 January 1792 revealed his growing confusion

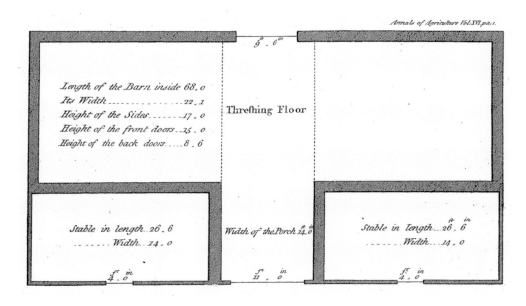

Annals of Agriculture Vol.XVI.pa.1.

Length of the Barn inside 68.0
Its Width 22.1
Height of the Sides 17.0
Height of the front doors .. 15.0
Height of the back doors 8.6

Threshing Floor

9.6"

Stable in length ..26.6
.... Width ..14.0

Width of the Porch 14.0

Stable in length ..26.6
.... Width ..14.0

4.0

11.0

4.0

56. Barn plan, plate from Arthur Young, *The Annals of Agriculture and Other Useful Arts*, 46 vols (Bury St Edmunds: Arthur Young, 1784–1815), 16, p. 791

and 'difficulties' with the barrage of information and particularly regarding 'labour' which was 'so lightly touched on that' he knew 'not how to estimate it' and wherein he recalled a former letter of Washington's[60] that acknowledged that 'all labour' was 'by slaves'. Ever the pedantic economist, Young set out to value a slave's labour comparatively with that of an English labourer, concluding that 'reckoning a negro at £50 sterl. & estimating his life how you will he must surely be cent per cent dearer than the labour of England'.[61]

In June 1792 Washington wrote one of his more open and detailed letters to Young wherein he endeavoured to 'solve the doubts which' Young had 'expressed' in his 'queries'. Explaining that 'south of Pennsylvania, hired labor' was 'not very common', Washington gave some outline of life for a 'black' individual, although any clear distinctions between servant, labourer and the enslaved worker, whether hired or unhired, remained ambiguous over the entire length of the letter:

> But high wages is not the worst evil attending the hire of white men in this Country, for being accustomed to better fare than I believe the labourers of almost any other Country, adds considerably to the expence of employing them; whilst blacks, on the contrary, are cheaper: the common food of them (even when well treated) being bread, made of Indian Corn, Buttermilk, Fish (pickled herrings) frequently, and meat now and then; with a blanket for bedding: In addition to these, ground is often allowed them for gardening, & priviledge given them to raise dung-hill fowls for their own use. With the farmer who has not more than two or three Negros, little difference is made in the manner of living between the master and the man; but far otherwise is the case with those who are owned in great numbers by the wealthy; who are not always as kind, and as attentive to their wants & usage as they ought to be; for by these, they are fed upon bread alone, which does not, on an average, cost more than seven dollars a head per Ann.[62]

Washington also wrote to his friend Richard Peters for help in answering Young's return barrage of questions but Peters refused to answer the issue that most puzzled Young and that Washington was probably most eager to deflect, responding, 'As to Slaves I have but a very imperfect, & you [Washington] a perfect Knowledge of what concerns their Value, Expence & Labour.'[63]

Washington also tried to educate Young in the American way of estimating the value of land. The 'English Statute acre' was 'the measure by which we have hitherto bought & sold land; and the price of land, as handed to you in my last, includes buildings, fences, arable, meadow, in short the improvements of every sort appertaining to the tract, on which they are placed'. He acknowledged that 'to a stranger at a distance, this aggregate mode, of estimating the value of a farm is, it must be confessed, dark, & unsatisfactory; but to the parties present, who see & examine every thing, & judge for themselves, it is quite immaterial'. The statement that 'fresh land without improvements' was 'more to be desired than worn' land, must have been difficult, if not impossible, for an arch-improver such as Young to comprehend, and Washington tempered this by categorising it as a 'general, not an invariable rule; for the better & more attentive farmers keep their farms in high order, and value the improvements accordingly'.[64] Moving to such larger, national economic questions as taxation, on 2 December 1792 Washington sent Young a list of the taxes paid on an anonymous Virginian estate. The estate in question was Mount Vernon but Washington concealed its identity from Young, possibly because the largest tax payment on capital, independent of that generated by land, was for Washington's 138 adult 'Negroes'. Washington had to pay the state of Virginia an annual tax of £17 and 10 shillings for their capital value.[65]

When Young wrote to Washington on 17 January 1793 to express his gratitude for all the 'information so truly valuable and important' that he had received, he also expressed his complete and utter confusion:

> Your information has thrown me affloat upon the High Seas. To analyze your husbandry has the difficulty of a problem: I cannot understand it; and the more I know of it the more surprizing it appears. Is it possible that the inhabitants of a great continent not new settlers who of course live only to hunt, to eat and to drink can carry on farming and planting as a business and yet never calculate the profit they make by percentage on their capital?[66]

For Young the American estate made no economic sense and, in a period where use and beauty were closely allied, this meant that he could not read the design logic of American estate landscape. Washington's response was again to redirect

Young's questions to Richard Peters, whom he introduced to Young as 'a man of humour' and 'one of the best practical farmers in *this* part of the State of Pennsylvania'.[67] Peters was accommodating, penning a long, impassioned missive on the American project for Washington, who then enclosed it with his own letter to Young of 1 September 1793. Responding to Young's powerful image of being all at sea, Peters employed 'facts well known & *felt* here, serving as Pilots to guide him [Young] into a safe Harbour' and which would 'enable him to arrive on a Shore pleasant in its Prospects & abundant in its Resources'. These included such familiar arguments as America's freedom from aristocracy, primogeniture inheritance and preying clergy, and a passage on how America was 'not so much indebted to Art as to Nature for its Beauties and Conveniencies' as the nations of Europe. Defensive and prickly, Peters refused to be drawn into exactitude: 'Not having the least Inclination, if it were in my Power, to disturb the Systems of other Nations, & wishing the Happiness of Mankind in their own Way, I do not mention either our positive or negative Prosperity, with a View to draw odious or disagreeable Comparisons.' Framing America as a nascent imperial power, he explained that 'tho' the Reflexion be painful to Humanity, it is justified, in Point of Fact, by Experience, that the Nations in Contact with the Whites always have been & ever will be exterminated' and that 'the Approaches of our Settlements always banish the Indians'. In a clear criticism of Young's tendency to myopic economic calculations Peters related his 'Facts, merely to shew why our Farmers need not make nice Calculations about per centage'.[68] His great omission was the calculation of labour. In a very long letter he makes no mention of slavery, not even by implication.

Young's confusion was a powerful form of criticism. It drew forth a powerful response – for in his next letter to Young, Washington enclosed a plan of how Mount Vernon was to be redesigned and this was subsequently engraved (Fig. 57). The plan also revealed Mount Vernon's true character, as Washington, by drawing it, exposed the number and location of the four outlying plantation 'farms', together with their barns, overseers' houses, 'negro' huts and intermediary tracts of woodland. It also revealed the relative scale of the mansion house farm to that of the tobacco 'farms'. That he took the step to draw Mount Vernon and represent it in a surveyed plan to scale seems to have occasioned substantial unease. Washington worried that something in 'the thoughts'

he was 'now about to disclose' to Young might 'in the opinion of others' contain some 'impropriety'.[69] He began with a statement that somewhat undermined his plain and simple farmer identity by admitting (with no concise figure) that much of his estate was leased out to others, in the manner of a typical British aristocrat: 'All my landed property East of the Apalachian Mountains is under Rent, except the Estate called Mount Vernon'. This he had 'kept in my own hands; but from' his 'present situation', 'advanced time' of life, 'a wish to live free from care, and as much at [his] ease as possible during the remainder of it' and 'from other causes' he did not consider 'necessary to detail' he had 'latterly, entertained serious thoughts of letting' Mount Vernon while 'reserving the mansion house farm for' his 'own residence – occupation – and amusement in agriculture'. He would do this only if he could obtain, 'in his own judgement' and 'in the opinion of others' he planned to consult, 'a low Rent' and 'provided also' he could 'settle it with good farmers'. A drawn plan was necessary to describe 'the quantity of ploughable land (including meadows) – the relative situation of the farms to one another; and the division of these farms into separate inclosures; with the quantity & situation of the Woodland appertaining to the tract'. Washington believed that all this would be 'better delineated' by the sketch he had 'made from actual surveys, subject nevertheless to revision & correction, than by a volume of words'.

The December 1793 letter positioned Mount Vernon geographically and comparatively. No estate in United America was 'more pleasantly situated' as it lay 'in a high, dry & healthy country, 300 miles by water from the Sea—and, as' Young would 'see by the plan, on one of the finest Rivers in the world'. With 'its margin is washed by more than ten miles of tidewater' a farmer could draw rich mud from the 'enumerable coves, inlets & small marshes with which it abounds … as a manure'. It was situated in a 'latitude between the extremes of heat & cold', and easily accessible 'from the Federal City, Alexandria & George town'.[70] Washington then proceeded to outline Mount Vernon's estate structure, writing that there were, as Young would 'perceive by the plan, four farms besides that at the Mansion house' and that these four contained 3,260 acres of cultivable land (Fig. 57). The boundaries of the four farms became mutable and slippery as Washington imagined 'some hundreds more [acres], adjoining, as may be seen, might be added, if a greater quantity should be required' while insisting that the farms were 'never designed for, so neither

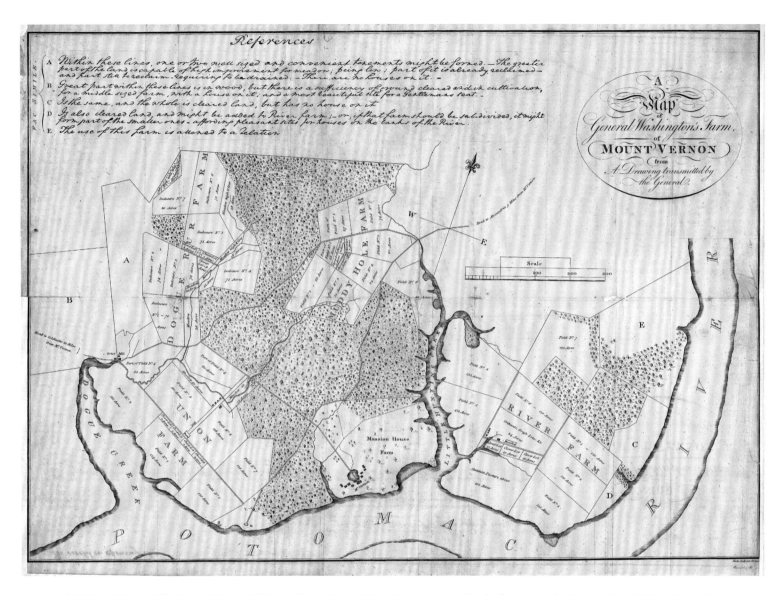

57. 'A Map of General Washington's Farm of Mount Vernon from A Drawing transmitted by the General 1793' in Letters from His Excellency General Washington, to Arthur Young ..., London, 1801. Library of Congress, G3882.M7 1793.W34 1801 TIL, loc.gov/item/99466780

can it be said they are calculated to suit tenants of either the first, or of the lower class; because those who have strength & resources proportioned to farms of from 500 to 1200 acres (which these contain) would hardly be contented to live in such houses [slaves huts] as are there on – and if they were to be divided and subdivided, so as to accommodate tenants of small means – say from 50 to one or 200 acres, there would be none'. Only on 'the lots which might happen to include the present dwelling houses of my Overlookers (called Bailiffs with you), Barns, & Negro Cabins' could an adequate standard

of accommodation for a farmer be said to exist. Estimating how the Mount Vernon 'farms' might be subdivided and then sublet into smaller and smaller farms suggested a patchwork of leaseholders, familiar to any estate manager of a British estate. It also invoked the spectre of the middleman, by then anathema to all improvers, due in part to Young's own publications. Washington seems to have been aware that much of British estate layout and design was determined by the relative standard of dwelling that the leasehold hierarchy created, and he balked at the idea of constructing such a hierarchy of farmhouses: 'Nor would I chuse to have the woodland (already too much pillaged of its timber) ransacked for the purpose of building many more.'[71] By equating the duties of Mount Vernon's four 'Overlookers' with those of bailiffs Washington misinterpreted the bailiff's role on a British or Irish estate. Typically charged with the estate's financial estate management, particularly the collection of rents and the even more onerous duty of eviction, four bailiffs were too many. Confusion as to the role of bailiff was also not uncommon in France, and the Marquis de Lafayette, who wrote to Young for advice on the layout of his French estate, was as confused as Washington in presuming that a bailiff's duties could include laying out an estate in the manner of Capability Brown or Humphry Repton.[72]

Washington's motive was to let the approximately equal 'four farms to four substantial farmers, of wealth & strength sufficient to cultivate them; and who would insure to me the regular payment of the Rents'. Washington's espousal of a tenant structure was not surprising. If Young thought the farms too large, Washington had no 'insuperable objection against dividing each into as many small ones as a society of them, formed for the purpose, could agree upon among themselves; even if it shd be by the fields as they are now arranged (which the plan would enable them to do) – provided such buildings as they would be content with, should be erected at their own expence'.[73] Large landowners were quick to appreciate the advantages of such a landlord and tenant structure. Leases formed the basis of aristocratic income in England and 'economic historians have shown that tenant farming was common in Virginia during the eighteenth century, a puzzling phenomenon if land was truly inexpensive and available'.[74] Yet Holly Brewer has contested the characterisation of American land as 'cheap and easily available',[75] arguing that 'colonists who wished to own "new" land had to win it from the Native Americans, and they did so only gradually and painfully' as 'individuals could not purchase land direct from the Indians'.[76] The large numbers of indentured servants resident in the United States, who aspired to purchase land once their term of indenture was over but who could not afford to, had to lease property rather than buy it. Yet even if tenant farming was common in Virginia, Washington found it very difficult to induce any Americans to lease his four farms. His proposed leases were very short – a mere fifteen or eighteen years, probably because the value of land was rising sharply and

Washington had made mistakes in leasing land in the Blue Mountains for periods of three lives. He would only let out all four farms at once, or none at all, and he outlined his reasons in detail, with those regarding the breakup of enslaved families indicting his moral and humanitarian intentions:

> The whole (except the Mansion house farm) or none, will be parted with, and that upon unequivocal terms; because my object is to fix my income (be it what it may) upon a solid basis in the hands of good farmers; because I am not inclined to make a medley of it [renting some and keeping other]; and above all, because I could not relinquish my present course without a moral certainty of the substitute which is contemplated: for to break up these farms – remove my Negroes – and to dispose of the property on them upon terms short of this would be ruinous.[77]

Arthur Young, who frequently preceded any analysis of an Irish gentleman's estate with a precise delineation of its area,[78] was kept in the dark as to the exact reach of Washington's estate until the close of their correspondence. This must have proved frustrating because many of the key agricultural writers of the second half of the eighteenth century did not address estate management issues without first classifying an estate by size, i.e. a 1,000-acre demesne demanded a different management schema to that of a 2,000-acre demesne and each was contingent upon the size of the wider estate. A great ducal estate of perhaps 100,000 acres was designed to express its superior scale and reach and could support much more 'model' farming activity than the typical gentry estate of a few thousand acres. Such analysis was not unknown in America, and Benjamin Latrobe carefully assessed Mount Vernon's economic scale as 'by no means above what would be expected in a plain English country gentleman's house of £500 or £600 a year'.[79] Such information on an estate's scale would have considered absolutely essential by the travel and agricultural writer Arthur Young. Visiting Mount Kennedy, Co. Wicklow, in 1776, he began his account by remarking that General Cunningham's estate was 'in the midst of a country almost all his own, for he has 10,000 Irish acres here'.[80] Young also frequently passed comment on the model improver's zeal for taking more land into his own hand, i.e. farming it directly. How much land you held in your own hand was an indication of your relative wealth, your residency status (as absentees generally held less) and your zeal for improvement. George Washington's overall estate is considered to have encompassed some 51,000 acres by the close of the eighteenth century and his estate at Mount Vernon consisted of approximately 8,000 acres, all in his own hand, although some assessed it at 10,000 acres.[81]

In 1777, having just returned from touring Ireland, Young had met Lord Kingsborough, heir to the Earl of Kingston, whose principal seat was Mitchelstown Castle, Co. Cork, and had lectured the young lord on the terrible effect of the middleman on Ireland's agriculture. Evidently convincing, he was appointed agent to the estate at a salary of 500 livres

per annum.[82] Taking up what was to be his only professional appointment as agricultural improver of a real landscape, Young set off on 1 September 1777 for Mitchelstown and his influence on Mitchelstown's extensive redesign may still be underappreciated (Fig. 58). Mitchelstown's eighteenth-century Palladian house (replaced by a castle in the 1820s) was set amidst the substantial parkland of a demesne that lay west and north of its estate town. The topographical pencil drawing Young made of Mitchelstown's prospects suggests he was involved in laying some out (Fig. 59). He praised Mitchelstown at length in his *Tour in Ireland*, although the many drawings of Blarney,

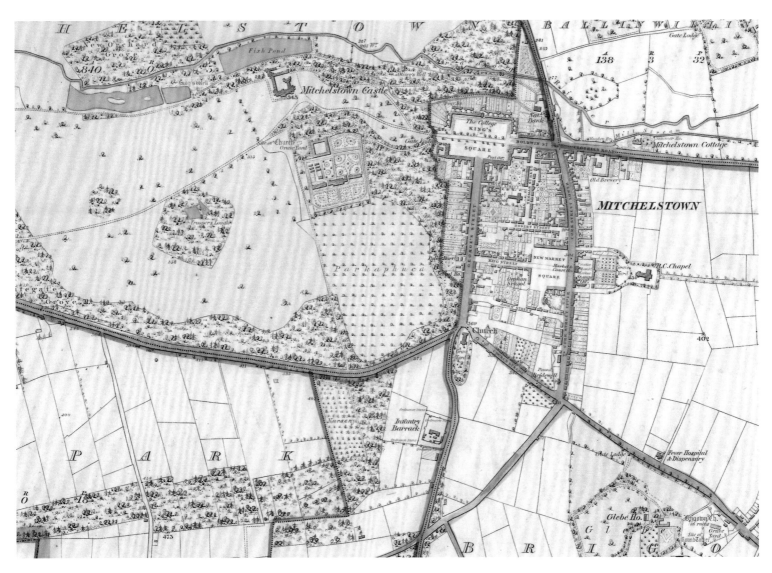

58. Mitchelstown, Co. Cork, depicting the nineteenth-century castle, on first edition OS map of Co. Cork, Sheet 19, Scale 1:10,560, surveyed 1841, printed 1844. Reproduced courtesy Trinity College Dublin

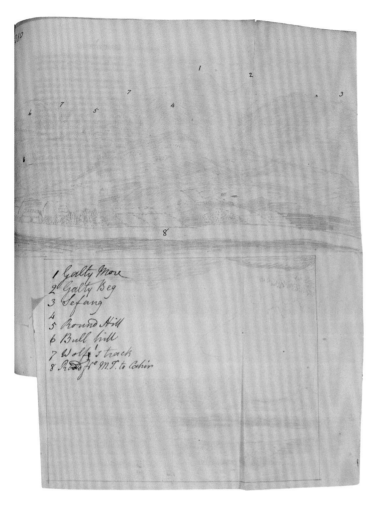

1 Galty More
2 Galty Beg
3 Sefang
4
5 Round Hill
6 Bull hill
7 Wolf's track
8 Road fr. M.T. to Cahir

59. The Galtee Mountains and Mitchelstown from extra-illustrated copy of Arthur Young's *A Tour in Ireland*, plate after p. 380. National Library of Ireland, LO 10203

Co. Cork, that he proposed initially as illustrations suggested that his employer, the Earl of Kingston, still had much to learn. The Mitchelstown estate became one of the most ambitiously improved landscapes in Ireland and the improvements extended into the design of a model estate town on a 138-acre site.

Close to Mitchelstown lay Castlemartyr, the Earl of Shannon's improved estate and the location of the admired barn that Young wrote to Washington about.[83] Young had included detailed descriptions of the Earl of Shannon's innovations to Castlemartyr in his *A Tour in Ireland, 1776–9*, including cross-sections of ditches and the great barn. He visited Castlemartyr on 17 September 1776, awarding Henry Boyle the distinction of being 'one of the most distinguished improvers

in Ireland … with a knowledge and ability which enabled him to do it most effectually'.[84] Its demesne plan reveals the Earl's farming interest in the very careful allocation of farming activities to particular locations in the landscape. Meticulously labelled, the agricultural landscape was quite segregated from the more ornamental areas and located in the western areas of the demesne. Such landscapes and their conventional representation in demesne maps were familiar to Young. The spare surveying technique of Washington's own map was not.

Drawings of dual identity and purpose, most eighteenth-century estate maps were both decorative and managerial in role and concept. Even maps depicting demesnes of a middling gentry size contained long legends to list the area and function of each numbered and bounded parcel of land, and (for estate maps of land lying beyond the demesne wall) of the occupant of each tenancy. They compressed the landscape's aesthetic and practical ambitions into one drawing, where use and beauty were united in their intention to improve the landscape (Fig. 60). In comparison, that produced by Washington for Arthur Young must have appeared strangely shorn of information (Fig. 53). Its departure from the prevailing conventions of eighteenth-century European estate maps betrayed as a consequence its departure from British and Irish estate structure. The map's small black squares of overseers' huts, each situated beside and yet separate from their charges, would not have mapped cleanly onto a typical British or Irish demesne plan in Young's mind. The map's very singularity betrays the pronounced absence of any other Mount Vernon estate plan, save for the other minor surveys of the separate farms (Fig. 52). The wider absence of Virginian estate plans, an accepted design tool in both estate design and management throughout Europe, remains puzzling, while the estate plan tradition of the Caribbean was also richer than its Virginian corollary.[85] In Virginia, South Carolina, Georgia and other parts of the South, the necessary conditions for the existence of estate maps, as enumerated by David Buisseret, had been met. These were 'agricultural organization in which land was divided into fairly large parcels', a 'felt need for such maps, and for this there had to be a landowning class interested at least in some degree in "improvements"', 'being able to visualize the land so as to exploit it more effectively', 'access to trained surveyors', and a 'certain degree of peace and civil order'.[86] Moreover, as Martin Bruckner has observed 'the purchase of American land was a highly charged act, emotionally and socially' and, unlike

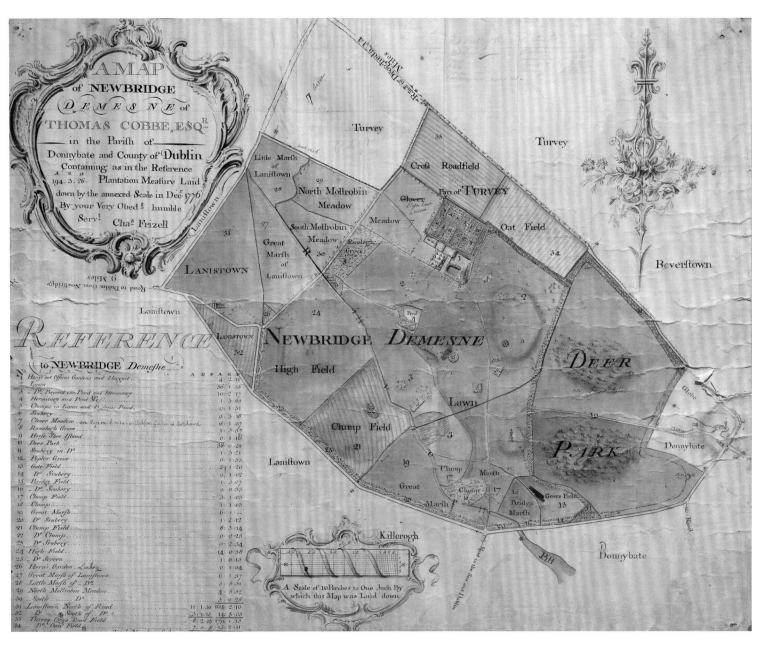

60. Charles Frizell, *A Map of Newbridge Demesne of Thomas Cobbe, Esqr in the Parish of Donnybate and County of Dublin containing as in the Reference 194 Acres, 3 Roads and 26 Perches*, December 1776. Private collection

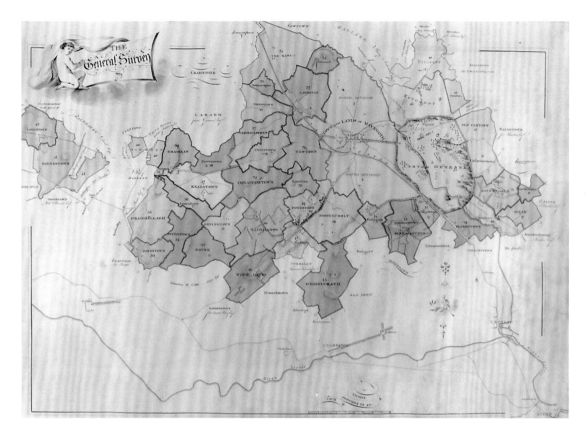

61. Sherrard, Brassingham &
Greene, *General Survey of Leinster
Estates*, 1821. This map shows the
Carton demesne towards the centre
surrounded by the Leinster estate's
other manors and tenanted lands.
Photo: Gerry Hayden

62. *(facing page)* Union Farm, detail,
from '*A Map of General Washington's
farm of Mount Vernon from a
transmitted drawing by the General
1793*' in *Letters from His Excellency
General Washington, to Arthur
Young ...*, London, 1801. Library of
Congress, G3882.M7 1793.W34 1801
TIL, loc.gov/item/99466780

in Europe, the authorship of 'this all-important document'
often lay with 'the owner himself'.[87] Such men, when they drew
maps, did so in a highly professional, formalised and abstracted
manner, making 'textbook examples of good geodetic writing' but not in the decorative manner of many estate maps of
Great Britain and Ireland or of some of the British Caribbean
islands. Estate maps were also arguably less necessary and useful in the United States. Unlike the Caribbean which had high
rates of absenteeism from 1700 onwards, American landowners
were generally in occupancy and busy carrying out design
themselves. Many of the most beautiful and communicative
demesne maps and plans in both the Caribbean and Ireland
were intended for the eyes of absentee landlords, who needed
help in imagining their landscapes, while professional landscape
designers such as Capability Brown had to produce professional
design drawings to charm clients into commissions.

Washington's plan cuts to the essential difference between
the American plantation and the British or Irish landed estate.
Here there is no grand design to link all 8,000 acres into a
demesne plan, despite it all being in Washington's own hand

(Fig. 57). Nor is it a key 'general survey' in the manner of a
British or Irish book of estate maps (Fig. 61), as the mansion farm is not distinguished sufficiently as demesne land
and separated from the other farms. This would entail a clear
boundary, by wall, tree belt, fence, road or walk, between the
bounds of the mansion farm and the other four farms. The
geometric patterning of the four satellite farms is comparable
enough to improved farming landscape in the British Isles, yet
the overseers' houses are far more axial and dominant than any
European farmhouse would be, with the rows of the enslaved
workers' huts too close, regimented and similar to be familiar to European eyes. Moreover, the tree plantations which
encircle the satellite farms form a convenient visual boundary
between the mansion house farm and its satellites, even allowing for the deep gullies and sharp topographical gradients that
exist in the woodland portions. Washington's disinclination
to use any woodland for housing may have been connected
to a role in screening the outlying farms from the eye of the
centre. Nor are the outlying farms bereft of any aesthetic
improvements. Clumps of trees were key ingredients in the

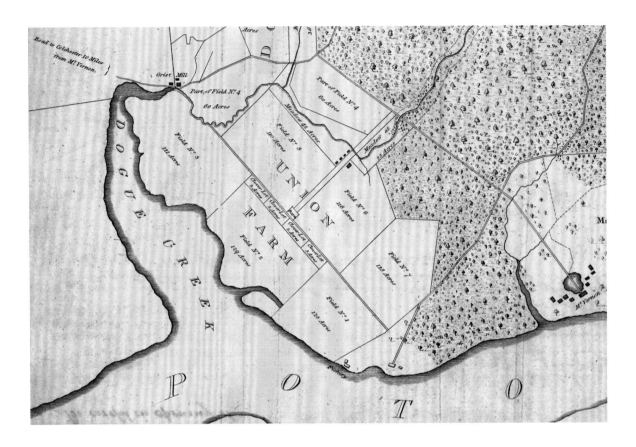

well-tempered British landscape garden, where they were popularised by Capability Brown in the mid-eighteenth century. In 1792, during the period of his most intense correspondence with Young, Washington was particularly engaged with designing Mount Vernon's clumps:

> I shall again express my wish ... to have all the ground (except single trees and clumps here and there) cleared, and well cleared, as mentioned in a former letter, between the old clover lot and the sunken ground ... In clearing the whole of this ground, let all the ivy and flowering trees and shrubs remain on it, over and above the clumps, and other single trees where they may be thought requisite, for ornament.[88]

The letter sent directly to the gardener instructed that the mulberry trees should be 'planted about in clumps'.[89] It is not surprising to find clumps in Mount Vernon's mansion house farm, what is surprising is the degree in which such aesthetic components of the landscape garden strayed beyond its polite boundary and into the tobacco plantation farms with their

enslaved workers. In his letter of 23 December 1793 to his manager William Pearce, Washington ordered that 'Whenever the field No. 3 at Union farm is prepared for a Crop, which was intended to be the case next year – if the piece of Wood within is touched at all, let there be a handsome clu[m]p of trees left at the further end of it – or more than one – according to the shape & growth of the Wood.'[90]

This indicates that Washington was employing key components of the landscape garden aesthetic, namely tree clumps, in his outlying farms. The number 3 field in Union farm was particularly visible from boats sailing along the Potomac River and up Dogue Creek (Fig. 62), but quite far and out of sight of the mansion house, and Washington was concerned about the prospects from the house's portico to the riverside and the reverse prospects of the house from the river (Fig. 63). Washington's planting instructions suggest that he intended the landscape garden aesthetic, which is so evident in the region south of the portico, to stretch along the riverside. Union farm was designed to be Washington's best model farm and this was not unconnected to its visibility, which also encouraged its planting with

63. Prospect southwards towards the mouth of the Potomac River from Mount Vernon. Author's photo, 2013

wheat (Fig. 62). It contained Washington's new brick barn, a commodious four-room new house for 'the Overlooker' and 'sufficient accommodation for fifty odd Negroes (old & young)' although their cabins 'might not be thought good enough for the workmen, or day labourers of England'. It also had 'two other houses very pleasantly situated' that could facilitate its division into smaller farms. Dogue farm was only marginally worse – its overlooker's house was 'small but new' and it had a new circular barn and 'covering for forty odd negroes'. Muddy Hole farm had an older version of the Dogue farm overlooker's house, a 'tolerable good barn', stables and 'covering for about thirty negroes'.[91] River farm, despite being the largest, had neither a new overlooker's house nor a new barn, with its large barn and stable 'gone much to decay', although plans to replace them in 1794 were in train. Yet despite such evidence that Mount Vernon's other farms are calculated works of landscape and architectural design, Washington's 'gardening schemes at Mount Vernon' continue to be generally assessed to be 'all (as far as we know) concentrated at the Mansion House Farm'.[92] The generally perceived character of American eighteenth-

century gardening and landscaping – that it exhibits a preference for the walled enclosure and the smaller scales of garden design – agrees with this assessment.[93] But what may be true of gardening is not correct for the larger and wider scale of landscaping and *all* of Washington's Mount Vernon landed estate was a designed landscape. The clear boundary between the Mansion House farm and the others was intended to make it seem like a small English gentleman's park. But the clumps, pathways, views and other elements that jumped the boundary between the Mansion House farm and surrounding plantation farms open up a profoundly American quality to its landed estates. These complex and ambiguous spaces reveal the intriguing and contradictory character of American estate landscape.

Young enclosed a copy of his just published *Travels in France* with his closing letter to Washington of 2 June 1794. He wrote that he had 'examined & reflected on the plan of your farms & the description', that they 'seem[ed]' to have 'been laid out & distributed with great judgment; and that the only drawback' he could find was 'the stock of negroes, w[hi]ch' Washington was 'so assiduous to keep in their envied situation'.

Evidently still bemused by Washington's insistence that his enslaved workers stay on the farms, Young wrote that he did 'not know enough of America to understand fully the effect of such a clause, but' that 'apparently it must have its difficulties',[94] perhaps not comprehending that Washington was hoping to avoid their sale. Ironically, the future King of France, Louis-Philippe, who visited Mount Vernon in 1797, understood that improving the lot of Mount Vernon's enslaved people would require the reversal of republican initiatives. The young prince argued that by reintroducing entailment and thus 'depriving their owners of the right to sell them', the enslaved might be gradually emancipated 'without upheaval'.[95] In his final letter of 9 November 1794, Washington assured Young that he had not intended 'to make it a *condition*' of leasing one of the farms 'that they [the slaves] should be annexed as an appendage' but that the farmer 'might, or might not as his inclination or interest should dictate, hire them, as he would do any other labourers which his necessities w[oul]d require him to employ'.[96]

Washington's project was unsuccessful. Young could find no emigrants willing to become tenants of the Mount Vernon farms. With Washington himself 'persuaded' that 'to acquire land in fee' or freehold was '*among*, if not the *first* inducement to emigration to the United States', he was 'sanguine'[97] in his disappointment. Despite a last request to publish their correspondence, Washington never granted Young permission, and the letters remained unpublished until after Washington's death. Washington's secretary Tobias Lear met Young in London in 1794 and the account of Young that he sent to Washington was not wholly positive.[98] Young's *Annals of Agriculture* had published many of his anti-slavery views, inspired in part by his friendship with William Wilberforce, and the problems of translating the Virginia's greatest 'farm' into British agricultural literature may have proved too great an ideological hurdle. George Washington's plan and letters tried to present to Young, with omissions of some finesse and calculation, his Virginian plantation/farm. Young's letters of response were determined by his own traditions of experiencing and reading landscape, and together they allow a comparison of the landscape design histories and theories of Great Britain, Ireland and the United States.

CHAPTER 3

Improving Mount Vernon

The Irish Mount Vernons

The landscape tour, promoted by Mary Delany in the English home counties in the mid-eighteenth century, soon jumped many scales of perception and practice. Transatlantic tourists, the last and most ambitious proponents of eighteenth-century tourism, generally continued to adopt the ethos of improvement – that people, places and countries could be designed into more profitable, more beautiful and more recognisably European versions of themselves. In countries with a colonial past, tourism is a stage in the appropriation of territory: an advanced stage, but part of the process by which land becomes worth owning, worth investing in, worth living in and finally worth presenting to relatives, visitors and outsiders. Travel rather than tourism is a more accurate description perhaps of what took place in the first half of the eighteenth century, as travel for practical, political, family or management reasons was not yet divorced from travel for leisure purposes alone. The visitor to the United States was rarely only a tourist, with many other agendas complicit in generating tours – economic, political and publishing ones in particular. Ambiguity as to the reason for travelling could remain, particularly when a traveller's identity could oscillate from planter to tourist over the course of a few miles. Nor was it necessary to experience important landscapes directly in person. Accounts, guides and images could be more influential than reality.

Vicarious tourism between America and Ireland was particularly common between men of the same political persuasion, and the American Revolution of 1776 inspired many Irish landed gentlemen to hope that their own country might achieve the same political and economic freedoms as the young United States. As president and the new nation's most prominent model farmer, George Washington became the revolutionary idol of his generation, and Sir Edward Newenham, an enthusiastic correspondent of Washington, Benjamin Franklin and the Marquis de Lafayette, was among the president's most fervent Irish admirers. Unlike Washington, whom he never met, Newenham did meet Franklin and the Marquis de Lafayette in France.[1] Described by James Kelly as 'a tenacious rather than a skilful politician', Newenham believed that the Glorious Revolution of 1688 had secured the finest constitution in human history but that it was 'being undermined by corrupt self-serving aristocrats', and he directed 'much of his energies to the pursuit of policies aimed at eradicating corruption and reforming the operation of parliament'.[2] Similar concerns occupied the Protestant Irishman Pierce Butler, signatory of the United States Constitution, first senator of Georgia and the subject of Chapters 5 and 6.

Newenham had sent a few letters to his idol before he eventually received a response. When Washington took up the correspondence in 1784, writing of how he had 'long known' of Newenham's 'worth' and 'political tenets', he formally rejoiced

(Facing page) Detail of fig. 74

64. Belcamp, Co. Dublin, west elevation.
South Dublin County Libraries,
Photo: Michael Fewer Collection

that his 'own conduct has been such as to acquire' Newenham's 'esteem, & to be invited to [his] friendship'.[3] One of Newenham's motives in writing to the president was to introduce his sons to Washington, thinking that they might one day have to emigrate to the United States. But in the early 1780s he was quite happy at home in Ireland, if not so happy with his old house of Belcamp set in a small demesne in north Dublin. A convenient inheritance gave him the means to replace it 'with one more appropriate to his status and aspirations,'[4] and thinking that architectural design, 'like pleading his many law cases', was a task 'he could best perform himself', he began drawing plans for a new mansion in the summer of 1780. His eventual design of a seven-bay three-storey brick house was of a similar scale to other houses in the vicinity, such as Santry Court, Lucan House or Newbridge House (Fig. 64). Many of Dublin's suburban mansions shared its east–west orientation, notably the nearly Breckdenston, where the garden front had allowed the 1720s politician Robert Molesworth to enjoy a view of the ships sailing into Dublin Bay. The bow-front that Newenham built onto the east-facing garden front provided the upper storeys with splayed sea vistas, while those looking west from the entrance front enjoyed the evening sun. The location of

this substantial suburban mansion 'four miles from Dublin'[5] meant that Newenham could walk briskly into the city centre to attend to his duties at parliament in two hours.

Like other suburban demesnes, Belcamp did not initially possess a substantial park, particularly because the family had no estate in the area. Leasing more land allowed Newenham to make Belcamp's demesne more proportional to its house and by 1781 he had amalgamated 125 acres. By the time of the first Ordnance Survey map of 1843, the first map known to exist for Belcamp, it had been reduced again to a 70-acre demesne footprint (Fig. 65). Its landscape design was modest but it did include two approach routes. The one from the south crossed the river before reaching the house, while the eastern approach from the Malahide road followed a serpentine route along the stream and south of the parkland that is reminiscent of the approach recorded in Samuel Vaughan's survey of Mount Vernon (Fig. 75) and Newenham may have learned of Mount Vernon's plan from American visitors or returning Irish travellers. Washington described Mount Vernon's character to Newenham in his first letter of 1784.[6] It was his 'retreat from the cares of public life; where in homespun & with rural fare' he would invite Newenham to 'bed & board', should

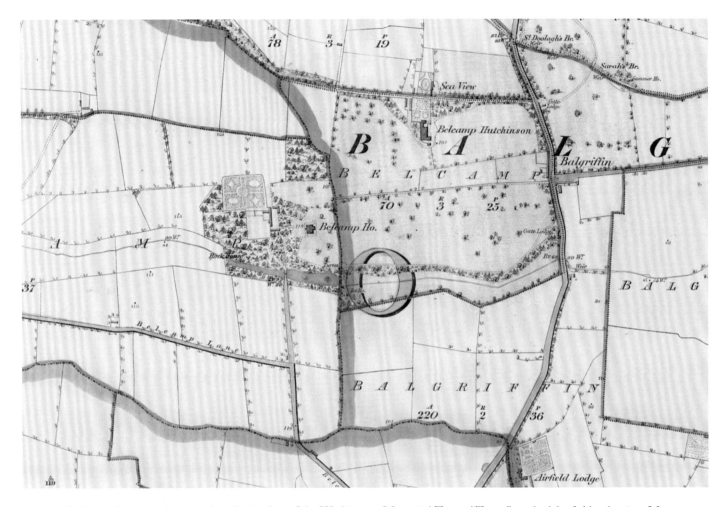

65. Belcamp demesne, showing the relationship of the Washington Memorial Tower ('Turret') to the lake fed by the river Mayne
and the curvilinear southern planting scheme of the garden front, reminiscent of Samuel Vaughan's plan of Mount Vernon.
First edition OS map of Co. Dublin, Sheet 115, Scale 1:10,560, surveyed 1837, printed 1843. Reproduced courtesy Trinity College Dublin

Newenham ever cross the Atlantic: 'Nothing would be more pleasing to me than the opportunity of welcoming you, or any of your family, to this land of liberty'.[7] Washington presented the self-sufficient, modest and humble lifestyle that he enjoyed at Mount Vernon as one that embodied all that European aristocratic life did not.

In 1784 Newenham also described his own 'delightful villa' in a letter to Benjamin Franklin, writing of how he had 'quitted the field of Politics and retired' to Belcamp with his children and grandchildren. The house boasted a new ground-floor room – a library 'called the *States*' that was nearly complete save for a niche designed to accommodate Franklin's bust. In the other niches Newenham had positioned General Washington and 'his worthy Friend the Marquis Le Fayette' on 'each side

of *Vir[gil]*'.[8] This careful selection of 'Revolutionary Worthies' is pointedly reminiscent of the 'Temple of British Worthies' constructed by Henry Cobham at his great landscape garden at Stowe in Buckinghamshire. Belcamp's interior plasterwork united Gothick and romantic themes and this most probably indicated his political alignments, as they had for Lord Cobham at Stowe (Fig. 66). More practical transatlantic transfers also took place, particularly those of expert labour, and Edward Newenham introduced an emigrating Irish stuccadore, Richard Thorpe (or Tharpe), to George Washington in a letter of 23 July 1785, now lost. By November Washington had 'neither seen, nor heard of Mr. Thorpe the stucco worker', conceding that a 'good man acquainted with that business would have come very opportunely' as he had 'a large room which' he was

66. Interior plaster roundel at Belcamp of weaponry and a landscape with a castle in the same eighteenth-century pastiche Gothick style as the George Washington temple. Photo: David Fleming

'about to finish'. He engaged 'one [John] Rawlins of Baltimore in Maryland (lately from England)' to do it instead, stressing how Rawlins 'from having no rival, impose[d] his own terms'. Washington considered these 'exorbitant' and wrote that 'good workmen of any profession, would meet encouragement in these States'.[9] Once Richard Thorpe had safely arrived in the United States, he was engaged by Rawlins 'to be the principal workman in the ornamental parts of' Washington's 'new room' and 'the person on whom Rawlins depended for the execution of the plan.'[10] This was Mount Vernon's great East Room where Washington was also following the Irishman Samuel Vaughan's advice on its décor.[11]

If Mount Vernon's East Room benefited from travelling Irishmen's decorating skills the décor of Belcamp's room 'The States' responded quickly to transatlantic current affairs. In 1784 Newenham bought 'paintings depicting the taking of Quebec'[12] and when Lady Ranelagh visited his 'American Room' in 1789 she viewed Washington's portrait among 'the pictures of all the Respectable Characters in America'. Those who fell out of favour were demoted, and while she viewed the 'Bust of the Venerable and Great Franklin with Sensible Emotion', she 'remarked with pleasure the picture of One Arnold *reversed* and his *Treason* wrote under it'.[13] Political speeches and texts were also framed and hung on Belcamp's

walls, making Newenham's politics ever more legible to visitors. The two men discussed their prints of dignitaries by letter,[14] and Newenham framed the president's 'late Address to Both houses', placing it 'in Company with [Franklin's] & Fayettes Picture'.[15] Print rooms were popular in Ireland in the 1780s, and the nearby Castletown, Co. Kildare, had a print room that made the Conolly family's networks and loyalties evident to visitors.[16]

By 1787 Washington imagined Belcamp as a model Irish version of the American villa, an ideal that was easy to imagine because it was never dulled by a more prosaic or contradictory reality:

> The manner in which you employ your time at Bell champ (in raising nurseries of fruit, forest trees, and shrubs) must not only contribute to your health & amusement, but it is certainly among the most rational avocations of life for what can be more pleasing, than to see the work of ones own hands, fostered by care and attention, rising to maturity in a beautiful display of those advantages and ornaments which by the Combination of Nature and taste of the projector in the disposal of them is always regaling to the eye at the sametime in their seasons they are a grateful to the palate. I should have much pleasure in admiring your skill in the propogation and desposal of these things in a visit to Bell Champ. but declining health and an anxious wish to spend the remainder of my days in retirement will fix me to Mount Vernon and a small circle round it whilst I tread on this Theatre.[17]

At Belcamp Newenham constructed the ideal Irish revolutionary villa, populating it with a suitable set of model men and explaining, via their speeches and published works, just why they were exemplary. Stretching his political agenda out into the landscape he built a Gothick tower to his hero George Washington with the inscription 'Oh, ill-fated Britain! The folly of Lexington and Concord will rend asunder, and forever disjoin America from thy empire', just in case its meaning should have escaped any visitors (Fig. 67). Visible from the southern approach route, where it stood across the piece of water on the opposing bank, again in the manner of the river Styx at Stowe, but with the river here representing the Atlantic, the tower was surrounded by 'autumn vegetation luxuriant to an amazing degree' from which Newenham 'pulled a cabbage rose of a second spring' in 1784 (Fig. 68).[18]

When a neighbour's house was destroyed by lightning in 1784 Newenham became 'anxious to fortify' his 'Expensive Edifice', against the 'powerfull actor' of electricity and although 'ignorant of the proper mode of doing' so he installed a lightning conductor. Building Belcamp had cost him £7,000 and he characteristically wrote to Benjamin Franklin, the most famous eighteenth-century scientist, for advice on how to 'preserve' it 'and have some amusement'. He also constructed 'a *Lillypution* air Balloon' in 1784, when his first 'query' to Franklin was 'How many feet *high* does your Excellency, or your Philosophick Brethern in Paris, imagine that it is possible for any Balloon to ascend, preserving the Life of the Aerial Traveller?', with the second, 'May it not arrive to Such a height as to render a more minute observation of the Moon, of use', and so the emulation continued.[19] He had ordered a bust of Franklin from Bordeaux, enquiring anxiously from every likely ship that sailed into Dublin port for news of the votive statue of a man equally 'revered and respected by' the Newenham family 'as by his grateful Countrymen in the United States'.[20]

Newenham well appreciated the significance Americans attached to personal farming and gardening achievements. Keen to present himself to his American friends as an avid gardener, planting was his 'chief amusement' in a 1786 letter that also informed Franklin of the 'valuable present of trees and seeds' he had received from the engineer and inventor Colonel Decius Wadsworth of Connecticut, possibly angling for some more. Claiming that he did 'all the nice parts' of planting himself, 'sowing the seed, pruning, budding etc.' and never leaving 'any thing to a gardiner', he had 'therefore one of the most healthy and promising plantations in the Kingdom'. Wadsworth's trees 'promised well' by 1786 when he had also planted 'the seeds of the largest fir trees' from the St Bernard Alps, which were 'in the most promising state'.[21] Adopting wholeheartedly the lifestyle of the American gentleman farmers he so admired, by the following August he was 'confined to a Little Politics, planting and Laying down Ground' and spent

67. *(above right)* Nineteenth-century photograph of the Washington Memorial Tower across the lake on the southern approach to Belcamp. Irish Architectural Archive

68. *(right)* Photograph of Washington Memorial Tower. Photo: Susan Roundtree, *c*.1995

69. Roxborough House, Co. Galway, seat of Colonel Persse, Irish Architectural Archive

'3 part out of 4 of the Day, in planting and Improving a Bad and Ungracious soil'. Colonel Wadsworth's 'Butter Nutts and Hiccory' from Connecticut were 'growing most Amazingly' and he mused that they liked Belcamp's newly 'Congenial Soil', because it had been so successfully improved.[22]

Beyond the suburban confines of Belcamp, Newenham was a staunch improver of the Irish countryside and its people. He spent much of the summer of 1787 at Colonel William Persse's house and demesne at Roxborough, Co. Galway, because his eldest son Edward Worth Newenham had married Persse's daughter Elizabeth in March 1787 and had done so despite her lack of a large dowry. He introduced William Persse to Benjamin Franklin in March 1787 as a gentleman who had taken 'a Conspicuous part, in this Kingdom (during the whole of the late war) in favor of America, and in all other respects ha[d] been a real Patriot'. Allowing his son to marry a poorer bride reflected well on Newenham's republican principles and he wrote to Franklin that 'loving Liberty' had inclined him not to meddle with the match.[23] Roxborough, the bride's father's house, despite her small dowry, was quite substantial. It was situated 'in delightful Country, the Land Naturaly luxuriant, all good natural Soil' with a large deer park and an overall estate that was 'wooded and watered in just proportions' (Fig.

69). Keen to describe Galway's unusual geology to Franklin, Newenham wrote of its many subterranean rivers where he had 'found trouts and eels in perfection' swimming 8 feet beneath the land's surface. Other local gentlemen were also engaged in improvement including a Mr Kirwan who had 'reclaimed many hundred acres of Black mountain' giving him 'a very *considerable* size of annual rent'.[24] Newenham also commissioned a version of the Irish jaunting car on Franklin's behalf from Colonel Persse's 'Car maker' who was 'a most ingenious man'. These cars could draw considerable loads, travel '92 miles in 4 days', and were pulled by little horses that required 'but little feeding'. He planned to send the jaunting car to Franklin 'by the first Ship that sail[ed] from Galway'.[25]

Plants could travel in the place of people, both initiating and cementing such transatlantic relationships, particularly those between people who had never met. Colonel William Persse must have been inspired by Newenham to contact George Washington in 1788, explaining how he had 'mentioned to Sr Edward Newenham' his 'intention to send' Washington 'some goosberry plants of a remarkable fine Line' by 'ship from the Port of Galway' and some grass seeds, but with Irish summers 'so uncertain' he could not get any that were 'fit to send'. Persse wrote long and careful instructions

70. 'An Irish Cabbin', plate from extra-illustrated copy of Arthur Young's *A Tour in Ireland.* National Library of Ireland, LO 10203

71. 'An Irish Cabbin', pen-and-wash drawing from extra-illustrated copy of Arthur Young's *A Tour in Ireland.* National Library of Ireland, LO 10203

as to the gooseberries' planting and care, stressing how the American climate would require modifications to Irish practices.[26] The gooseberries arrived in Baltimore in February 1789 when the merchant Hugh Young reported to Washington that they bore 'buds near an inch long'. He sent them on to Mount Vernon 'by the Land Stage, as the Jolting would effectually destroy the[m]'.[27]

Newenham was not, however, impressed with the Galway natives' unenthusiastic espousal of improvement, writing that 'if the Common People had the least Spirit of Industry, they might become rich Farmers' but that 'the sloth and Apathy of the Common Irish prevent[ed] Industry'. Offers had been made to them 'of Large Tracts of improveable Mountain and Bog, but not accepted of'. To his chagrin the locals did not believe that 'in a few years a man, with a wife and 2 or 3 Children from 12 to 16 years, would improve Several acres, which would then (in 5 years) prove worth 9*s.* an acre and his rent only 6*d.* an acre'. Writing of how 'any man (now)' could 'get a Lease for 999 years' he went out into the countryside and 'visited many of their wretched Hovels, and endeavoured to Convince them how Easy it was to better their station'. He 'explained the whole System of Agriculture to them; and promised that their Landlord would give them a long lease',

but to no avail. Despite having 'stated to them the Comfort of warm Cloathing and Comfortable houses' he got 'no answer, but that, if such things had been possible, their fathers would have done so'. Revealing his reading of Captain Cook's voyages to the Pacific, and the popular correlation of the Irish peasant with natives of the empire's more distant reaches, he wrote of how 'the Inhabitants of Otaheite [Tahiti]' were 'Intelligent Beings and Industrious People when compared to those wretches'.[28]

Newenham's analysis of Irish cottagers and their hovels differed substantially from that of Arthur Young who had used an engraving of 'An Irish Cabbin' as a frontispiece for volume two of the two-volume edition of *A Tour in Ireland, 1776–1779* (Fig. 70). Derived from a pen-and-wash drawing of a much more impoverished landscape, which either Young or his publisher did not choose to engrave in its full shocking detail (Fig. 71), the Irish cabin was beginning to personify Ireland, and her mode of governance. Choosing a decrepit hovel, rather than a great house or public building, as a frontispiece for a published tour of Ireland did have political overtones.[29] Arthur Young was aware of the fashion for the *cottage ornée* and had criticised the cottage 'made of rafters & thatched' but that looked like a 'wretched necessary house', or toilet, in the Luxembourg gardens.[30] Eighteenth-century English landscape painters, notably Gainsborough, used cottages to depict 'fantasies of rural England or "Happy Britannia" that never was',[31] described by John Barrell, and such views of English cottages invited the positive interpretation of 'the cottage family as the embodiment of the nation'.[32] The Luxembourg aristocratic *cottage ornée* was not the same as a real cottage with real inhabitants, and Young's aesthetic issues with the French translation of an English cottage did not complicate his honest representation of an Irish one. If he could denigrate the Luxembourg *cottage ornée*, why did his Irish frontispiece, which was arguably worse, stand for Ireland, if not to make a powerful critical comparison of Ireland and England?

It was difficult to understand a country's politics from a distance in the eighteenth century, particularly when reliant upon invariably biased accounts. Franklin was careful not to enter into a comparative discussion of Newenham's 'Common People' or anything touching upon the indigenous or enslaved people of the United States. Washington was highly adept at writing general statements that concurred with his correspondent's overall opinions but which never became so detailed as to cause offense:

> I am heartily glad to find that the prosperity of Ireland is on the encrease. It was afflicting for the Philanthropic mind, to consider the mass of People, inhabiting a Country naturally fertile in productions and full of resources, sunk to an abject degree of penury and depression. Such has been the picture we have received of the Peasantry.

Political speeches and tracts crossed the Atlantic relatively quickly and in August 1788 Washington 'gathered from the Spirited speech of Mr. [Henry] Gratton [sic] on the commutation of tythe', delivered in the Irish House of Commons on 14 February 1788, that the Irish common man's 'calamities' did not 'seem to be entirely removed yet'. He hoped 'ere long, matters will go right there and in the rest of the World' and that 'instead of the disconsolatory idea that every thing is growing worse' he 'would fain cheer [himself] with a hope that every thing is beginning to mend'. He agreed with Newenham that if 'Ireland was 500 miles farther distant from Great Britain the case with respect to the former would be as speedily as materially changed for the better'.[33] Both men's belief in practical farming as the bedrock of a country's civilised society and

fortune never faltered. In 1789 Washington wrote to Newenham of how he had been 'made more sensible, upon every new tryal, that this *country* [US]' was 'susceptible of various and great improvements in its agriculture' and that it was 'on *that resource* it must depend essentially for its prosperity'. Although the 'useful arts and commerce' should not be 'neglected', 'in comparison with the tillage of the earth' they were 'a subordinate concern'.[34]

In the aftermath of the French Revolution the correspondence between Washington and Newenham and between Franklin and Newenham became less georgic and pastoral, and much more political. With Ireland becoming 'more Violently agitated' by December 1791 than it had 'been since King James's Reign', Newenham described to Washington how 'the Papists' had 'formed Committees – adopted most Violent Resolutions – and declared that they must be put on the same Footing with the Protestants in *Every* respect, particularity in Voting for Members to serve in Parliament'. However much Newenham was 'inclined' to 'toleration', the realities and consequences of Ireland's sectarian condition required much transatlantic explanation, particularly the dangers posed to Protestant property:

> I cannot agree to give them [the Irish Catholics] half of what they ask – they are 4 to 1 in this Island, consequently they would become the Electers, & no real Protestant would be returned for any Free City, County or Town; more than half the members of the House of Commons would be Papists or Sons of Papists, & we, descendants of English, would not be Tolerated to be Chosen; they would also buy half the Boroughs; the Next Step would be to rescind all the Acts of Forfeitures & the Act of Settlement – this Island would be the Asylum for all the Bigoted Papists drove from other Countries, for I do assert, that the Irish Papists are the most Bigoted People under Heaven[35]

Comparing Ireland directly with America, he wrote that 'a Law might as well passed in America, that none but Refugies & Loyalists should have votes in Congress – if they had, could it be doubted, but they would repeal y[ou]r forfeiture Laws'. Going into further detail he explained how the Irish Catholics could 'never divest themselves of the Remembrance' the Protestant ascendancy 'enjoy[ed] what formerly belonging to their Ancestors'. Comparing Ireland with France was also very dangerous:

It is absurd to bring up the Acts of Toleration in France, as an Example for us; the Protestants there are about 200000 to 25,000000; and beside[s] the Protestants have no Ancient Claims to any forfeited Landed Property – they are too few ever to disturb the National Constitution, Laws, or Religion besides they have no inducement to hazard their present Situation.[36]

Newenham acknowledged openly that he and the Catholic Irish 'were never good friends'. Anxious about Ireland's future in the wake of the French Revolution, in 1791 he planned to dispose of his landed property in Ireland and cross the Atlantic with his wife and sons to become 'Citizens of New Yorke'. Events in France served to increase his anxiety and in December 1791 it 'astonish[ed]' him 'that the French Government [did] not immediat[e]ly Send an Army across the Rhone & disperse the Enemy at Coblintz & Worms'. As always, he compared the European condition with America's, reminding Washington of how Washington himself had 'Cross[e]d a more dangerous River & attacked a *Tenfold* more Numerous Army at Trenton, & in Consequence thereof, forced them to a Retreat' and maintaining that he could perceive and 'argue' this comparison 'from Geography & having often travelled that Country, in Germany & France'.[37] In January 1792 Newenham reached the peak of his anti-Catholic paranoia when at pains to point out that although it would 'Answer in the United States to give [the Papists] that Liberty, & in France to give the Protestants Votes' it would never do in Ireland because the American proportion of Protestants to Catholics was 'ten to one'. American Catholics also had 'no forfeited Estates to reclaim' and 'their obedience to the see of Rome' could not 'raise' even 'the most Trifling trouble'. He reiterated that in France the Protestants were 'but one to 25' French Catholics with 'no Claims on the Estates of the Catholics' and 'besides the Protestants there were always on the side of the Nation at Large'. Hoping to convince Washington that the Irish Catholics were 'Enemies in the Emancipation of America – not a Single address or Name came from them on that Cause of real Liberty',[38] merely occasioned a neutral response in the president's best diplomatic prose:

Of all the animosities which have existed among mankind those which are caused by a difference of sentiment in Religion appear to be the most inveterate and distressing

and ought most to be deprecated. I was in hopes that the enlightened & liberal policy which has marked the present age would at least have reconciled Christians of every denomination so far that we should never again see their religious disputes carried to such a pitch as to endanger the peace of Society.[39]

He reminded Newenham, a would-be émigré to the United States, of Americans' 'happiness which is scarcely known in any other Country; for such is the extent of the U.S. and so great a variety of climate and soil do they embrace, that we never need apprehend a universal failure of our crops and a consequent famine'.[40] Newenham's support for the settlement of the 'Glorious Revolution' of 1688 that had established Ireland's 'Protestant Ascendancy' never faltered. It eventually led to his support of loyalism over revolutionary patriotism and a complete rejection of the United Irishmen's ambitions for a non-confessional Irish nation.

Newenham's anxiety in the early 1790s was also borne of the ongoing financial difficulties occasioned by Belcamp's construction. Despite such worries, his planting preoccupations continued and in February 1792 he wrote to Washington of how he had received 'many Curious seeds of Trees & Shrubs from Mrs. [Janet] Montgomery',[41] one of their mutual acquaintances, then travelling in Ireland but did not describe where he had planted them. Despite the solace of Washington's letters, and that of his ongoing planting plans, Newenham was obliged to sell Belcamp in January 1793 having reached an agreement with Henry Otiwell, the collector of the Dublin excise, to sell the house and lands (then comprising 59 acres) 'on condition that Otiwell paid Newenham's debts to the tune of £5500'.[42] He had lived in the finished Belcamp for less than ten years before being obliged to sell it. Afterwards he led a somewhat itinerant existence, moving to Carrickmacross, Rathdrum and eventually to Bushfield, Nenagh, Co. Tipperary, on lands 'that were still within his control'.[43] Always believing that he would one day manage to cross the Atlantic and visit Mount Vernon, in 1794 he again 'laid Plans & regulations, for a few Weeks absence from this Island to pay my *Sincere Respects* at Mount Vernon'. Embroiled in legal proceedings, he bemoaned how 'law, Cursed Law, ha[d] prevented' him from doing so and despite a bad fall he still hoped to spend six months there: 'If I can do so, *I will* – and I shall consider it as the *Grandest* Period of a Long Life.'[44] Washington continued

72. *(top)* Mount Vernon, Co. Clare, probably constructed in the nineteenth century by the Persse family. Author's photo, 2010

73. *(bottom)* The suburban villa of Vernon Mount, Co. Cork, constructed *c.* 1784, with the city in the distance. IAA

to uphold their shared bucolic identity as independent improving gentlemen given to a life of rural calm and genteel enjoyments in his last letter of August 1797:

> I am now seated in the shade of my own Vine & Fig tree, and shall devote the remainder of a life – nearly worn out to such agricultural and rural amusements as will afford employment for myself, and cannot, or ought not, to give offence to anyone – offering while I am on this theatre, my sincere vows that the ravages of War, and the turbulance of passions may yield their sceptres to Peace and tranquillity, that the world may enjoy repose.[45]

Newenham's final letter to Washington on 30 October 1797 reported that 'Wall fruit was Scarse [sic]' in Nenagh, Co. Tipperary, where he was then living, but that other fruit was 'in *abundance*'. He closed the correspondence by hoping that Washington's Irish gooseberries and all other concerns remained in a 'thriving' condition.[46]

Belcamp's tower was only one instance of the many memorials to Washington constructed throughout Ireland in the final decades of the eighteenth century and long into the nineteenth (Fig. 72). Terraces or houses called 'Mount Vernon' were built in the villa suburbs of all the major Irish cities, but most notably in Cork, a major transit point for all British ships crossing the Atlantic. On its southern hills stood Vernon Mount, an elegant suburban villa of *c.*1784 constructed by the merchant prince Sir Henry Browne Hayes, until it was destroyed by fire in 2016 (Fig. 73). Neither Belcamp nor Vernon Mount, like their inspiration, Mount Vernon, are grandiose design statements, nor are they dependent on well-known architects or landscape designers for their significance. The scale, informality and amateur authorship of all three houses was intended to break from established aristocratic European tradition. At Belcamp Edward Newenham aspired to create an environment that reflected the optimistic Ireland of the late eighteenth century with its own parliament and ideally its own taxes, as had been achieved in America. Its comparatively small demesne had no defined encircling tree belt, no axial approach routes, no multiple lodges and no demesne stone wall. It set out to be a modest demesne for an independent gentleman, just like Washington. It was not identical to Mount Vernon because eighteenth-century gentlemen did not attempt to imitate each other's landscapes exactly – this would have gone against the *genius loci* spirit of Alexander Pope and his successors in the landscape garden who thought that each landscape should be designed to reflect the character of its distinct environment. Neither Belcamp nor Vernon Mount replicated Mount Vernon and, although informed and inspired by its design, they remained distinctively Irish versions of the ideal country house. Nor did Washington aim to replicate 'Belle Champ', even as he admired its design principles as filtered through letters and literature. Transatlantic design translation was not an exact science, particularly when some of the parties involved had never crossed the ocean. The revolutionary men of the Atlantic world passed ideas from country to country in the spirit of constructive comparison, if not in person. Newenham asked, 'How Noble does our Friend the Marquis de La Fayette appear? he is the Washington of Europe. If *France* had a *Franklin* for the *Civil* Government, all

would be Compleat.'[47] Their landscapes were equally transferable. Stray shoots of Belcamp's landscape crossed the Atlantic to take root in Mount Vernon's soil, as did wisps of Mount Vernon in Ireland.

The Other Mount Vernons

> The country is beautiful but it is like a beautiful scene in a theatre – the effect at proper distance is admirable but it will not bear a minute inspection, the features are large, the weeds rank, the grasses coarse, but distance blends all that and renders the whole a singular, certainly, and in my mind, a beautiful landscape.[48]

> Theobald Wolfe Tone, Philadelphia, to Thomas Russell, Belfast, 7 August 1795

Until the last decade of the eighteenth century tourism was almost invariably considered to be a positive thing, whether for engendering revolution at home, having more interesting plants in the garden, learning new farming techniques or for educating and expanding one's mind. Yet travel and tourism could work against the status quo. Touring America involved a complex set of comparative framing devices for the European eye. If plantation landscape had been tamed into a relatively calm oblivion in Ireland by 1770 this was not the case in either the Caribbean or the United States, where an enslaved labour force complicated its design and successful representation. This upset any happy equivalence between, on the one hand, improvement, subsequent increase and quality of life, and, on the other, freedom and equality. As Jean-Jacques Rousseau had argued in his highly influential pedagogical treatise *Émile*, the child learns to estimate scale and distance by travelling from his father's house to nearby places, slowly building up a spatial geography. This enables the child to orientate him/herself in the world and encourages him to make 'his own map, a very simple map, at first containing only two places; others may be added from time to time, as he is able to estimate their distance and position'.[49] Such initial early spatial experiences were profoundly formative, affecting a person's conception of the world and his or her place within it for life. The age of initial foreign travel and the order of its experience was significant and the home landscape (or *Hausberg* as Austrians might say) continued to be a fundamental measure of comparison.

Late eighteenth-century road maps of the British Isles featured the great houses that lay along each route. The approach to the house from the dominant road, in Ireland almost invariably that from Dublin, was a carefully choreographed exercise stretching far outside the boundaries of the estate itself. Books of views sometimes threaded such houses in sequence so that each estate's relative importance could be correctly deduced, with gate lodges also signposting their comparative significance.[50] Arthur Young approved of the way Irish roads 'were all found leading from houses like rays from a center … until in a short time, those rays, pointing from so many centers, met; and then the communication was complete'.[51] In contrast, American roads were not laid out to connect the great plantation houses as staged points in a designed route but rather to connect the plantation with the shipping wharves where the plantation's produce was loaded, almost invariably at a plantation's edge.[52] Some of the difficulty experienced by Europeans in discerning the American estate from the road was due to the absence of such expected markers. It was also related to the dearth of estate towns. In Europe generally, and particularly during the 'improvement' period in Britain and Ireland, the estate town was an important appendage to the great estate. Developed frequently by the estate itself, estate towns became models of urban improvement much as the demesne became the pinnacle of its rural and agricultural corollary. A family's ownership and political control of their estate town was expressed in many discreet and not so discreet ways. Most, and often all, of the public buildings, including the established church, school, market house, memorials, statues, barracks and latterly law courts and police stations, were built on land gifted or leased to the town by the estate's owner. The town's architectural expression was frequently designed to harmonise overtly with the great house and/or its lodge(s), gates and avenues that often linked the two physically. This cohesive patterning of estate, demesne/gentleman's park and town meant that Europeans found the less calculated urbanism of the United States difficult to read. For example, when the Irish tourist Isaac Weld visited Georgetown near Washington DC he argued that if its houses had 'been built situated in one place altogether, they would make a very respectable appearance, but scattered about as they are, a spectator' could 'scarcely perceive any thing like a town'.[53]

Wandering through the trees to find Mount Vernon, greatest of all American estates, was a matter of considerable bemusement to European visitors. How could one tell that this was a great estate if it did not project its lines of organisation far into the countryside, instead concealing its scale, location and boundary from the road? No avenue connected Mount Vernon to the wider road network and visitors commented on its sudden appearance, lodgeless, from the road.[54] When Benjamin Latrobe visited 'the farm of the President' that 'extend[ed] from the Mill to his house' in 1781 he remarked on its 'good fences, clear grounds and extensive cultivation strik[ing] the eye as something uncommon in this part of the World' but found the road 'bad enough'. Although the house became 'visible between two Groves of trees at about a mile's distance' it 'had no striking appearance, though superior to every other house' he had seen and the approach itself was 'not very well managed but leads you into the area between the Stables'.[55] The young Scotsman Robert Hunter when visiting Mount Vernon in 1785 wrote of the 'fine view of the Potomac' until the visitor 'entered a wood', where a 'small rivulet here divide[d] the General's estate from the neighboring farmer's' and where a vista of the house 'br[oke] out beautifully upon you when you little expect, being situated upon a most elegant rising ground on the banks of the Potomac'.[56] Isaac Weld set out from Alexandria in 1799 to visit Mount Vernon, located 9 miles away. He soon met the 'very thick woods' that remained 'standing within four or five miles of the place' with 'very bad' roads, 'so many of them cross[ing] one another in different directions, that it is a matter of very great difficulty to find out the right one'. Although he had taken care to 'set out from Alexandria with a gentleman who thought himself perfectly acquainted with the way' and had left 'ample time to have reached Mount Vernon before the close of day' at nightfall they were still 'wandering in the woods' with no 'vestige of a human being to set' them right. When they eventually reached Mount Vernon Weld heard of another gentleman who had been 'from ten o'clock in the morning till four in the afternoon on horseback, unable to find out the place, although within three or four miles of it the whole time'.[57]

In contrast to these Europeans, the American Samuel Powel considered 'the approach to this Seat' of Mount Vernon 'very pleasing' and found little to criticise in Mount Vernon's landscape structure:

At the Entrance from the Road you have a view of the House at the Distance of near a Mile. The Grounds on each side of the Road are cleared of the under wood & the Saplings neatly trimmed so as to promise to form a handsome Wood in future. Passing thro' this young Wood the Road lies thro' a bottom till you approach the House.[58]

Mount Vernon is situated on a height above Chesapeake Bay near or on top of an earlier house. Its river prospect was well described by such artists and visitors such as Benjamin Latrobe (Fig. 74), who wrote of how 'toward the east nature' had 'lavished magnificence' in the form of 'the mighty Potomac' that ran 'close under this bank, the elevation of which must be perhaps two hundred and fifty feet'. Many commented

on the scale and planting of the waterside area where 'down the steep slope' the trees and shrubs had been 'thickly planted' but 'kept so low as not to interrupt the view'.[59] Mount Vernon's site strategy of a 'hill at the top of which stood a rather spacious house'[60] was unusual and not particularly advantageous for British eighteenth-century landscape design, which sought a balanced composition of land, water and architecture. This was hard to achieve with the house so close to water yet perched so high above it. Ireland's leading families, like those of Virginia, rarely had funds for the wholesale redesign of house and landscape and the design norms of seventeenth-century houses rarely aligned with those of a later landscape garden. Houses built near rivers that were prone to periodic severe flooding were invariably located well above the

74. Benjamin Latrobe, 'View of Mount Vernon looking towards the South West', 16 July 1797.
Maryland Historical Society, Object i.d. 1960.108.1.2.11

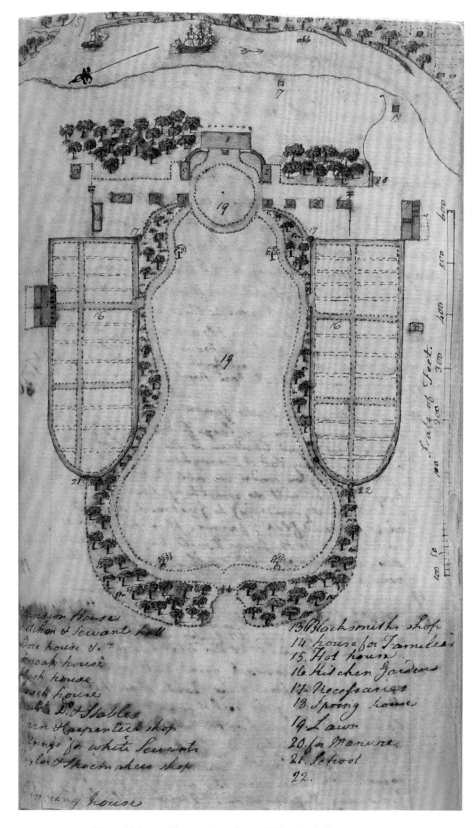

75. Plan of Mount Vernon from Samuel Vaughan's Diary, 1787, p. 56,
Mount Vernon, Ms-4996. Courtesy of Mount Vernon Ladies' Association

river's flood plain but the sensible precaution of building on higher ground, which had enhanced avenue planting in the seventeenth century, limited any connections between house, water and approach routes.[61] By placing the house on a hill, no lake or water feature could be contemplated easily, and many Virginian streams and creeks, such as those at Mount Vernon, were deeply incised into the ground, flood-prone and difficult to dam into elegant water features.

The transatlantic merchant Samuel Vaughan completed a small tour of Virginia in 1796. Born on 23 April 1720, he was the last and twelfth child of Benjamin Vaughan and Ann Wolf, who married in Dublin in 1700. Their fourth son, Samuel Frier Vaughan, was baptised by John Cooke, probably in the cathedral church of the Trinity and St Olave, Waterford city.[62] Often identified as an Englishman, Vaughan has been credited with the design of Philadelphia's first public park and with many other American parks and gardens. When he stopped at Mount Vernon on his 1787 tour of the east coast he drew the well-known plan of Mount Vernon's core mansion house landscape in his diary (Fig. 75), working it up subsequently as a presentation drawing for Washington (Fig. 76). An experienced transatlantic merchant, Vaughan also provided many luxury goods for Mount Vernon's furnishing and decoration, among them a mantelpiece, a set of three vases and a battle painting.[63]

A commonplace book typically recorded a family's births, marriages and deaths, and the 1892 publication *Miscellanea genealogica et heraldica* published that belonging to the Vaughan family of Wexford. Such a book could also record other key family events, including, in this case, the dates of travel by members of the Vaughan family. Samuel's father Benjamin had moved from Ballyboe near Clonmel, Co. Tipperary, in 1717 when he 'took a house in Waterford from Mr. Rodgers for 21 years'.[64] As Samuel Vaughan's preceding sister Hannah was born in Waterford in 1717, and there is no record of his father ever leaving Waterford save for a visit to his children in London in 1736,[65] all the sources and indications suggest that Samuel Vaughan was Irish and born in Waterford. Other published extracts from the family's commonplace book record that Samuel, then aged thirteen, went to London in 1733 to live with his married brother William, who had been living there since 1722.[66] After three years in London Samuel was apprenticed to the merchant Mather Corr who took him to Jamaica in 1736 at the age of sixteen.[67] On arriving in the Caribbean he completed some topographical profile drawings of the various islands,

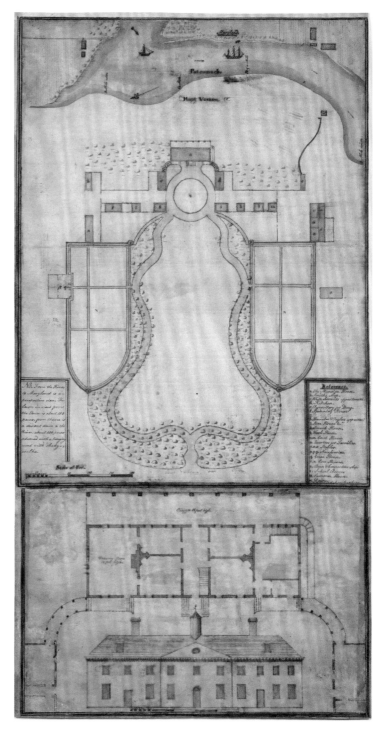

76. Presentation plan of Mount Vernon, from Samuel Vaughan's Diary, 1787, Mount Vernon, DI_1309-1_W-1434. Courtesy of Mount Vernon Ladies' Association

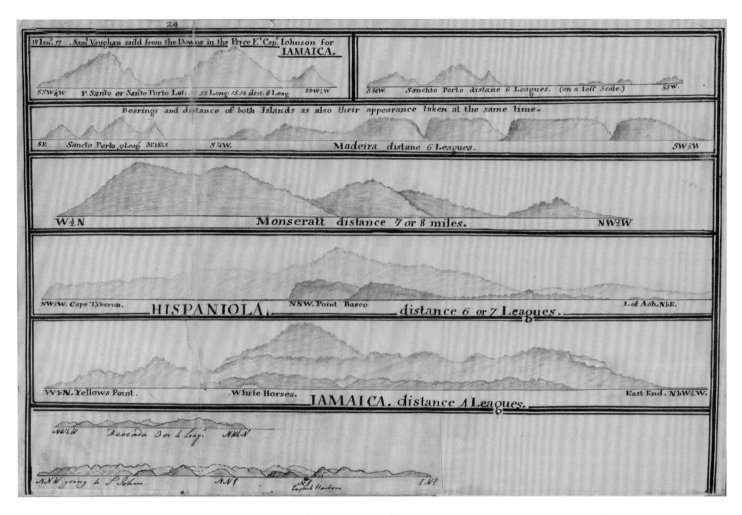

a common practice for military expeditions of the period (Fig. 77). During the sixteen years that he spent in Jamaica he acquired some substantial plantations before returning to London in 1752 as an absentee (Fig. 78).[68] There he became a successful banker, merchant, 'political radical and religious dissenter', if slightly tainted by the corruption scandal that resulted from his attempts to secure the plum job of Clerk to the Supreme Court of Jamaica for his family.[69] Frequently travelling back to the Caribbean and the United States, he became a quintessential transatlantic gentleman.

Samuel Vaughan's 1787 diary sketch of Mount Vernon had a legend that carefully listed Mount Vernon's principal features,[70] and when he revised it for the presentation drawing it remained substantially the same but for number 14 'house for Families' becoming 'n. Quarters for Families' and the '18. Spring house' by the river, perhaps indicating some water device, which was changed to 'w. Dairy' (Figs 75 and 76).[71] Vaughan's plan describes Washington's desire to make undulating curvilinear approaches to Mount Vernon, yet the approach options were in reality severely curtailed to one side or other of the main vista, if any travelling through the other four farms was to be avoided. Joseph Manca has carefully analysed Washington's evolving preference for a route that led past the bowling green and towards the coach house and stables, thereby eliminating any choice of route that might lead to the enslaved people's huts and quarters.[72] These were concealed behind a greenhouse that George Washington had designed with the help of 'Tench Tilghman, his former military aid, who had in turn enlisted

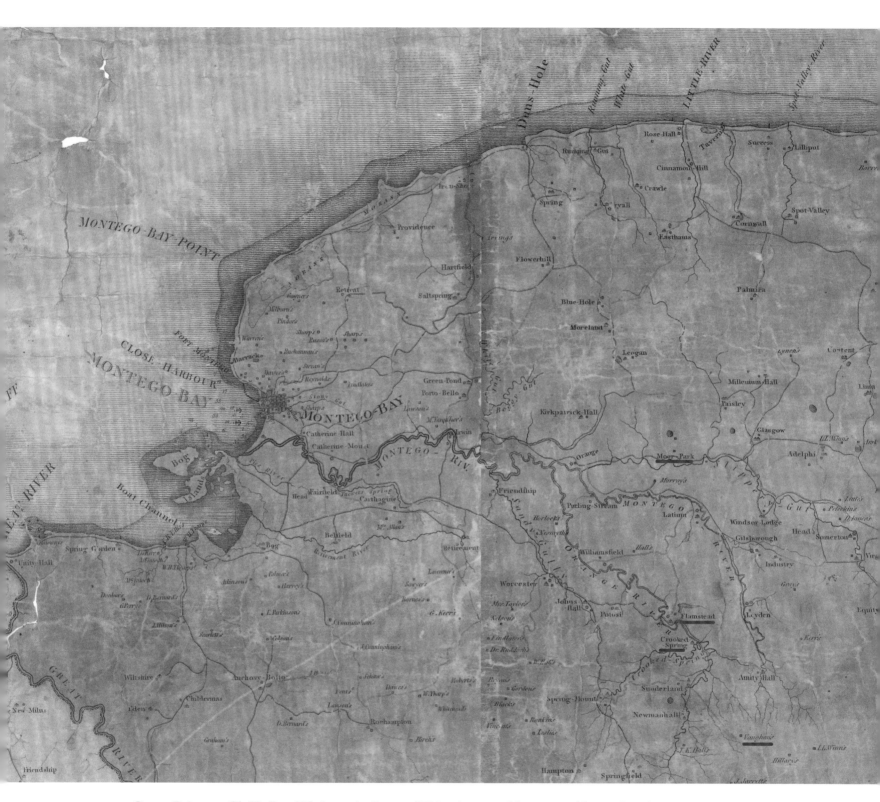

78. George Robertson, 'To His Royal Highness the Prince of Wales, this map of the county of Cornwall, in the island of Jamaica, constructed from actual surveys', 1804, National Library of Scotland. Detail with the Vaughan plantations underlined

79. Mount Vernon's greenhouse. The enslaved males' dormitories abut it directly to the rear. Author's photo, 2013

80. View towards Mount Vernon from the central gate of the bowling green. Author's photo, 2013

81. View from Mount Vernon looking over the serpentine bowling green, over the haha and the road to the distant parkland and the gateway framed now by lodges. Author's photo, 2013

82. Edward Savage, 'View of Mount Vernon from the North', *c*.1797, Courtesy of Mount Vernon Ladies' Association

the assistance of Mrs. Charles Carroll of Baltimore' (Fig. 79).[73] Unlike a British or Irish great estate, which would typically have a hierarchy of approaches from many directions, Mount Vernon could only have one. This limited the estate's possible vistas, as the interwoven approach routes of British and Irish great estates enabled a multitude of prospect points. The estate's only approach prospect – the view of the house from the north – was an artful and clever design given the severe constraints under which it operated (Fig. 80). Its corollary was the view from the house towards the entrance gates, where the serpentine bowling green and dividing haha structured a composition of foreground, middle ground and rear ground, the last punctuated only by the entrance gates in the eighteenth century, as the lodges were built later (Fig. 81). Estate portraits of Mount Vernon often tried to suggest the existence of other approach routes

and by extension prospect points, but these did not exist on the ground. Edward Savage's *c*.1792 view suggested that it had been taken from a track approaching the house from the east (Fig. 82) but any approach route from that direction would have had to negotiate the steep topography of Little Hunting Creek (Figs 52 and 53), where a vista of River Farm's overseer's house and the cabins of its enslaved workers was particularly undesirable.

The history of Mount Vernon's landscape, and by extension that of eighteenth-century American landscape design, has been substantially derived from Vaughan's and Washington's two maps. Like Washington, Vaughan was very familiar with plantation landscapes, having spent sixteen years in Jamaica surveying, drawing and designing the family plantations of Flamstead and Crooked Spring. Vaughan drew Mount Vernon at the scale of 50 feet to an inch, a much larger scale than that

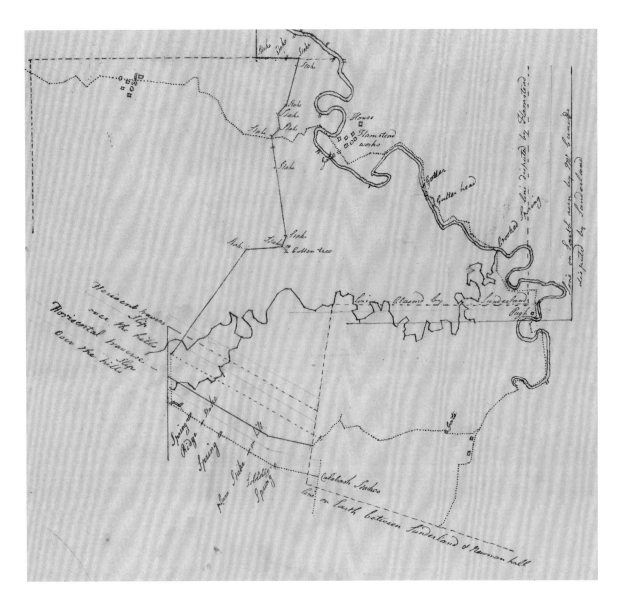

83. Plan of Jamaican river system with inset plan of 'Flamstead works'. Samuel Vaughan Album, Bowdoin College Library, George J. Mitchell Department of Special Collections & Archives

84. *(facing page, top)* Landscape (probably of a Jamaican plantation). Samuel Vaughan Album: 17b verso. Bowdoin College Library, George J. Mitchell Department of Special Collections & Archives

85. *(facing page, bottom)* Samuel Vaughan's plan of Flamstead? recording in red those portions of the buildings he had himself built. Samuel Vaughan Folio, Bowdoin College Library, George J. Mitchell Department of Special Collections & Archives

employed by Washington in the map he produced for Arthur Young which was drawn at 50 rods to an inch, with 16.5 feet in a rod. Vaughan's plan differs from Washington's in the scale and extent of what he chose to exclude from view – he drew only the mansion house farm. But why did Vaughan, who produced or commissioned the interconnected diagram map of his estates of Flamstead and Crooked Spring, Jamaica (Fig. 83), cut such a sharp frame around his plan of Mount Vernon? Why not include the wider plantation estate, as he did in his watercolour view of an unidentified Jamaican plantation sugar works, but probably that of his own Flamstead (Fig. 84)? His very familiarity with plantation structure allowed him to accurately record the uses of Mount Vernon's service buildings,

as he had also done for one of his plantation houses (probably Flamstead), where 'the Buildings Erected by Mr. Vaughan' were highlighted in red (Fig. 85). As a capitalist entrepreneur, he knew the financial cost of reducing an estate's tobacco acreage and he carefully depicted tiny portions of the fields and buildings that lay across the river from Mount Vernon, but none on the estate itself (Figs 75 and 76). In contrast, Benjamin Latrobe's view of the same opposing riverside omitted the buildings that Vaughan depicted in plan and also excluded any suggestion of a working, farmed landscape, save for one long field boundary on the left-hand side, carefully interrupted by a lone broadleaf tree (Fig. 86). But Vaughan did not care to draw at a scale that would include the buildings that lay on Mount

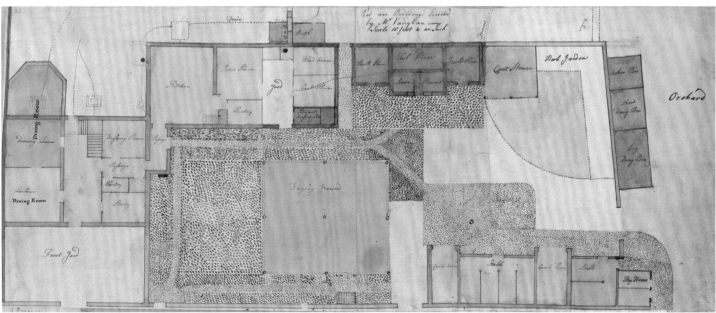

86. Benjamin Latrobe, 'View to the North from the Lawn at Mount Vernon', 16 July 1797. Maryland Historical Society, Object ID 1960.108.1.2.10

Vernon's other 'farms' on his plans of Mount Vernon. The plan of Moore Park's substantial Jamaican sugar works proves that he was more than capable of reading or producing detailed technical information when required (Fig. 87). Careful to reveal none of his own substantial experience as a Caribbean planter, his drawing and plan of Mount Vernon are as interesting for what they exclude as for what they include.[74]

Scale was used and manipulated in the design of colonial space. In America the nested hierarchy so beloved of European Cartesian geometry was imperfectly translated, leaving some scales conspicuously absent, or overtly preferred. Scale is used extensively in any design process, as drawings of different scales change or set the knowledge of a place, while the absence or presence of particular design scales reveals local, national or international spatial hierarchies. Visitors consistently found the scale of Mount Vernon hard to assess. The Scottish visitor Robert Hunter incorrectly assessed its extent at 4,000 acres in 1785, when it encompassed approximately 8,000 acres, and 'people frequently over or underestimated its size'.[75] An overlay of Samuel Vaughan's 1786 garden plan onto George Washington's 1793 survey of Mount Vernon reveals the discrepancy in design scale between the garden core and the wider plantation estate of four tobacco farms (Fig. 88).[76] Design scale, in both the landscapes and their traditions of representation, manipulated perceptions of the individual plantation, the individual planter and, for a nation that identified itself as a

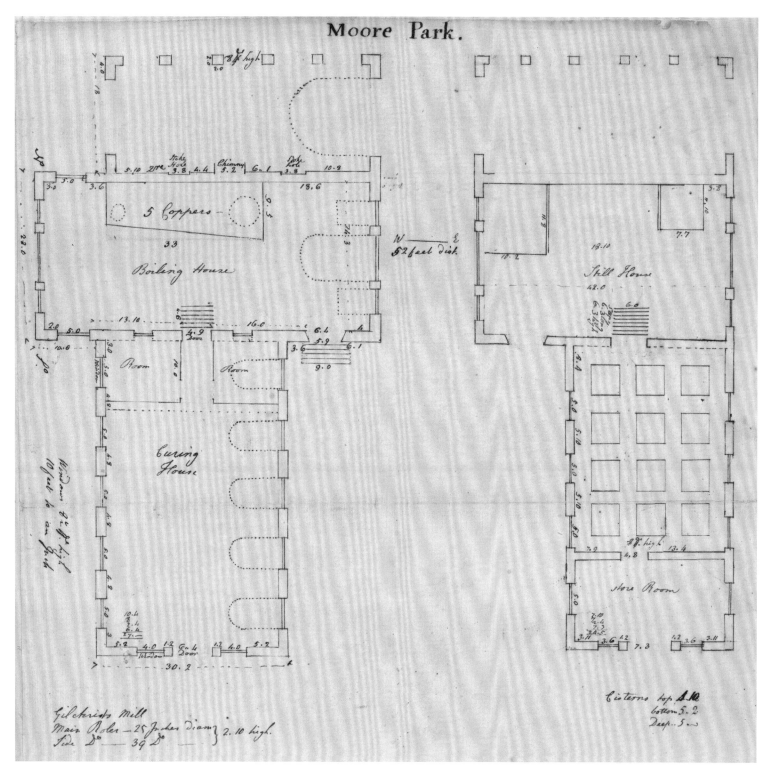

87. 'Moore Park' sugar works. Samuel Vaughan Folio, Bowdoin College Library, George J. Mitchell Department of Special Collections & Archives

nation of farmers, the state itself. Manipulating scale has both design and ideological consequences, and George Washington's manipulated scales of house, garden, farm, estate and national identity were a carefully calibrated design project.[77]

On his presentation map Vaughan took care to 'nota bene' that 'from the house to Maryland is a perspective view' and that 'the lawn in view from the House is about 100 paces' and that 'from thence is a descent down to the River, about 400 paces adorned with a hanging wood with shady walks' (Fig. 76). Including such measurements indicates a desire to compare and measure Mount Vernon against other sites, as Arthur Young had frequently done in his books. Was Vaughan comparing it with the Flamstead, Crooked Spring or Penn Plantations in Jamaica, the presumptive sources of his own wealth and where he had spent his formative years aged sixteen to thirty-two? Maybe he was thinking of his childhood landscapes of the Blackwater River that flows into his birthplace of Waterford, where many old houses, such as 'Dromana Castle, seat of Lord Grandison', sit high above a topography that differs substantially from the flat oxbows of the Thames.

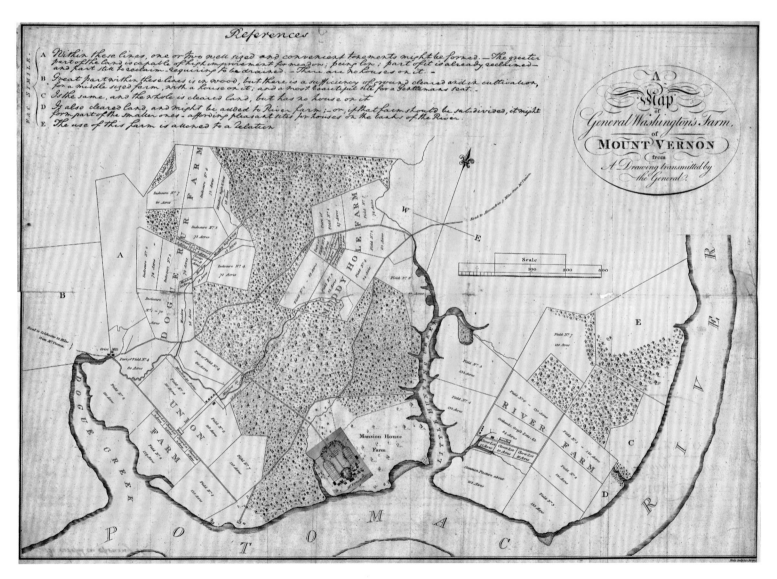

88. Neil Crimmins, overlay of plan of Mount Vernon from Samuel Vaughan's diary, 1796, p. 56, Mount Vernon, Ms-4996, Courtesy of Mount Vernon Ladies' Association onto *A Map of General Washington's Farm of Mount Vernon from A Drawing transmitted by the General 1793' in Letters from His Excellency General Washington, to Arthur Young ...*, London, 1801. Library of Congress G3882.M7 1793.W34 1801 TIL, loc.gov/item/99466780

89. Charles Fraser,
'Dromana, seat of
Ld. Grandison (Co.
Waterford), Benson Castle'.
Untitled sketchbook,
p. 47. Gibbes Museum,
Charleston, SC, Accession
no. 1938.036.0024

Copied carefully by the American landscape artist Charles
Fraser into his practice sketchbook (Fig. 89), such scenes from
published books of views assisted in the correct composition of
picturesque views (Fig. 90).

Other eighteenth-century American landscape designs also
puzzled Europeans. Three of the most prominent tourists of
the late eighteenth century visited Monticello, the Marquis
de Chastellux in 1782, and both Isaac Weld and the Duc de la
Rochefoucauld-Liancourt in 1796. De Chastellux felt obliged
to inform his readers that Thomas Jefferson had 'himself built
it and chose the site, for although he already owned fairly
extensive lands in the neighbourhood, there was nothing in
such an unsettled country, to prevent him from fixing his
residence wherever he wanted' (Fig. 91). This implicit question-
ing of Jefferson's site selection was resolved by the explanation
of the name 'Monticello (in Italian, little mountain) a very
modest title, for it is situated upon a very lofty one, but which
announces the owner's attachment to the language of Italy;

90. 'Dromana, seat of Lord Grandison', plate from Paul Sandby,
The Virtuosi's Museum (London: G. Kearsly, 1778–81)

91. *(top)* View of Thomas Jefferson's Monticello house. Author's photo, 2013

92. *(bottom)* Monticello's northern vista. Author's photo, 2013

and above all to the fine arts, of which that country was the cradle and is still the asylum'. Further musing on the site's logic is suggested by de Chastellux's comment that 'Mr. Jefferson is the first American who has consulted the Fine Arts to know how he should shelter himself from the weather'.[78] Yet such a position was far from elite British landscape taste in 1789 when Humphry Repton wrote that 'the House which stands upon the highest Ground in the Park, is not placed in the best Situation that might have been chosen, from the unfortunate Mistake so often made in not distinguishing between an extensive Prospect and a pleasing Landscape'. It had a corollary effect on any landscape views made of the house as 'in proportion as we are lifted above the Tops of the Trees we lose the advantage of a foreground which is essential to a good Composition.'[79]

Arthur Young's friend the Duc de la Rochefoucauld-Liancourt was similarly preoccupied with Monticello's composition when he visited in 1796. He found that 'on the east side, the front of the building, the eye is not checked by any object, since the mountain on which the house is seated, commands

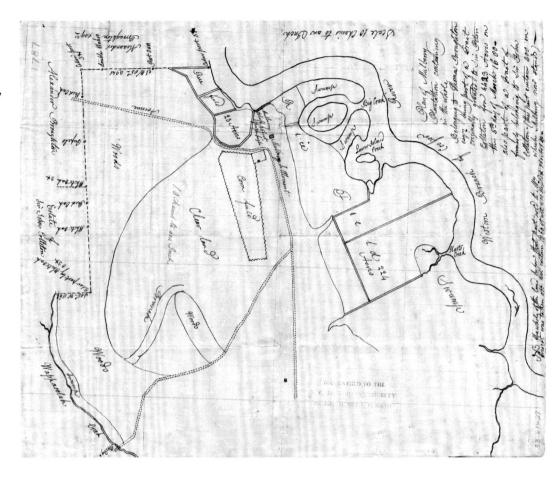

93. John Diamond, *Plat of Mulberry Plantation*, Cooper River, land of Thomas Broughton, adjoining property of Mrs Trescot and others, 1787. South Carolina Historical Society, Maps/plats, Call no. 33-61-27

all the neighbouring heights as far as the Chesapeake'.[80] He liked the contained garden front where 'the bounds of the view on this point, at so small a distance, form a pleasant resting-place' and wondered if the entrance front's 'immensity of prospect' was 'perhaps, already too vast'. Although he approved of the distant dots of 'cultivated fields, houses and barns' that enlivened the extensive landscape, they were too few and too far away. With eighteenth-century landscape painting convention in mind, 'the aid of fancy' was 'required to complete the enjoyment of this magnificent view; and she must picture to us those plains and mountains such as population and culture will render them in a greater or smaller number of years'.[81] Essentially, Monticello had no middle ground (Fig. 92). By placing his villa on top of a hill and his tobacco plantations in the valleys below, Jefferson could only enjoy distant views from his hilltop station. As at Mount Vernon, the position of the house had determined and limited the range of prospects available. Excluding views of Virginian tobacco fields was as important for the estate's successful design as including other ones.

At Mount Vernon there could not be a landscape garden. The surrounding context, for many reasons, could not adopt its aesthetic with any degree of conviction, and its vocabulary of boundary, route and oblique vista was frustrated at every turn. This extended into the American tradition of landscape painting where the wider point of view became linguistically inappropriate. Key American estates such as Mount Vernon were painted repetitively from the same short-range points of view.[82] Oblique approach views of Mount Vernon from the middle distance are hard to position on the ground and very limited in their viewpoint, with the same imagined view from the north-eastern approach appearing again and again (Fig. 82). Some estates such as Monticello were entirely unsuited to any such tradition of estate portraiture because of their site and situation.[83]

The plantation of Mulberry, South Carolina, was surveyed by John Diamond in 1787 (Fig. 93) and then depicted in a series of seven exceptional estate portraits by Thomas Coram in *c*.1800. The leading portrait showed the axial approach view

94. Thomas Coram, 'View of Mulberry, House and Street', *c*.1800. Gibbes Museum of Art/Carolina Art Association Charleston, SC. Accession no. 1938.018.0001

of the mansion, where it was flanked on one side by a line of enslaved workers' huts (Fig. 94). Remarkable for both its honesty and its rarity, the lone tree to the left-hand side does not accomplish its intention of making the scene picturesque. The other six views were very constrained in their viewpoints, and none of them depicted the extensive rice paddies that lay to the right-hand side of the approach avenue and which were drawn in Diamond's map (Fig. 93). They bear little evidence of the estate's full scale and reach, remaining focused on the perimeter road and the Cooper River (Fig. 95).[84]

The Irishman Isaac Weld, author of a grumpy, condescending 1797 *Tour of America*, had been introduced to George Washington by Sir Edward Newenham in 1795 as the 'Son of an old & truly respectable Friend of Mine … of an Amiable Character & Virtuous Character' who was embarking on 'a Tour of pleasure & Curiosity to Visit' Washington's 'Happy Country'.[85] Weld had been 'induced to cross the Atlantic' when 'storms' were 'gathering over his native country' for the purpose of 'examining with his own eyes the truth of the various accounts which had been given of the flourishing and happy condition of the United States of America, and of ascertaining whether, in case of future emergency, any

part of those territories might be looked to, as an eligible and agreeable place of abode'.[86] Sir Edward Newenham had dabbled in tour-writing himself and was 'especially proud of the accounts he wrote of his tours to Europe in 1751, 1759, 1761, 1772, 1778–9 and 1782–3 and confident that his description of his "tour to Norway, Sweden, Lapland and the Baltick would get a rapid sale"'[87] if he published it. At only twenty years of age, the route Isaac Weld followed over two years took him from Philadelphia, where he landed, northwards to Baltimore, Boston and the shores of Lake Erie. He then travelled southwards to Washington DC and deep into Virginia. Arriving into Philadelphia by ship, Weld distinguished carefully between long- and close-range views of American landscape. The former were positive, the latter much less so:

> Philadelphia, as you approach by the river, is not seen further off than three miles, a point of land covered with trees concealing it from view. On weathering this point it suddenly opens upon you, and at that distance it looks extremely well; but on a nearer approach, the city makes a poor appearance.[88]

95. Thomas Coram, 'View of Road at Mulberry', *c.1800*. Gibbes Museum of Art/
Carolina Art Association Charleston, SC. Accession no. 1938.018.0005

His book *Travels through the States of North America, and the Provinces of Upper and Lower Canada, during the Years 1795, 1796, and 1797* was controversial in America,[89] although it did give him an introduction to European society when he returned, notably at the *l'Insitut de France*.[90] Like Arthur Young, who had compared Ireland to England to find some of the intermediary scales absent, Weld tried to scale the components of American landscape for his European readers. Of Virginia's property mosaic he wrote that 'instead of lands being equally divided, immense estates' were 'held by a few individuals', who derived 'large incomes from them, whilst the generality of the people' were 'in a state of mediocrity'.[91] The 'farms and plantations in Maryland' varied from 'one hundred to one thousand acres' with those 'in the lower parts' more 'extensive' with 'large quantities of tobacco' grown using 'labour performed almost entirely by negroes'. This allowed their enslavers to live in a manner 'very similar to the planters of Virginia' with stewards and overseers to carry out 'the management of their lands'.[92] Weld observed that such men had often received 'liberal educations' with some sending their sons to England to be educated 'as the veneration for that country from whence their ancestors came' was 'by no means extinguished'.[93]

Somewhat chastised perhaps by his book's anticipated and eventual American reception,[94] Weld's next travel publication was a highly conservative and limited example of the genre. His 1812 *Illustrations of the Scenery of Killarney and the Surrounding Country* reduced his route from the many thousands of miles he covered in the United States to approximately five around Killarney's famous Lough Léin. He argued erroneously that the book covered a 'part of the united kingdom' that was 'very imperfectly known' and could not resist comparing Killarney with America, despite the ridiculous disparity in scale, with the 'apparent wildness' of the bay of Glena incapable of being 'surpassed by that of the forests of America'.[95]

Emphatically not a child of the French Revolution, Weld was not impressed by the equality the United States had achieved: 'Poverty is also as much unknown in this country as great wealth. Each man owns the house he lives in and the land which he cultivates, and every one appears to be in a happy state of mediocrity, and unambitious of a more elevated situation that what he himself enjoys.'[96] Comparing the various nationalities that made up the American population (he did not like Germans), he concluded his tour with an extensive comparison of Canada and the United States.

Hungry at a roadside tavern at Ticonderoga, before crossing the border, Weld and his companions were surprised when the tavern keeper departed 'from the system of equality' they were familiar with in the United States, where they might be 'kept an hour or two till sufficient supper was prepared for the whole company, so that all might sit down together'.[97] In contrast, in Canada he was agreeably surprised to be served quickly, because their hostess had identified them as important guests, and where a 'variety of objects' served to 'forcibly' remind him that he had 'got into a new country':

> The British flag, the soldiers on duty, the French inhabitants running around in their red nightcaps, the children coming to the door to salute you as you pass, a thing unknown in any part of the United States; the compact and neat appearance of the houses, the calashes, the bons dieux, the large Roman Catholic churches and chapels, the convents, the priests in their robes, the friars; all serve to convince you that you are no longer in any part of the United States: the language also differs, French being here universally spoken.[98]

At Mount Vernon, Isaac Weld was struck that 'concealed behind the house's wings, on the one side' lay 'the different offices belonging to the house, and also to the farm, and on the other, the cabins for the SLAVES [sic]' explaining in a footnote that these were 'amongst the first of the buildings which are seen on coming to Mount Vernon'. It was 'not without astonishment and regret they are surveyed by the stranger, whose mind has dwelt with admiration upon the inestimable blessings of liberty, whilst approaching the residence of that man who has distinguished himself so gloriously in its cause'.[99] Weld excluded the slave quarters from his published view, with the house abruptly chopped in half as a consequence (Fig. 96). Once his tour was published Weld became an authority on the Americas and patterns of travelling to it. On his return to Ireland he was summoned to see the Irish Lord Lieutenant, Lord Hardwicke, and to give his views on the emigration which 'had become very general in Ireland, especially in the northern provinces'. Weld advised directing the stream of emigration to Britain's 'own American colonies', namely Canada, 'instead of suffering it to flow to the United States' and he was soon occupied in drawing up a 'compendium of those parts of his work which dealt with the subject of emigration' for Lord Hardwicke.[100] Samuel Vaughan's politics, in contrast to Weld's,

retained a radical and republican cast which he transferred to his son Benjamin, who 'fearing he would be arrested during a government investigation of revolutionaries in 1794 ... fled to France and later to America'.[101] There he arranged the Maine publication in 1800 of 'The Rural Socrates' or 'An Account of a celebrated Philosophical Farmer lately living in Switzerland, and known by the name of Kliyogg'[102] that owed its origin to Arthur Young's translation and inclusion of *The Rural Socrates, being the Memoirs of a Country Philosopher* in his 1770 book *Rural Oeconomy or Essays on the Practical Parts of Husbandry*.[103]

Such European visitors to Mount Vernon always brought their own particular order of landscape experience to bear on their interpretations of that site.[104] Most of them documented not only what they saw in reality but also the presence of absence, the gaps that they did not expect, the boundaries they had expected to pass, the vistas they had expected to see. Most potent at the time of initial experience, this presence of absence can be felt not only in the landscape itself but also in its documentary record. The divergence of American landscape design from European tradition, fashion and practice occurred particularly along estate boundaries – frontiers of landscape design. Creating an American landscape garden required a special new boundary between the inner house core of improved mixed agriculture and the surrounding plantation monoculture. How to conceal this junction became the key landscape design decision for men such as George Washington, Thomas Jefferson and Carter Burwell, who wished to adopt English landscaping and farming practices. Some managed to conceal the transition by virtue of their choice of site, as at Monticello. Others segregated off farms and surrounded them with woodland to affect a central and distinct core, such as at Mount Vernon. In contrast, others retained the old geometrical approach, so evident at Mulberry and Gunston Hall, sensing perhaps that the American estate, if it abandoned geometry for the landscape garden, would create a new and paradoxical paradigm. This relative proportion of monoculture/plantation land to the more leisured, elite and visible landscape surrounding the plantation mansion was central to eighteenth-century American landscape design. Both areas were designed landscapes, one concerned that white visitors should see and interpret it narrowly, the other equally concerned that it remained hidden from such eyes.

Seventeenth-century plantation design in the United States took European land survey and distribution methods but

96. 'Mount Vernon', plate from Isaac Weld, *Travels through the States of North America, and the Provinces of Upper and Lower Canada, during the years 1795, 1796, and 1797* (London: John Stockdale, 1800)

remoulded them for effective use in new environments. As the colonies grew in wealth and design ambition, the eighteenth-century landscape garden and the picturesque tour brought new challenges to colonial design. These dynamic and route-based designs manipulated the perception of scale to achieve layered and duplicitous spatial effects, particularly in the design of boundary, approach and vista. Translations of their design vocabulary into the Americas had to contend with a larger scale of plantation monoculture coupled with a smaller scale of architecture, rendering many intermediate scales absent, compressed or expanded. This also occurred in the landscape's many representations, with scalar curtailment affecting a similar compression in the tradition of landscape painting. Estate maps carefully edited their information, typically advancing one design scale at the expense of others. The aesthetic attention lavished on each central great house declined very sharply to an invidious edge of monoculture agriculture, chattel slavery and industrialised production. For many Caribbean or American planters such translation issues could be unimportant, but for men such as George Washington, colonial insecurity and national pride demanded European approval.

The history of eighteenth-century landscape design in the United States is more than 'the study of the integration of European gardens styles with the physical conditions of the unspoiled natural environment of the New World'.[105] Much of the eastern seaboard had lost its unspoiled and natural status some two hundred years before 1800. The great estates of the tidewater Chesapeake, the James, Rappahannock and Ashley river valleys and the sea islands of Georgia's coastline are designed landscapes, demonstrating as controlled and intentional a design language as any of their European counterparts. George Washington's and Thomas Jefferson's serpentine walks around a carefully delimited lawn are not poor approximations of the English landscape garden. They are landscape designs that resolve and express the particular challenges of the landed estate in the United States.

CHAPTER 4

Subversive Suburbias

Rousseau's Landscapes

This chapter explores Jean-Jacques Rousseau's radical reformation of eighteenth-century villa structure and lifestyle in
his suburban farmhouse of Les Charmettes on the outskirts of
Chambéry in the alpine Savoie department of eastern France.
It investigates why Arthur Young and many other eighteenth-
century writers and travellers found his innovations so inspir-
ational, among them two leading United Irishmen, Lord
Edward FitzGerald and Arthur O'Connor. At Les Charmettes
Rousseau's habits of walking, farming and botanising combined
with his writings' comparative analysis of countries and their
people to inspire such men to replicate his lifestyle in their own
environments at home. His innovations were later coupled with
the French Revolution's iconography, as exemplified particularly
in its choreographed festivals and rituals. These upset traditional spatial hierarchies by placing landscape – mountains,
plains and countryside – as the virtuous corollary to architecture, particularly by undermining such traditional spaces as the
cathedral, the square and the city. Creating a heady ferment
of political, cultural and spatial ideas, every gesture – how
you picked flowers in your cottage garden, how you drew and
coloured your survey drawing or hopped over the garden wall –
became ways to express individual identity and thereby revolutionary intent. The reasons why FitzGerald and O'Connor
travelled and landscaped with such performative conviction
to inspire revolution in Ireland can be unpicked by tracking
their biographical and spatial trajectories. Their perceptions, as
recorded in their letters and memoirs, reveal the role of landscape in narrating their changing physical and mental world-
views, and in shifting their national and political identities. For
O'Connor, visiting France, Switzerland and monasteries, and
for FitzGerald plantation islands, American wildernesses and
indigenous tribes, gave each of them the comparative sources
that they later employed with some effect as revolutionaries.
The extent to which they imbibed the French Revolution's
key spatial and representational strategies is revealed in their
choices and designs for Irish environments when they came
home. Rousseau's suburban bolthole became a powerful
model in the repressive sectarian society of eighteenth-
century Dublin, then caught in a complex web of penal laws.
The hidden landscapes that Catholics (and revolutionaries)
were obliged to inhabit led to an exodus from the city to the
mountains of Wicklow and the plains of Kildare. Plotting revolution took them back again to Europe, where they concealed
their activities behind a polite veil of tourism. O'Connor's
unpublished autobiographical memoirs, the manuscript of
which is now held in his descendants' château outside Paris,
are affected by their degree of distant recall, unlike Edward
FitzGerald's less filtered and immediate letters to his family.

(Facing page) Detail of fig. 97

97. Joseph François Marie de Martinel, *Vue générale de Chambéry/Chambéry a la fin du XVIIIe siècle*, c.1780.
Musée des Beaux-arts de Chambéry. Crédit photographique: Musées de Chambéry-Didier Gourbin

To reach Chambéry from Paris the road extends south-east across the plain of the Ile de France when it dips and bobs over Burgundy's low hills to cross the Rhone and veer towards the Préalpes. Chambéry lies in these alpine foot-hills with the great Massif des Bauges separating it from the higher lake Annecy (Fig. 97). Built to a general southerly aspect, the town happily avoids the deep valleys and dark declivities of the more upper Alps. In 1732 the twenty-year-old Jean-Jacques Rousseau, employed in the King's service as a land surveyor, arrived in Chambéry.[1] Although not wholly enamoured by the discipline of mapping, he acknowledged that making cadastral maps gave him drawing skills that he retained for life (Fig. 98).[2] Cadastral maps are those that provide 'public register of the quantity, value, and ownership of the real property of a country'.[3] Usually compiled by the state or monarch for taxation purposes, drawing such maps requires an ability to measure, scale and represent space accurately in two dimensions. Making the maps gave Rousseau an understanding and a taste for drawing and design ('le goût du dessin') and he also made some landscape and flower paintings. He did not rate his talent highly, but later recalled his total preoccupation with such activities during this period of his life.[4]

Rousseau lived initially with his mentor and sometime partner Madame de Warens in a Chambéry townhouse. It had no garden and he disliked their cramped and poorly ventilated dark room that had but a wall and cul-de-sac as a view. Combined with the crickets, rats and disintegrating floorboards, it was not a pleasant place in which to live.[5] The couple escaped their 'stifling dungeon' by renting a garden in one of Chambéry's suburbs, a 'little retreat' where they grew plants and botanised – gathering plants in the wild and carefully drying their samples before cataloguing them.[6] After various escapades, including much music teaching, a failed attempt to set up a botanical garden (with Rousseau as botanist) and some periods of ill-health, the pair became disenchanted in turn with this suburban garden. It could not be a true rural retreat when it was so surrounded by other houses and gardens.[7] They set out to look for a more ideal and peaceful location, one far enough from the town and undesirable visitors yet close enough for any necessary or occasional visits.[8] They found Les Charmettes, a small estate close to Chambéry, but as 'retired and solitary as if it had been a hundred leagues away'[9] (Figs 99 and 100). Situated beside a stream in a valley that ran north–south between two reasonably high hills, the neighbouring houses were so sparsely distributed that it proved a little 'wild and retired asylum'.[10] It had a stepped garden with a vineyard on the upper terrace and an orchard on the lower. Close by lay a fountain and a grove of chestnut trees, while further up the hillside was a pasture for animals. Finding it to contain everything necessary for their ideal establishment, they moved in at the end of summer 1736.[11]

Rousseau was overjoyed with his new environment.[12] Although he and Madame de Warens continued to return to the Chambéry townhouse for the winter, as soon as the snow had begun to melt they left for Les Charmettes in time to hear the first notes of the nightingale. A typical day began before sunrise when Rousseau climbed through the orchard to reach a very pretty path.[13] As he walked he prayed and contemplated the rural landscape, finding it the only thing of which the heart and eye never tired.[14] Later, recalling his time there as 'the brief happiness' of his life, he reminisced that such brief yet moving experiences had given him 'the right to say, I have lived'.[15]

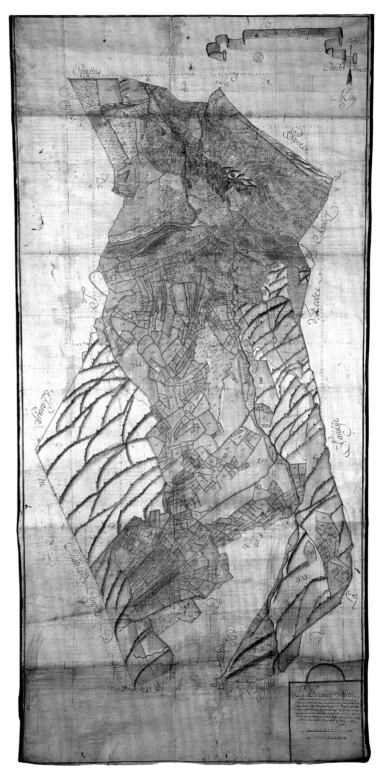

98. Example of a 1732 cadastral survey of La Compôte, Savoie, on which Rousseau worked, Département de la Savoie, Archives départementales, C 2650

99. View of Les Charmettes house and gatehouse. Author's photo, 2014

100. View from the terraced gardens to the house. Author's photo, 2014

101. View from the terraced gardens looking towards Chambéry and the mountain. Author's photo, 2014

The farmhouse of Les Charmettes can still be reached by walking southwards out of Chambéry. Winding paths and roads lead to a gatehouse set in high perimeter walls enclosing gardens, outbuildings and a substantial stone farmhouse (Figs 99 and 100). Its principal rooms are well proportioned if shy of the conscious elegance of perfect geometry, and look out on the north-facing terraces that step down the hill. Long perspective lines link the garden via the town to the Roc du Margériaz, its stone cliffs rising behind the church spires of Chambéry (Fig. 101). Rousseau, when not preoccupied with country matters and working 'like a peasant',[16] continued his intellectual education, fussing that he was not doing anything well. He and Madame de Warens enjoyed 'dinners on the grass at Montagnole, suppers under the trees, harvesting the fruit, the grape harvest, scutching the hemp from the flax' and these became their 'festivals'. Yet he found his more solitary walks to possess an even greater charm, because his heart could then be more 'en liberté'.[17] Walking, together with the sights, feelings, emotions and meditative processes that it could inspire, became the cornerstone of his way of life, and when he left for Paris in 1741 he claimed that he had left his heart at Les Charmettes.[18]

As Rousseau's fame and reputation grew over the course of the eighteenth century more and more people made the pilgrimage to see the place where the philosopher had been happiest. Unlike a humanist prince in Renaissance Italy, Rousseau did not have a court of scholars or artists – his ideal life was one of repeated simple daily rituals that humans of every estate could emulate. His political tract *Letters from the Mountains* (1762–5) positioned radical thought in mountainous environments, while his *Reveries of the Solitary Walker* (1776–8) emphasised personal communion with nature as the path to self-knowledge and awareness. Slowly the comparatively small and innocuous outer suburban farmhouse of Les Charmettes established a way of living that found its inheritance in many subsequent suburban dreams. Middling in scale and modest in ambition, the landscape's vistas might stretch to the mountain but its designed elements did not. Although reminiscent of any traditional villa in its view towards the city and the staged route required to reach it, it broke from aristocratic precedent in its modest design ambition and practical function. Its value for revolutionaries lay in its scale as an unpretentious complex of buildings and gardens, its connected views linking town and mountains, and its location on the border of Switzerland.

Caught between city and country, townhouse and country house, Les Charmettes became the ideal middle ground.

Switzerland had been incorporated into the European grand tour as a key approach route to Italy over the course of the eighteenth century, particularly for tourists of the Protestant north who wished to avoid France. As the country increased in perceived beauty and symbolic power, it became the apogée of picturesque landscape and then of romantic landscape.[19] Rousseau's publications, and his reputation as *le philosophe de Genève*, contributed to this rise, and in 1780 Jean-Benjamin de Laborde's *Tableaux topographiques, pittoresques, physiques, historiques, moraux, politiques, littéraires, de la Suisse* included views of places whose principal significance lay in being 'near the house of Jean-Jacques Rousseau' (Fig. 102). As the country became a destination in its own right it resulted in an inevitable reordering of itineraries with Les Charmettes incorporated into tours and tour guides because of its central role in Rousseau's spatial biography (Fig. 103).

Rousseau's promotion of walking as a prescribed practice led people to perceive spatial relationships from a lower level and at a more ruminative pace. Landscapes that demanded a walking acquaintance, being difficult to travel through on wheels, such as those of Switzerland, became ever more significant as destinations. A logical consequence of the growing appreciation for natural and romantic landscape, walking in the mountains became the apex of landscape experience and pedestrian travel the authentic way to experience nature. Walking in contrary motion also acquired some potency, as reversing the route, much like upsetting the mode of transport, creates a discernible shift in perception.[20] As the tourist gaze dropped and slowed other issues came into focus, particularly those relating to local people's lives and relationships. Close and comparative landscape analysis competed with the broader strokes of landscape aesthetics and botanising myopically began to challenge the wider prospect view.

Among those who followed such an itinerary was Arthur Young. During his *Travels in France during the Years 1787, 1788 and 1789* Young visited Érmenonville, Rousseau's memorial garden close to Paris. He described its 'three distinct water scenes'[21] but did not publish a detailed overview of the whole site, reasoning that it had been comprehensively described and published by others (Fig. 104).[22] In a letter to an anonymous friend he was charmed by the 'rude simplicity which one meets with in the walks on one side of the forest, where little

102. Claude Louis Chatelet, *Torrent du Val-Travers. Vue a peu de distance de la Maison du Philosophe de Genève, dans le Comte de Neuchâtel*, c.1780, engraved by Louis-Joseph Masquelier I, Bibliothèque de Genève, Gir 0819/03 also plate CXXXIVV from Jean-Benjamin de Laborde, *Tableaux topographiques, pittoresques, physiques, historiques, moraux, politiques, littéraires, de la Suisse, Tome 3*, p. 223 (Paris: Née & Masquelier & Ruault, 1780–8)

103. Print of Les Charmettes, engraved by Forbier. Alamy

rivulets, Swiss bridges, seats à la rustique & c. present themselves every moment'.[23] Young's more personal inclination, however, was for Les Charmettes – 'the road, the house of Madame de Warens, the vineyard, the garden, every thing, in a word, that had been described by the inimitable pencil of Rousseau'.[24] Situated 'about a mile from Chambery, fronting the rocky road' and small, being 'much of the same size as we should suppose, in England, would be found on a farm of one hundred acres, without the least luxury or pretension', the garden was noteworthy for being 'confined, as well as unassuming'. Young, who was profoundly influenced by Rousseau, asserting that he had never been 'prevented by rain from taking a walk every day',[25] could not but be interested in Les Charmettes, viewing 'it with a degree of emotion; even in the leafless melancholy of December' when he wandered 'about some hills, which were assuredly the walks' Rousseau had 'so agreeably described'.[26] Treading physically in the philosopher's footsteps, Young adopted Rousseau's aesthetic preferences so as to re-enact the same spatial experiences.

104. View of Rousseau's tomb on the island at Érmenonville with the château in the background. Author's photo, 2014

Arthur Young's *Travels in France during the Years 1787, 1788 and 1789* was first published in 1792 and remains one of the foremost sources for the general condition of France on the eve of revolution.[27] Modelled on his *A Tour in Ireland, 1776–1779*[28] it was also a sustained exploration of an entire country, unlike his tours of the northern or eastern English counties. He took care to publicise his project to such French gentlemen as he happened to meet along the way, as he had done in Ireland. In Ireland, Young had adopted the tone and eye of the disinterested foreign observer, which was harder for him to affect in the home counties of England, and Ireland became a stepping stone to his comparative assessment of nations. He compared the French town of Luzarches with Derry/Londonderry, which had 'something of its form' but wanted 'some of its richest features',[29] while his first view of 'the Pyrenees at the distance of 150 miles' brought his experience of seeing Ireland's Wicklow mountains from Holyhead, Wales, 'at a distance of 60 or 70 miles'[30] to mind. Although Ireland was the dominant landscape comparison of choice for Young when touring France, he still considered Ireland to be part of the British Isles, and visiting it was not really going abroad. Describing his French tours as the 'first of [his] foreign travels', they had 'confirmed the

idea, that to know your own country well, we must see something of others'. Countries 'figure[d] by comparison; and those ought to be esteemed the benefactors of the human race, who have most established public prosperity on the basis of private happiness'.[31] His French tour directly equated political and landscape structures, enabling his British, Irish and American readers to imbibe his method of agricultural observation, landscape description and comparative analysis to arrive at similar conclusions for themselves. His mentor in France, the Duc de la Rochefoucauld-Liancourt, as the preceding chapter has explored, would practice the same comparative analysis during his own travels in America.[32]

Young began his French travels with a route that ran down the central spine of France via Limoges to reach Bagnères-de-Luchon at the foot of the Pyrenees. Swinging around to Bordeaux, he returned to Paris via the Loire valley before going home briefly to England. Next he made a counterclockwise tour of Brittany before returning home again from Nantes via Paris. His next trip traced a north-eastern loop from Paris to Strasbourg, Besançon and Lille before striking south to Lyon, the Rhone valley, Savoy and then home. He published a map of his French touring routes, an item he had

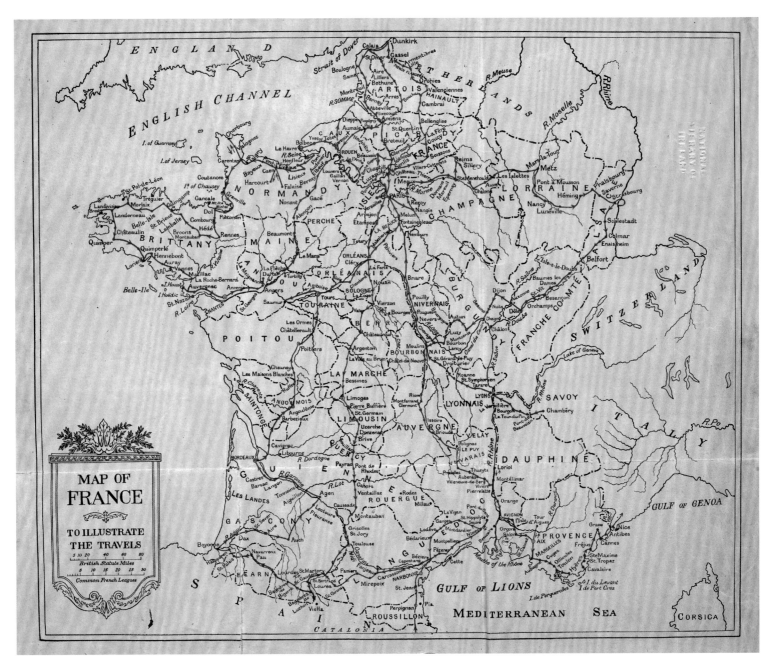

105. Arthur Young, 'A New Map of the Author's Route' from his *Travels in France during the years 1787, 1788 & 1789*, first published in vol. 1 of the two-volume edition (Dublin: Richard Cross, 1793). Reproduced here from the work edited by Constantia Maxwell (Cambridge: Cambridge University Press, 1929).

omitted from his *Tour in Ireland, 1776–1779*, as the frontispiece for his *Travels in France* (Fig. 105). It clarified the course, direction and sequence of his tours and gave his French travels a pronounced point of view. It also made the route by which he perceived France its representative image. The Irish tour, in contrast, had fixed Ireland's identity through the power of two stationary images; a view of Powerscourt Waterfall for volume one (Fig. 39) and a view of 'An Irish Cabbin' for volume two (Fig. 70).

Young re-ordered the relative beauty of France's landscapes in his tour through the composition of his routes and his choice of spatial emphasis. The Loire 'for so considerable a river, and for being boasted as the most beautiful in Europe' exhibited 'such a breadth of shoals and sands as to be almost subversive of beauty'.[33] His first and central spinal route, from Paris to the Pyrenees, had been decided for him by the Duc de la Rochefoucauld-Liancourt's invitation and he found the landscape between La Ville au Brun and Bessines in La Marche by 'far the most beautiful'[34] that he had yet seen in France. There a 'mountain of chestnut copse' commanded 'a scene of a character different from any' he had viewed either in France or England, with 'a great range of hill and dale all covered with forest, and bounded by distant mountains'. It had 'not a vestige of human residence; no village: no house or hut, no smoke to raise the idea of a peopled country; an American scene; wild enough for the tomohawk of the savage'.[35] French mountains grew slowly 'more interesting', with Young proclaiming 'their beauty to northern eyes' to be 'very singular'[36] and contrasting the 'black and dreary prospects' of British mountains with their wooded French counterparts.[37]

Young also set out to describe the general spatial and social structure of France.[38] He placed much of the blame for the country's rural poverty at the doors of its absentee noblemen carousing at court and on the French nobility's predilection for hunting, which placed large tracts of forest out of improvement's reach and in the service of *la chasse*. Young credited England and Rousseau's writings with the great change that had occurred in French habits:

> The present fashion in France, of passing some time in the country is new; at this time of the year, and for many weeks past, Paris is, comparatively speaking, empty. Every body that have country-seats are at them; and those who have none visit others who have. This remarkable revolution in French manners is certainly one of the best customs they have taken

from England; and its introduction was effected the easier, being assisted by the magic of Rousseau's writings. Mankind are much indebted to that splendid genius.[39]

French country houses were not really situated in the country, with the château of the Duc d'Aguillon 'badly situated, according to all rural ideas; but a town is ever an accompanyment of a chateau in France'. He thought 'that banishment alone', from Paris and the court, would 'force the French nobility to execute what the English do for pleasure – reside upon and adorn their estates.'[40] Entering 'Paris for the fourth time' he became 'confirmed in the idea that the roads immediately leading to the capital' were 'deserts, comparatively speaking, with those of London', concluding that circulation was 'stagnant in France'[41] with the French 'the most stationary people on earth'. In contrast, the English had to be 'the most restless' finding 'more pleasure in moving from one place to another, than in resting to enjoy life in either'.[42] France and Britain differed at the close of the eighteenth century in their relative adoption of the picturesque tour. In Great Britain and Ireland the landscape garden had been projected out into the countryside to create the wider tourist routes, and tourists and travel writers, such as Young, noticed that this manner of experiencing and perceiving landscape was not yet general in France. The many inns that serviced British and Irish tourist spots by the late eighteenth century were also lacking, leading to Young's conclusion that France did not enjoy 'the same quantity of motion' as the British Isles. Generally France had 'less wealth, less consumption, and less enjoyment'[43] than Great Britain and these, combined with immobility, had agricultural, aesthetic, economic and political consequences.

As in Ireland, Young was concerned to delineate French property structure, particularly the presence or absence of long leasehold tenure. The scale of French landholdings could be exemplary, when 'all in the hands of little proprietors, without the farms being so small as to occasion a vicious and miserable population'.[44] At Ganges, located inland and close to Périgueux, secure tenure and the consequent 'enjoyment of property' had 'swept away all difficulties', covering 'the very rocks with verdure' and inspiring Young's aphorism: 'Give a man secure possession of a bleak rock, and he will turn it into a garden; give him a nine years lease of a garden, and he will convert it into a desert.'[45] But he found little general evidence of improvement on French soil, despite other estimates finding that French 'taste for agriculture and rural economics developed after 1748, was accentuated around 1756, became a major preoccupation through the sixties, and declined slowly after 1770'.[46] This suggests that Young knew little of French improved landscapes, save when he admired and was acquainted with their owners, such as his mentor the Duc de la Rochefoucauld-Liancourt. Generally projecting the English tenurial system onto French soil, he was probably unaware of its 'complexity of seigneurial rights'.[47]

If Young had found it difficult to reconcile the landscape garden with Ireland's fitful and uneven property structure in *A Tour in Ireland, 1776–1779*, as discussed in Chapter 2, its French corollary was also problematic. Although 'the attention of the rich & great' in 1780s France was 'given to English gardens', Young found their reproduction generally implausible, wondering whether 'a walk ten times more winding than a snake, a ditch near it, & a bad piece of grass' could be 'dignified with the name of an English garden'.[48] The landscape garden in France, frequently translated as the *jardin anglaise* or picturesque garden, was generally smaller and more filled with follies and other designed and manmade elements than in England.[49] Young observed how Louis XVI's brother, 'not content with the Luxembourg garden', had made an adjoining small English garden that contained an 'English cottage, made of rafters & thatched' but which looked like 'a wretched necessary house', a description somewhat reminiscent of 'An Irish Cabbin' (Figs 70 and 71).[50] Nearby at Versailles, Marie Antoinette's *Hameau* dreamt of a simple yet pleasurable rural life set amidst cottages, mill buildings and carefully curated farm animals. Its creation in 1783–6 by the Queen and her architect Richard Mique played with the *ferme ornée*'s incendiary mixture of utility and pleasure and, as Jill Casid has explored, the Hameau's eleven cottages exhibited substantial levels of contradiction. When coupled with the defamatory print-culture of revolutionary France, the Queen's lifestyle and improvements at the Hameau became politically charged.[51] Its position on the borders of a *jardin anglais* set in the environs of the Petit Trianon, which was itself an enclave within the large royal parkland of Versailles, gave it the dangerously elevated levels of seclusion and delusion that encouraged incendiary journalism. Young's private letters of the period reveal a strong initial enthusiasm for the French Revolution but one that rapidly dissipated following the execution of Louis XVI in 1793.[52]

The French Revolution, in its ambition to restructure society and its governance, also sought to restructure the world spatially. This could be achieved by overturning and complicating the classical oppositions of city/country and art/nature. If the city represented the apex of human political, artistic and spatial achievement, the countryside was its natural, wholesome, uncomplicated corrollary and Rousseau's writings helped to position the countryside as the uncorrupted free space of revolution. This was of course a very old idea, stemming from classical Greek and Roman precedents and invoked in virtually all villa landscapes. He had also undermined the status of great capital cities by arguing that when the state could not be 'reduced to proper limits' or an ideal scale, 'one resource still' remained: 'not to allow any capital, but to make the government sit alternately in each town'. Imagining a future equality of towns, he argued that 'the walls of the towns' were 'formed solely of the remains of houses in the country', stressing again the countryside's inviable supremacy.[53]

The spatial theories of the French Revolution promoted new rituals and routes in order to subvert older practices. Walking was intrinsic to their design, and many festivals, follies and monuments required and designed the ascent of man by foot. The great revolutionary festivals were typically held in vast unrestricted open spaces on the edges of Paris, such as the Champ des Mars. Often former military spaces where the revolution's spatial concepts were tested and articulated, festival design replaced permanent buildings with point monuments that took up mostly impermanent forms as statues, columns, obelisks or Liberty Trees (Fig. 106). More choreography than architecture, a festival's processional route tied together its complex iconography. Inherently unstable, the character of such revolutionary spaces changed rapidly over set periods of time, whether hours, days or months. Peopled with such symbolic characters as Hercules and Marianne, festival design could also propose new global geographies by incorporating 'the civilized nations of the New World' who 'had returned to the principles of Nature herself' and, in homage to Rousseau, 'the simple inhabitants of happy Helvetia', or Switzerland.[54]

During the French Revolutionary period the mountain was established as a design typology. Representing nature at liberty, mountains infiltrated such unexpected contexts as church interiors while also forming the focus of the great

VUE DE LA MONTAGNE ELEVÉE AU CHAMP DE LA REUNION

pour la fête qui y a été célébrée en l'honneur de l'Etre Suprême le Decadi 20 Prairial de l'an 2.me de la Republique Française.

A Paris chez Chéreau Rue Jacques, aux deux Colonnes, près la Fontaine Severin, n.° 25.

106. *Vue de la montagne elevée au champ de la reunion pour la fête qui y a été célébrée en l'honneur de l'Etre Suprême le Decadi 20 Priairial de l'an 2me de la Republique Française.* Print. Library of Congress Call. co. PC 5 - 1794, no. 2 (B size). Paris: Chez Chéreau, Rue Jacques, aux deux Colonnes, près la Fontaine Sevrein, No. 257, 1794

revolutionary festivals. Heroic mountain-climbers en masse celebrated the new pedestrian equality of man and the repetition of particular spatial types, and their patterns of use, reinforced revolutionary ideals. As Lynn Hunt has argued, 'the political culture of revolution was made up of symbolic practices, such as language, imagery, and gestures'[55] and its 'social sources of coherence included the appearance of the same kinds of leaders in different places and the same kinds of places in the forefront of politial action'.[56] Hunt also argues that 'paradoxically, while multiplying the forms and mean-

ings of politics, the most revolutionary of the French acted out of a profound distrust of anything explicitly political'.[57] Spaces were important because they were not explicit and could represent the new society and its values in oblique ways. Repeating selected spatial types, and their patterns of use, reinforced revolutionary ideals.

The most subversive spatial projects of the revolutionary period were those that literally replaced architecture with landscape. Of these, the mountain projects are arguably the most spectacular, certainly in their many representations, where

107. Dutour (ingenieur), 'Projet pour un Montagne Symbolique. Bordeaux, 5 Fructidor an II'. Archives Nationales de France, Cartes et Plans, F$_{14}$10216, no. 62

the structural issues that compromised their successful realisation could be sidestepped. The engineer-architect Dutour designed an inhabited symbolic mountain, complete with rocks, plants and follies, for Bordeaux (Fig. 107). Bearing more than a passing similarity to the French picturesque garden and the landscape paintings of Hubert Robert, its compression of the French landscape garden's often contorted route, numerous follies and cross-sectional complexity into one dense hollowed-out building is shocking and thus effective. Spatial

and scalar precedents had been dramatically overturned – landscape became building, building became landscape, and all at a small symbolic scale. Mountains inside churches were also popular resolutions of the revolution's subversion of spatial and scaler precedents (Fig. 108). To find a 'Mountain erected at the end of the church' could not but have the 'surprising impact'[58] that its architect Alexandre-Théodore Brongniart ascribed to his design for turning the church interior of Saint Jean, Lyon, into a festival for the goddess of Reason. With nature invading the cathedral – the summit of architectural sacred space – existing spatial order was completely overwhelmed. Paris, the centre of much revolutionary drama, was not however the ideal revolutionary space. The ideal space was unenclosed, unbounded and possessed of many long-distant views that were preferably not axial. It was in effect the opposite of architecture, if the role of architecture is to enclose space in three dimensions, and over the course of the revolutionary period horizontal open space increased in status.[59] Military spaces of the old régime such as forts and prisons were sometimes converted into gardens – again an instance of a formal architectural space, bearing a precise and regimented use, being converted into a natural space that foregrounded trees, walks and landscape design rather than walls, rooms and architecture (Fig. 109). Such church/mountain and fort/garden projects invoked less mythic space than the festivals and represented many of the revolution's place-making ambitions, few of which survived.[60]

108. Alexandre-Théodore Brongniart, 'Dessin de la Fête de la Déesse Raison à St-Jean'. Bibliothèque Municipale Garde-Dieu, Lyon, Ms. 2394-1. Photo: Vincent Lefebvre

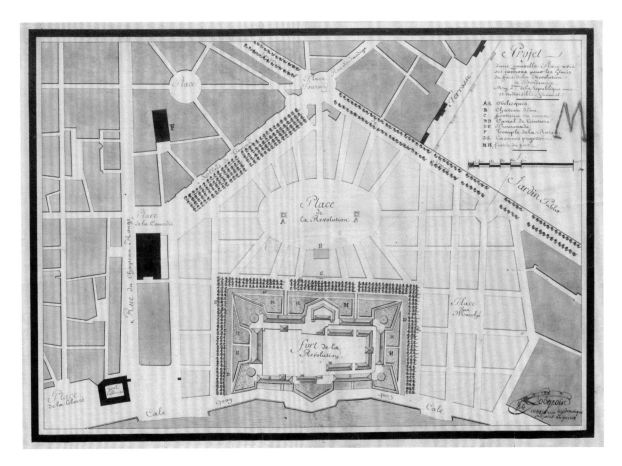

109. Lobgeois, Fort de la Revolution Garden on the site of Château de la Trompette, Bordeaux, France, An II, 1794, Archives Nationales de France F/13/1713

Touring Revolutionaries

Rousseau linked spatial experience and education in his writings. He typically wrote from a precise situation, whether mountain or plain, hamlet or city, to analyse how a space, and its relation to other spaces, affected his own and other people's lives. His 1762 novel *Émile* explored the formative effects of childhood spatial experiences. Positioned as the founding bedrock, childhood landscape grounded and bequeathed psychological ownership of territory, even to the most peripatetic individual. *Émile* exerted considerable influence over children's education in the closing decades of the eighteenth century, when fashionable Francophile families throughout Europe tried to emulate Rousseau's pedagogical precepts.[61] Mary Delany, the well-travelled letter-writer and cultural barometer, recounted in wonder in 1766 that Emily, Duchess

of Leinster, Ireland's premier noblewoman, had offered Rousseau 'an elegant retreat *if he would educate her children!*'.[62] Children brought up in such pedagogical environments and who later became revolutionaries could not but attach significance to their surroundings, projecting ideal societies onto suitable landscapes.

The spatial biographies of the Irish revolutionaries Arthur O'Connor and Edward FitzGerald align closely. Both men experienced similar Rousseauian educations, as documented in their writings:

> You know our characters are formed for us not <u>by</u> us we are what our early impressions have made us of? education that makes the man and this comes from the laws, customs, institutions, family, neighbourhood in which we are born and bred and the books we have studied.[63]

110. Hugh Douglas Hamilton, *Lord Edward Fitzgerald, c.*1796–8. National Gallery of Ireland, NGI.195

Both men travelled in their youth and compared countries, landscapes and the people who inhabited them. Both younger sons, neither man experienced the grand tour's traditional trajectory of great cities arrived at in sequence, an experience more generally reserved for an eldest son and heir. Of the two, FitzGerald was the more widely travelled (Fig. 110). A scion of a family whose tree stretched between England, France and Ireland, his spatial education began in his mother's radical model school in Blackrock, Co. Dublin. Long experience of travel in various guises, *en famille*, as a professional soldier and as an independent gentleman, saw him develop a distinctive mode of travel. Peculiar to this was a close and reciprocal regard for the local people, a preference for walking, over carriage or horseback, and an observant eye for the character of each place and how it differed from others he had experienced in the past.

Landscape, for an educated officer in the late eighteenth century, even if appreciated for its beauty, also had to be drawn, surveyed, improved and defended. The oppositional concepts of use and beauty, military urgency and leisured appreciation, were often conflated with the word 'tour' used to describe both military tours of duty and the leisure activities of tourism. Such an amalgamation of military and polite experience, and of military and tourist routes and spaces, affected how such men, subsequently revolutionaries or counter-revolutionaries, ordered and designed their worlds. The younger son of a duke, primogeniture had destined Lord Edward for the army, and many of his teenage hours were spent drawing plans of fortifications, barrack layouts and territorial surveys. When in France at the age of seventeen, he wrote to his mother that he had 'erected a beautiful fortification in the Orangerie' and of how he had also made a 'very pretty Survey of the fields round the Garonne' river, drawing 'the borders of the fields' in colour but leaving fields themselves white with 'very good Effect' and with 'all the Trees in Indian Ink'.[64] In 1780, when at military camp, he helped his superior officer, his uncle the Duke of Richmond, to improve the camp's plan, which had been 'quite wrongly marked out'. Edward was entrusted with 'pitching' a company of soldiers and his set-out 'was not one Inch wrong when all the Tents were up'.[65] Travelling to the United States as a teenage British military officer, he served in Charleston and at the battle of Eutaw Springs, where he was wounded and rescued by a black man called Tony, who became his constant travelling companion. By 1783 he was in Saint Lucia in the Caribbean 'working hard at the fortifications' despite 'unluckily' having 'three Blockheads of Engineers' to help. Ever the Francophile, when he returned some prisoners to the French island of Martinique he found it 'a much finer island than ours and much better peopled'[66] and unlike his older brother Charles who hated 'every thing French', he soon made a second trip to spend 'a week very pleasantly',[67] attending a ball every night. But he needed to return to Europe for promotion and opportunity, and by October 1783 he was home.[68]

When posted to the Channel Islands by 1786, Edward warned his mother not 'expect a Description' of Jersey because 'the whole Tour' was 'a kind of military Survey' for his superior officers to choose the positions of new defence works 'in case of an attack'.[69] But by 1787 he was firmly in a tourist cast of mind when planning 'to rejoin his mother at Nice, and from thence proceed, in the summer' to meet friends in Switzerland.

III. William Ashford, *Gibraltar*, 1775. Private collection

Describing this tour as a 'pleasant foolish plan', he anticipated that the holiday 'would certainly be charming', when compared with the sober prospect of staying at Woolwich and furthering his military education. Foiled inexplicably from carrying it out, he had to settle instead for a tour of the Iberian peninsula that began in Gibraltar and proceeded to Cadiz via 'Portugal to avoid a [Spanish] quarantine'.[70] Landscape analysis did feature, with the countryside between Cadiz and Granada described as 'very beautiful' with 'all about Malaga … mountainous, charming'. Granada's valley was 'highly cultivated, full of the finest Trees and Shrubs of all kinds' and the Spanish could 'manage the water so well' that even 'in the Dog days' of August everything was green. He visited the Alhambra where 'the colouring and the finishing' of the surviving painted rooms was 'much beyond anything' in Ireland. Surprised to find that most 'modern patte[r]ns' were 'taken from' non-figurative Moorish precedents, he compared one of its painted rooms with 'the Gallery at Castletown' when he exhibited little

national or familial chauvinism in judging it far superior to one of Ireland's (and his Aunt Louisa Conolly's) most treasured interiors. As in the West Indies, when Edward had jumped to French Martinique to escape the tedium of British Saint Lucia, the existence of political borders or complexities rarely prevented him from reaching his desired destination. Despite indications that Spain and England were not wholly in agreement on the status of Gibraltar, he remained 'delighted with Spain, the Country, the people, and their manners', travelling about with some evident naivety and accompanied only by Tony and a muleteer.[71] His 'travelling *en Philosophe*' in emulation of Rousseau led him to preference rural contexts and to sometimes think longingly 'on a little Town profligacy and Dissipation' while his comparative analysis of people's 'appearance in travelling tro' the Country' was often youthfully banal, with Spanish women 'very pretty' and 'delightful' in 'their own dress and manners' but in French or English dress 'detestable'.[72] Recalling Edward Newenham's disapproval of the

Galway peasants, if the Spaniards had not been 'such an indo-lent people it would be a paradise on earth; for by the smallest care you could have the plants of all climates'.[73]

Edward FitzGerald's travelling practice was to 'always set out about three in the evening and travel till one or two; and then to walk the next morning about the' town or village. Gibraltar was a 'high rugged rock, separated by a small neck of land from a vast track of mountainous' country and Edward was quick to compare its situation with the much larger 'rocks' of Great Britain and Ireland (Fig. 111). Walking over its higher parts made him 'feel quite proud to think you are a set of islanders from a remote little corner of the world surrounded by Enemies thousands of times your numbers after all the struggles both of them and the french to beat you out of it keeping it in spite of all their Efforts'.[74] Together with General O'Hara, a fellow Irishman and Gibraltar's commanding officer, whom he knew from the West Indies, he 'walk[ed] the whole day, from five in the morning till eight or nine at night'.[75] While the self-sufficient bravery of the British Isles made him 'proud', Gibraltar's exceptional views were also carefully ana-lysed for scale, sublime potential and the aesthetic sensibility that the experience inspired:

> all this makes you proud yet the still greater greatness of the Scene the immense depth of the Sea under you, the view of a great Tract of Land whose numerous inhabitants are scarcely known, the littleness of your own works in comparison with those of nature make you feel nothing – in short you have Scenes and feels here you can have nowhere else.[76]

Perceived as a British mountain fastness on mainland Europe, Gibraltar, for Edward FitzGerald, was a British Switzerland.

Edward FitzGerald's identity in Spain was mostly that of a titled English officer and he believed that the local people were 'so fond of the English that *Cavallero Ingles*' (himself) was 'asked into almost every house and made to sit down and eat or drink something'.[77] A naturally friendly and attrac-tive individual, if perhaps somewhat gullible, he claimed to have made some acquaintance in every part of Spain. But his identity remained in flux, such as when he 'happened to get in among the French nobility' in 1787 in Lisbon and planned to 'proffit of the occasion and see their Manners and Customs'. Pronouncing them as 'a very odd people',[78] he ignored just how many of his own relatives and acquaintances identified with

that body. Still firmly loyal to Great Britain and its monarchy in 1787, he would imbibe the radical and revolutionary ideals of the French Revolution over the next few years. The Irish identity that slowly replaced his British identity was acquired between 1787 and 1791 in order to lead his own countrymen to rebellion. It was not born in Gibraltar, but the associations between mountains and liberty that he found there would prove useful to the United Irishmen in the years to come.

In 1788 Edward FitzGerald again crossed the Atlantic, landing in Halifax, New Brunswick, to find the country 'almost in a state of nature, as well as its inhabitants' and appreciating 'the equality of every body and of their manner of life'. There were no gentlemen, everybody was 'on a footing, providing he works and wants nothing; every man is exactly what he can make himself, or has made himself by industry'.[79] Travelling to St John's he planned to avoid the 'common route' of sailing across the Bay of Fundy with its 'very disagreeable navigation', and to take a longer but 'very wild and beautiful' route through 'rivers and lakes of which one has no idea in England', their banks covered with 'the finest wood and pasture but quite in the state of nature'. A 'journey after [his] own heart', he intended to keep a journal to send to his doting mother.[80] On another tour 'in canoes up to the Grand Falls of St. John's' he found the contrast between Canada and France 'very great: the one all wild, the other all high cultivation' and instead of Blois, Tours and other great French towns only 'a few Indian bark huts'. Recalling again the Georgic tradition, Edward was 'not quite certain which' he preferred:

> Ogilvie says I ought to have been a savage, and if it were not that the people I love and wish to live with are civilized people, and like houses, &c., &c., I really would join the savages; and leaving all our fictitious, ridiculous wants, be what nature intended we should be. Savages have all the real happiness of life, without any of those inconveniences, or ridiculous obstacles to it, which custom has introduced among us ... no separations in families, one in Ireland, one in England: no devilish politics, no fashions, customs, duties, or appearances to the world ... Instead of being served and supported by servants, every thing here is done by one's relations.[81]

Canada had four sorts of inhabitants – 'the Indians, the French, the old English settlers' – with 'the refugees from the other parts of America' judged 'the most civilized'. The

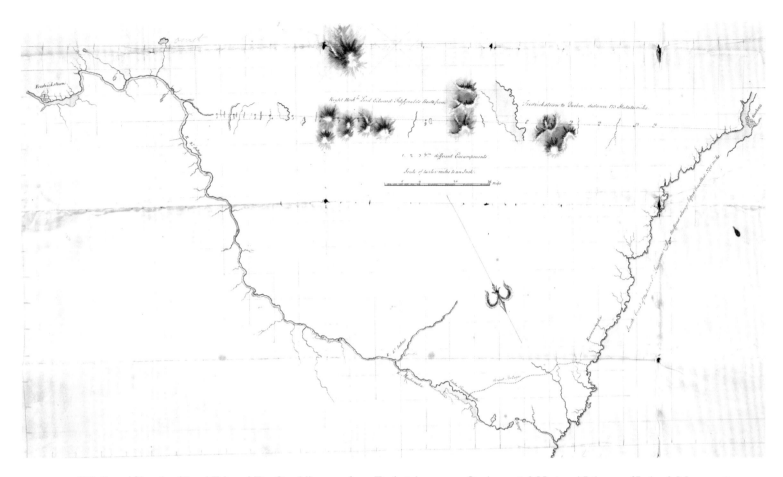

112. 'Mr. Jones' Sketch of Lord Edward FitzGerald's route from Frederickstown to Quebec, 1789'. National Library of Ireland, Ms. 35,008

American old settlers were almost as wild as the Indians, but led a 'very comfortable life'. They were 'all Farmers' supplying 'all their own wants by their contrivances, so that they seldom buy anything' and he reasoned that 'they ought to be the happiest people in the world, but they do not seem to know it, they imagine themselves poor because they have no money, without considering they do not want it'. In America commerce was 'done by barter' and 'any man that will work is sure in a few years to have a comfortable farm'.[82]

Edward FitzGerald slowly became a highly competent traveller and explorer, beyond that of the typical well-travelled military man. On 22 May 1789 a Mr Hamilton Moore sent Edward's brother, the 2nd Duke of Leinster, a 'Sketch of Lord Edward's Route' from Frederickstown, New Brunswick, to Quebec, drawn by a Mr Jones (Fig. 112). He described it as an 'arduous & dangerous undertaking, entirely through uninhabited woods, morasses and mountains', which had been, somewhat questionably, 'never before attempted, even by the Indians'.[83] Edward was accompanied by another officer, a Mr Brisbane, and his own servant, with each man carrying his own luggage and provisions. Their route reduced a journey of 375 miles to 175 miles, which they accomplished in twenty-six days with all the military advantages that such brevity and mobility implied. The sketch was particular insistent on the straightness of their route and their correct use of the compass in making it so.[84]

Edward also made the requisite landscape pilgrimage to the Niagara Falls in 1789, the pinnacle of American tourism for all visiting Europeans:

Imagine the sea tumbling from an immense rock 630 foot high, divided by an island covered with fine wood, the high rocks on either side of the River covered with fine open wood, and close to the waterside, great rocks which have tumbled from the top covered with cedars growing in the soil that has

113. *Arthur O'Connor*, hand-coloured etching, published by John Aikin, 26 April 1798. NPG D15641 © National Portrait Gallery, London

fallen down – the immense height and noise of the falls, the spray the rises to clouds

It made 'a scene that pays well the trouble of coming from Europe to see', particularly 'the Greenness of everything about, the quiet of the immense Forest around, the violence of everything close to the Falls'. The experience so affected him that he warned his mother that 'Ireland and England [would] be too little for' him when he got home.[85] Slowly splintering between two countries, his fluctuating identities were complicated by his new indigenous friends, who were only too happy to compare countries and cultures, often with negative results. Visiting Detroit in 1789 'with one of the Indian chiefs,

Joseph Brant' who had been in England, he thought that Brant would entertain his mother 'very much with his remarks on England, and the English'.[86] The two had 'taken very much to one another', so well in fact that in less than three weeks the young Irish lord had been 'adopted by one of the Nations, and' was 'now a thorough Indian'.[87] 'David Hill, Chief of the Six Nations' gave Edward the new name of Eghnidal, 'a name belonging to the Bear Tribe'[88] and he left Quebec 'in high health and spirits, on his Route to Europe, by the River Mississippi and the Gul[f] of Mexico and through Spain'. Others predicted 'a tedious Journey', with the Mississippi 'upward of six hundred Leagues'[89] away, but Edward reached New Orleans in December 1789 nevertheless, where his plans to tour the silver mines of Mexico and the city of Havana were frustrated by worsening political relations between the British and the Spanish.[90]

Returning to Europe for the last time in 1790, Edward FitzGerald lived initially in London but moved to Paris in October 1792. There he was profoundly influenced by his acquaintance with Thomas Paine and other revolutionary radicals of the period. Although traces of revolutionary and republican sympathy may be found in his letters before 1792, particularly as filtered through the writings of Rousseau, his political conversion to radical republicanism appears to have been relatively sudden and complete. Writing to his mother from Paris on the 30 October, '1st Year of the Republic, 1792', from the 'Hotel de White, au passage des Petits, pres du Palais Royal' where he lodged with his 'friend [Thomas] Paine', he signed himself 'Le Citoyen Edouard Fitzgerald'.[91] The Paris newspapers reported on the party of foreigners who had arrived at White's 'to celebrate the triumph of victories gained over their late invaders by the armies of France'. Clearly treasonous in their intentions, 'the festival' that they celebrated conspired to produce a seditious address to the National Convention.[92] During the festivities both Sir Robert Smith and Lord Edward FitzGerald publicly renounced their aristocratic titles, with Smith proposing a toast to 'the speedy abolition of all hereditary titles and feudal distinctions'.[93]

Arthur O'Connor was Edward FitzGerald's closest friend, travelling companion and fellow United Irishman (Fig. 113). A few months older than Edward, he was born Arthur Conner on 4 July 1763 and grew up in his father's house at Connersville just outside Ballineen in Co. Cork.[94] Independently wealthy at a young age, his inheritance funded early excursions into parts of England and Wales and gave him reasons for 'seeing the immense contrast between England and Ireland between the state of prosperity, industry and comforts of a people who have a national government and one that has not, between a nation whose legislature are the traitors largely paid, for reducing the people to misery'.[95] The memoirs he wrote many years afterwards and which exist in manuscript form credited the 'possession of liberty' for England's superiority 'to Ireland for in Ireland the heart fails and the soul sickens for want of the recompense of industry'. England's 'immense wealth and industry in commerce in manufactures in agriculture and in extent of dominions' was 'extremely recent', as was 'every improvement in agriculture'. Before 1745 no English ground had been 'fallowed: no peas, grass, turnips, nor potatoes were then raised, no cattle were fattened and little grain was exported', while 'the produce of the farm was barely sufficient to enable the tenant to pay a trifling rent'.[96]

In 1784 O'Connor visited France for the first time. The country's government gave her 'an immense advantage over Ireland whose government was the corrupted agents to another nation', but France was still 'far inferior to England from the whole people being debased to exalt … Court, the nobles and the clergy'.[97] He was forcibly struck by the contrast between Paris and London, finding Parisian society 'divided into two classes the one that rode in carriage the other that went a foot', an observation that suggests a close reading of Arthur Young's analysis of French mobility in *Travels in France*. 'Such was the filth, mud and insecurity' of Parisian streets 'that one would have imagined the ease and well-being of the people made no part of the object of Government'. The city had 'no flagways' and 'the carriages went so rapidly the drivers seemed to take pleasure in splashing the citizens, the houses were bespotted with the seas of gutter the streets were filled with; the iron bars that protected the shops gave the houses the appearance of prisons'.[98]

The French countryside fared no better in O'Connor's analysis, approaching 'the disorder and slovenlyness of Ireland'. He could find no evidence of improved varieties of artificial grasses, turnips, or beetroot while 'all means of manure' were found wanting with wheat and oats particularly inferior to that grown in England and Ireland, 'especially the oats'.[99] O'Connor travelled with two men of his own age, identified as Walter and Mr O'Grady in his memoirs. On their journey south to Dijon they fell into company with an older man, who became their wise guide because he 'had travelled in most

countries in Europe and had acquired considerable knowledge of their manners and characters'. O'Connor employed the navigational compass as a verb to describe how the older man by 'compas[s]ing' the countries he visited 'had attained the most unprejudiced & philosophical opinions on all he had seen & studied'. The man, whom O'Connor never identified by name, was 'a solid, moral republican' who 'was convinced the affairs of nations went best and more for the happiness of people' when they were ruled 'by agents of their choosing than when by a Court and its Courtiers who lived but taking the produce of the people's labor'. Evidently anti-Catholic, he bemoaned the Church's influence over 'all Italy to Spain to Portugal and to every country where the influence of those papist priests existed'. The 'experience of his life' had shown 'that every people must be incapable of possessing or defending liberty who possess a religion that enacts the abandonment of their own judgement and reason to a priest'.[100]

Leaving Mr O'Grady studying in Dijon, O'Connor then made an excursion to Lyons and into Switzerland with his other friend Walter. They travelled in a diligence carriage in the upsetting company of two monks and two prostitutes, and like many picturesque travellers, they reached an abbey before they reached the mountains. The Carthusian monastery of the Great Chartreuse near Grenoble 'then contained a numerous assembly' and the visit confirmed O'Connor's deeply seated prejudices about Catholic monastic life and religion. His analysis of the allegedly parasitical economy of the great abbey descended from the rhetoric of the dissolution of the monasteries and was reminiscent of eighteenth-century books of British and Irish antiquities, with their particular nuances for a Protestant Irishman. Despite his anti-aristocratic republican beliefs, he did not compare the monastic foundations with the aristocratic estates that acquired their lands in Great Britain and Ireland in the aftermath of the English Reformation. Preferring to employ dry economic analysis in the manner of Arthur Young, he credited the abbey with the consumption of 400,000 francs 'without sending a single sliver to the nation, though those lusty monks did nothing but eat, drink, sleep and pray' and in a later reflection thought the monks had begun 'to entertain some fears' for 'their rich establishment'. When revisiting the monastery in 1802 on his way to Italy 'all that remained of this vast family was one old monk, who though 80 years of age performed more useful work than all his predecessors' by mending 'the shoes of the neighbouring peasants'.[101]

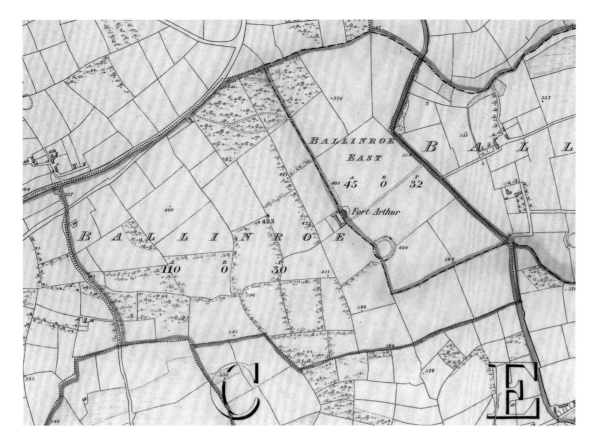

114. Fort Arthur on first edition OS map of Co. Cork, Sheet 124, Scale 1:10,560, surveyed 1841–2, printed 1844. Reproduced courtesy Trinity College Dublin

115. *(below)* Carrigmore (Connersville), Manch House and Demesne and Fort Robert, Ballineen, on the first edition OS map of Co. Cork, Sheet 108, Scale 1:10,560, surveyed 1841–2, printed 1844. Reproduced courtesy Trinity College Dublin

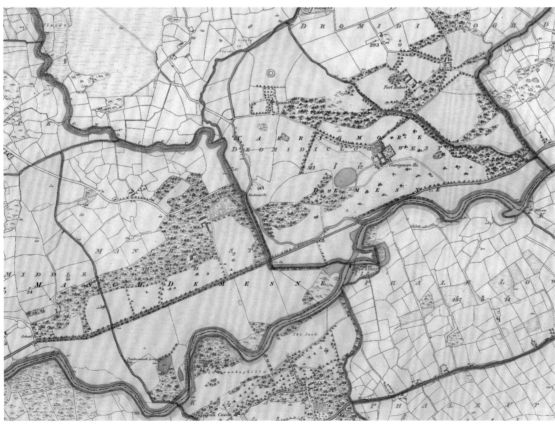

O'Connor and his friend then then moved onto Switzerland – 'the antidote to French despotism' and the 'opposite to English aristocracy'. It had 'the manners of a Republic which seemed to nest on the air, in the soil & in the heads and nature of the people'.[102] Describing the 'little Country' as the 'plank' that kept 'republicanism from sinking in the seas of despotism' it was also 'the most beautiful country in the world' and 'so covered with woods, waters and mountains' that all who laboured frugally could procure for themselves 'the comforts of life from the culture of the little portion of vegetable earth that was left them'. The 'all-consuming drones of other countries' were not to be found in Switzerland because they were excluded by necessity from a place where 'frugality and industry' were the principal virtues.[103] In Switzerland, for the first time, O'Connor 'saw the fruits of Equality – a Society where no man was exalted at the debasement of his fellow Citizens' and where every citizen 'from the highest to the lowest, from the richest to the poorest, possessed the consciousness he was a free and independent man'. Yet it was still easy 'to distinguish the Cantons where the papist religion prevailed'.[104] He dined frequently at the *tables d'hotes*[105] of travellers' inns 'with the peasants and the artisans', and whose 'good common sense' convinced him that 'they knew the value of the liberty' that they enjoyed. It gave them 'an ease and urbanity that was as far from servility as from vulgar familiarity' and such men, 'never having felt oppression' also 'knew how to respect the men of superior education', such as O'Connor himself. What most impressed O'Connor, and 'what distinguished Switzerland from nearly all the rest of Europe' was that it was 'a country where the produce of labor of other Nations' was not taxed and he asked his readers to notice 'that the nations which adopt this liberal commercial principle are those whose industry is most profitable and that have fewer beggars'. Concluding his 'just tribute to the Swiss' for what was 'liberal in their institutions', he did not however forget that in 1784, when he had first visited, the Swiss were 'exercising domination' from Berne over the Pays de Vaux 'under the debasing title of *pays conques*'[106] or conquered country. In noting this, he revealed his sensitivity, as an Irishman, to instances of conquest and colonisation.

Arthur O'Connor returned to London in 1785 approximately, where, as a barrister, he became interested in the debates taking place in the House of Commons. He visited his fellow Corkman Edmund Burke to ask him to 'class' the

barristers of the time 'according to their abilities and eloquence'.[107] But by 1787 'things were passing in France' that made him very 'desirous to revisit it'. Once there he 'was struck with the rapid progress the public mind had made in the three years', crediting it to 'the American Revolution and the part the French Government had taken in it'.[108] Returning to his native Cork he sought a 'retreat' where he 'might be whole master of' his 'time and studies' and where he needed to 'arrange' his 'fortune which had suffered some confusion' in his absence. He began by purchasing 'a large estate in the neighbourhood of Kinsale' that required some complicated legal and family buy-outs to make him, eventually, its sole possessor.[109] There he 'sat down to cultivate' his property, and his mind, building 'a handsome house with numerous out offices together with several farm houses' that became known as Fort Arthur, the name probably inspired by the French Revolution's subversive reconfiguration of military spaces as public gardens or domestic idylls, as discussed above (Fig. 114). At Fort Arthur he 'undertook the culture of a considerable Domain on the best English system' and as yet another eighteenth-century 'practical farmer'.[110] Still political if not yet politicised, he was 'disgusted with the narrowness of mind of Lord Charlemont and all the protestant Volunteers' – the militia raised to defend Ireland in the aftermath of the French Revolution and who had 'made Ireland lose her liberty by the sole possible means' she had of acquiring it, namely 'the Union of her people'. Choosing to remain secluded in his farming idyll, O'Connor resolved to make it an exemplary estate by farming his 'lands upon the new improved principles' whilst 'always devoting a great part of' his time to the study of his 'favorite Sciences of Legislation and Political Economy'.

The French Revolution's architectural paradox of the domestic fort was introduced by O'Connor to west Cork where his solid farmhouse of Fort Arthur looked eastward to address a distant prospect of Kinsale harbour. Behind the house lay an enclosing U-shaped range of service buildings containing the improving ambitions of his 'practical' farm (Fig. 114). Unusual in their immediate adjacency to the house, O'Connor had no evening views of lawns and flower gardens, more one of cows and farming utensils, such as Arthur Young might have enjoyed. The Conner family's ancestral house at Manch, Manchdemesne, Ballineen, Co. Cork, was a solid Georgian house of middle size with extensive walled gardens and service buildings but no grand approach route. Nearby lay

Connersville (now Carrigmore) demesne, its eighteenth-century house long demolished, while to the north-east the ruins of Fort Robert, built by Arthur's older brother, still stand (Fig. 115). An austere eight-bay house, bearing little similarity to a fort beyond its name, it was photographed by William Lawrence in the early twentieth century (Fig. 116).

Citoyen Edward FitzGerald returned to Blackrock from Paris in 1792, fresh from breakfasting with Thomas Paine and renouncing his title. He set up home with his wife Pamela, soi-disant daughter of the Duc d'Orléans, in his mother's suburban villa, Frescati, in Blackrock, Co. Dublin. 'A noble village, situated about three miles from the north-east corner of Stephen's Green, on a rising ground south of the Bay of Dublin', Blackrock contained 'a considerable number of elegant country houses, and in summer, when 'much resorted to by the

116. 'Fort Robert, Ballineen, Co. Cork'. National Library of Ireland, William Lawrence Collection, L_ROY_10259

117. Photograph of the garden front of Frescati House, Blackrock, Co. Dublin, with Lord Fitzwilliam's 'Porter's Lodge' bordering it to the upper left. National Library of Ireland, Morgan Aerial photographic collection, NPA MOR170. Photo: Alexander Campbell Morgan

citizens for the purpose of bathing', it was 'as much crowded with carriages as the most populous streets in the city'. One of its principal attractions was the 'number of genteel families' who 'resid[ed] there at this season of the year', ensuring that they had 'drums and assemblies as in town'.[111] Emily, Duchess of Leinster, Edward's mother, leased Frescati from the ground landlord, Richard, Viscount Fitzwilliam (Fig. 117). Initially conceived as a school modelled on Rousseau's pedagogy for the Duke's nineteen children, among them Lord Edward, its radical educational phase was managed and directed by William Ogilvie, a conscientious Scottish teacher. When Ogilvie married Emily, Duchess of Leinster, his employer's widow, his spectacular reversal of fortune saw Frescati become the newly-weds' suburban home, where they could be somewhat concealed from the censure of both city and country. Designed to express Rousseau's controversial pedagogical agenda and to transfer educational and political ideas of a radical cast to the Duke of Leinster's children,[112] it also became a bolthole for successive members of the FitzGerald family, whenever the necessity arose.

Edward and Pamela cultivated a contrived Rousseauian identity in suburban Dublin, complete with a Herculean son, a pretty flower garden and no gardener but Edward himself, much like the frontispiece to Rousseau's *Émile* (Fig. 118). Dublin celebrities, they were constantly in the public gaze, with the FitzGerald family 'so conspicuous and so much talked of' that William Ogilvie warned Edward's sister Sophia, in a letter of 1 March 1793, of the 'very false and malicious Reports that have gone about of poor Edwards being in rebellion'. The watchful stepfather saw 'a disposition to misrepresent everything belonging to the Fitz-geralds – from their Politicks and the Envy they exite'.[113] The rumours, however, were true. Edward had become involved with the United Irishmen and had begun to plot the rebellion of 1798 from his childhood home. Although obliged to make the requisite country house visits to his various aristocratic relatives, Frescati became his seditious escape, its smaller suburban character clearly distinguished from that of the aristocratic country house. The ideal revolutionary's abode, Frescati's location, out of sight and out of mind in an anomalous, egalitarian suburb owned by an absentee landlord, was useful. It became a focus for their revolutionary activities, which were initially of a cultural and pedagogical cast but became progressively more political and subversive in the 1790s.

118. Plate by Pierre-Philippe Choffard after Jean-Michel Moreau, 'Chacun respecte le travail des autres, afin que le sien soit en sûreté', from Jean-Jacques Rousseau, *Émile, ou De l'éducation*, vol. 3, p. 98

When his mother's financial problems eventually obliged Edward to look for another home in 1794 he was nevertheless loath to resign himself to the plains of Kildare, where his uncle, Thomas Conolly, had offered him a small house and farm. Initially seeking 'a small house with 40 acres of land some trees upon it near the seaside' in the 'beautiful country between Wicklow and Arklow',[114] his disinclination to settle in Conolly's Kildare Lodge, situated on the outskirts of Kildare town, arose partly from the county's identity as a FitzGerald aristocratic stronghold and his sensitivity to any suggestion of noblesse oblige.[115] Most of Kildare town itself lay on the estate of his brother the 2nd Duke of Leinster and Conolly also

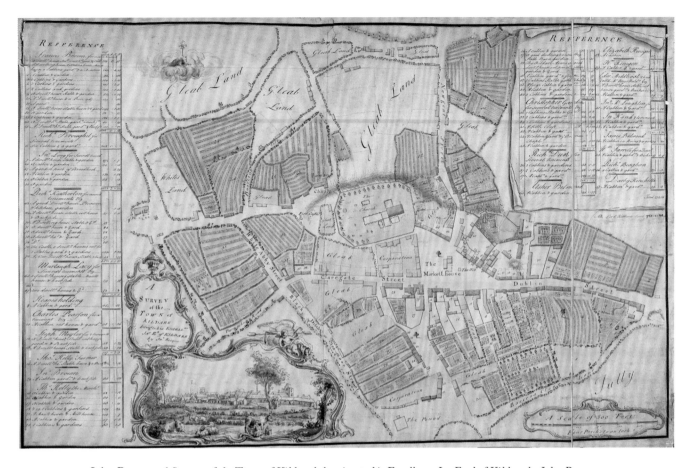

119. John Rocque, *A Survey of the Town of Kildare belonging to his Excellency Jas Earl of Kildare by John Rocque*, 1757.
National Library of Ireland, Ms. 22,004 (5)

120. John Rocque, *A Survey of the Town of Kildare belonging to his Excellency Jas Earl of Kildare by John Rocque*, 1757,
vignette detail. National Library of Ireland, Ms. 22,004 (5)

leased Kildare Lodge from the Duke. 'Parting with poor dear Frescati' made him 'melancholy' and he argued that although Kildare Lodge was 'in a good county', unlike Wicklow it had not 'mountains and rocks'. He moved in June 1794, despite his qualms and delighting in its ideal scale: 'I write to you in the middle of settling and arranging my little family here … How you would like this little spot! it is – the smallest thing imaginable, and to numbers would have no beauty; but there is a comfort and moderation in it that delights me'.[116]

Kildare Lodge appears in plan on the 1757 map of Kildare town that Edward's father had commissioned from the renowned Hugeunot cartographer John Rocque (Fig. 119).[117] The map's vignette view concealed Kildare Lodge but did depict the FitzGerald tower house (Fig. 120). Although the view depicts the town thirty-seven years before Edward's arrival, this plan (Fig. 121) agrees very well with the description of Kildare Lodge Edward provided for his mother in 1794. He began with the approach:

> After going up a little lane, and in at a close gate, you come upon a little white house, with a small gravel court before it. You see but three small windows, the court surrounded by large old elms; one side of the house covered with shrubs, on the other side a tolerable large ash; upon the stairs going up to the house, two wicker cages, in which there are at this moment two thrushes, singing à gorge deployée [with open mouths].

To the right of the gate in the garden wall lay the old Norman FitzGerald castle, which still stands today (Fig. 122). He then described in detail the plan of his new home:

> In coming into the house, you find a small passage hall, very clean, the floor tiled; upon your left, a small room; on the right, the staircase. In front you come into the parlour, a good room, with a bow window looking into the garden, which is a small green plot surrounded by good trees, and in it three of the finest thorns I ever saw, and all the trees so placed that you may shade yourself from the sun all hours of the day; the bow window, covered with honeysuckle, and up to the window some roses.

The front parlour with its bow window appeared on a later 1798 plan of Kildare by Thomas Sherrard (Fig. 123) where the western part of the site had acquired the requisite flower garden:

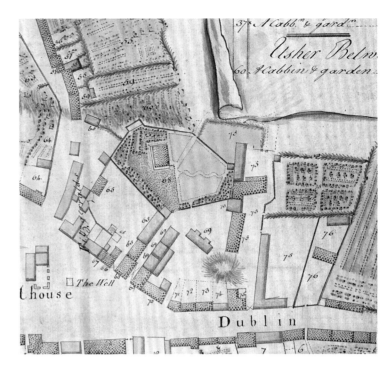

121. John Rocque, *A Survey of the Town of Kildare belonging to his Excellency Jas Earl of Kildare by John Rocque*, 1757, detail showing Kildare Lodge (no. 68) and the old Kildare Castle (75). National Library of Ireland, Ms. 22,004 (5)

122. Photograph of the FitzGerald tower looking towards the enclosure of Lord Edward's garden. Author's photo, 2013

123. Thomas Sherrard, *A Survey of the Town of Kildare, The Estate of His Grace the Duke of Leinster*, 1798, detail.
Edward FitzGerald's house is no. 36, not the lodge indicated. National Library of Ireland, Ms. 22,004 (6)

Going up the stair you find another bow-room, the honeysuckle almost up to it, and a little room the same size as that below; this with a kitchen or servants' hall below, is the whole house. There is, on the left, in the court-yard, another building which makes a kitchen; it is covered by trees, so as to look pretty; at the back of it, there is a yard, &c, which looks into a lane. On the side of the house opposite the grass plot, there is ground enough for a flower-garden, communicating with the front garden by a little walk.

The house, outhouses and garden all stood in the castle's old keep and 'the whole place' was 'situated on a kind of rampart, of a circular form, surrounded by a wall; which wall, towards the village and lane, is high, but covered with trees and shrubs; – the trees old and large, giving a great deal of shade'. The garden looked 'towards the country' where the garden wall was 'not higher than your knee' and 'from these open parts you have a view of a pretty cultivated country, till your eye is stopped by the Curragh', Kildare's heathland, too poor to be improved or to be grazed by any animal but sheep (Fig. 124). Edward and

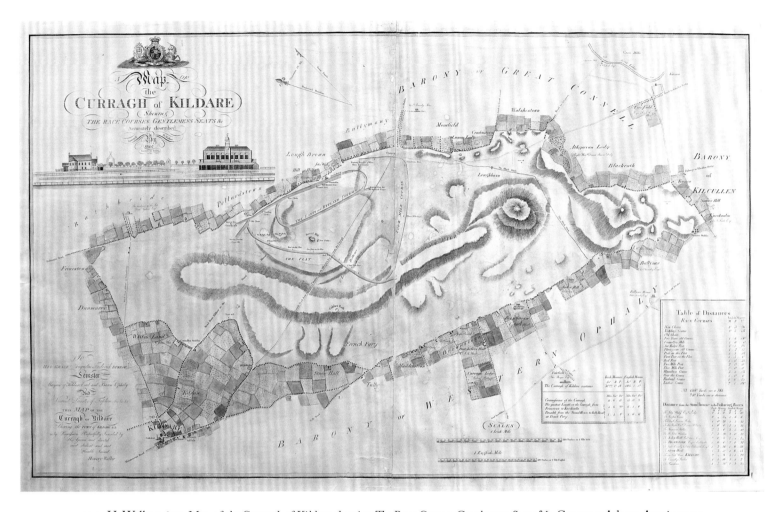

124. H. Walker 1807, *Map of the Curragh of Kildare showing The Race Courses Gentlemens Seats &c.* Courtesy Adams Auctioneers

his fellow revolutionaries could hop over this garden wall to the Curragh, bypassing the town and its many peeping windows, an important consideration for their later, more seditious, tours: 'From our place there is a back way to these fields, so as to go out and walk, without having to do with the town.'[118] William Beaufort's view of Kildare in April 1794 did depict Kildare Lodge, probably the higher building lying immediately to the right of the FitzGerald tower house (Fig. 125). Beaufort's view, taken from the northern approach to Kildare, depicts a route with far fewer houses than Rocque's and consequently fewer watching eyes. How easy for the revolutionary *citoyen* to jump those hedges and set out to foment rebellion in the countryside.

Kildare soon began to replace Frescati in Edward's affections and he revived there the modest, unassuming but affected lifestyle he had cultivated in Blackrock: 'I have been very

busy since I am here we both doat on this little place & enjoy it completely … we generally dine out under the Trees.' The county was delightful for riding, its roads 'like Gravel walks' and they went out in their curricle every evening.[119] Initially Edward was kept busy 'about the militia' – enlisting men into the Volunteers for his brother the Duke of Leinster although the 'common people and farmers' did not 'thoroughly come into' the process and Edward approved of their reluctance to be 'entirely led by names', even when the aristocratic surname was his own.[120] He began to chafe further against aristocratic authority, particularly when staying in the FitzGerald family's townhouse, and in March 1794 he and Pamela were so uncomfortable in Leinster House that they planned to stay in the Leinster Hotel instead. Today the seat of Dáil Éireann, Leinster House was for them a 'melancholy house', where

125. William Beaufort, *Anthologica Hibernia*, Plate 1, 'Kildare, April 1794'. View from the north

their poor country housemaid had 'cried for two days and said she thought she was in prison' and which did 'not inspire the brightest ideas'. In Dublin the young couple 'amuse[d] [them] selves a good deal by walking about the streets' which shocked Edward's sister Emily 'not a little', while Edward's brother the Duke and his wife, or their retinue, were not 'pleasant' to them, suggesting some frosty disapproval of their behaviour.[121] Aristocrats were supposed to be carried by sedan chair or carriage through the streets of Dublin, not walk by themselves.

Edward FitzGerald and Arthur O'Connor first met in around 1793. Together they employed lifestyle and spatial setting as indicators of political position, now accomplished in tandem, and their seemingly innocent 'native' Kildare activities of drinking whiskey, speaking Irish and dancing jigs also included enlisting locals to the United Irishmen.[122] Escaping through the back gate of Kildare Lodge 'without having to do with the town' concealed their revolutionary activity behind the polite pastime of touring the countryside. They believed that their Kildare habits of 'the dear song, & the old dance, the conversation, the humble meal & the jug of native punch' had the power to 'change this monotonous lonesome ever-reigning solitude into mere mist',[123] while their political discussions

won them some staunch converts among Edward's younger sisters. One unidentified sister wrote to the youngest sister Lucy, Edward's most loyal foot soldier, of how her brother 'was mad about the French affairs – the levelling principle, and indeed seems intirely engrossed by these subjects, upon which he converses in a charming pleasant way'. This more sensible sister feared that he had 'made out a system to himself too perfect for this world and which to bring about would be the cause of much disorder and much blood would be spilt'. Her brother had denied this charge but she correctly surmised that the United Irishmen's plot would 'but too soon shew itself – for it gains by his accounts great grounds – one must not say the mob before him but the people, and he has put out of all Mama's French books Priviligeux[?] du Roi'.[124] Transparent and communicative, Edward found secrecy difficult and, despite the gaps in the Leinster archive, his brothers and sisters seem to have been well aware of his plans. Political divisions within the FitzGerald family were very much in evidence by 1797 when the unidentified sister found all the revolutionary ardour 'perfectly odious'. She thought 'it charming to hear talked of' but believed that Edward and his cohort would 'never realise it'. Somewhat guilty by having been seduced by their ideas, she explained how 'hearing them all talk so much in this way lately' had drawn her 'without intention into it'.[125]

Enlarging their touring routes, Edward and Arthur's revolutionary activity soon demanded a European tour to Hamburg and thence to Switzerland, again partially if unsuccessfully concealed behind a veil of landscape tourism. Hamburg was the spy capital of Europe, its identity as a free Hanseatic city relieving its inhabitants of the rigorous social controls being enacted by other European monarchies and governments in the aftermath of the French Revolution.[126] Hamburg, however, did not remain their abode for long and their walking tour 'to Berne, Freibourg, Lausanne and Lake Geneva, returning by Lake Neuchatel' in 1796 was not the innocent enjoyment of landscape that it appeared to be.[127] Describing to his mother how they had begun their tour 'with true Rousseau enthusiasm',[128] Edward forbore to mention how O'Connor had continued into France to make plans with General Lazare Hoche for the planned French invasion of Ireland.[129]

> I had a very pleasant Tour, am in raptures with Switzerland. I left my Friend O'Connor in Switzer-land taking another Tour. There never were two persons who more thoroughly admired Switzerland than we did. We saw it with the true Rousseau enthusiasm: He is as fond of Rousseau as I am, so you may conceive how we enjoyed our journey.[130]

O'Connor 'entered completely' into Edward's 'way of travelling, which was walking most of the way, getting into a Boat when we could, taking our dinner in some pretty spot, and swimming when we could'. The two men 'agreed in everything' with their seemingly innocent pleasures designed to pass the censor's eye. Arthur O'Connor's unpublished memoirs reveal another, quite different, purpose.[131] Their tour was also inspired by 'a Swiss order that no stranger should abide in Ba[s]le longer than three days' and the concerns occasioned by an English agent promising 'English gold to every one he could find to undertake the works of disorder, anarchy and insurrection'.[132] When they returned to Basel they received 'an answer from the Directory in which they said they would willing enter into the treaty such as' the United Irishmen 'had demanded', with General Hoche appointed as negotiator. Edward and Pamela's famous, and often notorious, families made discreet diplomacy very difficult and the French ambas-

sador had to explain that it was impossible Edward could be permitted to enter France because of a rumour that 'a member of the Directory had been in treaty with the Duke of Orléans [Pamela's soi-disant father] to be King of France'.[133] O'Connor, in contrast, experienced no trouble in France because he 'passed for an American'[134] and he went to Reims alone to meet Hoche while Edward returned to Hamburg. The United Irishman Wolfe Tone's presence was requested as 'indispensible'[135] for the planned French landing and O'Connor was 'greatly disappointed to find that instead of Tone they had sent a low presumptuous blackard of the name of Ducket' who 'at a dinner of patriots at Killarney' had drunk 'to the memory of Robespierre, Coullon & Ld Juste', by then out of favour.[136] He promised General Hoche that he would 'lose no time in returning to Ireland' travelling 'night and day without stopping … passing by Pays Bas Holland Westphaly & Luxembourg to Hambourg'. There he was reunited with Edward and rather prematurely 'overjoyed' at O'Connor's 'complete success' they 'lost not an instant in going to England'.[137] Edward 'returned in a Dilligence, by way of Schaffhouse, Ausbourg, Nuremburg, Brunswick' and although the journey was 'troublesome enough as to the Body'[138] the enthusiastic revolutionary did not mind.

When Arthur O'Connor reached England his promise to Hoche not to lose a minute was somewhat forgotten, overwhelmed by the duties of a returning tourist. It was only after he had visited all of his 'beloved friends' to give them some 'little presents', among them the Duchess of Devonshire, to whom he gave 'a memorial' from a Lausanne professor and 'some beautiful landscapes of Switzerland', did O'Connor 'set out for Belfast by Portpatrick and Donaghdea'.[139] When he reached Dublin he and Edward were determined to 'leave nothing undone that could prepare support for the arrival' of their allies and they soon departed for 'Connaught to examine the line of operation from Galway Bay & see' for themselves 'the state of the peoples' minds'. Surveying the territory for its military capabilities, Edward, an erstwhile British officer, examined the Shannon river towns of Athlone and Banagher, particularly the river crossings.[140] But when back home in Kildare Lodge they still found time to go to the races.[141]

O'Connor's Irish and European tours and experiences, both with and without Edward, gave him enough comparative landscape experience to write *The State of Ireland* address in 1797, where revolution resulted in clear examples of successful landscape improvements:

Look to Holland! from the moment she threw off the Spanish yoke, and established Liberty, how she converted swamps, rescued from the sea, into a garden! Look to Switzerland! from the moment she threw off the Austrian yoke, how she has cultivated her mountains to the highest summit! Look to America! from the day she freed herself and her industry from the domination of England, with what rapidity she has cleared her woods and drained her morasses![142]

Recalling William Gilpin, Arthur Young, and many other tourists and tour guides, O'Connor compared the 'beauteous island' of Ireland with 'the swamps of Holland, the mountains of Switzerland, the diminutiveness of Geneva or Genoa, or the sterility of Portugal' to conclude, somewhat ambiguously, that 'the people of Ireland should be satisfied'.[143]

Edward FitzGerald and Arthur O'Connor used travel to define their own identities. These fluctuated over time, as they met new men or visited new nations. They employed comparative analysis to define the state of their own country and to propose a future for it. These comparisons combined with repeated habits of lifestyle to reinforce and communicate their changing political perspectives. Moving between his British, French, American and Irish identities, Edward FitzGerald tried them all out for size, before eventually becoming an Irish revolutionary. Arthur O'Connor, if less mutable in his national identity, travelled critically through France, Switzerland and London, before arriving home to Cork to practise farming. Both men experienced France in the critical years of 1784 to 1791 when the spatial precepts of the revolution, grounded in such tropes as the mountain and the plain, were being tested and refined. Arthur Young wrote his important French tour in the same critical years of 1787, 1788, 1789, when the French experiments in weighting city and countryside, and in estimating the limits of both, may be discerned in his writings and letters.[144] All three men followed the precepts of Jean-Jacques Rousseau, where to follow in his footsteps was to enact revolution spatially. O'Connor and FitzGerald then identified the anomalous suburban town of Blackrock, Co. Dublin, as the ideal setting for their seditious activities. Located on the fringes of the great absentee Fitzwilliam estate, there they could exploit the strangely egalitarian principles that had informed its

development and which Chapter 6 will explore, whilst avoiding the aristocratic townhouses and formal squares of Dublin city. When eventually forced to abandon Blackrock they moved to the rural idyll of Kildare Lodge with its honeysuckle bowers and small flower gardens. In these locations they explored how a landscape of equality might be designed, what kind of views it should address, how it should be planted and how best it could be used, often adopting an affected choreography to act out their revolutionary roles for interested observers.

The United Irishmen's revolutionary dreams were ultimately defeated in the rising of 1798 and by its aftermath. General Hoche's 1796 expedition to Ireland failed for a variety of reasons, not least bad weather, and was replaced with a new plan for a 1798 landing under General Humbert. Frescati, which the Duchess found difficult to divest herself of, continued to be a meeting place for the United Irishmen, and in 1798 the government informer Reynolds reported that on 24 February 1798 he had gone to Blackrock 'to dine with Lord Edward' and to be given 'the Resolutions and returns of the National Committee',[145] which he then betrayed to the authorities in Dublin Castle. When the United Irishmen rose on 24 May 1798 in Dublin, the rebellion spread rapidly to Wicklow, Waterford and Wexford but eventually failed, riddled with security breaches and abortive communications. Edward FitzGerald was shot in a Dublin townhouse and died of his injuries on 4 June 1798, and a few weeks later on 21 June the decisive Battle of Vinegar Hill, Co. Wexford, defeated a substantial force of United Irishmen. The French landing in Killala, Co. Mayo, in August 1798 by General Humbert and his men led to a series of other battles and skirmishes that were ultimately defeated at Ballinamuck, Co. Longford, on 8 September. The French invasion that Wolfe Tone led was defeated off the coast of Donegal on 12 October 1798. Revolutionary dreams were also extinguished by the prosaic realities of growing older, acquiring new responsibilities and ensuring that a revolutionary past did not affect their children's future. But the tradition of projecting revolutionary ideas onto the landscape continued to run through the history of Ireland and the United States, and how those ideas (and their contradictions) were translated into landscape design are subjects the next chapters will explore.

CHAPTER 5

The Plantation Revolution

Pierce Butler's Plantations

> One hundred years hence, no one will care whether you have
> slaved yourself in trying to have an Estate as it ought to be;
> or my trying to make it so.[1]
>
> Roswell King, Butler's Island, 3 January 1813

In 1793 George Washington observed that 'few Ships, of late' had 'arrived from any part of G[reat] Britain or Ireland without a number of emigrants, and some of them, by report, very respectable & full handed farmers'.[2] They were not only farmers – many Irishmen travelling to the United States in the eighteenth century did not do so for financial motives. Forced to emigrate by political necessity rather than free choice, such men fled capture rather than starvation. Carrying money and assets with them, once in America they had the time and leisure to travel and make spatial choices, unlike the impoverished, famine-fleeing Irish emigrants of the nineteenth century. Eighteenth-century Irish émigrés, and particularly the radical revolutionaries of the 1790s, typically landed in Philadelphia. There they found a tolerant environment for their revolutionary ideas among the many Irish men and women who preceded them.[3] William Duane, publisher of Philadelphia's radical newspaper the *Aurora*, had unusually emigrated in his youth from America to Dublin, where he learnt the newspaper and publishing trade. The printing culture he then brought home to America gave radical Irishmen a voice in the new republic.[4] Other Irish emigrants cast their lot with the burgeoning American nursery trade rather than with farming,

particularly if they did not have the wherewithal to buy land. 'Bernard Mac Mahon … County of Tyrone' who had signed the 'Petition of Catholics of Ireland',[5] making him a prominent revolutionary sympathiser, concealed both the Mac origin of his name and much else besides during his metamorphosis into Philadelphia's primary nurseryman, receiver of the Lewis and Clark plant samples, a correspondent of Thomas Jefferson's and author of America's first gardening book *The American Gardener's Calendar*.[6] The plants he provided for Thomas Jefferson were carried to Monticello by Mr Duane, keeping the Irish radical network intact, if more botanically occupied, in their new home.[7]

One of Ireland's most notable eighteenth-century emigrants was the planter and politician Pierce Butler who was born in Co. Carlow in 1744. The son of Sir Richard Butler, a scion of a minor branch of the Ormond dukedom, he was most probably commissioned into the 29th Regiment of the British army in 1759 at the age of fourteen. Initially stationed in Limerick, he crossed the Atlantic to Nova Scotia, Canada, where he was made a major on 23 April 1766. By 1767 he was living in Charleston, South Carolina, where he began courting Mary Middleton of a powerful landowning family and heiress to substantial plantations, whom he married in 1771. He resigned from the British army in 1773, sold his commission and became caught up in the American Revolution on the patriot side. The first senator of the state of South Carolina and a great planter in the state of Georgia, he was one of the thirty-nine signatories of the Constitution of the United States (Fig. 126). As an author of its fugitive slave clause,

126. Max Rosenthal, 'Pierce Butler, Signer of the Constitution of the U.S.' Print. New York Public Library, Digital Library, https://digitalcollections.nypl.org

for America, Wolfe Tone, in the company of the other United Irishmen, had sworn their formation oath in McArt's Fort on the mountain of Cave Hill outside Belfast in the north of Ireland:

> On the first [June, 1795], Russell, Neilson, Simms, M'Cracken, and one or two more of us, on the summit of M'Art's fort, took a solemn obligation, which, I think I may say, I have, on my part, endeavored to fulfil – never to desist in our efforts, until we have subverted the authority of England over our country, and asserted our independence.[8]

A suitably ancient and agreeably symbolic Celtic promontory fortification, McArt's Fort still looms over the town of Belfast and the Lagan valley (Fig. 127) and views positioned the city against the Cave Hill outcrop (Fig. 128). Mythologised subsequently in printed images, the oath's backdrop of bare rocks and soil and low-flying birds indicated the height and exposure of the location (Fig. 129). The day after the ceremony the revolutionaries pitched a tent in Belfast Castle's deer park, where they 'dined and spent the day together deliciously' while the following day was recalled as 'one of the most agreeable in their lives' because of their 'excursion to Ram's Island, a beautiful and romantic spot in Lough Neagh'.[9] This rather strange conjoining of tourism with militant and seditious insurgency was not uncommon in Ireland at this period. Conventional tourism generally reinforces national identity as tourists typically follow agreed routes, visit well-known places and make traditional comparisons, and Tone and his companions had completed an established circuit of Belfast tourist sites while also carrying out such prescribed leisure activities as picnicking, strolling and boating. They also assessed the landscape beauty of such sites and carefully labelled them under the aesthetic criteria of the period. Their oath-taking ceremony on top of McArt's Fort, an interesting antiquity, agreed with the romantic tour's precepts but took it a step further by using the landscape to invoke Irish nationalism and incite revolution.

Although this leisurely tour of the Belfast region somewhat contradicted any sense of imminent danger, Wolfe Tone and his comrades did finally embark on board the ship *Cincinnatus* for Philadelphia on 13 June 1795.[10] Two days after landing Tone wrote to his friend Thomas Russell in Belfast to describe his new environment:

he ensured that the southern states' voting rights were proportional to the number of their enslaved people, with many terrible consequences.

Pierce Butler was often asked to advise other Irish gentlemen emigrants, among them two of the most prominent United Irishmen, Archibald Hamilton Rowan and Theobald Wolfe Tone who arrived in Philadelphia fleeing British spies and warships in 1795 and 1796 respectively. Before embarking

127. Andrew Nicholl, *McArt's Fort, from the Mountain*, *c.*1828. Ulster Museum BELUM.U250, © National Museums NI Collection Ulster Museum

The country is beautiful but it is like a beautiful scene in a theatre – the effect at a proper distance is admirable but it will not bear a minute inspection, the features are large, the Weeds rank, the grasses coarse, but distance blends all that and renders the whole a singular, certainly, and, in my mind, a beautiful landscape.

His immediate impressions of Philadelphia conformed to the strictures and ideal distances of foreground, middle ground and rear ground of the picturesque tour he had just experienced. Although he could write positively of America's comparative beauty and abstract composition, appreciating it as a composed landscape, he nevertheless realised that this neatly sidestepped any detailed analysis. He was also aware of his incompetency in judging adequately what he saw: 'I am obliged to speak of the face of the country, for as yet I know so little of the people that it would not be candid to speak what I am inclined to think of them.'[11] His more general knowledge of the principles of landscape analysis can be extrapolated from a later lengthy written assessment of the beauties of Dutch landscape (or the lack of them). Touring the Low Countries in 1797 Tone found that there was 'something, after all, in the view of Holland, notwithstanding its monotony, which to me, at least, is not disagreeable'. He carefully and accurately listed

128. Thomas Thompson, *A View of Belfast from the Banks of the Lagan*, 1805. Engraved by F. Jukes, Belfast.
Published 1 December 1805 by T. Thompson No. 6 High St: 'From an Original Drawing by T. Thompson'. British Library, Ktop LI, 41.e

the fundamental 'features of a Dutch landscape' as 'an immense tract of meadows till the view is lost in the distance, intersected either by deep and wide ditches, or by fences of wicker, made as neat as basket-work; large plantations of willows; small brick houses covered with red tiles, and in excellent order'. 'Here and there a chateau of a Seigneur' was 'surrounded by a garden in the true Dutch taste' and he was 'not sure that, for a small garden, that taste is a bad one; its neatness, exactitude and regularity agree admirably with what one expects to find there'. His command of the nuances of contemporary landscape design was also impressive. The Dutch garden had 'not the picturesque beauty of an English garden, but it ha[d] notwithstanding, its own merits' and he liked it 'well enough in miniature', concluding that 'in a Dutch garden all is straight lines and right angles; in an English, all is sinuosity'.[12]

Once in America, the politics of the new world proved very confusing. Rowan was very puzzled by the 1796 presidential contest between John Adams and Thomas Jefferson, a contest that Adams won. He found it 'not a little remarkable, that all the eastern that were the great republican states' were 'in favour of Adams … while the southern states support Jefferson – themselves and he slaveholders, but great republicans – and at the revolution much less in earnest than the eastern states?'[13] Critical comparison was particularly acute in the first few months of residency when Tone found that 'the spirit of commerce hath eaten up all other feeling' in the United States with the status of mercantile wealth 'little beneath the lofty pretensions of your aristocracy'. Already invoking a new mixed identity, he wrote, 'We are splintering fast here into two parties, the rich and the poor … The real state is Aristocracy against Democracy.' Tone was particularly sensitive to the concealment of aristocratic values behind a republican farmer veneer, with Washington singled out for particular censure:

> Washington is an honest man and a sincere American, according to his own theory. But he is a high-flying aristocrat … What is it to me whether it is an Aristocracy of Merchants or of Peers, elective or hereditary? It is still an aristocracy, incompatible with the existence of genuine liberty.[14]

Both Rowan and Tone chose to become farmers of northern states while in America, and this spatial choice was not taken lightly. In 1795 Tone bought a 'plantation of 180 acres, beautifully situated within two miles of Princeton, and half of it under timber', for £1,180, believing it to be 'worth the money'.[15]

129. John D. Reigh, *The Cave Hill, Belfast. Formation of the Society of United Irishmen by Wolfe Tone, Samuel Neilson, and Thomas Russell*, Supplement gratis with Christmas Number of the Shamrock, December 1890. National Library of Ireland, PD Shamrock 1890 December (A)

He moved his family to New Jersey and 'began to think that' his 'lot was cast to be an American farmer'.[16] By September he had cleared 90 acres and was planning 'to bring fifty of them into English cultivation'.[17]

Archibald Hamilton Rowan took advice from Pierce Butler a mere three days after landing in Philadelphia on 18 July 1795, describing him as a man of 'good sense, good manners and good fortune, respected by all'. As their acquaintance grew, Butler introduced Rowan to such distinguished visitors as 'the famous traveller Volney' and he planned to give a party for the visiting Duc de la Rochefoucauld-Liancourt, habitué of Arthur Young, to which Rowan would be invited. Yet Rowan declined Major Butler's friendly offer of 2,000 acres of land in the South and chose instead, like Tone, to buy a farm in Pennsylvania, explaining his choice in a commendable passage in a letter to his wife: 'Now let me assure you, that I am acting quite by myself, and contrary to advice; for one wants me to remain in Philadelphia, and another, to buy a small farm in a settled country. But I will do neither; I will go to the woods; but I will not kill Indians, nor keep slaves.'[18] Uncomfortable with the young country's 'aristocracy of wealth', Rowan had found Butler to be 'as much disgusted with' America as himself and as every 'man must be who has lived in Europe'.[19] Butler's family were 'calumniated' in American society because they did 'not associate indiscriminately' and, despite the principles of republican equality that both men officially espoused, Rowan approved of Butler's selective behaviour. He thought that there were 'agreeable persons to be found' in America but that they were 'so rare', and 'so nearly impossible to keep' separate from the others that he considered 'the woods the most eligible situation'[20] for his family.

Pierce Butler rarely advised Irishmen to emigrate to the United States. He could not recommend that anyone, in specific economic terms, 'give up two hundred a year in Ireland, a healthy and a cheap country, to move a family to America on a capital of £5000'. Although a 'farm might be bought in the interior country for £1000 which would give food to' a 'family & a comfortable lodging', the emigrants 'would have no society, no opportunity of educating your Children unless you sent them from you'.[21] If emigration from Ireland was inevitable he advised 'a total remove to Georgia', above all other states, where the emigrant would 'save greatly' and would 'be the sooner an independent Man'. Probably recalling his own considerable forays into debt, Butler warned that 'dependence on the will of others' was 'a great curse'.[22] His advice was frequently sought

by British and Irish men of independent means who hoped to increase their fortunes by investing in American land, without necessarily intending to live there permanently themselves:

> You ask me what part of America I wou'd recommend. Much depends on your plan & the Capital you wou'd wish to realise in America. If a landed estate, without trouble, with a moderate Interest is Your object I recommend the State of Pennsylvania. If an encrease of property is your object I prefer the State of Georgia to any part of the United States … If you visit us I will cheerfully make a tour of the States with You & You shall judge for Yourself.[23]

Butler could present his adopted country positively when he wanted to, employing comparative examples to help procrastinating Europeans imagine America. Its climates 'resemble[d] those of Italy' where 'the lower part' was 'hot and sickly' but just like approaching 'the foot of The Alps' it became 'cool and healthy' at the higher elevations. His own position was described with great exactitude. When 'seated about 220 miles from Charleston, South Carolina' at his plantation of Mary Ville 'on top of a hill' he enjoyed 'a view exceeding in extent that from the terrace at Windsor Castle, though not to be compared to it in any other sense'. In America there was 'nothing but Nature' whilst in Berkshire there was 'Nature highly improved by Art and Industry'. He might almost be writing a personal tour guide for his London cousin Weedon Butler:

> The eye here is lost in space, having nothing to impede its view. No mosquito or insect here to disturb our repose as in the low country. Intermittants, the bane of the rice country, are strangers here. And the children of the inhabitants look as ruddy as those in the Highlands of Scotland. So would the grown people if they could be prevailed upon to drink less rum. Every man here is lord of the soil he lives on, happy and independent if they are sensible of it, the earth yielding generously. People are not very industrious; having no landlord to fear, they cultivate enough to give them plenty for their own use.[24]

Pierce Butler was, however, somewhat silent on the real differences between European and American landscapes in his letters to Europe, and as Rowan and Tone's land purchases indicate, Europeans were not unaware of the impact of slavery on many issues. His explanation that 'the manners of the northern and southern states differ much'[25] seems somewhat disingenuous in its degree of understatement, and his present of 'some silk that was made in South Carolina near to a farm of mine, or as we term it, a "plantation"', when combined with the suggestion that the recipient would be 'honouring the State to convert it into stockings and wear them'[26] strangely calculated.

These United Irishmen who headed across the Atlantic had to take decisions there that no European had to take at home – whether to become free republican yeoman farmers or to own slaves. Established Irish-Americans, like Pierce Butler, could offer advice but were ultimately compromised and conflicted by the choices they had made themselves. Tone soon recovered from his initial reluctance to pass judgement

on American society with the results of his 'observation … a most unqualified dislike of the people'.[27] He reasoned that his friend Thomas Russell would be 'amused with the idea' of Tone becoming 'the father of a farming club after assisting in framing societies of so very different a nature', in Ireland, namely the revolutionary United Irishmen. He argued that he saw no other way of 'being useful' in America, having 'determined not to interfere in any degree, directly or indirectly, with their politics' and to 'never assume the rights of citizenship'.[28] The United Irishman Thomas Russell, convinced that the republican principles of equality should apply also to countries, had argued with Tone before he left Ireland 'that all countries were alike to the well-regulated mind'. But Tone responded that were Russell to try his 'experiment' of a few months residency in America, he too 'would feel the irresistible affection with which a man is drawn to his native soil and how flat and uninteresting the politics and parties of other countries appear'. Tone's travels within the United States, particularly his comparative assessment of Philadelphia, New Jersey and Rhode Island, had converted him into 'an inflexible Irishman',[29] and not long afterwards he left America for good.

In contrast, Pierce Butler, as a resident planter and politician, had made many decisions and compromises in the United States, particularly relating to landscape design and management, and these reveal much about the challenges of landscaping the American landed estate in the 1795–1815 period. How did his native Irish-born knowledge of the Irish and European landscapes affect what he did in the United States, if at all? Did concepts of improvement, so general in

130. Ballintemple House, Co. Carlow, constructed *c.*1770, burnt down 1917. IAA

131. Ballintemple House and demesne on the first edition OS map of Co. Carlow, Sheets 14 and 18, Scale 1:10,560, surveyed 1839, printed 1840. Reproduced courtesy Trinity College Dublin

eighteenth-century Ireland, work in practice in the American South? The extensive letters, drawings and directions Butler wrote to his successive estate managers George Valley, William Page, Roswell King and his son of the same name, allow an accurate picture of the land management and design of his Georgian estate to be created. Some of Butler's papers have been well excavated by American historians, but not the full logic of their transatlantic origin nor the difficult translation of Irish and European landed estate concepts into the state of Georgia.[30] What balance was struck between farming, economic and aesthetic concerns, and how did this reflect the compromises that slavery exerted on concepts of improvement?

Pierce Butler was born in the great house of Ballintemple, Co. Carlow, in 1744 (Fig. 130).[31] Located in a region of comparatively fertile soil, ideally suited to tillage farming, the family's highly worked and manipulated demesne of approximately 1,000 acres was one of the many that lined the banks of the river Slaney (Fig. 131). Ballintemple's great house was positioned well above the riverside, with its entrance front facing east and its garden front west (Fig. 132). Only the stone temple front of the entrance façade still stands, now bereft of a large turning circle for carriages (Fig. 133).[32] People approaching the house from the north were greeted by a gate lodge before entering Brownian parkland, where clumps of trees picked out prospects towards the house, the western parkland and the river. The service road that bisects the demesne became the spinal support of the estate's improvement and drainage endeavours. Protected by high ditches and walls and sunken in sections, the road linked the house, its various service buildings, the walled garden complex and the demesne's many fields. Flanked by a retaining wall and ditch on one side, and a double ditch with a central bank and hedge on the other, it corralled the estate's drainage into an ordered network that discharged eventually into the river (Fig. 134). The wider Butler family was well versed in drainage and water infrastructural improvements, with Pierce Butler's eldest brother Sir Thomas Butler taking a 'leading part in the legislation for improving the Navigation of the River Barrow'.[33] One of Ireland's most ambitious eighteenth-century public engineering projects, it canalised the Barrow laterally with locks that allowed ships and barges to proceed further upstream (1756–c.1800).

How to make and bound a field in an unpredictable hydraulic environment was a problem for farmers on both sides of the Atlantic. Despite the difference in climate between

132. Photograph of the view westward from Ballintemple's garden front. Author's photo, 2017

133. *(below)* Approach to the ruin of Ballintemple House portico today. Author's photo, 2017

134. Transverse route through Ballintemple demesne showing large banked walls. Author's photo, 2017

Ireland and the American South, the design problem remained substantially the same – how to control the level of water within a field by making banks and ditches, and how to vary the water level using drainage channels and sluice gates when required. In eighteenth-century Ireland this improved farmland produced oats or wheat, in Maryland tobacco and in Georgia, rice, indigo or cotton. By the mid-eighteenth century, at the peak of the ideology of improvement, Ireland's advancement was so completely equated with drainage and reclamation projects that they were at times ideologically powerful enough to proceed without a full calculation of their economic benefit.[34] Where the land was too wet, which was nearly everywhere owing to the country's precipitation rates, wall and

ditch were combined together into a reclined S-section. This provided the farmer with a boundary to his property, shelter for his animals and drainage channel or 'ditch'. The mound of earth was sometimes faced in stone and often planted with a blackthorn or other 'quickset' hedge on top.

In 1719 the distinguished Maryland planter James Carroll, nephew of Irish-born Charles Carroll 'the Settler',[35] paid his uncle John Carroll 'the Ditcher' for making ditches on some of the Carrolls' extensive land holdings around Annapolis (Fig. 135).[36] Although the brother of one of America's richest planters, John 'the Ditcher' lacked his brother's formal education, and depended on such manual labour for his livelihood. He brought an indentured servant, Thomas Maguire, over from Ireland to help him build ditches on neighbours' plantations where the men's expertise in draining the Irish midlands' water-logged fields was re-employed to lay out the Chesapeake's tobacco plantations.[37] Such practical experience of Irish landscape improvement, although acquired on the other side of the Atlantic, was valued in the United States, and in 1785 Pierce Butler also brought William Payne, 'the son of a faithful old Servant' of his father's, who had been 'brought up on the family estate', back with him to America, thinking that he 'might be [in] some way useful'.[38]

Pierce Butler's first experience of plantation landscape was of those plantations owned by his wife Mary Middleton, particularly the complex at Euhaws on the Ashley River, not far from Charleston, where in the 1780s he learnt the practice and price of becoming a southern gentleman.[39] When Sauney, the young couple's enslaved cook and butler, was 'insolent to his Mistress' Pierce Butler put him 'in the field to punish him'. Only when Sauney had been 'pretty well humbled', by the experience of field labour at the hands of overseers and drivers, did Butler think that he might 'forgive him'.[40] Close by lay another Ashley River plantation called Maryville where prominent trees such as a 'dead old Oak' and a 'light wood pine'[41] had fixed the points between the chain survey length measurements. Access to the river was very important and although very little information on the plot's interior was provided, the owners of neighbouring plots were carefully recorded (Fig. 136).

Butler's own principal Georgian plantation was at Hampton Point, on St Simon's Island, one of Georgia's many barrier low-lying sea islands.[42] Located at the mouth of the Altamaha River, Butler bought the initial 600 acres from James Graham in 1774 (Fig. 137).[43] One of the patchwork of

135. Carroll House, Baltimore. Author's photo, 2013

136. *(below)* Pierce Butler's estate on the east side of the Ashley River, probably Mary Ville, 'Copy of a plan of a tract of land or Plantation containing 1002 acres on Ashley River, on the east side belonging to Major Butler's estate from a survey taken the 19th April 1759 by Nathaniel Bradwell'. South Carolina Historical Society, maps/plats, Call no. 33-39-87

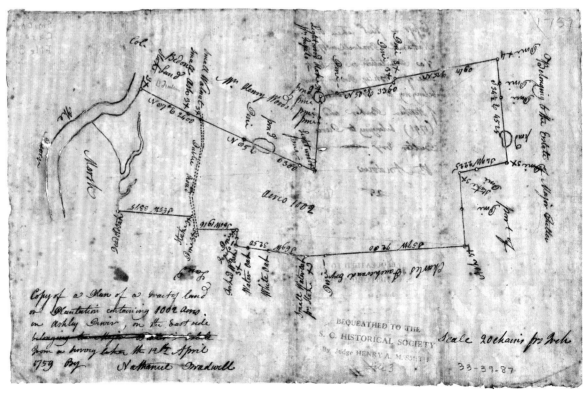

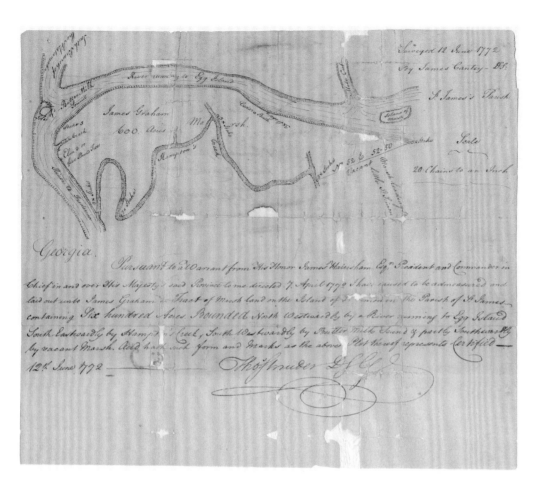

137. Survey for James Graham of 600 acres in Parish of St James, 12 June 1772, Georgia. Private collection

138. *(below)* De Brahm/Thomas Jefferys, *A Map of South Carolina and a Part of Georgia*, 1757. Detail showing St Simon's Island. British Library Maps 1.Tab.44

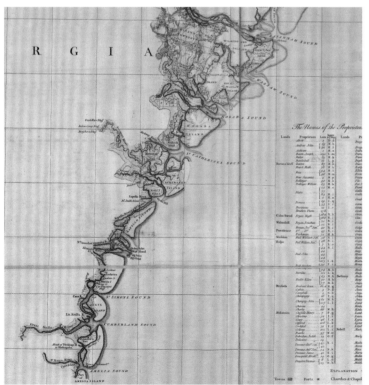

planters' plots that soon stretched south of Savannah along the entire coast of Georgia (Fig. 138), Butler slowly accumulated more and more of St Simon's Island and then began purchasing more islands, bluffs and other holdings upstream on the Altamaha (Fig. 139).[44] By 1780 St Simon's Island contained Hall's, Harrison's, Major McIntosh's and T. Spalding's houses and although the 'Hon. P. Butler Esq.' was inscribed on the map and evidently ensconced at Hampton Point, he had not yet built a house (Fig. 140). A 1797 watercolour map of Hampton Point and Little St Simon's Island carefully itemised the island's various landscapes of interest to potential purchasers and planters, namely the soft marshland that was only profitable when drained, the marshes for cotton and for feeding livestock, the oak and pine lands and the ponds.[45] It carefully depicted the fractal geometries of creeks interspersed with oak, pine and myrtle groves, and dotted with pink ponds (Fig. 141). This was the environment that was quartered and

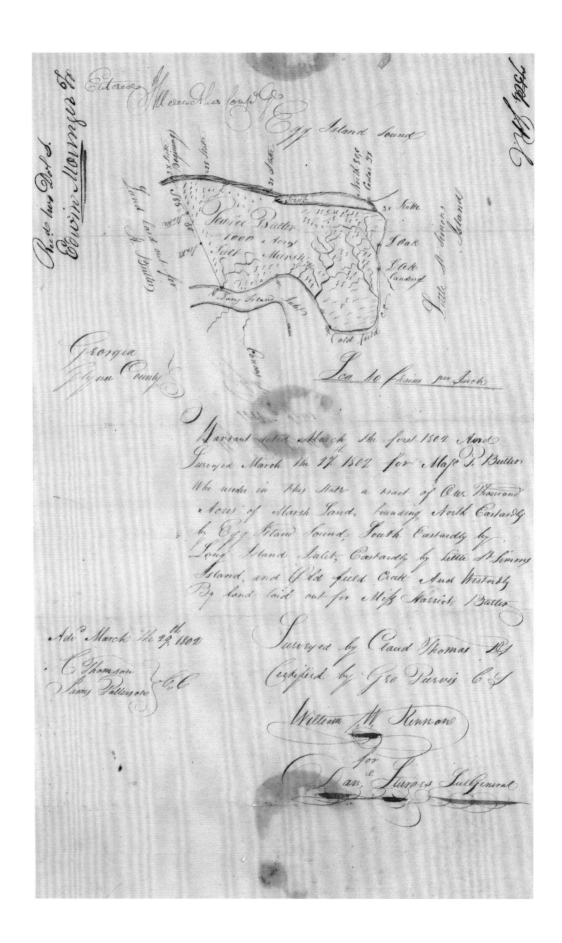

139. *Survey for Pierce Butler, 1,000 acres,*
29 March 1802. Private collection

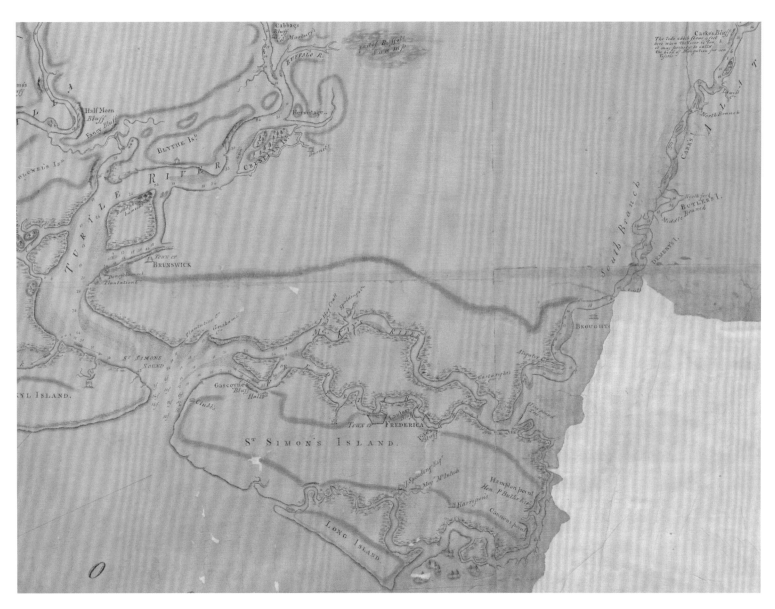

140. Anon, *c.1780*, *Map of the coast of Georgia, bordering on Camden and Glynn counties, showing the course and soundings of the Altamaha, Turtle, Crooked, St. Mary's, Great Satilla, and Little Satilla rivers.* Detail showing Butler's holding at Hampton and Butler's Island further upstream on the Altamaha River. Library of Congress, G3922.C6 178.M3 Vault

gridded into the dykes and squares of Butler's extensive cotton and rice plantations between 1790 and 1815.

In 1785 Pierce Butler travelled to Europe, spending time initially in Carlow and Dublin, and then in London where his son was at school. He then visited Holland and the Low Countries, making an extensive 700-mile tour into the German region of Westphalia and along the Rhine, 'a charming country and well cultivated'.[46] Returning to America,

he set about developing his Georgian plantations in earnest, taking inspiration from Dutch dykes and dams[47] and bringing his accumulated expertise of managing his wife's South Carolina interests to his Georgian plantations. When his wife Mary died in 1790 Butler began to move her enslaved workers, left in trust to her children, from South Carolina to his plantations in Georgia. He had lost the vast part of his South Carolina property during the British troop invasion of 1780

141. Hand-drawn map of Little St Simon's Island, partially in watercolours,
from a survey done by Hopkins and Parker in 1790 (oversize), 1797. Private collection

and was keen to separate his own personal wealth from that of his in-laws. This was illegal, as the enslaved were entailed with the land, and Butler, as trustee of his children's estate, was not entitled to move them outside South Carolina. Doing so involved him in lengthy legal proceedings with his wife's family.

Despite expanding his landholdings and purchasing more enslaved people, Butler never seems to have had any intention of moving to Georgia permanently. An ambitious man, his social and political milieu remained that of Philadelphia and the other principal cities of the northern states. This required him to manage his plantations by proxy, sending written instructions and drawings, initially to a series of fellow planters and then to his appointed agents. As his plantation management structure became slowly more secure his visits to Georgia decreased in both length and frequency.

In 1790 Butler instructed Captain Roger Saunders, a fellow Carolina planter, to move 'some 15 or 20 people, from the plantations of Mary Ville and Euhaws',[48] to 'Hampton Point, on Great St Simon's Island; in order to prepare for planting about 130 acres of cotton'. Only the 'most orderly' enslaved workers were to go, accompanied by the senior enslaved driver Sambo, and some corn and tools. The carpenters were to put up the enslaved workers' housing, a corn house and 'some little shelter' for Butler and any visitors.[49] Focused on 'resettling' his lands at Hampton and the Altamaha River, by August 1792 he was 'bent on' making it 'a right good Establishment'. If the overseer had been sufficiently 'industrious' and had got 'the land ready', he intended to move a further 'three hundred Negroes there, in the course of a year' leaving 'in Carolina 130, or 140' enslaved workers on the Middleton plantations. He was also planning to build 'a House at Hampton' and have 'things comfortable' ordering 'a dozen of the very best Orange Trees' from Augustine, Florida.[50] 'Anxious' to get the 'settlements under way', he intended 'on making a large crop of cotton & putting a number of hands to ditch' on his Tide Island.[51] With so many they could 'get four hundred Acres in order for Cotton' at Hampton and he could then move forty enslaved workers to his promising Tide 'Island up the River', which later became known as Butler's Island.[52]

As in all plantations across the Caribbean and the United States, much time was expended in evaluating the merits of different crops and the machines used to process them. Butler plumped first for cotton, claiming that 'Georgia Cotton' was 'not so long as the Surinam, Demerara or Esequibo Cotton' but that it had a 'much finer' texture and 'sold higher than any other at the London market'.[53] Cotton gin machines separated the cotton fibres from their seeds, and in 1793 Butler wrote to Nathaniel Hall of Great Exuma Island in the Bahamas to ask if his 'famous Ginn Maker' Eli Whitney, could 'be prevailed on to come to America' if Butler got him a patent for his machine.[54] Indigo might have replaced cotton at Hampton in 1793 when the cotton failed from an unprecedented attack of caterpillars, 'devoured just as it was opening in two nights'.[55] But Butler considered indigo to be 'as subject to Grasshoppers, as the Cotton' with 'the chance' on the crop 'equal on the ground of insect.' After 'weighing the subject' he decided that the land at St Simons was 'too light for Indigo' because 'the Sea-Islands generally' were 'at some part of the Summer, subject to a drought' and 'the leaves of Indigo in which the

dye lies' did not stand drought as well as cotton. Sowing a portion of each crop spread the risk, but although the cotton and indigo planting cycles did 'not much interfere' with each other and were 'a kind of succession of Work; yet from the great difference in the process', Butler worried that 'they might confuse' his enslaved labour force.[56] After this consideration of indigo, the Butler estate was primarily planted with cotton and rice and from 1812, approximately, sugar cane, with all the crops intended primarily for the European markets. Shipped via Savannah to Liverpool, the 'Pierce Butler cotton' became known for its quality.[57] Corn was also grown on the plantation as food for the enslaved workforce who were only given rice when damage had prevented its sale, when it could not be transported to market quickly enough or when they were considered run down or ill.

Butler sought a mortgage on his 'four cotton plantations and the Negroes that cultivate them' from the London merchant house of Simpson & Davisson to recover from the 1793 onslaught of caterpillars.[58] He planned also to mortgage his Tide Island, known subsequently as Butler's Island, where he 'had sixty odd Negroes at work' in 1793 'ditching, and Carpenters erecting Buildings'. Already convinced of his Tide Island's extraordinary money-making potential, he vowed he would not take 'a bill of exchange on London for 10,000 Guineas for that island alone'.[59] Hampton was the centrepiece of Butler's plantation jigsaw, partly because Butler intended to locate his house there, with the whole frequently referred to as 'the estate' by Roswell King in his letters. After Hampton, which remained the pre-eminent portion, whether financially in the ascendant or not, the hierarchy of the various other plantation divisions took a while to settle. The standing of the Tide Island (also called Rice Island and then Butler's Island) became more significant as its financial value increased. At the mouth of the Altamaha lay Butler's 'Experiment' Plantation, where cotton was grown, while his Little St Simons Island was devoted to stock farming. Experiment Plantation may have been more of a social experiment than a botanical or infrastructural one, and what exactly was experimental about it remains frustratingly unclear. King's information that he had not sent a female enslaved worker there because she had 'now two Children to suckle' and instead kept 'her at moating' cotton in Hampton[60] suggests that the work at the Butler's Island and Experiment portions was considered harder, probably because the enslaved had to work standing in flooded fields

and canals that contained poisonous snakes and where some
sections may have been used as punishment areas.

At first Butler relied on fellow planters to visit Hampton
and communicate his orders, which he sent them by letter,
and they would then send him back reports. Initially the
planter Thomas Young would travel from his own plantation to
Hampton and instruct George Valley, Hampton's first general
manager, but over time this led to management problems and
frustrations. Slowly, as Butler's ambitions expanded and he
began planning to 'go more largely on Cotton than any planter
in America',[61] he began to communicate with Young using
drawings, sending him 'a sketch of the plan' he had drawn of
'four distinct settlements' in 1794.[62] So began his search for
a 'real good Manager for' his 'planting interest in Georgia',
someone who would allow him to 'to be saved the necessity
of ever going to see' his estate. He intended to 'vest such a
Manager with full powers to do anything' he might need to do
in Butler's absence. Archibald Brown, a South Carolina merchant and a Cooper River planter, was asked to find a suitable
candidate at a salary of £150 or £200 a year and Butler expected
the successful candidate to live on the estate 'either on the Sea
Coast or River lands' with the sweetener that he could use 'the
produce of the Estate for his table'. The successful candidate
'should take a ride' over the estate with Butler to understand
the intended plan and Butler also intended to employ one or
two overseers as the manager's assistants, who had to 'understand ditching'.[63] Recruitment proved difficult, however, and
the planter William Page managed Butler's plantations from
1796 to 1802, while developing his own Retreat Plantation on
the southern tip of St Simon's Island. This was not ideal, as his
focus obviously tended towards improving his own land ahead
of Butler's. Matters improved for Butler when Roswell King
was appointed as manager in 1802 (Fig. 142).

Roswell King wrote to Pierce Butler approximately once
a week, give or take a few days. It was his practice to tour
all the plantations each week, probably staying overnight on
occasion at Tide Island, gradually known as Butler's Island,
its name definitively changed by July 1806. A section of
each letter was devoted to each plantation portion in turn –
Hampton, Butler's/Tide Island, Experiment, Little St Simon's
Island – and each letter generally closed with a brief report on
the enslaved workers' levels of sickness and rates of death.[64]
Overall, the correspondence described the backbreaking work
of constructing the canals, dams, ditches and sluice gates that

142. Portrait of Roswell King. Courtesy Georgia Archives,
Vanishing Georgia Collection, ful0522

were necessary to protect the low-lying islands from tidal and
hurricane surges, to control water levels in the irrigated squares
and to create the optimal growing conditions for cotton, rice
and sugar cane, all crops that Butler eventually grew in very
large quantities on his various islands. Each island was initially
assessed as to its suitability for a particular crop, observed for
a while under that crop and then rotated with other crops to
prevent soil depletion. Slowly the landscape was altered to
encourage and sustain the preferred crop's optimal production
with Irish and Dutch practices for compacting clay into an
impermeable layer and for building the simple wooden sluice
gates – crucial for keeping saltwater away from young plants –
pressed into use.[65] Butler continued to plant a mixture of crops
because it protected him financially from the failure of any one
of them and, because he had so much land, he could experiment. King's 'Statements of Planting' were usually submitted
in January to give Butler a complete picture of the estate's crop
acreage and demography. In the 1803 statement the rice acreage
more than doubled that of cotton while the total number of
enslaved workers stood at 194.75 people, with the children enumerated as adult percentages and concentrated at Tide Island
and Experiment Plantations.

	No. drivers	No. hands	Acr[e]s Rice	Acr[e]s Cotton	Acres Potato	Acres Pease	Acre[s] Corn	Acre[s] Oats
Hampton Plantation No. 1	1	16.75	"	75	5	3	"	3
ditto No. 2	1	17	"	75	5	3	"	3
ditto No. 3	1	32	"	150	10	6	"	6
Experiment No. 5	2	62.5	"	250	"	"	"	"
Tide Island No. 4	3	66.5	179[?]	194	3	"	11	5
Amo Total	8	194.75	1792	744	23	12	11	17

Roswell King's familiarity with compass-and-chain survey was useful, particularly as the low-lying nature of the sea islands presented interesting legal challenges for land purchasers, with his drawing and sketching abilities communicating such problems very effectively to Butler by letter (Fig. 143). When Butler bought Carr's Island in the Altamaha River from Major Lee McIntosh in 1804, McIntosh estimated its size at 700 to 800 acres while Roswell King thought it had an area of 450 acres. It was resurveyed before the sale, 'by land & not by water', and King calculated that this would 'save 50 acres from low water mark'. King nevertheless contracted to buy 300 acres for $3000. If it transpired that the island was bigger than 500 acres McIntosh would receive 10 dollars per acre 'for all surplus over one hundred acres' with a piece of pine land thrown into the bargain. Pine land, which provided timber for the estate's many construction projects, was highly sought after. It was used for piling, in buildings, fences and sluice gates and for making the flat boats that carried goods and people along the estate's growing number of waterways. All land seems to have been sold with pine land attached, much as turbary rights to cut turf were attached automatically to many leases in Ireland.

Tide Island or Butler's Island, was effectively Butler's gold mine. Planted with tracts of both rice and cotton, Butler maintained that concern for the enslaved workers' health had set the crop ratio. He believed cotton to be the healthier crop, while King, who generally chose profit over care, invariably disagreed.[67] The rice was planted in squares and enclosed within a grid of dykes, canals, ditches and sluice gates. The rise and fall of the tide was used to flood the squares of the rice land periodically with fresh water, allowing for the rapid hydration and growth of the young rice plants. The ideal landscape condition of such rice fields was as flat as possible, with a precise standard datum and no mounds, hills or hummocks. If the enslaved workers 'could not flow [flood] the high places' the rice 'came up badly, and what did come up was much [eaten] by the worms'. This was 'strong proof' that any 'high places should be thrown into the creeks which are near at hand' but, as ever in American plantation farming, whether rice, tobacco, indigo, cotton or sugar cane, the price of improving it, or in this case flattening it, had to contend with the mostly cheaper option of just clearing more of it.[68] Many of King's letters document the careful management of the fresh water level within the rice squares. Such geometrical divisions were both sensible and necessary, although the scale of the squares that made up the grid of banks, ditches, dams and canals inspired much design discussion: 'I enclose you a sketch of divisions no. 2 & 3 for your perusal. I am not pleased with the Divisions & still I am fond of small squares' (Figs 144 and 145). When the enslaved driver Morris had finished ditching a new rice square in 1804 King wrote that the job had been 'too heavy' for him. King had 'wished to have it in a proper shape' and consequently had not wanted to make the square smaller, even though this would have made Morris's job more manageable.[69] By 1806 King was proud of the fact that the dykes at Butler's Island had been constructed 'much higher … than other people's' and also 'so much more cut by the water'.[70] This comparatively high datum

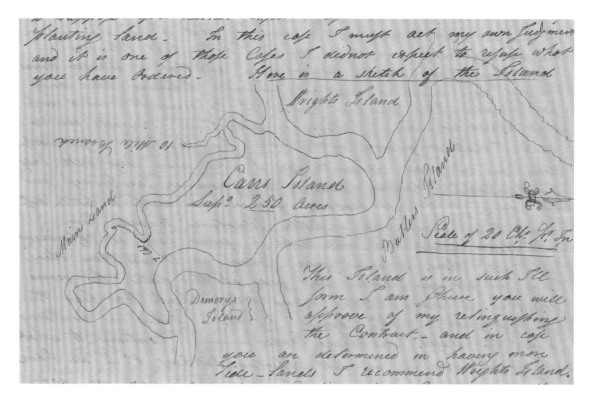

143. Roswell King, drawing of Carr's Island, 1804, from Historical Society of Pennsylvania, Butler Family Papers [1447]. Box 2 Folder 12: Roswell King, Tide Island, to Pierce Butler, 2 June 1804

and small scale of lattice was struck early on in the set out of the rice squares and it was partly an aesthetic decision.

Once divided into squares the land had to be desalinated. This does not appear to have been as onerous a job as it was in Holland or parts of Ireland, where specific crops were carefully rotated to progressively remove excess salt from the soil.[71] On the Butler plantations a rice or cotton crop was planted immediately, with no preceding plants to desalinate the soil, either because such practices would have delayed the plantation's profits or because these crops were considered more salt-tolerant than oats or wheat. Other Irish habits, such as manuring, a matter of almost fanatical principle for many of Ireland's eighteenth-century gentlemen, did die hard. Ireland's land, frequently so stony, acid and wet as to be virtually impossible to grow crops on, was copiously manured – by seaweed, lime, dung or any material that might feasibly improve it, often at a great cost in labour and to little effect.[72] Butler's constant instructions to manure the extremely rich soil of the Altamaha delta's islands (in an environment where land was relatively plentiful and under-exploited) met with obsequious written indulgence and almost utter practical neglect from Roswell King: 'As for manuring land it is of material Consequence

but how to do it to proffit is what I am not fully satisfied with; when you have so much rich Tide lands uncultivated.'[73] Marsh-grass was sometimes allowed to rot into 'dung' and then applied to the new rice squares as manure. Again, if the labour was judged to be more valuably expended elsewhere on the plantation, then this was not done. When it was proposed to bring some 500 or 600 tons of 'excellent manure' to Hampton in 1803, King thought the distance too great to be profitable. If the manure could be procured close to where it was required, then King acknowledged that manured land that had 'never produced well before' could grow 'very excellent Rice far superior' to land that had none.[74] In March 1804 King claimed that it was out of his 'power to manure the Marsh squares' and remarked that if other planters could grow good rice without manure then surely Butler could too.[75] He concluded firmly that he did 'not think manuring on a large scale profitable' and that while it might 'do for a small planter', Butler emphatically was not of that cohort.[76]

Making a rice landscape was back-breaking work and Butler's strongest enslaved workers, presumably male, toiled in the rice plantations.[77] They began by making banks that were sloped for structural stability, as was typical for polder

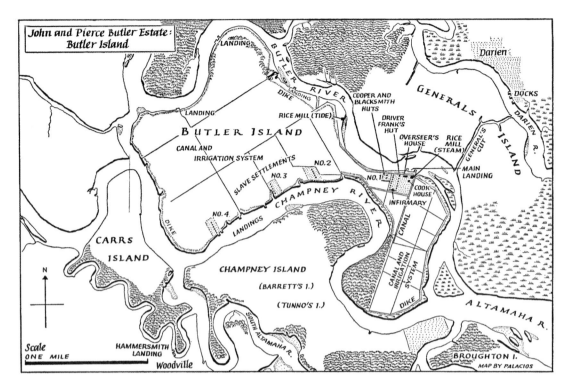

144. Drawing of Butler's Island by Palacios from nineteenth-century plan of Butler's Island, from Fanny Kemble, *Journal of a Residence on a Georgian Plantation in 1838–1839* (Athens: University of Georgia Press, 1984)

145. Butler's Island dykes, canals and ditches. Google Maps, 1 June 2017

landscapes, and with ditches on both sides.[78] As more and more land was reclaimed, requiring more and more embankments, there was 'no end of work' for the ditchers,[79] and Butler and King tried to purchase enslaved workers with experience of such estuarine and tidewater environments. When King informed Butler of the 'rejoicing when they [the enslaved] found they could drink the water out of the River' in 1803, they took this as 'a proof that they' had 'been acquainted with the same soil' in Africa.[80] Rice landscapes required constant oversight, maintenance and regular reconstruction, particularly in the aftermath of the many hurricanes that hit the sea islands every few years. Despite extensive work to Butler's Island in the period 1803–6 they were obliged to take 'very considerable pains' again in 1812, digging another 'ditch all round within, and divid[ing] it into four squares'.[81]

The technique and finish of the ditchers' work, who were all enslaved, inspired substantial comment and not all of it utilitarian. In 1804 King admired how the experienced ditcher Morris had 'done 4360 feet of River Bank & dressed it in a handsome manner'.[82] One of the most renowned American rice plantations is that of Mulberry, South Carolina (Fig. 94). There the approach to the house was by a causeway positioned above low-lying rice fields that stretched away eastwards towards the Cooper River (Fig. 93). Long prospects of water channels enclosing rectangles of rice were framed by the great Virginia oaks of the causeway's avenue, with the oblongs of young green rice shoots providing a pleasing tonal contrast to the dark trees (Fig. 146). Much as the good burghers of late seventeenth-century Holland enjoyed their vistas of dykes and canals, so the planters of the American South enjoyed their controlling geometries and long perspectival lines of water channels and soil embankments, revelling in their precise mastery of level. Citrus trees were planted along such dykes and embankments to strengthen them with their root systems, particularly relevant during high tides or spring floods, while also emphasising the pleasing axial water vistas. All the lemon trees were alive on Butler's Island in 1806 when King planned to send one thousand lemons to Butler's grandchildren in Philadelphia. He wondered if the two dozen oranges he had sent previously 'in Rice chaff' had arrived safely.[83]

146. Photograph of the rice fields of Mulberry Rice Plantation, Moncks Corner. Library of Congress, LC-J7-SC-1523-....03872u.tif

Many practical decisions have an aesthetic dimension and this is sometimes but lightly acknowledged in design history, where it is generally simpler to segregate the useful and the beautiful. Finding the optimum width of bank and ditch was also accomplished through trial and error. When King made a 'very correct' survey of the ditches at Settlement No. 1 in 1806 he found them 'so wide' that the 'loss of land' was about 22 feet, a substantial area when multiplied by their length. 'Cold & sickly to clean out in Winter and very troublesome', the ditches' margins were so narrow that they were 'always subject to break' and cleaning them left the enslaved 'up to their knees in mud' all day. King proposed to make new ditches with '30 foot' margins and requiring a very substantial outlay of labour but Butler would thereby 'save 14 or 15 feet of land, have a handsome margin, a strong bank and a clean ditch'.[84] The extraordinary intensity of ditching work saw King incentivise the enslaved workers by selling them 'meat at a cost of 3 cents per day' that he claimed was 'eas[ily] earned in heaving mud'. Yet ditching and banking continued to be essential for the plantation's success and when 'the prospect of the times' in the aftermath of the war of 1812 was so bad that 'the moving of dirt appear[ed] more perminant than erecting buildings' King carefully computed his complete responsibility for 'more than $400,000 of perrishable prop[er]ty (besides the crop on the ground)'.[85]

Technological expertise was acquired slowly. Whether Butler or King realised that the level of polder land continues to fall after it has been drained, requiring higher and higher dykes to protect it over time, is unclear. King's 1804 observation that generally the banks had 'settled very much', with three 'frames', or squares 'settled beyond calculation' and needing to be 'raised & margins made' suggests some awareness. [86] These margins amounted to a 'very considerable number' of acres, and King identified the design 'question between loss and gain' as one for Butler to judge.[87] Butler preferred the banks to rise straight from the level of the rice fields with small ditches between them, and this involved an overall increase in finished design level. Growing higher and wider over time, when some diverged from 'other banks in proportion', King planned to put 'a tuft of grass all over' them in 1812 for some visual harmony.[88] Although King was 'fearful of the Bermuda grass ruining the margins' it was very valuable for strengthening the banks and the 'great quantity of work' on the settlement bank of No. 1 square in 1812, raising it by 'about 18 inches', saw him

query whether he should continue, considering that 'to make such banks without ditches' was very costly. He agreed with Butler that 'large ditches [did] look very ugly' and wished to please Butler but 'was fearful of laying out any more labour'.[89] Despite the evidence of such aesthetic ambitions at a personal level, the public perception of plantation landscapes as purely economic, practical and mundane creations continued. When Aaron Burr fled to Hampton in 1804, in the aftermath of his duel with Andrew Hamilton, he found that its 'landscape of course, present[ed] no scenes for a painter'.[90]

'Great Works Want Great Power'[91]

As in all new world plantations, technological advances were highly desirable so that crop production could approach a factory-like efficiency. By the late eighteenth century this had been achieved in the sugar works of many Caribbean islands and their technological push for new machinery, together with the connected labour paradigm of gang or shift-work, was gradually transferred to the southern United States. Butler's estate bought in technological expertise when required, invariably doing so for large investments in machinery. Wishing to minimise the manual labour required to separate the rice grains from the chaff, in 1803 the structural foundation for a heavy rice machine was begun. This proved very troublesome as the land, lying low, flooded when it was dug.[92] Mr Sherman, the rice machine expert, advised 'a solid bed of Timber' as the best foundation in swamps. It was preferable to piling, which could fail, even when the timber piles were driven into the ground 'as far as possible' because the 'quicksands' often gave way afterwards. Roswell King's plans invariably differed from any visiting expert's and he preferred piles to raft foundations, advising Butler to spend $1,000 on driving 'down several 100 pine-trees' some 50 feet 'to stand like table-legs to support the whole of the machinery, the Morters as well as the waterworks'. He warned Butler that 'mills and particularly Rice Mills' were 'very apt to fail … for the want of good foundation – for if one corner of the machine sinks or such the whole of the machinery'[93] would soon wear out.

Powerful pumping machines were required to control the rice squares' precise interior water levels and they were also needed for making and strengthening the island's many canals. King imagined a machine that would 'take full 25 Tons of Water per minute … to give all parts full power of motion' and that could 'work with three feet head of water'. A constant head of pressure ensured a canal's consistent water level and some enslaved men became highly expert at making the banks and ditches that controlled the water levels.[94] The driver Morris had never had 'a creek to break' on him in his life and King estimated that 'it would about kill him in his Old age to meet with that misfortune'. It was 'useless to pretend to say that there' was 'anyone more skillful in banking against water than Morris', and King thought it 'justifiable' to 'indulge' him with one plum job, despite the 'detention' Morris had accumulated for disrespectful behaviour, which somewhat undermined King's veneer of respect for Morris's expertise. There were five 'head men' among the enslaved workers – George, Santee, Bram, Morris and Sambo – and King's management policies ensured that they also had to participate in the discipline and punishment actions of the regime: 'Morris is a brave old man has got his people tolerable well at work again, tho he says he cannot git them to pick cotton enough. I told him if coaxing would not work flogging must.'[95]

By 1808 more advanced rice mill technology was required and the rice machine expert Mr Sweeney visited Hampton that August to advise. He found that neither 'the Iron work of the old rice mill' nor the old building in which it was housed would answer, but acknowledged it a 'pity to pull down the Barn & old works' that 'might last this number of years with small repairs'. But the old mill was in the wrong place and the workmen never had 'water enough, on an average through the winter, than to beat [the rice] more than one third of the time'. King disagreed with Butler again and vowed that if the old rice mill was rebuilt, instead of repaired, he would spend half a day writing a letter containing all of his objections. He thought that any new one, if built at all, should be built on Hampton Creek, where there was plenty of water and where it would be a 'proffit and credit' to the country as a whole. Manipulative to the bone, King needled Butler that Mr Sweeney's machine would cost an astronomical $5,000 because of Butler's fondness for 'having everything … a little better than' the neighbours.[96]

King's interest in such industrial and agricultural buildings affected the overall plan of the estate. On plantations where the mansion acted as a true plantation great house it was generally the sun about which the lesser buildings spun. John Michael Vlach has categorised the overall plans of many plan-

tations in his book *Back of the Big House*, particularly the 'block plan' type where the service buildings and slave quarters were placed in close, strictly geometric and spatially subservient relationships to the great house.[97] At Butler's Island the estate's design did not have to respect the position of a great house either spatially or ideologically because there was no grand seat in the manner of a traditional villa or country house landscape. This resulted in the estate's fragmentation, with the separate plantations (Hampton, Butler's/Tide Island, Little St Simon's, Experiment) and their numbered settlements designed to operate as separate entities, each with its own internal logic and without the benefit of a masterplan, such as that employed by George Washington at Mount Vernon and explored in Chapter 2. This splintered estate structure freed King from observing any centralised and aesthetically coherent plan. Because buildings such as the rice machine house could be positioned at their optimum location the landscape was more economically focused and probably more profitable. Some of the more technically complex projects also inspired the use of innovative materials. The long process of piling to find a source of fresh water at Experiment Plantation led to King's 'extraordinary' discovery of a 37-foot-thick stratum of 'sand, stone and shells without hard Earth'.[98] This became tabby – the raw material used to construct many of South Carolina and Georgia's most distinctive coastal vernacular buildings.[99]

Despite Hampton's unimpressive domestic architecture, gardening was still important, if a little mundane. The main house at Hampton had a garden and in June 1804 King's list of garden seeds included spinach, cabbage, carrots, parsnips, beets and onions, lettuce and radishes, and he asked Butler to add 'any other vegetable that' Butler 'might think proper' to grow. By 1808 King was busy trying to make Butler 'a good garden' for his anticipated visit to Georgia,[100] expanding the shopping list to include 'Savoy, early York & Sugar Loaf Cabbage, Marrow fat & Sugar Loaf Pease, Salmon Radish – Carrot – broad and narrow leaf spinage' and 'some good turnip'. Hampton had no recorded orchard, unlike any comparable European estate where it invariably accompanied the kitchen garden, and it is likely that the apple trees Butler sent to his niece Dorothea of Co. Mayo in 1790 originated in New York.[101] The garden was probably enclosed by the estate's ubiquitous timber fences with King convinced that a 'poor fence looks worse on an Estate than even poor Mules & Oxen'.[102] Botanical experimentation took place at a small scale and King probably planted the 'two seeds of Mauritius Cotton' he was sent in 1803 in the sheltered confines of the house garden, where they could be more easily observed than in the wider landscape. Despite planting them 'very carefully' they did not sprout, suggesting that the estate would have benefited from a potting shed or greenhouse.[103] Sometimes neighbouring planters gave them plants or seeds with which to experiment, such as Dr Grant's 'ten bushells of a new kind of large grain'd rice' that King considered his 'duty to plant' in 1807.[104] In 1808 they experimented with the 'Magetha' bean, a black bean favoured by the Kikuyu people of Kenya. Unfortunately, of this effort to provide African foodstuffs, 'not one seed came up', although Butler was asked to procure some more.[105] King had his own garden at Hampton where he grew thirty sugar canes 'from a few hills of rattoon' in 1813. The estate's first foray into sugar production, he later moved them to the main house garden.[106]

Much building activity was generated by the hurricanes that hit the Georgian coastline every few years. The estate was so low-lying and coastal that their tidal surges proved particularly destructive. In 1804 and 1813 the tide rose to '6 feet over the whole of' Butler's Island, as measured 'by marks within the buildings', when it 'carried off every loose article'. The buildings emerged relatively unscathed in 1813 when the water rose 'so very fast' that the banks were 'not so very much broken as in 1804' because they were 'stronger and in places grassy', and Experiment Plantation then had an intriguing 'hurricane house' that 'did not shake' in the storm.[107] If the damage to buildings from the hurricane of September 1813 was bad, 'such a stench' was created by the rotting plant material that it was 'enough to poison the island'. It left King 'quite out of heart' with 'the trouble' he had 'taken, in trees, banks, fences' in order 'to beautify' Butler's 'different places; and now all gone to destruction!'. Not only were the low-lying plantations of Butler's and Experiment Islands affected but also Hampton, where not 'a panel of fence' was left standing. The whole estate looked 'like a ship-[w]reck and, what' was 'more discouraging', the enslaved workers were 'out of heart' at the loss of most of their poultry. King 'tried to reconcile them' to their loss by sending 'to Savannah for a hogshead of Whiskey to help keep their spirits up'.[108]

When searching out the most innovative plantation management, farming and industrial practices Butler and King looked to the West Indies and more specifically Jamaica for inspiration. As the British empire's most financially successful colony for most of the eighteenth century, Jamaica's agriculture had generated extraordinary amounts of money for its planter class, and by extension the British state. It became the model for other Anglosphere planter societies while Saint-Domingue, now Haiti, occupied a similar position in the French empire until its revolution of 1791. Many Caribbean islands had been extensively colonised, improved and landscaped well before the American South, and this gave them more advanced expertise in many areas, particularly medicine, which was very important for maintaining the health and value of the enslaved, with West Indian doctors acknowledged to know 'more of the nature' of medicine in a hot climate than others.[109] Pierce Butler was aware that Jamaica's fortunes were founded on the total violation of the enslaved workers' freedom and other rights, compounded by the extraordinary violence and repression required to keep some 90 per cent of that island's population by the mid-eighteenth century in servitude.[110] Mr Richards, a 'very intelligent, though not the most polished' acquaintance, was described by Butler as 'a West Indian, yet a friend to the rights of man', suggesting prevailing perceptions of West Indian planters as uncivilised, boorish and repressive.[111] Such a reputation was undesirable, and King preferred for Butler to be 'cheated out of a little work' than for King and the estate to acquire 'the name of Cruel & Unjust'.[112] Whether such reputational concern was directed towards fellow planters, society as a whole, or a local audience (that might affect the hiring of additional slaves from neighbouring plantations) is difficult to discern. Other letters were more ambiguous as to Jamaica's reputation, particularly any excessive expenditure on the enslaved workers' comfort. When King bought blankets for the enslaved workers in 1813 Butler estimated that such expenditure 'could have reasonably been done without', leading King to accuse Butler of thinking that he was trying to 'make a Jamaica estate' of Butler's plantations.[113]

The war of 1812 blockaded many Caribbean and American ports, leading to a rise in the value of tropical commodities throughout the Atlantic world. Any plantation with the soil and climate to grow sugar began to consider it seriously as a potential crop, if the Haitian revolution and subsequent economic collapse had not inspired them to enter the market earlier. Roswell King was converted to sugar well before Pierce Butler. His enthusiasm began in 1812, when he estimated that they could 'make from 3 to 4 puncheons of Rum per Acre', of a quality 'equal to Jamaica' and 'superior' in profit to anything else they could grow. By November 1812 many Georgian planters were busy experimenting with the 'various ways of planting sugar cane', and when King heard of the Philadelphia publication of Bryan Higgins's 1812 *Treatise for the Improvement of the Manufactory of Muscovado Sugar and Rum In Jamaica*' he asked Butler to buy it at 'the first convenient opportunity'.[114] Learning fast, he wrote to Butler that those planters who had 'planted on the Jamaica plan' had 'failed in a great measure' because they could not believe that 'the cold sand of Georgia, was equal to the rich clay of Jamaica'.[115] The general upheaval of wartime created an appetite for change, with King acknowledging that although 'it appear[ed] to be idle business to talk of Improving these times' he nevertheless thought it 'correct to study and act, as if we were to live forever, or die tomorrow'.[116]

In the early decades of the nineteenth century Jamaica was replaced as a model plantation environment by interstate competition closer to home. When a New Orleans planter wrote to Butler that planters in the United States lacked 'experience and workmen for the very many different branches' of sugar production, King interpreted the letter rather differently. Although most of the 'observations' were 'very correct', King claimed that its author's motive was to discourage Butler from entering the market, writing, 'Georgia planters can outdo New Orleans planters in sugar making. It is true we make the best cotton <u>and we can make the best Sugar.</u>'[117] Despite King's efforts, Butler continued to be 'much opposed to sugar making', perhaps because of its notoriously cruel labour practices, although this is not entirely clear from the correspondence. The steady trickle of negative reports on the habits and labour practices of the British West Indian plantocracy, when combined with the copious anti-slavery literature emanating from the London printing presses, probably had an effect on one as inclined as Butler to preserve his European identity and to purchase English books, pamphlets and newspapers. King did not deny that sugar making was 'hard work; but Negroes' were 'very fond of the work' and his manipulative logic argued that 'on the score of humanity' it was better to give 'the Negro his choice of work'. Plenty of molasses were also hailed as 'a blessed thing for their children'.[118] Despite such specious arguments, and the perennial cry of sugar's extraordinary returns, King did not manage to convince his master.

Managing enslaved workers was very different from managing tenants. The most disagreeable part of an Irish estate agent's job was ejecting tenants for not paying their rent, not disciplining the enslaved. Although bigotry arguably coloured relations between the Irish and the English in eighteenth-century Ireland, it pales when compared with the naked disrespect for slaves' lives, persons and families that runs through Roswell King's and Pierce Butler's letters. Although King's letters offer a less mediated and more damning picture of the plantation's design mentality, Butler is complicit despite his absence, or even more so. He received and read the letters, answered them and evidently approved of much of what King did. He funded the workings of the plantation, made all the most important decisions and benefited by far the most financially. Despite the imbalanced record of the correspondence, with many more of King's letters surviving than Butler's, the evidence does indicate that Butler remained uncomfortable with King's more overt racism, although this appears to have declined as Butler became progressively more integrated into American society, as the next chapter will explore. His close attention to Irish politics, together with the latent sensitivity to racial slurs that most Anglo-Irish gentlemen possessed, inclined him to suppress or conceal his collusion with the racism that underpinned slavery. His letters reveal a consistent discomfort with slavery and its consequences for estate management and this discomfort must have encouraged his absenteeism. King was 'doubtfull' that Butler would visit in 1806 'to see the deranged affairs'[119] on his estate and when 'truly sorry to hear' that Butler's health would 'not admit' of his visiting that autumn, it was with a slight sense of resignation.[120] Although King had 'no doubt' that Butler and his children 'wish[ed] to expend as little' in Georgia 'as possible' in 1808, he had to recommend some modicum of expenditure on the estate and some oversight by its owner.[121] Advising 'nothing better' in 1809 for Butler's 'health & comfort than to leave Philadelphia early in October for' Hampton, he recommended that Butler take his time 'and travel l[eisure]ly and return in April the same way'.[122]

Butler's steady purchasing of new enslaved workers together with their natural increase saw the estate's population leap to an estimated total of 417 hands, or working adult labourers, by 1811. Roswell King sent a 'List of Negroes' to accompany the 'Statement of Planting' that he sent to Butler every January, enumerating the enslaved workers by age. If the columns for those aged under 10 and over 60 are included (and most of these people worked in various capacities) there were 632 enslaved people on the estate in 1811.

	under 10	10 to 20	20 to 45	45 to 60	over 60	amt Total
Hampton No. 1	23	27	19	9	10	88
Hampton No 2	17	8	16	5	8	54
Hampton No. 4	31	30	24	3	5	93
St. Simons	3	2	11	1	–	17
Experiment	32	13	27	–	5	77
Butlers Island No. 1	17	13	32	8	2	72
" " No. 2	21	16	31	7	3	78
" " No. 3	14	10	27	4	5	60
" " No. 4	17	8	22	1	1	49
Mechanicks	–	12	27	4	1	44
	------	------	------	------	------	------
	175	139	236	42	40	632

The estate preferred to buy and enslave those who knew 'nothing of trade' and who were 'not acquainted with Town-tricks'. When they bought some of the neighbouring Profford estate's enslaved workers in 1811, and not the 'rice field Negroes' they really needed, their urban innocence was thought to compensate 'for their not knowing Rice from Grass'.[124] As a manager, King was aware that the enslaved workers were often far more highly expert than the men who 'owned' or commanded them. If Butler wanted him 'to be accountable for the work' of building the rice machine, he would 'not hire a white man' but would trust the enslaved worker 'York to lay the foundation'. The irony of his assessment and the upside-down hierarchy that it exposed escaped him: 'If I am to have a man under me give me one I can control, no master workman will suffer one to dictate that is no workman.'[125]

Roswell King was an employee, not a planter in his own right, although he subsequently became one. This lends some of his correspondence a fawning tone, which would in the Irish language be called *plámás* – an obsequious and ingratiating deference that is also somewhat duplicitous.[126] In 1804 his ambitions were 'to know how to plant more Rice & Cotton to the hand; Beat the Rice better; put double or threefold the labour in moating Cotton, than any other person and all other things in rotation'. Such early letters tried to give Butler proof of his suitability for the job and were peppered with such aphorisms as 'No good can arise to the Owner, from the Manager & Overseer or Drivers, working one against the other'. He sought to convince Butler that the principal drivers always paid King 'due Respect' as did all Butler's 'People', a euphemism for his enslaved workers.[127] A plantation's economic success lay in the rigorous management and often violent control of its enslaved workforce, and King constantly reassured Butler of his ability to do this: 'You may rest contented your negroes never behaved more orderly nor so well to me as they do this year.'[128] As Butler's absenteeism became more entrenched, King's tone became less fawning and his writing more open, and as his job security increased over time he slowly revealed his own character and preferences. A man who pushed for change in all areas of estate management and much harder than Butler ever did, by 1809 King accused Butler 'as regards the improvements of' the estate of having 'always cramped' his ambitions.[129]

Harvest times were periods of peak labour when 'one single day's extraordinary exertion' from the enslaved workforce could optimise the harvest's yield, while also reducing the risk of storms or drought. King adopted a carrot-and-stick approach to obtaining an increased work rate. During the rice harvest of July 1806 he asked Butler for 'something to heat the People' advising that '100 dollars spent on rum & pork' would save Butler 500 dollars. He also gave the enslaved workers a 'good talk some severe, and a little whipping' which led the 22 women and 18 men 'to thrash in a tolerable manner in two days' 1,500 bushels of rice, at an average individual rate of 19 bushels a day. Nevertheless, he was 'not satisfied' with the 'most able & stoutest men' who were 'not in good temper'. He suspected the enslaved driver Sambo of sowing dissent among the enslaved workforce but because it was 'so difficult to find out the ground work of difficulty among Negroes' he was 'very cautious' about how to proceed. The estate's enslaved drivers, like Sambo, were in positions of substantial power, and the violence that King habitually employed to drive up work rates also trickled downwards.[130] When Sambo, drunk on bribes of rum, was thought to have whipped several of the 'prime men' in 1806, King threatened that he would 'pay for it' if it was true.[131] These are complex, horrible letters, that reveal the twisted and layered rationales of power that were common to all such landscapes of slavery, violence and subjection.

Butler continued to try to convince himself that he was a good planter with a benevolent concern for his 'people'. This belief was easier to uphold when he did not have to do the onerous and debased managing and disciplinary actions himself. He could maintain a façade of benevolence and care from Philadelphia while his employees carried out the 'necessary' management duties far away in the South. Such was Butler's identification with benevolence in the early years that King was 'fearful' of giving Butler any 'information that tend[ed] to the Discredit' of the enslaved with Butler 'hardly willing to believe or hear anything against them'. In Philadelphia Butler could enjoy 'so high an opinion of' his workforce that anyone who said 'aught against them' was thought to do so 'in anger'. With the confidence of one in situ, King maintained that it would be 'a valuable fund' of knowledge for Butler to know the enslaved workers as well as King, who had made it his 'sole and whole study to manage' them. Yet even if King did conceal from Butler some of the everyday cruelty of the plantation system, the many written accounts of its punitive and common-place violence could not have left Butler innocent of what was being carried out in his name and for his benefit.[132] Complicity must attach to such aphorisms as 'After a Negroe is 50 years of age he is not worth the Expence of Cutting off a Leg particularly against his will',[133] or statements like 'Be assured Bram [the driver] is not neglected, I should not have valued him at $3000 and then neglect him'.[134] The absentee mentality of 'out of sight, out of mind' must have failed, when the weekly letters prove the extent of Butler's knowledge.

Over time King appears to have partially moved towards managing the enslaved workforce with a food barter system rather than one of violence. Whether he presented this seeming greater humanity to his master as a benevolent façade is not easy to discern but it seems of a piece with his growing commercial interests and the likely societal pressure to abandon whipping in favour of extra food and medical care, particularly for the enslaved women and children. The scale of Butler's operation in both land and enslaved workers allowed him to allocate workers to specific areas according to their physical strength. When the 'number of weakly Negroes' that were 'not fit to thrash' rice was high, it was 'as well to plant part cotton'. Weaker people were generally transferred from the rice to the cotton plantations, particularly during the hoeing and picking periods of the crop cycle. In 1811 King was about to 'bring down a number of the most useless women from T[ide] Island'[135] to Hampton where he would put 'all the ablest' clearing land while 'the balance' would 'put the settlements in order and sort cotton'. Butler worried that the slaves were left idling in those periods of the year when there was little to do except wait for the next crop to mature and in 1812 this led King to reassure him that the enslaved were 'beginning to put water on' the rice they had just finished hoeing on Butler's Island and to warn Butler, who had evidently been complaining, that only when they were finished with this task could they be described as 'out of work'.[136] Although it continued to be easier for Butler to claim the advantage in benevolence, on occasion King proved to be the softer of the two, as in the case of blanket purchasing described above. His 'singular and uncommon way of managing' the enslaved workers was to give them 'many comforts other people do not' and this ensured that when he 'wanted them' he could 'find them, and they work[ed] as if it was for themselves'.[137] King summarised their two approaches in 1813:

> I am apt to think we both give ourselves trouble owing to the principles of economy, and quantity of work should be done, you calculate closely. I consent to try to do more than is in my power you fret that all calculations are not fulfilled; I fret that I cannot fulfil your wishes, and so I suppose we shall both make ourselves miserable as long as we live.[138]

The two men were highly competitive and compared the estate constantly with those of their neighbours. In 1813 King postured that he 'would not own a planting interest' and keep it in 'the state most planters keep their Plantations'. If the Butler plantations 'were in no better order than Grant's Major Woods and many others' of their neighbours, King would 'feel humbled', evidently not a good thing. Butler 'would be exceedingly mortified' at being on par with such neighbours as he had 'always evidenced a pride in having things in the best order'. A planter's success, or the lack of it, was closely identified with his character, and when their neighbour Mr Baillie 'the unfortunate man' had 'a sorry crop; hardly enough to feed and clothe his Negroes' this was because Baillie's 'ill mind' had led to such 'ill luck'.[139] Writing of their own relationship, Butler judged that King did him 'ample justice' given that he could 'never relinquish the right of directing and controlling' and proclaimed himself 'entirely satisfied' with King's share of the estate's 'management'. He managed to congratulate them

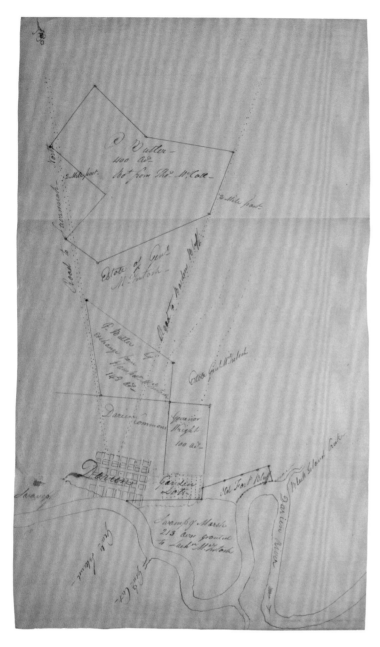

147. Plan of Darien, Georgia, c.1800. Historical Society of Pennsylvania, Butler Plantation Papers, Butler Family Papers [1447]. Box 10 Folder 23

both: 'you enter thoroughly, and with good judgement into my views; and no man of my knowledge more capable of executing them'.[140] In 1813 they were thoroughly delighted with each other, a situation the ongoing war would soon crack. Although King was 'doubly gratified to think' that Butler was 'pleased with the order & repute' of his rice crop and promised to do his 'best to keep the good name it ha[d] got', he still warned Butler of the essential difference between owner and employer. While Butler had 'two views in it – the name of being a great planter and a correct planter', King had 'but one which [was] to be correct'.[141] As the war progressed the estate manager's many roles began to take their toll and King found it impossible to 'conduct so many branches correctly': 'I can build you a Rice mill. I can build you a Chip. I can build you a House. I can be your factor. I can be your planter, and many other things; but if you depend on me for all those things, you must expect that some will be found wanting'.[142]

The war also threatened to upset the South's delicate balance. Standing on the knife-edge of entrenched, and yet unstable, racism, its whirling subcurrents of liberty saw King acknowledge in writing that the enslaved were more than capable of freedom. Whilst flattering Butler 'that no negroes like their master better than yours like you', he nevertheless knew that Butler's many enslaved people would sell them both 'cheap, if they had a good chance'. Undermining the racist opinions he had consistently held about the enslaved people's alleged preference for manual labour, and overall intelligence,[143] he acknowledged in 1813 that their 'smartness' was 'sufficient to convince us both [that] they would a number of them rather manage for themselves'. The adjacency of war led to other thoughts of a strangely unconscious equality that must have reminded Butler, a one-time British officer, of other times and places: 'You have experience of war with the <u>savage British</u> – I have seen 7000 Black troops at their exercise in a line! and smart fellows they were.'[144]

If enslavement profoundly affected the design of Georgia's plantations or landed estates, how did it affect the larger scale of the countryside and specifically the position and form of urban settlements? As James Ackerman has explored, colonial villa and plantation landscapes 'in un-urbanized territories often spawned towns, reversing the normal dependence of the villa on the city' and 'these were not the great metropolitan centres that grew up as administrative centres but more modest market towns'.[145] The town of Darien, Georgia, originally named New

Inverness, had been laid out in the early eighteenth century by Scottish colonists. Located at the mouth of the Altamaha River, as the rice plantations that surrounded it developed and grew, so did the town. The Butler manuscripts document Darien's various functions – as a market town, an administrative centre and a place where news and information of the surrounding countryside and from further afield could be obtained. The United States postal service ran from Darien, and the estate bought many commodities there, although large volumes of corn, timber and iron were generally bought in Philadelphia or New York. Butler, like many great planters, always speculated in land, and he bought up many tracts that had once belonged to Darien's founding McIntosh family (Fig. 147). The local road commissioners met in Darien, and Butler, despite his Irish experience of local gentlemen funding road construction, was heavily fined for refusing to contribute his share of enslaved labour for building the new road from Darien to Barrington, probably because he did not own land in that direction.[146] On 17 September 1808 the local planters Spalding, Hopkins and Gignilliar, the 'Commissioners for Barrington Road', met at Darien and decreed that Butler should pay $6 for each of his absent forty-six enslaved workers, a cumulative fine of $276.[147]

Towns provided enslaved people with opportunities to sell their own work or produce, or the estate's pilfered crops. These were illegal activities and a Major Hopkins, a neighbouring planter, informed on the Butler's Island slaves, who 'had more to sell' in the market in Darien 'than any Negroes he ever knew' in 1806 and whose marketeering 'mostly supported Darien in Corn'. King presumed that the enslaved had had 'recourse to the Corn House key'[148] and had stolen the estate's own produce. Tradesmen were legally prohibited from either selling to enslaved people or buying from them. In 1808 King attended a prosecution against Darien's traders 'for dealing with Negroes',[149] where a coalition of planters brought proceedings against fifteen traders, fining them $30 each. Despite approving of the exclusion of the vast majority of the population from trading in the town, a strategy that contradicts all principles of urban economic expansion and success, and which sharply diverges from European, British and Irish principles of urban improvement, in 1810 King still believed that the 'great number of Boats building' in Darien would make it 'a great place of Trade' in the future (Fig. 148).[150]

Towns also had defensive uses and in 1815, during the British navy's blockade of the American coastline, one local planter decided to move his family from a sea island to Darien for safety. Roswell King's wife Catherine wrote that her husband would never think of moving to town and she considered some parts of Hampton Island much safer than Darien, particularly its main house.[151] Towns were also developed to increase the value of land that might one day become suburban. King found it irrelevant for Butler to wonder what price he might achieve for part of Hampton in 1818. If Butler would 'only establish a Village' it would soon make the 'other lands valuable but it want[ed] beginning'.[152] Never only a plantation manager, in 1818 King mused poetically that 'prices of property rise and fall and shift their course like rivers'. If Butler could 'find out what course' and direction 'the City of Philadelphia's development was likely to follow', he estimated that property there would rise 500 per cent in value before Butler's estate in Georgia rose 50 per cent. In all Butler's time spent planting in Georgia he 'could have purchased in Philadelphia for $300,000 what would now sell for $3,000,000'.[153]

Ireland was no stranger to the foundation of towns with little hope of success. Mostly established during the great wave of eighteenth-century improvement in Ireland, many estate towns such as Dromana, Co. Waterford, Heywood, Co. Westmeath or Strokestown, Co. Roscommon, never achieved the demographic size and economic impact that their design had intended.[154] Strokestown's unconvincing urbanity was dependent on its great house for both its origin and any possibility of growth and it remains today much as it was laid out, a thin, one-house deep town of overblown ambition and little trade (Fig. 149). Darien, despite his interests in its surrounding territory, and the necessary facilities its markets and quays provided to all planters, did not inspire much civic feeling in Pierce Butler. As an absentee he had little need to shop or socialise in Darien himself, and the many buildings that Irish landlords would have been obliged to fund and build in Ireland, such as churches and other community buildings, were actively discouraged in such plantation environments. In 1804 King plotted 'to break up so much preaching' as there was on the estate, with some 'Negroes dy[ing] for the Love of God & some through the fear of him'. Thinking that dancing would 'give the negroes a better appetite for sleep than preaching', he asked Butler to buy 'a full dozen of Fiddles' costing 'from one to two dollars cash' each.[155] In the aftermath of the hurricane of 1804, when preaching was again increasing on the estate, another 'half dozen' fiddles were ordered from Philadelphia.[156]

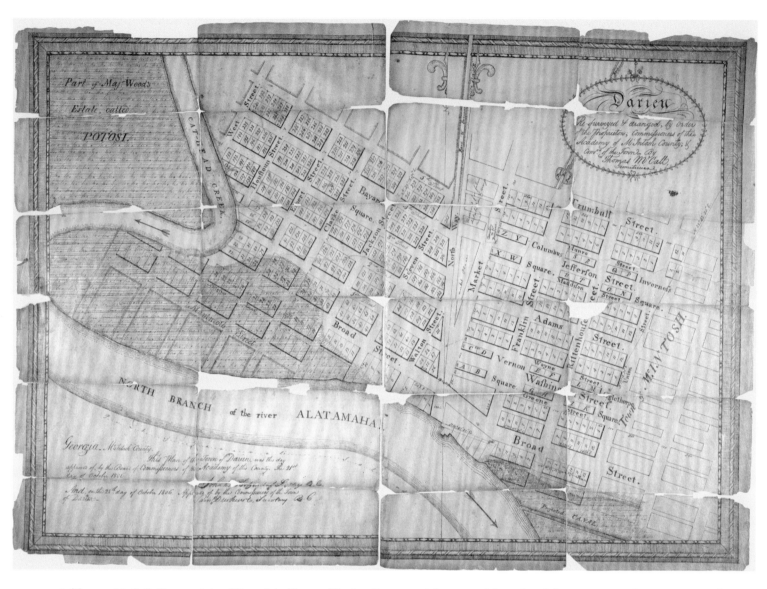

148. Thomas McCall, Geometrician, 'Plan of the Town of Darien. Resurveyed & arranged, by order of the proprietors; Commissioners of the Academy of McIntosh County; & Comrs. of the Town', 1806. Courtesy Georgia Archives, Historic Map File Collection hmf0045

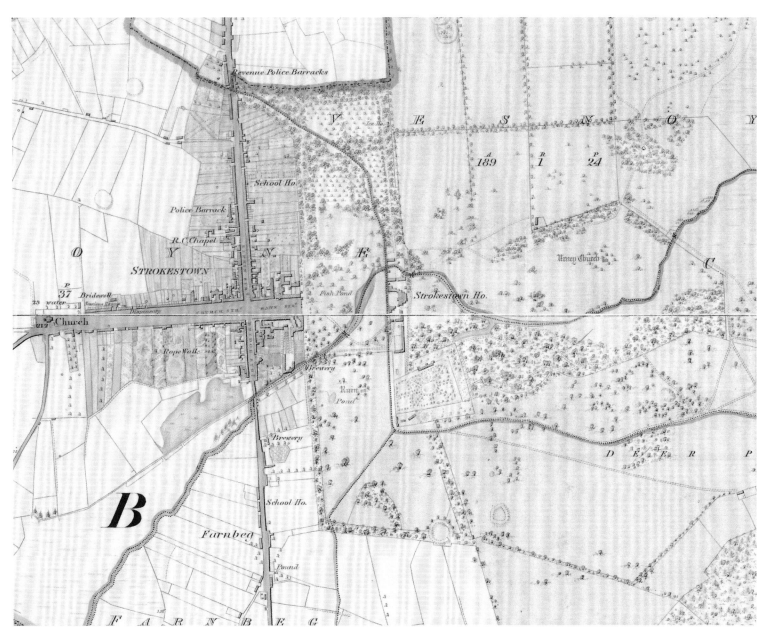

149. Strokestown House, town & demesne, house constructed *c*.1690, modified by Richard Castle 1730. First edition OS map of Co. Roscommon, Sheets 23 and 29, Scale 1:10,560, surveyed 1837, printed 1838. Reproduced courtesy Trinity College Dublin

If religion was regarded as a threat to the estate, there was little likelihood of church-building nor of the many buildings, such as schools or community halls, that followed a church's construction.

Butler's landscapes were complex pieces of design – fluid in their motives, origins, uses, vocabularies and authorships. They were profoundly trilingual, with each agent in the design process – master, manager and the enslaved, electing to describe and read the landscape according to their own experience and perception of its structure, hierarchy and purpose. Plantation design was concerned sometimes with aesthetic issues but mostly with purely economic profit. Whereas some decisions were made ethically, founded in the eighteenth-century idea of improvement and benevolence as eventually, if not essentially, good for all members of society, most decisions were made according to the exploitative and demeaning values of chattel slavery, which corrupted all who came in contact with it. Every design decision in the polder islands of the Altamaha River delta of Georgia derived from the original grid of ditches, canals, dykes and carefully controlled water levels that Pierce Butler laid out and modified from 1794 to 1822, with the substantial assistance and interference of his agent Roswell King. A ditch does not exist in isolation. It is part of a complex lattice of interventions that turns one environment into a more productive and economically profitable one. The design of a ditch is invariably affected by anticipated water volume, its identity as a legal boundary line or field division, and the technological expertise, whether vernacular or professionally acquired, of those making it. Where the water went was key, and a building's level revealed much about its status, material, occupants and construction sequence. Buildings frequently came last in the order of priorities for highly exploitative, industrial and absentee landscapes because although their destruction could be unfortunate it was not catastrophic, unlike the failure of a dyke. Technological ingenuity and focus fell on the construction of the landscape – and the various machines used to process the crops. These are the highly designed entities – more than the buildings that sat on top – and landscape took precedence over architecture, because that

is where the most money was spent and made. Butler's Island of 1,792 acres, now covered again with swamp and scrub (Fig. 145), was the scene of an extraordinary design transformation in the 1790s, when the high price achieved by long-fibre sea island cotton on the Liverpool and London stock exchanges saw one of Georgia's greatest fortunes derived from a small Altamaha delta island. There the architecture was vernacular, but the landscape was emphatically not.

Some of what may be considered to define plantation landscape – the military and exploitative mentality required to re-organise land into a productive machine – was somewhat familiar in Ireland. There too, land had been surveyed by the military, portioned out into long rectangular plots and efficiently re-organised for profit. The local inhabitants were conceived (if not converted) as cogs in a machine, and the protective concepts of a yeoman farmer, common land, entailment and secure leasehold roughly prohibited for those who had been dispossessed, mostly Catholic and (frequently but not always) native. The concept of 'improvement', whereby Ireland was not redistributed but 'improved', could serve to salve an Irish conscience abroad, where the many greater evils of matrilineal chattel slavery were all too evident. Pierce Butler's easy transfer of the enslaved from one plantation to another and from South Carolina to Georgia, in violation of their legal entailment to defined landholdings, shares a similar insouciance with the vast transfers of property and people that were a feature of seventeenth-century Ireland. The legal contortions demanded by the Irish penal laws and their legacy of complex and concealed leases, mortgages and other economic devices served the Butler, Carroll and other Irish-American slave-owning families very well in Pennsylvania, Maryland, South Carolina and Georgia. In a more material way, canals, ditches and sluicegates, descended from those of Carlow, Dublin and Amsterdam, appeared both in the sea islands of Georgia and the tobacco fields of Virginia. Butler's landscapes were also emphatically republican and revolutionary, twisting political concepts of freedom to commercial and capitalist ends, and it is these contradictions that the following chapter will explore.

CHAPTER 6

In Absentia, Arcadia?

Absentee Landscapes in Ireland

This chapter sets out to explore the design impact of absenteeism. Very prevalent throughout the Caribbean by the mid-eighteenth century, absenteeism was then also increasing among landlords in Ireland, a consequence partly of great magnate families, such as the Petty-Fitzmaurices, Earls of Kerry, choosing to live permanently at their principal seats, almost invariably located in England. Absenteeism from a local or regional environment was not unusual – more a common condition for the aristocracy and gentry of Great Britain and Ireland in the eighteenth century, when preserving a family's power and influence often demanded lengthy periods of attendance at court or in the capital. Mostly in possession of more than one residence, wealthy men and women were typically peripatetic, moving from one seat to another, from court to countryside and from one country to another. They switched environments as the seasons changed, to enjoy more varied society, to grasp opportunities for advancement and taste the delights of travel, tourism and change, in and of itself. But absenteeism at an international scale was unusual in western Europe and the absence of owners on the ground led to a decline in such positive aristocratic values as benevolence or the duty of care to one's dependants and wider local community. 'The landlord, at such a great distance' was 'out of the way of all complaints, or, which is the same thing, of examining into and remedying evils; miseries of which he can see nothing, and probably hear as little of, can make no impression.'[1] At the larger international scale, absenteeism was a natural consequence of imperialism, that had created a global hierarchy of countries, nationalities, residences and identities. It required representatives from the imperial core to rule over the conquered territories, and these men were typically dispatched from the imperial heartland, if they could be convinced to go.

Arthur Young was agitated by Irish absenteeism, while acknowledging that 'very few countries in the world' did not experience 'the disadvantage of remitting a part of their rents to landlords who reside elsewhere; and it must ever be so while there is any liberty left to mankind of living where they please'. Estimating that Ireland had more absentees 'proportional to the territory'[2] than elsewhere, Young claimed another disadvantage for Ireland in the lack of free trade with England which meant that returning absentee money was effectively taxed, encouraging residency in London or England. Young made his claim for Ireland's exceptionalism more convincing by compiling his own list of absentees for his *Tour in Ireland, 1776–1779*. Calculating how many thousands of pounds each absentee had lost the Irish economy, he compiled his data from interviews with resident landowners, computing an overall annual national loss of £732,200. Acknowledging the likelihood of some mistakes in his calculations, he argued that absenteeism was 'not the simple amount of the rental being remitted into another country, but the damp on all sorts of improvements'.[3]

Absenteeism was also a consequence of modernity, as the streams of income that enabled great patrician lifestyles became ever more divorced from the real sources of their wealth, and the advantages of concealing such wealth more apparent. Some countries, notably Holland, had managed to diversify almost entirely into funding or insuring the Atlantic triangular trade through complex financial instruments, with many families successfully disassociating themselves from any visible complicity by the 1700s. Ireland was a particularly transnational place in the early eighteenth century when many of its great families, their Irish nationalism muted by seventeenth-century events, developed pronounced transnational identities. Migrant flows between France and Ireland were substantial and reciprocal during the period 1640–1700, when as Tom Truxes writes, 'protestants and catholics alike, to a degree unparalleled for other ports in the British Isles, moved regularly between the two countries'.[4] Such families often had good reason to leave home for patronage, trade and networking opportunities and, for Catholics, more accommodating religious, political and economic environments. Irish ports continued to benefit from long-established connections to Caribbean and American ports, plantations and extended family networks throughout the eighteenth century, a period when Irish men also profited from their mutable identity in European courts. Presumed to be disloyal to Great Britain by virtue of their Catholicism, they took up powerful positions in all the European empires. Often forced to emigrate by the Cromwellian upheavals of the mid-seventeenth century, or by the Glorious Revolution of 1688, such Irish émigré families were trans-imperial in their outlook and operations[5] and Ireland, although much closer to the global centres of political power than any part of the Americas, was similarly affected by an intervening area of sea. This maritime space created a delay between decisions, whether design or political, and their enactment. Dublin, despite its size and significance in the eighteenth century, still had to await the final passing of its parliamentary bills in London, where legislation was eventually passed into law and where the final courts of appeal were situated. This time interval gave Ireland and the Americas similar governance problems – how to manage countries, estates and people at a distance and across an interstitial maritime space.

Although absenteeism from one's locality was prevalent among the elite classes of Great Britain, absenteeism from one's home country was less common, and its incidence in Ireland was consistently higher than in England, Scotland or Wales.[6] It was more generally prevalent where landowners were required to carry out unpleasant activities or adopt problematic identities, and these were a feature of colonial and plantation environments. Many British plantation owners, once their fortunes had been made, aspired to return home while in the French empire, 'three out of four white people who settled in the colonies returned to France'.[7] Irish absentees, unlike their French or British Caribbean counterparts, did not necessarily regard moving back to Europe as their ultimate goal, with home ground often poorer than any new environment and difficult to mythologise as a distant Eden. Absenteeism with a few removes, such as those made by Pierce Butler, who moved from Ireland to South Carolina to Georgia to Philadelphia, was common with many such Irish transatlantic gentlemen moving between multiple locations of varying religious and political hues, often abandoning traditional markers of identity in their new environments. John Black, an Ulster slave-owner of Trinidad, preferred to be ruled by a British administration, but his complaint in one letter that he had 'no desire to be a Spaniard again'[8] suggested many identities, lightly made and easily discarded. Nor was his Irish Protestant identity impervious to alteration – he was 'almost indifferent' as to whether his daughter became 'Protestant or Romish', whilst being educated in Belfast.[9]

Pierce Butler, once an Irish gentleman, then a British military officer, followed by stints as an American revolutionary, senator of the state of Georgia and a successful plantation owner, had no difficulty with claiming to be either Irish, British or American, or all three at once. It often suited such men not to have a national identity, appropriating bits and pieces of other nations when and if required. His high quotient of absenteeism created a conflicted, cosmopolitan and transnational identity that led him to design landscapes of substantial contradiction. Landscapes created by men or women of such mutable national identity contradict established narratives of landscape design and their neat opposition of national styles, particular the opposition of French, English and Dutch styles of landscaping over the course of the eighteenth century. These are mostly predicated on the stylistic analysis of royal or aristocratic gardens, where landscape design and national loyalty are perfectly synchronous.[10] Not only do Butler's landscapes exhibit an almost total insouciance for national classifications, but they also contradict landscape history's preferred neat opposition of utility and beauty. This occurs when a plantation's productive landscape, stretching from the house kitchen garden to the industrial monoculture of the rice squares, becomes wholly interwoven with such design features as avenues, dressed inclines, and abstract geometric and proportional concerns. Design decisions in such plantation landscapes are also concerned to increase the productivity of plants and people, to advance an estate's technological prowess and to improve the management of the enslaved. Butler's extensive correspondence with estate managers George Valley, William Page and Roswell King (father and son) allow his Georgian landscapes to be compared with Irish absentee landscapes of the second half of the eighteenth century, some of which are equally well documented, and although American historians have long researched Butler's life and letters, the full logic of their absentee mentality and design, and their strange connection to radical Irish eighteenth-century politics, has not been hitherto explored.[11]

How does absenteeism affect landscape design? Very often absentees had a very imperfect understanding of what their landed property was like in reality and an incomplete or incorrect knowledge of its geographical structure, climate, flora, fauna, occupants, constraints, risks and patterns of use and management, and this could profoundly affect its design over time. When the owner was replaced on the ground by an agent, attorney, family member or neighbouring landowner this impacted the decision-making process. Who was designing the landscape and for what purpose? Was it for economic gain, for visual beauty, for a rich experience or for a quiet life? The delayed transmission of design decisions often led to mistranslations – where the design intention was imperfectly conveyed to those charged with carrying it out.[12] Mostly communicated on paper in stages, the projects were often not logically sequential, and strange disjunctions between paper and completed projects occurred.

The absentee mentality was particularly evident in the developments promoted and rejected by the Fitzwilliam family in the period 1730–1800 in Dublin, where their estate of 2,700[13] acres stretched from Merrion Square in Dublin's city centre to Bray, Co. Wicklow. Resident in London from the 1720s, the family exhibited little interest in any Irish project that might foreground social or community values as distinct from purely financial ones. Free of any obligation to build and maintain a great seat in Ireland, successive Viscounts Fitzwilliam ruled at one remove through their agents, benefiting from the anonymity provided by the intervening sea. The stream of drawings and letters that crisscrossed the Irish sea kept them informed of their Dublin developments and remains invaluable for constructing an absentee's mentality and its spatial consequences.

It reveals how they managed to conceal the extraordinary extent and reach of the estate from tenants, developers and other interested observers in Dublin by embracing ambiguity – of size, scale, religious identity and intention. Designs for villas, townhouses and churches that explicitly expressed and revealed their own or the wider Irish social and religious hierarchy were frowned upon. This created a disconnected landscape with patterns of ownership, management and confession, when translated into walls, fields and houses, that were difficult to read and interpret.[14] This was what its owners intended. In a city and country where Protestantism represented the establishment position any clear expression of the estate's spatial reach could make the Fitzwilliam family's cultural, political and religious position legible, and was to be avoided.

For Fitzwilliam's agent in Dublin, Richard Mathew, there was 'no doubting' the 6th Viscount's attachment 'to Liberty and Equality', a strangely revolutionary phrase to employ in 1749. His attachment had led him to 'employ Popish Agents, and abominate Confinement, in any sort'.[15] Convert and most probably closet Catholics, the Viscounts Fitzwilliam concealed their religion from society and most particularly from the Dublin authorities. Their removal to London had helped them avoid Dublin's strict sectarian environment and the full consequences of the Irish penal laws, and their various contorted methods for subverting these laws gave the estate a particularly duplicitous and somewhat anarchic character. Notably free of hierarchy, the estate's development precepts promoted an equality of plot and building scale and an anonymous, discrete and quotidien style of architecture. When in Ireland, which was rare, the Viscounts' secondary residence of choice was the Old Court of Simmons Court and Old Merrion, the manor from which they derived their title. This they let to their agents Bryan and Elizabeth Fagan, sometimes staying with them instead of bothering to rent a suitable residence, or inhabit their great house in Mount Merrion, which they also typically leased out to others. This implicit overturning of the principles of aristocratic residence and ownership distracted attention from the estate's true reach, and also enabled successive viscounts to shirk any hierarchical privileges and appearances they might otherwise have been required to adopt. With the visiting Viscount mostly staying in his agent's castle, the respective powers of landlord and agent appeared reversed to interested Dublin onlookers.

From the distant and more tolerant environment of Richmond-upon-Thames, the Viscounts Fitzwilliam encouraged their Catholic agents to accommodate Catholic tenants on their Dublin estate and to provide such tenants with as much security of tenure as possible, whilst also permitting their agents to develop housing projects. The family's ambiguous approach to estate management is most visible in the strategies they adopted to aid their Catholic tenants. The 1703 penal law had ensured that Catholic estates could not be inherited in their entirety under primogeniture by the family's eldest son, thereby ensuring that Catholic landownership was splintered by gavelkind into smaller and smaller units. The 1709 law ensured that 'no lease to a catholic could exceed 31 years' and introduced the idea of 'leaving the operation of the law in the hands of individual "Protestant discoverers" who could file a bill in the Chancery Court against any lease which infringed the laws'. If the bill proved successful, the discoverer could then take the lease himself as a reward. The operation of the law in practice was, as ever, more complicated. While some people did operate as discoverers in the spirit of the law, many were 'but front men allowing their names to be used by lawyers on behalf of clients'.[16] Some of these clients were really intent on taking over a lease held by a Catholic; others were using discovery to create a smokescreen of protection around a Catholic's property. These practices served to make the identification of the true holder of the land difficult. The straightforward expression of authorship and patronage, so essential for determining architectural motive and design intent, was muddied and concealed by these dissimulating practices of ownership and counter-ownership.

Irish Catholic families mostly held lands not just in fee simple (which was difficult to pass on by inheritance and impossible to purchase) but also through a combination of leasehold interests of varying terms.[17] Length of lease impacted on the design and management of both landscapes and buildings. Richard Mathew's 1749 prayer for 'an Act of Parlement be obtained; or some other Modus printed out, to Qualifie your Lordsp, to give a Term of years, sufficient to Encourage Improveing Tenants', associated improvement directly with the award of a long-term lease.[18] People would not invest money in land they were not legally entitled to hold for long and this particularly affected architecture and building practice, with Mathew reassuring the Viscount that improvements at the Viscount's Dublin seat of Mount Merrion were 'carrying on, without thinking of our short term' in 1735.[19] In the same year he wrote of how Simmonscourt house would

only become a gentleman's residence if 'the whole [was] Rebuilt, the whole Composition' because it was constructed 'of miserable Materials *adapted to the Term*' (emphasis added).[20] Designers made decisions based on length of lease and a poorly built house reflected how long the lessor thought he might be in residence. Catholic houses were thus, by logical extension, more poorly built than those of their Protestant neighbours, as the benefits of improvement were more evident and attractive to those who were legally permitted to hold long leases.

An example of such contorted practices was Bryan Fagan who had 'built a house of Bricke' at Old Merrion and 'a large Garden with a Stone wall nine feet high'. Very uneasy by having 'expended much more than his Covenant', the problem was also that 'being a Roman' he 'could not take a longer Term than 21 years'.[21] To extend his potential interest in the property Fagan came to an agreement with the Protestant Thomas Bomford, who took out a lease of three lives as a front for Fagan.[22] In a letter to the Viscount, Mathew tried to anticipate what would happen if 'a Discoverer Apear[ed]', who might expose Bomford's holding of the lease in trust for Fagan because he believed that Fitzwilliam 'woude willingly defeat such Gentry'. The land was 'to be ploughed in high Ridges' and 'demonstrate tis for Meadow the first seven years' with Mathew also assuring the Viscount that Fagan had 'dunged five acres, with dung from Dublin and seawreke, and will dunge the whole for ploughing on anny other consideration'. A complex letter, delineating a design strategy of calculated dissimulation, fear of discovery probably required Fagan to plough the land 'in high Ridges' and demonstrate that it would be managed as 'Meadow the first seven years', with no ploughing for crops permitted. Such a management schema demonstrated a long-term interest in the land (such as that held by a Protestant lessor, such as Bomford) and not one consistent with the short-term profits that a Catholic might generate by the rapid rotation of crops.[23]

As Catholics, Richard Mathew and Bryan and Elizabeth Fagan lived under threat of discovery against their own leases, and as agents they also had to fear both reprisal and blackmail from others. In 1748 Fagan was 'somewhat Aprehensive of a Discovery against him in regarde to the Lease he holds under Mr William Fitzwilliam' and thought it 'adviseable' for the Viscount's brother William Fitzwilliam, who had taken the lease, presumably much as Bomford had done for Fagan, to send him as 'soone as may be, a letter to Impower me, as his attorney to Accept of a Surrender of said Lease'.[24] By surrendering the lease the fear of discovery was removed and it seems likely that the lease was then redrawn at a later date, once the fear of discovery had passed. More complex again was the manipulated use of discovery by those who wished to extract themselves from unwanted leases. One such gentleman was the Protestant Mr Quin who held 'a Lease for 3 lives of part of the Lands of Owenstown' close to the Mount Merrion estate. Being 'anxious to get rid of it' Mr Quin had 'taken the opinion of Coun[sel]' who said it was a 'discoverable Lease, liable to Popery laws', and that a Court of Equity would 'release him'. William Fitzwilliam thought that it would be 'prudent' of his brother to accept the surrender, as he would probably 'be forced to do it' anyway.[25] The Fitzwilliam family continued to stay abreast of events in Dublin that might harm the Catholic leaseholder's interest such as when a 1772 parliamentary bill 'to enable Roman Catholicks to take Building Leases' was 'thrown out' by the Irish House of Lords but a 'Popish Mortgage Bill' passed.[26] They were often unsuccessful in their efforts and in 1763 William Fitzwilliam wrote to appraise his brother that their dissimulation strategies for Stephen Browne, another Catholic tenant, had failed because it had been 'necessary to mention in [tha]t signed by him that He was a Roman Catholick'.[27]

Apparently, lands were managed and farmed to conceal or reveal length of lease depending on a tenant's confession. If Catholics had to farm as though they had no expectation of a long lease their lands probably looked different as a result. Whether all people could perceive such distinctions or only those familiar with farming practice remains unclear, but the Fitzwilliam correspondence raises important questions as to how landscape may have been perceived and developed in eighteenth-century Ireland. These obtuse and frequently ambiguous examples from the Fitzwilliam estate are presented as suggestive of the complex reach of leases in design decisions and practices. They are not conclusive but indicate that a less straightforward reading of design motive and language may be required in some circumstances. Such questions also make the interpretation of 'improvement' more complex. Its implicit rhetoric – that Ireland should look more like England and that indigenous farming and architectural practice should be replaced by improved and imported practices – is complicated by the design repercussions attached to length of lease. Short leases begot poor buildings and leached soil, long leases the

reverse, yet only one sector of society was allowed and encouraged by law to adopt and demonstrate good practice.

With no real intention of removing permanently from Richmond to Ireland, successive viscounts rarely resisted the temptation of renting out the family's suburban seat of Mount Merrion, and Jonathan Barker's 1762 map of Mount Merrion was one of many maps commissioned to send a complete picture of the estate to London. The vignette drawing in the top left-hand corner of the map succinctly documents Mount Merrion's principal anomaly among Irish country houses – where the house should have been lay a vacant area of grass (Fig. 150). Close to Mount Merrion lay the seaside town of Blackrock. The estate tried but failed to connect the town and demesne successfully by axis, and the entrance avenue to the Fitzwilliam's vacant house plot remained irritatingly offset from the long suburban road of Mount Merrion Avenue (Fig. 151). A new Protestant church was a key building project in any Irish eighteenth-century estate town, where its typical position as the focus of the central urban space professed the town's spatial allegiance to the established Church and the local Protestant landlord, who had often given both site and funds for its construction. Viscount Fitzwilliam was unusual in that he did not fund such set pieces on either his urban or his suburban lands, where new churches were unceremoniously slotted into vacant plots. The 'Roman Chapel' of no. 5 on Jonathan Barker's 1762 map of Booterstown (Fig. 151) was constructed on Fitzwilliam land before any of the area's Protestant churches, a most unusual design order of precedence for the Irish environment. The area's Protestant church was eventually positioned midway along Booterstown (now Church) Avenue, where it took up its entitled position on the superior avenue, yet one bearing little urban design intention or effect. With no clear spatial expression of spiritual and temporal authority, Booterstown, and its sister suburban town of Blackrock, were spatially subversive in the confessional environment of eighteenth-century Ireland. The absence of any patriarchal oversight left such suburbs relatively free of the benevolent and improving instincts of many Irish estates and ripe for the revolutionary activities of such residents as Edward FitzGerald.

Absenteeism had many advantages. Although William Fitzwilliam, sent over from London to provide a family member's oversight, encouraged his brother, Richard, 6th Viscount Fitzwilliam, to move back to Dublin from London

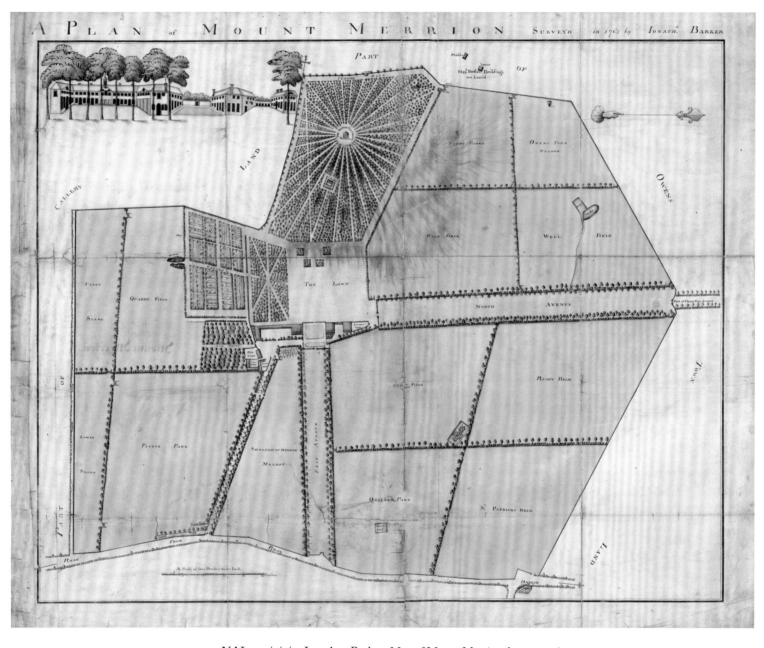

150. NAI 2011/2/2/11, Jonathan Barker, *Map of Mount Merrion demesne*, 1762

151. *(facing page)* NAI 2011/2/2/7, Jonathan Barker, *Map of Booterstown*, 1762. A indicates the offset between the position
of the entrance avenue to Mount Merrion House and Black Rock Avenue. B indicates the 'Roman chapel'

A MAP OF BOOTERSTOWN AND ALL ITS SUBDENOMINATIONS SURVEY'D IN 1762 BY IONTHAN BARKER

in 1753, writing that all debts would be 'made Easy' when the Viscount came 'over and settle[d]',[28] on another occasion he advised his brother to 'be in no hast to take a journey hither; the less you appear among these People the better'. William himself would 'deal with' the estate's Dublin clients and 'give them a fair hearing, tho' with a deaf ear'.[29] Busy developing the south-eastern quarter of Dublin city, he found that his 'bargains succeed[ed] better without' the Viscount's appearance. If the Viscount did visit he 'would be way laid & got at; & beat down in your Price', for an absentee could not 'stand against the haggering & chattering'[30] of the locals. Less likely to be influenced by local predilections for particular traditions, styles or architects, an absentee's weak local presence gave the estate's economic rationale increased prominence and legitimacy. What was considered appropriate locally could be conveniently ignored from afar, and distant oversight reinforced its financial focus. Yet successful improvement could also be thwarted by a landlord's absence, his siblings and servants on the ground sometimes paralysed by his indecision and inaction. In 1747 Richard Mathew bemoaned that they had not 'the Pleasure of yr Lordsps Presence here, as soone as Expected' and reminded the Viscount there were 'many things to be considered' that he could not 'take upon my Selfe to Transact'.[31] Regarding the ambitious development of Merrion Street and Square, Fagan wrote that his lordship's presence would 'induce the Builders to Build thereon, which heretofore has been but slow'.[32] If the agents remained unfailingly civil in their prose, brothers could afford to lose their temper, with William Fitzwilliam reaching the end of his tether in 1757:

> If I can make any thing from my Br. Johns discourse, I apprehend you are very uncertain whether you will come to Ireland this year or not. Fix your resolutions & come, your Presence is absolutely wanted, your affairs are in a way I do not like, there are some Leases you muct sign yourself, & some surrenders to be made that you must yourself accept.

The Viscount had put off travelling to Ireland and his brother was quite 'tired of Lying' for him in his absence.[33] William Fitzwilliam's pleas for his brother's physical presence in Dublin match the later entreaties sent by Roswell King for Pierce Butler's presence in Georgia.

On the west side of Merrion Square stands Leinster House, built partly on Fitzwilliam land by the FitzGerald family, Earls of Kildare and subsequently Dukes of Leinster, in 1740. When the Fitzwilliam family began to lay out Dublin's pre-eminent Georgian square on the south side of the city from 1750 onwards they took pains to ensure that the central axis of Leinster House's garden front did not determine their square's geometry. The resulting offset irritated the ducal family and also rendered the square's design somewhat irrational and haphazard – a spatial character created in part by the absent landlord's point of view.[34] The Fitzwilliams felt no obligation to bow to a dominant house or family in any of their developments, directing their agents to meticulously place the Earl of Kildare 'on the same footing'[35] as the estate's other tenants and warning that 'the Grandees' had been observed 'to pay the worse'.[36] The knock-on effect was the creation of an aristocratic quarter, where the absence of a resident landlord left all its aristocrats much more equal to each other.

Lying at the end of the long axis of Booterstown Avenue and neighbour to Frescati House stood a mansion whose name 'Lord Fitzwilliam's Porter's Lodge' expressed a paradoxical equality of both tenant and architecture (Fig. 152). William Fitzwilliam wrote to his brother in 1755 of the property's inherent problem:

> He [Judge French] intends going to see your lodge as you call it near the Black Rock; so I must tell you tho' I diminished yr plan, tis still rather a Palace, than anything else: I am actually ashamed of it, & think I must find out some scheme, to get it off your hands to advantage. Tis much too grand for the design'd use.[37]

This strange assessment is explained by the drawing of the house that Barker included in his survey book (Fig. 153). Evidently 'too grand' to be a porter's lodge, the house had been built on a suburban plot that was too small for such a mansion. It did not have, and never could have, the gardens and landscape appropriate to its scale and which genteel tenants required, such as those of the neighbouring Frescati (Fig. 117). Suburban housing, as revealed by the housing developments that the estate permitted its tenants to build in Blackrock and Booterstown, had an ideal scale; not too large and not too small. It approved most of houses that were five bays in width and two storeys in height, constructed in groups of five or seven (Fig. 153), and such egalitarian suburban housing, when coupled with an ecumenical preference for few churches

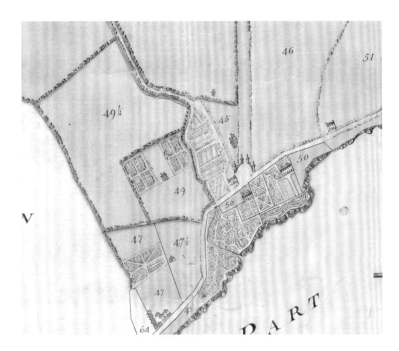

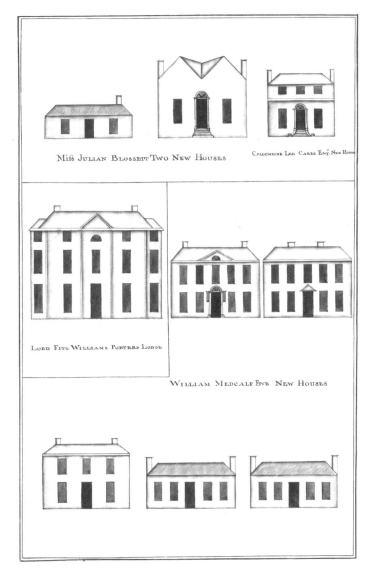

152. *(above)* Jonathan Barker, *Map of Booterstown*, 1762. Detail showing Frescati (no. 49), the 'Porter's Lodge' (no. 45) and William Metcalf's (no. 50). National Archives of Ireland 2011/2/2/7

153. *(right)* 'Lord Fitzwilliams Porters Lodge & William Metcalf's five houses', unnumbered inventory of drawings, from Jonathan Barker, 'A Book of Maps and References to the Estate of the Right Honourable Richard Lord Viscount FitzWilliam', 1762, p. 7. National Archives of Ireland, Fitzwilliam Mss. 2011/3/1

placed in positions of little urban design consequence, made for an interesting and puzzling suburban spatial structure. 'The porter's lodge' misnomer is emblematic of a general pattern of misrepresentation in this corner of eighteenth-century Dublin where an absentee's purely economic interests left the spatial and social hierarchies deliberately obtuse.

But how distinctively Irish is this case study of the Fitzwilliam family, and how Irish their absent point of view? The strategies adopted by the Fitzwilliams to protect their property and tenants derived from the strictures of the penal laws, which only applied to Catholic or dissenting families, and were particular to Ireland's confessional history. Protestant

absentees had no need of such contorted logic nor of the many veils of dissimulation and manipulation that were brought into play. Yet, the depths of manipulation and subterfuge employed makes the Fitzwilliam estate a formidable *ne plus ultra* example of calculated transnational strategy, where pure economic interest, mostly uncomplicated by local attachments, engendered a highly successful landed estate. This is the ambition of most absenteeism, to stand clear of messy local issues while quietly extracting an estate's monetary potential. When power is located elsewhere, the spatial expression of that power becomes de-centred and oblique, its force deflected by interstitial local objects that are hard to read or irrelevant from a distance. Planned avenues, churches, great houses and housing projects may initially exhibit a puzzling incoherence. This derives from their less than straightforward formation and is characteristic of much colonial space.

Conflicted Identities

The Philadelphia publisher Thomas Stephens dedicated his 1795 edition of the *Proceedings of the United Irishmen of Dublin* 'To Pierce Butler, A senator of the United States of America; an enemy of Aristocracy, and a Friend of Man, who preferring virtue to titles, has relinquished the distinctions conferred on the House of Ormond, to promote the dignity of human nature, and the cause of equality' (Figs 154 and 155).[38] The *Proceedings* were those 'of a band of his Countrymen, who not debased by Slavery' had 'preserved their freedom of mind in the midst of chains', and they left Butler's identity as successful planter with large and highly productive plantations scattered across

Georgia and South Carolina, a great speculator in land (like George Washington) and the owner of many enslaved people somewhat elided.[39] The *Proceedings* do reveal Butler's fervent support of the French Revolution and suggest how helpful he could be to the radical Irish arriving in Philadelphia.[40] Butler's politics, more generally, were republican, with his formative years in Carlow playing some part in his rejection of aristocracy and of any inherited or purchased position.[41] Like the Fitzwilliams of Dublin, some aspects of his identity were concealed from particular individuals or groups and only found voice in his letters home. Privately appreciating the opportunities that America presented for amassing a great fortune, he nevertheless considered it unfit for the education of his son and for the society of his daughters. The façade he presented in Philadelphia, and at a further remove in London and Dublin, frequently contradicted the reality, as the previous chapter has explored.

Emigration to the United States did not inhibit Butler's critical observation of Irish society; it seemed more to encourage it. In 1791 he was 'not surprised' at the number of Irish

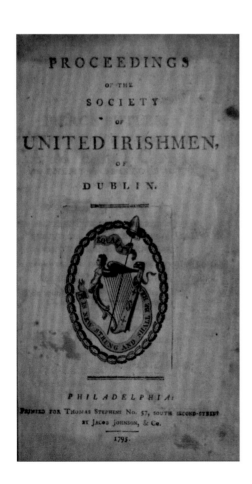

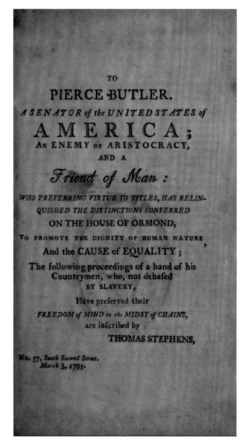

154. *(far left)* Frontispiece to *Proceedings of the United Irishmen of Dublin* (Philadelphia: Printed for Thomas Stephens, of No. 57, South Second Street, by Jacob Johnson, & Co., 1795)

155. *(left)* Dedication to *Proceedings of the United Irishmen of Dublin*, 1795

emigrating to the United States, crediting 'the injudicious deportment of too many of the Land Lords, the oppressive tythes' and 'the religious discriminations' as 'more than sufficient' reasons for the Irish to emigrate. The 'certainty of asylum' in the United States 'where a comfortable living may be had with moderate exertions, where the natural, civil & equal rights of Man are well secured' left him wondering why more Irish did not cross the Atlantic. The 'address from the Belfast Volunteers that pleased' him very much in 1791 led him to speculate that Ireland was 'ripe for some change'.[42] The Volunteers had gathered in Belfast to celebrate the second anniversary of the fall of the Bastille. Their published address, authored by Wolfe Tone, included the three resolutions of the newly formed Society of United Irishmen:

I. Resolved, That the weight of English influence in the Government of this Country, is so great as to require a Cordial Union among all the people of Ireland, to maintain that ballance which is essential to the preservation of our Liberties, and the extension of our Commerce.

II. That the sole constitutional mode by which this influence can be opposed, is by a complete and radical reform of the Representation of the People in Parliament.

III. That no Reform is practicable, efficaceous or just, which shall not include Irishmen of every Religious Persuasion.[43]

The declaration that all religions would be treated equally was particularly radical in Ireland, where the established Protestant Church claimed the allegiance of a small minority of the population and Butler's actions in America indicate that he too worked to undermine religious bias in his new country. Less than enthusiastic about his appointment to the Protestant General Episcopal Convention in South Carolina in 1792, he took pains to introduce a Roman Catholic priest to Charleston's Protestant minister, writing that although he was 'not of your [not our] church' he was sure that the priest would 'not, on that account meet with less attention' from his religious counterpart.[44] Contradicting his later suppression of his enslaved workers' devotions, he pontificated that 'if none but one denomination of Christians' were 'to be admitted to the throne of mercy, for what purpose were the rest of mankind created?'[45] But in practice he generally conformed closely to the traditions of the Anglican Church, particularly when planning his own funeral arrangements.[46]

Butler, despite his criticism of American society as outlined in Chapter 5, was very proud of his new nation's achievements and of how the United States had 'affected a revolution in our form, nay in the spirit of our government, not only without bloodshed but even the smallest strife'. An exceptional strength of 'citizens of the United States' was to have 'a pretty accurate knowledge of the principles and tenderness of the different forms of government' from which the 'more civilised nations of Europe' could learn 'a useful lesson'.[47] His letters reveal the political principles that had inspired and confirmed his new nationality. Entitled men 'who thought that all was made for them',[48] were problematic, particularly the King of Great Britain and Ireland who controlled 'not only all executive power' but was 'himself also a very important and essential branch of the Legislature' and 'head of the church'. Unlike the 'elected and curtailed power of the American President', monarchy was abhorrent for being hereditary where a 'weak man, or a mad man, may, as heir, ascend to the throne'.[49] He strongly disapproved of the purchased nature of British military officers' commissions, writing that he would be 'much hurt' if his own son Thomas 'should make choice of that profession'. Butler had become a military man 'not by choice but from that necessity which flows from the injustice of a feudal system, giving to the first-born all'.[50]

Pierce Butler followed the French Revolution's stages, observing in 1788 how France and other parts of Europe had 'again got an inclination to taste the sweets of free government' but that the King of France had 'gained nothing by the American Revolution'. America was 'the means of opening the eyes of the enslaved, as to make them cast off their chains' and such references to political slavery did not leave him blind to the irony of an American slaveholder espousing revolutionary sentiments. Excusing slavery demanded some tortured reasoning in his letters to his English cousin, Weedon Butler, who was then schooling Butler's first-born son in London:

You may naturally ask me: 'Why, with these sentiments, do you hold so many in bondage'. I answer you, that I would free every one of them tomorrow if I could do it, that is if the Legislature would permit it. I ardently wish I never had anything to do with such property. I daily beg of them to seek some master that they think they would be happy with, that

I may get done with them. But though it is an indulgence, not unusual here, they will not try one … If I could part with lands here for near their value, you should soon see me in England, but in a private station. So great is the scarcity of money all through America that property will not sell for one half its real worth.[51]

George Mason, Butler's fellow signatory of the American Constitution and neighbour of George Washington in Gunston Hall on the Potomac (Fig. 8), sent Butler 'French news' and in 1790 Butler wrote to Mason of how he 'ardently hope[d]' that the 'French Nation' would 'accomplish their object & secure to themselves & their posterity the equal operation of Laws' and 'perfect freedom and enjoyment of property'. Gushing on the 'phenomenon' of 'a real free Government in Europe', he considered the French to have 'a claim to the respect & admiration of every generous breast'.[52] Reading Thomas Paine, not wholly uncritically, he hoped that 'every peasant in Europe' would 'know what are the rights of Man.'[53] It was 'a century of Revolutions' with 'the troubles in France' holding 'out another useful lesson to monarchs'.[54]

Butler made his money from agriculture – from perfecting the monocultural system of plantation farming, explored in Chapter 5, that slavery both engendered and facilitated. He associated activities such as banking or investment with the formation of a new quasi-aristocracy and believed that wealth should derive instead from land and farming:

> Principles teach us that commerce should be the consequence not the means of Agriculture; Agriculture being the basis. Arts Manufactures and Commerce follow of course & progressively in their order but to begin with commerce and in an inverse method through Arts and Manufactures arrive at the culture of land is a reversal of all order in the oeconomy of things.

In 1791 he suspected that the 'wealth & influence' of the fledgling Bank of North America would lead it to become an '[im]proper engine in the hands of a few', who were bent on 'establishing an Aristocratick influence subversive of the spirit of our free, equal government'.[55] The 'landed Interest' had been 'left to shift for itself'[56] and only the election of staunch republicans would avoid 'rivitting an aristocratick Tyranny over the people' of Carolina in 1792. A free yeomanry, owning their

farms in freehold and making their money from agriculture, was the solution, as it had been for George Washington and Arthur Young, and Butler found it an 'evident truth' that 'so long as the yeomanry of a Country are virtuous the Country will be free & happy'.[57] His suspicion of the banking interest was probably affected by his own substantial and serious levels of debt. A natural consequence of his speculation in land and his questionable trusteeship of his wife's estate of enslaved workers, it continued to affect his financial freedom to a distressing degree.

Despite his admiration for what had been achieved politically by the United States, Butler, like Archibald Hamilton Rowan and Wolfe Tone, his fellow United Irishmen, still awarded Europe cultural supremacy. This underlying sense of inferiority led Butler, as it had Washington and others, to seek European approval of the actions of the United States. He longed for when 'Europe, enlightened Europe, must ere long be forced to acknowledge that we are not so entirely in the dark as we may be thought to be' and protested, somewhat too much, that while 'Britain' might 'enjoy her opinion of our darkness and barbarism – thanks to the God of Nature we see light enough, & feel ourselves so advancing in civilization as to be content'.[58] The British government saw 'with different Eyes from those', like Butler, who had experienced both countries and who could correctly 'view the interests of both'. Britain's politicians had 'never been in America', only forming 'their opinions on the Reports & judgements of others', while Butler and others like him had made their 'own conclusions from' their 'own observations'.[59] Pierce Butler often acted in ways that revealed both the caution and the cunning of the first-generation immigrant. At vulnerable moments, such as the period following his wife's death in 1790, Butler's insecurity became palpable. 'Left alone' and 'charged with the care of four daughters' who had 'no Guide, no near Relative, perhaps no real friend' in America but himself,[60] he longed for 'the society of a few'[61] London friends and relations. He wrote to his mother, perhaps inspired by filial duty, that if he were not 'still tied' to the United States he would 'willingly return' to Ireland.[62] Yet Pierce Butler was also Irish enough to appreciate the full advantages of absenteeism, where ownership of land did not require or encourage residence on that land.

Pierce Butler, like Lord Edward FitzGerald and many other younger sons of the gentry and aristocracy, had been commissioned into the military at a young age. Chapter 4 explored how young officers were taught how to survey land and draw plans of the territory, particularly fortifications, barrack layouts and other important topographical features. They then directed their men, often pressed from the peasantry of the locality, into building ditches, dugouts and other simulacra of combat as a training for wartime. When such men became property owners and land speculators they continued to use drawing as a tool for visualising their acquired territories.[63] A drawing could represent a complex, messy, real place as an ideal, abstract space. The seemingly inevitable logic and inordinate success of plantation design, with its overtones both of the landed estate and the factory, derived from this ability to abstract a place into a space, and drawing became the necessary facilitator of absenteeism. As absentees came to believe in the power of the *plat* to accurately delineate their design intentions, they sought drawing skills in their agents and overseers.

Butler, like George Washington, invested substantial amounts of money in purchasing land that he did not intend to cultivate, but to hold and only sell once its value had increased. Drawing and surveying skills were absolutely essential for successful land speculators. Concerned that his eldest son and heir would learn such skills in London, Butler wondered suspiciously if his son's drawing had been given 'the last touch' by the drawing master before being posted across the Atlantic.[64] Even if such men did not survey the land themselves they needed to employ expert surveyors to ensure that the land that they bought was properly surveyed (deriving its area), accurately represented in plan to scale and then legally registered. If a speculator had not the skills to read drawings closely he was likely to make a bad purchase. Short of money in 1791, Butler had ready 'land purchasers' but they would make him no offer until they saw the 'platt or map of the land'. He carefully commissioned a 'resurvey' of his Salvadore lands in 1793 at 'very heavy expence' so as to 'ascertain the quantity of every acre'[65] and then hired the superlative Charleston surveyor James Purcell, who had previously mapped the Middleton properties (Fig. 14), to 'copy every platt',[66] with Purcell paid out of the eventual sales. In 1791 only two states, Pennsylvania and South Carolina, permitted 'aliens to hold land' because 'the Laws enabling them to do so' had 'passed previous to the adoption of the Federal Constitution'.[67] Butler looked forward to substantial windfalls from Europeans purchasing land in those states and as soon as a treaty was 'closed with the Indians' surveyors were to 'be engaged, handsome platts made out, & sent

to Europe'.[68] By January 1793 land values in the northern and eastern states had within 'six months doubled in value' with large tracts 'bought up by Europeans', and Butler reasoned that 'the distracted state of Europe' would 'oblige many even in Great Britain to think of' America as a 'retreat'.[69] Land was more valuable when sold in a homogenous block than when shot through with other people's holdings and in 1794 Butler determined to hold onto his own land for as long as possible in the rising market.[70]

In 1794 Major Pierce Butler made a plan for his sea island plantations on the coast of Georgia that 'saved the necessity of ever going to see [his] Estate'.[71] He considered slavery an inappropriate sight for his children and, as a widower, did not like to leave them on their own in Philadelphia. In 1793 his daughter Sarah wrote of how her father had 'gone to Carolina and Georgia for the purpose' of 'arrang[ing] *his troublesome kind of property* [a euphemism for slavery] so as not to require his presence'. The children 'could not accompany him' and it was 'the first time for many years that' they had been separated from their father.[72] As one of very few absentee plantation owners in Georgia, and 'the only exception to the rule' of owners-in-residence in the sea islands, Pierce Butler's enthusiasm for absenteeism made him unusually dependent on his agents and on drawings as a method of communication.[73] The masterplan of numbered rectilinear divisions that he produced for each of his expanding series of sea island plantations allowed him to refer easily to a particular area of the landscape in a letter (Figs 144 and 145).[74] His agents' ambivalent tolerance of such a regular stream of drawings was suggested by Roswell King in his response to yet another drawing in 1803: 'As for the plat of your land I am silent, have my hands full, shall attend to it when I possibly can.'[75] Such correspondence also presents interesting issues of design authorship as the professional estate manager invariably demonstrated his expertise by tinkering with his absent master's design. In December 1803 King sent Butler a drawing of 'another alteration for settlement No. 4' and apologised for making 'so many alterations from former plans'. But he could not 'in principal let slip anything' that was in Butler's interest and 'truly regret[ted]' that he had 'not the first direction of laying out Tide Island'.[76] Butler's older enslaved workers, who laid out his original system of dykes, canals and polder squares in the late 1790s, were also loath to abandon it. They tended to prefer the absent master to the resident manager and tried to undermine Roswell King's

156. Charles Ellet, *A Map of the County of Philadelphia: From Actual Survey*, Philadelphia, 1834.
Detail with the location of Butler's land holdings underlined. Library of Congress, G3824.P5 1843.E4

authority at available opportunities, particularly in the early years. When remaking the 'Old Square' and its beds at Experiment Plantation in 1804 the driver Morris 'after agreeing' with King 'to plant in the old beds – flew the way – saying he was fearfull' that Butler 'would not like it'.[77] When King had moved on to inspect another part of the estate, Morris reverted to Butler's layout.

Butler led a peripatetic existence in the early 1790s, residing seasonally in Georgia, Charleston, Washington DC, Philadelphia and New York. He was renting a house in Philadelphia in 1791, 'tho' only a hired one' and it gave him a

foothold in the 'handsome, large City, eminent for its order and regularity' where, to Butler's satisfaction, the 'principles and Interests of the Quakers prevailed' and whose 'wisdom and economy' had increased land values.[78] He also began to spend time at York Farm – his suburban retreat from the streets of Philadelphia – and in 1794 his daughter Sarah wrote a letter from 'German Town' to her brother, indicating that the family were then resident.[79] Located north of Philadelphia on the Old York Road, Butler's 'farm' lay near Germantown – a prominent Philadelphia suburb within easy commuting distance from the town centre (Fig. 156). In 1810 Butler enlarged the

OLD BUTLER PLACE, OLD YORK ROAD, BRANCHTOWN, PHILA.

157. 'Old Butler Place, Old York Road, Branchtown, Phila.' from
the garden front. Historical Society of Pennsylvania, Jane Campbell
scrapbook collection [V71]. Box 23A, p. 196

THE OLD BUTLER GARDENS, BRANCHTOWN, PHILA.

158. 'The Old Butler Gardens, Branchtown, Phila.'. Historical Society of
Pennsylvania, Jane Campbell scrapbook collection [V71]. Box 23A, p.196

site to 107 acres when he bought a nearby country house that a
Frenchman, named Boullange, had built in 1791 (Fig. 157). This
gave him 'an extended frontage on Old York Road on the east,
on Thorp's Lane on the south, and on Branchtown turnpike
on the west' where it was 'skirted by Thorp's dam – a beautiful
sheet of water'.[80] Described as 'undulating and picturesque' in
1892, one of the landscape's 'most unique and attractive features' was the principal approach route to the house from the
south, where a 'beautiful avenue of broad-spreading maple
trees whose interlacing branches form[ed] a complete archway'
cast 'a deep shade over the drive of several hundred yards from
Thorp's Lane to the mansion'. A 'babbling stream' wound its
way 'round the foot of a wooded hill', before 'finding its way,
ultimately, into Thorp's dam', suggesting an artful use of water
features in the landscape's design. It also had 'an old fashioned,
walled garden' described as 'rare in this country, though usually
attached to venerable country-houses of England', where 'figs,
and other semi-tropical trees flourish[ed], and mature[d] their
fruit in perfection' (Fig. 158).[81] No peas, corn, rice and cotton
featured in these descriptions of a Philadelphian suburban
mansion but instead a calculated display of imperial bounty,
grown by one of its most materially rewarded sons. Surrounded
by similar villa-style residences with large gardens, the spatial

hierarchy, as in other suburban contexts, was relatively muted,
when compared to Butler's prominent and very large townhouse that he had finally completed purchasing in 1798 (Fig.
159). It was situated on Chestnut Street, described by Jeffrey
Cohen as 'the city's preeminent corridor of urban visibility
shared with government, hotels, theaters, fine shops, and other
houses' by 1807.[82] York Farm's 107 acres encompassed a much
smaller area than that of his Georgian plantation jigsaw or of
Washington's Mount Vernon. Butler's Place was not a productive, working farm but an elegant suburban villa built to escape
the urban grid and grit of Philadelphia's core.

Butler's habitual residency in a Philadelphia suburb
reduced the status of the principal house on his plantations
and in a manner similar to the Fitzwilliam estate in Dublin,
where Mount Merrion's status was consistently demoted, such
absentee properties developed a distinctive structure over time.
Although Butler had intended to build 'a House at Hampton'
a few years after purchasing the estate and make 'things
comfortable',[83] as his absenteeism became more entrenched,
his ambitions for his own domestic arrangements at Hampton
became less and less significant. This was also Roswell King's
doing. Despite Butler's plans to alter and expand the rudi-
mentary house William Page had constructed in 1798, in 1803

At this date January 1st 1891, Fanny Kemble (Mrs Butler) is eighty two years old,
and feeble. She lives with a daughter in Surrey, England.
Died, at the residence of her son in law Canon Leigh 86 Gloucester place June 16th/93.& interred in Kensal Green Cemetery beside her father)

159. 'The Old Butler Mansion', 1836. It was located on Chestnut St and 8th St, Philadelphia.
Historical Society of Pennsylvania, K: 2-3. David J. Kennedy watercolors [V61]

King diverted labour and materials towards making ever more polders and ditches, and towards the various expensive phases of constructing the rice machines. When Butler asked about 'the enlargement' of the house in 1804 King admitted that he had made no progress, primarily because of the 'very heavy job created' by the rice machine and the construction of other necessary buildings on the estate. King chided Butler that if he had wanted his house badly enough he 'would have repeated [his] orders'.[84] King's growing abilities as a manager enabled

Butler's absenteeism, and as their communication system by drawings and letters became more successful it made the likelihood of visitors to Hampton ever more remote.

In 1813, once the new rice machine had been finished, Butler's attention again turned to his house 'addition'. This time work began in earnest and the timber frame was up by June 1813 when King wrote that he could finish it by December if provided with 'Glass & locks for the Doors'. As a good financial manager, he carefully calculated the number of doors, windows and panes of glass.[85] Despite the threat of British invasion that year, when 'talk of expecting the British to burn' buildings, and 'talk of building' did 'not well hang together', King considered it as well to be building as doing anything else.[86] On 20 June 1813 he sent Butler 'a rough sketch of the intended addition' because he wanted Butler's 'consent to move the door leading from the parlour, to the one intended; on the other side of the chimney from the former plan, (which was the corner marked waiting table)' (Fig. 160). He had observed that that corner was Butler's favourite place to sit and 'to cut a Door through there' would totally 'deprive' Butler of his chosen spot. Confident that Butler would approve of his new plan, which stood 'uniform', he made sure that it contained the same number of doors and windows as the former plan. He tried to tempt Butler to Georgia by writing that if Butler brought his family that winter they would 'find great convenience in it'.[87] The hurricane later that year, in September 1813, damaged Butler's residence. Its roof had been 'improperly built, or the Chimney would not have broke it in' and King, with his usual confidence, promised that the new chimneys would 'never fall again with such winds' because he was going to 'direct the building of them' himself. The house project's levels of architectural ambition, and specifically its decoration, continued to be affected by whether Butler intended to visit Georgia or not. King would 'put off' plastering the ceilings until the following summer if Butler 'should conclude not to come' but if Butler did decide to come it would be possible to make in 'tenantable' in a few weeks, but only if Butler sent some wallpaper for the rooms.[88]

Slowly Pierce Butler's many conflicting identities were translated to his landscapes. In the manner of a typical Irish absentee landlord he controlled his southern plantations from the comforts of his Philadelphia mansion and suburban villa. Despite the scale and value of his Georgian estates, he continued to feel little compunction to build an impressive southern mansion. When in Philadelphia he could play the part of a radical United Irishman by mixing with such revolutionary émigrés as Archibald Hamilton Rowan, all the while trying to entice them to buy southern plantations. His American revolutionary sympathies led in turn to his active support for the United Irishmen's rebellion of 1798, yet his growing reputation as a leading southern planter led to many duplicitous and tortured letters to his relatives at home, where the European interpretation of 'the rights of man' was hard to reconcile with owning more than six hundred slaves. Throughout his life

Butler remained *au fait* with the political, social and economic situation of his homeland, where the worsening conditions of the Irish poor, and more specifically their housing, continued to give rise to much aggrieved public commentary, particularly in the radical Philadelphia press, often controlled by the same radical Irish émigrés. The parallels between the Irish landscape and Georgia's landscape, particularly on the issue of exploitative farming practices, probably proved too uncomfortable a comparison to fully address in his letters to Ireland and London.

Butler's views on slavery were profoundly conflicted as, Janus-like, he presented one face to those across the Atlantic and another to the American South. He thanked the Quaker John Leckey of Ballykealey, Ireland, in 1791 for his 'generous opinion' of Butler's 'treatment of the wrettched Affricans' while tortuously attempting to place the blame for their enslavement on the workers themselves:

> Had it pleased God to allow the benign beam of Civilization to reach their Country, it would not be in the power of Europe to enslave them. I am not a friend to the trafick in Human kind. Yet upon strict enquiry I much doubt if their situation in their own Country is freer or better. However this does not perhaps justify the trade. We should leave them to Their own fate. Indeed I wish I had never owned one of them.[89]

Sometimes he was utterly oblivious to his own inherent contradictions, although rarely in his letters to Europe. His support for the French Revolution was tested by the sack and burning of Cap Français, Saint Domingue (modern Haiti), in June 1793 that led to the exodus of thousands of planters and other refugees to the southern states.[90] The extraordinary formation of an independent black republic in Saint Domingue made it a warning to other plantocracies rather than an inspiration. The planter revolutionary Butler thought that the October 1793 'insurrection among the Negroes of Carolina on Mr. Hayward's plantation' might have been inspired by events in Saint Domingue. The 'Eastern & French friends', whom he had cultivated previously, could 'do no good to our Blacks' leading him to 'wish they wou'd mind their own Affairs' when it came to the American South.[91] When his own enslaved workers in Georgia had become 'intollerable' in 1793 he worked to prevent their contamination by those returning from the northern states (where they were sometimes taken by

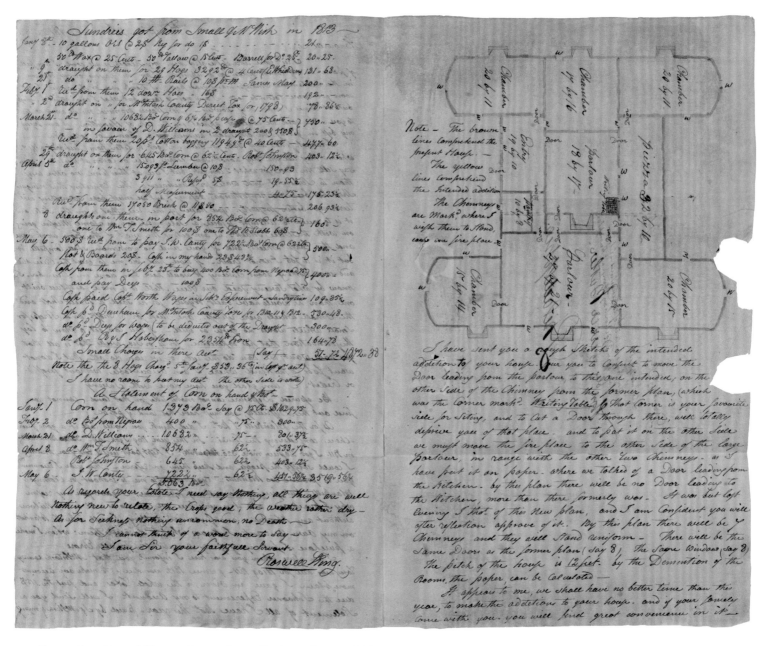

160. 'Letter from Roswell King to Senator Pierce Butler, 20 June, 1813'. This shows Roswell King's drawing of his proposed 1813 addition and alteration of Hampton plantation house. Historical Society of Pennsylvania, Butler Family Papers [1447]. Box 2, Folder 24

slaveholders) or those fleeing the Caribbean with foreign ideas of freedom. Describing how his enslaved people had become 'more luxurious and more insolent that any person, who ha[d] not witnessed it' could credit he reached the apex of his many contradictions by maintaining that their behaviour was 'one of the many abuses of the rights of Man'![92]

It was a disadvantage not to be native-born in the young United States, where loyalty and national identity were generally assigned to country of birth.[93] Many of its founding gentlemen had not been born there, and such men were aware of the questionable and mutable character of their identity, particularly when the various aliens acts of the 1790s brought national identity, and its connected voting and property rights, into focus. But if identity is widely connected to residency, rather than place of birth, then moving position manipulates identity, and the residency distinction could be invoked at smaller scales, many of them convenient for a plantation owner. How useful was his identity as an Irishman in deflecting accusations of complicity as a United States senator? If Butler was not resident in Georgia then how could he be fully responsible for what took place there? One of the most fundamental statements of identity that anyone makes is where one educates one's children. Butler's eldest son Thomas Butler was born in America on the 13 August 1778, the only one of Butler and Mary Middleton's four sons to survive infancy.[94] At the age of six he was sent to London to be educated in a school run by Weedon Butler, his father's cousin. He did not return to America until the age of seventeen, having seen his father just once in the eleven formative intervening years. That Butler was severely interrogated and at times chastised by his American peers for sending his son to Europe is evident in a letter where just such an exchange was recorded verbatim:

> I am often asked why I would not educate my son here, under my own eye. I have one uniform answer:
> 'You are unacquainted with his situation, Gentlemen, and my plans, or you would cease to ask the question. I would rather, Gentlemen, pay £500 a year for him where he is than have him educated here for one shilling'.
> – 'Then you don't think well of American education'.
> – 'Yes, I do but I take leave to judge for myself'.
> – 'Are you attached to America (?to) educate your son out of it?'
> – 'Yes.'[95]

The extraordinary effort Butler made to educate his only son 4,000 miles away from his home had unfortunate consequences. Butler sent an endless stream of directions to Weedon Butler on every aspect of son's ideal education, such as one that stipulated 'that he should possess that just sentiment of viewing none as his superiors but those who may excel him in virtue or knowledge, that he should not put too great a value on money, yet not too little, that he should be brought up to turn with abhorrence from every idea of getting it even by the smallest measures'.[96] For an avowed opponent of aristocracy the elitist nature of instructing Weedon Butler to provide his son with 'every master, every advantage, that the heir to a Crown could have', seems to have escaped him.[97] Trying to control his son's acquaintance from a distance, he instructed Weedon that Tom should never leave the school 'to visit any person, not even' his 'nearest relations', but such transatlantic micro-management appears to have been futile.[98] As they became progressively more detached, Pierce, the father, began to wish for Tom, the son, 'to be as perfect as possible before' he saw him again and, most worryingly, that he would then only 'love him in proportion to his knowledge and good qualities'.[99] Growing progressively colder and more distant, in 1792 he wrote that 'so long as' Tom 'deserve[d] it, and not one moment longer, he' would 'find in [Pierce Butler] a good father'.[100]

Similar concerns regarding children's education may be found the Fitzwilliam family's correspondence. William Fitzwilliam chastised his older brother, the Viscount, in 1757 for having 'month after month put off' his journey to Dublin.[101] The Viscount evidently preferred to stay at home in Richmond with his children rather than travel to Ireland, and William had little patience with his brother's excuses, writing that he should 'send [his] Boy to School' and then travel over to Ireland, which was 'no Place' for that boy, although the heir to a large part of its capital city. William Fitzwilliam, in turn, became concerned for his daughter's education. Although only 'three and a quarter years old' she was 'too old to remain' in Dublin and 'too young to send to a Boarding School'. Her father's 'best Thought' was to sell his Dublin townhouse and 'get rid of all Irish Connections as fast as I can; & go over & fix myself in some cheap part of London, where I may do my Duty by her under my own Eye'. William Fitzwilliam was 'quite sick of this Country [Ireland] after a residence of Eleven years'[102] and clearly balked at having an Irishwoman as a daughter. If he managed to 'quit this Country' he vowed to wash his 'hands of all connections with it'.[103]

Unlike Butler in the United States, the Fitzwilliam family had acquired almost wholly English, if covertly Catholic, identities once they moved to London in the 1730s. Butler's error was to try to give his son, as he saw it, the best of both worlds – an English education and an American future. He completely underestimated the degree to which his son's political sentiments would be formed by his environment, with Tom imbibing many of the aristocratic sentiments so abominable to his father in London, particularly in the aftermath of the French Revolution. Of the family's revolutionary leanings and sentiments, the most extreme were held, somewhat unexpectedly, by Pierce Butler's favourite daughter Sarah. Protected by her residence in Philadelphia from her father's 'troublesome sort of property' in Georgia, and by her gender from having to cross the Atlantic for her education, Sarah's letters to her brother reveal an ideal, pure and somewhat innocent form of Butler's republicanism, uncomplicated by the contradictions that plantation and slaveholding had created in her father. In April 1793 when she sincerely wished 'the French complete success' in the war that had been declared with England on 1 February 1793 but suspecting that Tom might 'be so much of an Englishman as to be surprised at' her sentiments, she joined with him 'in pitying the King of France and his family'. Although she did 'hate Kings', she worried that Louis XVI 'might not be spared' execution, but then observed, 'Yet why should the death of one man, perhaps deserving death, excite such emotions? The life of the honest peasant is equally dear to him'.[104] For Tom, who had spent the majority of his life in London with his loyalist and monarchist cousins, the strength of his sister's republican sentiments must have proved rather shocking.

Sarah also counselled her brother, somewhat presciently, to 'be in favour of' his 'native country', where he would eventually live, and which was 'now probably the freest in the world'.[105] She considered that the French, 'a people who have had the courage to assert their own independence', could 'never be the friends of those who submit to arbitrary government, and still more who advocate hereditary monarchy – a system that Americans hold in derision, and think a reflection on human understanding; yet it has its advocates in Britain'. According to Sarah Butler, citizens believed that 'all men [were] equal as to rights in society', and she prayed that the French might 'taste

the fruits of their virtues, and after humbling the haughty insolence of Britain as it deserves … teach all nations that the will of an uncorrupted majority, the natural law of every society, is the only safeguard of the right of man'. Unlike her father, Sarah saw clearly how conflicted her brother would be on his return to the United States. She warned that if he was 'not a warm friend' to the French Revolution he would 'not suit the meridean of' his own country 'and need never return to be happy', alerting him also to the 'disappointment it must be to Papa' to have a son who did not share his political views. She 'conjured' Tom not to 'adopt the political principles or opinions of the English Ministry or courtiers', because they were the 'subjects of a British King' while Tom was a 'citizen of the United States'. The British were 'educated in prejudices against America and against France – taught long to fancy themselves the only people great enough to be free'.[106] When Weedon Butler, who read any letters that Tom received, wrote to Pierce Butler from London to express his horror at such revolutionary sentiments being written by a woman, Butler, to his credit, moved to defend his daughter:

> For my daughter's anxiety respecting her brother's political principles there is some excuse. She justly observes that the smallest occurrence of a predilection for monarchy would deprive him for ever of the esteem or confidence of his country, would frustrate all my views for him, render residence in America ineligible and be highly mortifying to me who am from conviction and principle a friend to a republican form of government.[107]

By sending Thomas Butler to Europe his father deprived him of childhood and first-hand experience of his own country's design and creation, and as Sarah had predicted when Thomas Butler stood on his native soil once more, he was not charmed by the young United States. He read the young American environment as unformed and unimproved, when compared with London and its surrounding countryside, while the great experiment of the United States was not easily mapped onto the suburbs of Philadelphia and its farming hinterlands: 'Now, those parts that I have seen ought (from what I have said) to be the best cultivated. But, as all that I have noticed is a badly fertilized, heavy, clay soil, I think (speaking from the foregoing observations) that there can be nothing very promising in appearance anywhere.' The spatial disconnection that Pierce

Butler had achieved by living in Philadelphia rather than Georgia was even more profoundly transferred to his children. Utterly unaware of the plantations that sustained his lifestyle, and that he seems never to have visited, Tom's first impressions of Philadelphia were those of a transient, detail-observant tourist and far from a native's perspective: 'Of this country, even if I were capable, I could give no description at present, not having seen more than the city, which is considerable in its size. The plan is, as you know, regular. There are many good and handsome houses here. The brickwork is remarkably well executed.'[108]

Absenteeism from eighteenth-century Dublin is not comparable, on many levels, to absenteeism from the eighteenth-century sea islands of Georgia. The Fitzwilliams' tenants were Irish – they had not been forcibly transported across a great ocean in horrendous conditions to be seasoned, sold, bought and terrorised as the plantation system might devise. Some of them had to face the difficulties of being Catholic in a Protestant sectarian environment but this was not that unusual in eighteenth-century Europe and they always had the option of conversion, or covert behaviour, such as the Fitzwilliam family practised in London. So why compare the Fitzwilliam design precepts with those of Pierce Butler? Because the absenteeism that creates the palpable design disconnection in Dublin is of a piece with Butler's design practice in Georgia – where the utter breakdown of the traditional aristocratic estate reached its logical resolution. The Butler and Fitzwilliam families held similar Irish Norman lordships, acquired in distant medieval periods for military service to the Crown. The men of both families imbibed from childhood the aristocratic principle that wealth, land and position derived from loyal military and community service to the Crown. Absenteeism in both families had staged spatial consequences that stemmed from the loss of that benevolent tradition and its connected justification of aristocratic power. Aristocratic benevolence was never that general or convincing in eighteenth-century Ireland, and utterly unconvincing on a slave plantation. Merrion Square's purely economic design motives and subsequent loss of design coherence exposed some of the particular spatial consequences of an absentee's gradual withdrawal from spaces that they own but do not see. Fitzwilliam disconnection created Mount Merrion demesne's gaping lack of a great house from which to oversee the design of Dublin city, and the family's withdrawal encouraged the construction of humdrum suburban housing estates rather than grand suburban villas. Although Fitzwilliam sent a younger brother to oversee his developments in Dublin, he had no particularly onerous duties.

William Fitzwilliam's principal duties were to ensure that the family made no serious political mistakes and that when negotiating with the tenants the family had a loyal representative to defend their less-than benevolent interests on the ground. Although he did eventually buy and reside in one of the houses on Merrion Street to 'promote' the Viscount's 'designs', the fact that he had to beg for some financial 'little assistance' from his brother and mother in order to do so revealed his impotent status as a younger son.[109] Butler's relationship with his agent Roswell King is clarified by these comparisons, as no such delicacies were necessary in Georgia, where Butler's absence and the precepts of matrilineal chattel slavery placed Roswell King in a position of extraordinary power.

The indistinct geography of Philadelphia's suburbs allowed Butler to disappear into its growing homogeneity. His land and enslaved people rendered invisible through geographical distance, like his fellow Norman Irish aristocrats the Fitzwilliams, resident permanently in the London suburb of Richmond upon Thames, such fluid identities and geographies of residence and absence cannot be understood from one national viewpoint. Much as the protagonists were a mixture of Irish, American, Dutch or British identities, so their geographies are trans-imperial, transnational and fluid to their foundations. Such families created and occupied not one space but many, concurrently and simultaneously, in a shifting and dissimulating manner. When expressed spatially the character of such spaces can be most easily defined by what was absent (such as a house), what hierarchies were not upheld (such as those of churches and streets) and what design strategies were employed to subvert tradition rather than uphold it. Dell Upton has written of 'white and black landscapes in eighteenth-century Virginia' where 'all points are related to one's own customary location, rather than to the current position of the observer',[110] correcting the bias of history by perceiving and structuring the plantation from the point of view of the enslaved rather than its owner. This chapter has attempted to analyse that other customary location for many plantation owners – the off-site position.

Why compare these various instances, degrees and distances of absenteeism? All are qualified by circumstances, particularly the key absence of slavery. But the comparison shows how deep and lasting the consequences of absenteeism could be, at local, national and international scales of activity. Butler lived in a suburban villa on Philadelphia's Old York Road, as did the Viscount Fitzwilliam in Richmond upon Thames, and no great ocean separated either of them from their properties. But some residents of Dublin's villas, such as the Latouche and Massey-Dawson families, who owned extensive Jamaican plantations, did exploit the transatlantic scale of absenteeism.[111] Many early nineteenth-century British and Irish heirs to Caribbean plantations never crossed the Atlantic, their lands managed by a complex structure of attorneys and agents, and this is arguably a more insidious form of absenteeism because of the sheer scale of geographical displacement. Butler in Philadelphia and Fitzwilliam in London were still close enough to their estates to retain some recent knowledge of what took place on the ground, derived from the speed of personal and postal travel. Their spatial, personal and societal legacies were more traditionally recorded and are more easily unpicked. The crucial early and lasting difference between eighteenth-century American planters and their European gentlemen counterparts, as discussed in Chapter 1, is that Europeans generally did not depend solely on their plantation investments for their economic wellbeing or social status. Their diversified, transnational and transatlantic income streams then served them well by muddying the extent of their colonial property and by allowing the asset transfer of colonial profits to be overlaid by layers and layers of other investments, inheritances, dowries, mortgages, bank accounts, leases and subleases. Such Europeans, and particularly royal and aristocratic families, continued to benefit from being so distant that they could often disassociate themselves completely from the legacies of European transatlantic imperialism and its roots in chattel slavery, while the plantation landscapes they created from Europe are, for the most part, inadequately researched.[112] Yet they did not forget to claim compensation for the loss of their enslaved workers in Britain or for plantation property in France, a contradiction staggering for its moral bankruptcy. Attention is still grabbed by local and national stories while the international imperial narratives sail blithely on.

CHAPTER 7

Landscapes of Contradiction

Undermining the Picturesque

> Strange to tell the tract of county now occupied by the rebels, though little more than from ten to twenty miles distant from this city, has long been, and still continues to be as little known to us as any of the wildest parts of America; a rude and barren extent of heath, moor, bog and mountain, it has been hitherto considered as scarcely penetrable by the most adventurous sportsman.
>
> Saunders' Newsletter, 13 July 1798

Earlier chapters have explored how comparing countries, landscapes and lived experiences became a means of encouraging revolution. Route reversal upset established hierarchies of route, sites, views and landscapes to change perceptions of a place and its people to revolutionary ends. Unexpected and inappropriate translations had revolutionary consequences. The travels of Lord Edward FitzGerald and Arthur O'Connor manipulated the picturesque tour as a guise to conceal intent, using leisure activity to conceal political activity. Revolution was often soon followed by counter-revolution. The brief formation of a United Belgian States in 1789–90 led Pierce Butler to worry (with no sense of irony) whether the poor Brabanter revolutionaries were 'to be returned to their slavery'. Their harsh suppression by the Habsburg armies had created a people whose 'situation' should become 'a caution to the French to guard against counter-revolution'.[1] This chapter will explore how revolutionary landscape was successfully inverted during the counter-revolutionary phase that followed. By concealing

overtly military activity behind a mask of picturesque scenery, reversing the route back on itself and using text to complicate and undermine images, counter-revolutionary landscape restructured what it found. The restructuring was accomplished in various ways. Military roads altered the country's infrastructure and enabled its oversight and control. Visual images targeted perceptions of specific revolutionary landscapes and reframed them to reflect the government's point of view. Board games taught people, children especially, how to perceive the United Kingdom and the British empire.[2]

Few counties were as enthusiastic as Co. Wicklow in the 1798 rebellion. Its United Irishmen even managed to recruit 'a surprising number of cells from the supposedly loyalist King's County Militia' and the regiment had to be 'removed from Wicklow on account of its unacceptably high level of fraternization with rebels' in 1797. Ruan O'Donnell has written of how the county's religious diversity was relatively low-key with none of the 'violent economic inspired "sectarian" rivalry witnessed in south Ulster in the late 1780s'. This helped Wicklow to amass the 'largest United Irish organization in Leinster' and to embrace 'the inter-denominational and egalitarian ideals of the United Irishmen' with 'surprising ease'.[3] Like Lord Edward's position in County Kildare, it had a resident subversive nobleman in the Earl of Leeson, who was 'charged, at least privately, with overt United Irish tendencies' and such subversive aristocrats made the rebellion in Wicklow attractive to all classes.[4]

In the years before the rebellion the overhanging proximity of the Wicklow mountains became a matter of grave concern for the British administration in Dublin city. The adjacency of

such wild mountainous uplands, dominated by barren reaches of heather and gorse, to the city had always surprised visitors to Dublin – it was rather as if a large chunk of the Scottish Highlands was located as close to London as Lambeth. It would continue to surprise Victorian tourists who found it 'singular' that 'so wild a district should be found so near the principal city of Ireland' (Fig. 161).[5] The county's geography splintered the county into various distinct areas and this fractured character proved strategically helpful to the United Irishmen's rebellion, while also encouraging 'the protracted guerilla war fought in Wicklow from 1798 to 1803'.[6] With no spinal roads to provide safe passage for the military, the county's valleys, bogs and mountainsides became the haunts of such mythic rebels as Michael Dwyer and 'General' Joseph Holt.

Such naturally revolutionary landscapes were also worrisome for Wicklow's landed gentry and they submitted a 'Reason for making the new Military Road in the County of Wicklow' to the Lord Lieutenant, Charles Cornwallis in February 1800, which was the mountains' dangerous

'contiguity' to Dublin from 'which a [rebel] army might pour down in a few hours'. Arguing for a new road to open 'the whole range of mountains from nearly south to north', they hoped to separate the eastern rebel strongholds of Aghavannagh, Glenmalure and Seven Churches from their western haunts of Blackditches, the Glen of Imaal, Blackmoor Hill and Whelp Rock. They analysed Wicklow's road structure of three 'almost parallel' east–west roads that had no 'communication from any of these roads to the other', enabling the rebels to find 'safe retreats' in the mountains in between. Unless the mountains were 'laid open by Cross Roads a Banditti' would 'resort to them for years to come' and they included a map of the road's proposed route with the memorandum.[7] The government then moved to instruct the military engineer, surveyor and cartographer Alexander Taylor 'to examine and to reconnoitre the ground'.[8] Born in Aberdeen, Taylor had cut his teeth as a military land surveyor in Scotland, joining the army as a lieutenant in the 81st Regiment of Foot, before transferring to the Royal Irish Engineers in 1778.[9] His brother

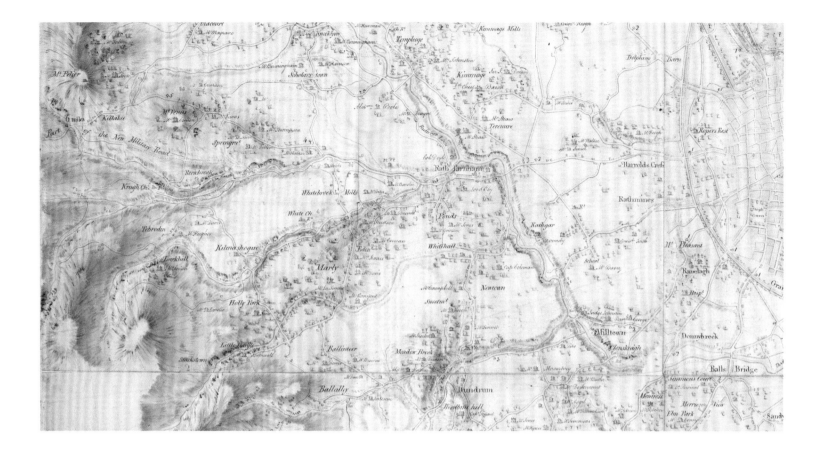

George was also a surveyor and cartographer, and they colla-borated with Andrew Skinner on the book *Maps of the Roads of Ireland* and a survey of Co. Louth, both published in 1778.[10] Construction of the military road began in August 1801 and continued until 1809. In 1801 Alexander Taylor wrote of the road's 'considerable advantage, in civilizing and improving' the country, recommending that barracks be built along its route to facilitate law enforcement. Believing that 'the greatest & most useful improvement'[11] that a country could know of was good roads, Taylor drew many of the surveys and maps himself.

The government's plans to improve the military road network aligned neatly with Wicklow's promotion as a picturesque destination. The county had become an impor-tant tourist site for Dublin's landscape enthusiasts over the course of the eighteenth century when day trips to see the Powerscourt and Dargle waterfalls, the Sugarloaf Mountain, Glendalough and the county's wealth of valleys and mountain passes became increasingly popular. The county's landowners, such as Viscount Powerscourt, encouraged visitors to visit their picturesque properties and to spend time (and money) in villages such as Bray or Enniskerry. Tour guides and books of views described many Wicklow sites, yet the Wicklow tour was never as much of a circuit as Killarney's, Ireland's pre-eminent tourist site by the close of the century.[12] Again, the Wicklow mountains' geography led tourists to visit separate and contained valleys, from which they could not easily travel to other sites. Unlike Ireland's other key tourist areas that were structured around a group of lakes (Killarney, Lough Erne) or along a river (the Liffey, the Boyne, the Blackwater, the Lee), Wicklow was difficult to tour, with many cul-de-sacs. A comparatively large county, many of its most picturesque sites were inconveniently far apart. Some cohesion occurred around Glendalough, Powerscourt and the river Dargle but other sites remained discrete and disconnected. The taste for the sea prospect, which saw Wicklow's seafront towns develop substantial tourist agendas later in the nineteenth century, was mostly overwhelmed by the overtly military functions of Dun Laoghaire and Arklow harbours.

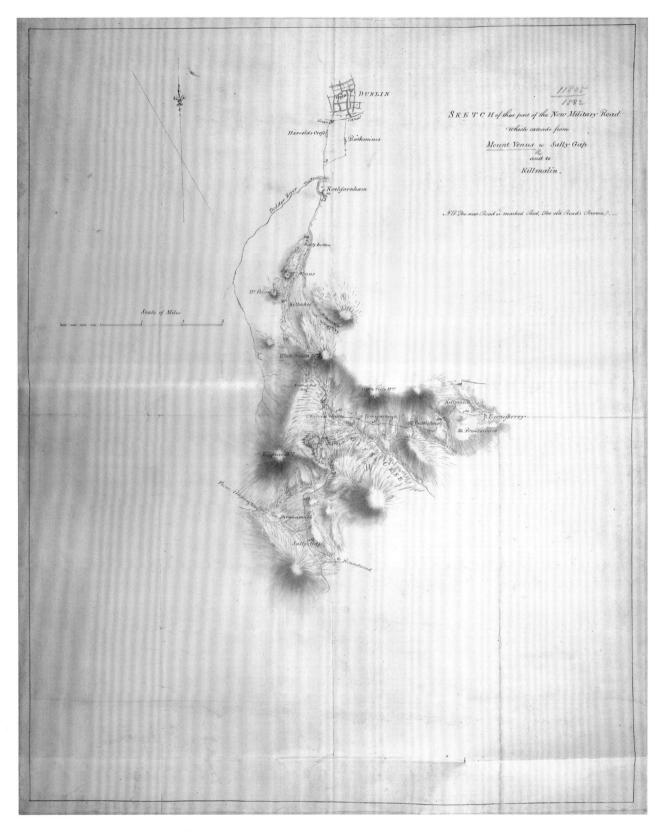

163. Major Alexander Taylor, *Map of the New Military Road, from Mount Venus to Sally Gap and Killmalin, near Dublin, Ireland*, 1801. British Library, Add. Ms. 32451 E

In Wicklow the eye of the roving tourist, concerned to see the most picturesque prospects, neatly coincided with that of the military road surveyor and strategist. Military roads had been adopted by picturesque tourists before, notably in Scotland, where the military roads of the 1740s accommodated later tours of the Highlands.[13] Yet it was rare for military and tourism projects to proceed so blatantly in tandem and with such evident design intent. The complicit cast of characters included the Lord Lieutenant, Philip Yorke 3rd Earl of Hardwicke, Chief Secretary the Hon. Charles Abbot, Alexander Taylor, the painter Thomas Sautelle Roberts and the dramatist John O'Keeffe. Philip Yorke and Charles Abbot had penned many letters and descriptions of their own earlier tours of the Irish landscape in 1781 and 1792 respectively.[14] As Lord Lieutenant, Yorke commissioned surveyors, road-builders, an artist and a dramatist to draw, design, improve, aestheticise and build a changed Wicklow. All these men were intimately acquainted with the proscribed modes for seeing, touring and appreciating landscape, and were connected by ties of patronage, professional association or acquaintance. Soldiers, road-builders, surveyors, politicians, artists and playwrights became simultaneously engaged in a spatial and ideological tug-of-war in the mountains, and the fluid translation of military and engineering projects into topographical watercolours and prints as well as to plays and the theatre, helped to pacify and amalgamate Ireland into the new United Kingdom, formed by the Act of Union of 1800.

Felicity Myrone has described topography as 'a complex, highly organised field of variegated visual and textual activity, reproduction and categorisation, involving the makers of images, antiquarians, collectors and entrepreneurs'.[15] The connection between representing space to scale and in two dimensions on plan, and its subsequent representation as a view, was widely used to denigrate practitioners of topographical drawing when compared to the 'greater' landscape artists. Topographical drawing, in its insistence on being a place, is a type of 'map-work' and its effects in real space may be as pronounced. The watercolours and prints that the Military Road project engendered were all intimately connected with the 'kind of map-work'[16] that accompanies the violent process of conquest and colonisation. Wicklow's maps, drawings and views generated an infrastructural re-design much as the topographical prospect views of Drogheda and Derry had generated landscape designs that responded to the military events of

1641, 1688 and 1690. Road-building had supported the ideology of improvement that characterised Irish eighteenth-century design practice more generally, and the correct representation of improvement in paintings and prints formed part of the general project of improving Ireland. But road-building and infrastructural reform also followed in the wake of insurrection and such projects were hard to frame simply as improvements, particularly when they came hard upon a period of violence and suppression. The close temporal alignment of the insurrection to the infrastructural projects it created and the representational projects it inspired was complex and contradictory.

In 1801 Alexander Taylor completed a *Sketch of the Environs of Dublin* in which he drew the beginning of a new military road leading out of Rathfarnham and southwards into the Wicklow mountains (Fig. 162). That year he also prepared a more detailed *Map of the New Military Road, from Mount Venus to Sally Gap and Killmalin* to set out a design for the northern reaches of the road, including its spur towards the demesne of Powerscourt (Fig. 163). Work on the new military road began on 12 August 1800 and continued throughout 1801. Taylor wrote to Lieut. Colonel Edward Baker Littlehales, Under-Secretary at the Military Department, in August 1801 to outline the road's rationale and to argue for the 'extension of Military Roads' as a means of 'civilizing and improving the Country'. Roads in 'mountainous tracts where there are now no Roads, or where they are so bad, & in such improper directions, as to be the greater part of the year, nearly impassable & useless' would first enable 'proprietor[s] to improve the Soil' and secondly 'would civilize the Country, by giving access with promptitude, & dispatch, to the march of Troops, from the nearest Military Posts, or Quarters, to those places, which had been heretofore the Haunts of Outlaws, Rebels, & Robbers'.[17] He suggested that 'Military Posts' or barracks 'might be established, on the new Roads, at the most proper places, for securing the Country' and so as to 'completely cut off the hopes of any party of Banditti; from making them places of shelter'. Such barracks would 'at the same time show the Inhabitants of the Vallies the readiness, & facility of affording them protection, & thereby remove the fear, or pretended fear, which they have been held in, by these Plunderers'. Despite the many references to improvement as a motive for road-building, Taylor acknowledged that the primary inspiration was the rebellion itself:

Tho the Rebellion has been suppressed, it has not been crushed. The spirit, the hopes, & the intentions of Rebellion, are as much cherished now, as at any period, & nothing is wanting to the bursting forth of the smothered flame, but some successful effort of the Enemy to land in this Country, in such a situation, every new communication which will lay open, any impenetrable part, of the interior of the Country, must depress the hopes of successful insurrection by destroying their Citadels.

If the government directed its attention towards the Wicklow and Wexford mountains that gave 'shelter to Rebels, Robbers & outlaws … at the Door of the Capital' this 'would certainly produce the most happy effects'. Its cost when compared to its advantages was 'inconsiderable' and when considered as a 'National object, of no account' whatsoever. Wicklow's contamination by the even more seditious neighbouring counties of Wexford and Kildare continued to be a concern and Taylor advised opening 'cross Roads, to facilitate the intercourse, with Kildare, & Carlow on the West, & with improved parts of Wicklow, & Wexford, on the East'.[18] The 'Military Road Financial Agreement' recorded that '200 Soldiers, 3 Subalterns, and a Pay Clerk' were 'constantly employed besides a certain number of Country People' and an 'Overseer of the Works'. All payments were approved by Taylor himself, who left the mundane work to others but retained his supervisory role. Six miles of road had been finished by 10 February 1802, when Taylor's progress report to Dublin Castle listed the many 'small bridges, sewers and water pavements' that its safe construction had required.[19]

Peter J. O'Keeffe's book *Alexander Taylor's Roadworks in Ireland, 1780–1827* includes an analysis of why the road's exact course was chosen and describes the slow process of driving the road southwards.[20] Much of the route's rationale was derived from land gradient. Richard Griffith, the author of the 1813 'Bog Survey Report on the mountainous parts of Counties Dublin and Wicklow'[21] found the road 'wonderfully level and straight' and observed that 'throughout the whole extent, the Engineer found no vallies which he could possibly take advantage of, consistently with his direction, except that of Glen Mackanass'.[22] Robert Fraser's 1801 *General View of the Agriculture and Mineralogy, Present State and Circumstances of the County Wicklow* was the first book to publish a map of the new military road, together with a very long list of the many

places it passed through from Rathfarnham to Aghavannagh (Fig. 164).[23] Its northern reaches were depicted in John Taylor's map of 1816 and in Baldwin, Cradock and Jay's 1822 *Map of the County of Wicklow*. The government followed Taylor's advice that a suite of barracks accompany the road, and by the end of 1802 barracks were planned for Glencree and/or Liffey Head, Laragh (Glendalough), Drumgoff (Glenmalure), Aghavannagh and Leitrim (Imaal). These placed soldiers permanently in the mountains and in positions where they could 'keep the mountaineers in subjection'. As the natives were suspect, soldiers 'belonging to some Scotch Fencible Regiments' were drafted in to build the road.[24] Modelled on Scotland's military roads and built by Scottish engineers and soldiers, the road drove a model of loyal Scottish expertise through a less than receptive Irish environment.

In March 1801 Major Cornwallis was replaced as Lord Lieutenant of Ireland by Philip Yorke, 3rd Earl of Hardwicke. Yorke, who had toured Ireland comprehensively in 1781 with his younger brother Charles, was well-versed in picturesque tourism. They had found the Giant's Causeway a 'wonderful production of Nature' and travelling southwards towards Dublin they stopped to view the Boyne obelisk, where they 'trace[d] out the principal ocurrances' of the battle on site to find that it agreeably 'conform[ed] a good deal' to a print they had seen of it in the London print shop Hamels.[25] They thought that the battle 'must have been a very hazardous enterprize, as the ground' was 'exceedingly strong on the banks' while Drogheda was remarkable for its 'remains of the old walls battered down by Cromwell'. When they eventually arrived in Dublin in late August they were keen to 'see the County of Wicklow to advantage', intending 'to make a tour' with Dublin 'so empty' that it was 'necessary to employ oneself in rambling about the Country in order not to waste time'. They spent a full five days touring Wicklow and also 'meditated a tour to Limerick Killarney and Corke' but resisted the temptation. A letter from Charles Yorke to his mother reveals just how well acquainted the future Lord Lieutenant was with Wicklow before any hint of the military road's conception. On 2 September 1781 the brothers had ascended the Sugarloaf Mountain and marched along one of the 'Ridges which form the Glen of the Downs (a pass between the Mountains much like the Dargle, only upon a larger Scale and without Water)'. The Devil's Glen was 'an extraordinary feature of Nature', resembling 'the approaches to some of the mountains in

Switzerland'. Their host, Mr Tottenham, was 'carrying a road along the woody side, with seats disposed at 'the most advantageous point of View'. This had improved the 'present' situation where tourists were 'obliged to scramble over large Masses of Rock which obstruct[ed]' their way. Summoned back to Dublin to see the then Lord Lieutenant, Lord Carlisle, they found him 'reserved and solemn' and saying 'little of public affairs'[26] but open to discussing their Wicklow tour.

When Philip Yorke returned to Ireland in 1801 to take up his difficult duties as Lord Lieutenant in the aftermath of the 1798 rebellion he was well-positioned to address the many challenges that Wicklow then presented to the British government. His Chief Secretary Charles Abbot had also toured Wicklow, visiting Powerscourt, the Dargle, Powerscourt Waterfall and the Devil's Glen in 1792. Travelling with Arthur Young's *A Tour in Ireland, 1776–1779* in hand, Abbot admired Young's 'great truth and propriety of representation' but criticised the view of the Powerscourt Waterfall as 'a very bad one' (Fig. 39). The Dargle resembled the river valley of Hackfall in Yorkshire except that Hackfall was 'a degree broader and the stream larger', and he preferred the route from 'Dublin thro' Bray and thence going up the Glen of the Downs' to the one through Enniskerry. Like Charles Yorke he was concerned about access to the Devil's Glen where 'the carriageway out of the high road' was only 'about half a mile long, down to the gate of the glen' and only those on horseback could pass 'very easily though the whole glen itself'.[27] In August 1801 these two well-versed Wicklow tourists set off again on a 'short tour' of the county as Lord Lieutenant and Chief Secretary of Ireland. They first visited the military road before proceeding 'to the Gold Mines of Croaghan, and to Arklow' to see 'the field of battle between the rebels and General Needham'. Abbot recalled in his diary that 'in consequence of this tour a large extension of the Military Road was resolved upon' with 'special reports' commissioned for 'a more effectual plan for working the Gold Mine, and also for improving the Harbour of Wicklow'.[28]

Amalgamating and overlaying the military and tourist tours encouraged improvements that served both agendas. Surveyors such as Robert Fraser, charged with producing a *General View of the Agriculture and Mineralogy, Present State and Circumstances of the County Wicklow* for the Royal Dublin Society, subsequently converted his findings into one of Wicklow's first tour guides.[29] The 'Statistical Survey' he made

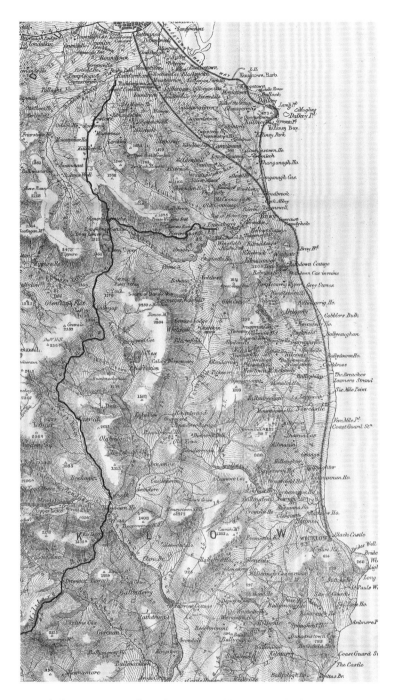

164. 'A General View of the County Wicklow in which the general features of the County are Determined', map of Co. Wicklow from Robert Fraser, *General view of the agriculture and mineralogy, present state and circumstances of the County Wicklow* (Dublin: Graisberry and Campbell, 1801). The military road is outlined in blue.

of the area around Lugnaquilla, Wicklow's highest mountain, saw his host Mr Hume 'pitch a marquee' for the party 'on the top of Knocknamunion, a very high mountain, at the head of the glen of Imale' thus providing Fraser with 'a convenient opportunity of choosing a clear atmosphere for exploring the extensive mountain of Lugnaquilla, from the summit of which you obtain by far the most expanded view of the whole range of mountains and adjacent country'.[30] Such viewpoints were then perpetuated in other tour guides. The Rev. G. N. Wright recalled Fraser's experience in his own 1822 tour guide *A Guide to the County of Wicklow* so as to introduce a frisson of past dangers, now tamed and averted, into his narrative. He recalled how Fraser's party had 'spent some time beneath a marquee upon the mountains, during which a party of armed rebels lay concealed in a cave amongst the precipices, fortunately both parties were then ignorant of each other's presence'.[31]

Staging the Status Quo

Art was also pressed into military service. The painter Thomas Sautelle Roberts, younger brother of the landscape artist Thomas Roberts, gave an 'exhibition of landscapes' that had been 'chiefly executed for his excellency the Lord Lieutenant [Philip Yorke] and the Right. Hon. Charles Abbot' in Dublin's old Parliament House in January 1802. According to the *Freeman's Journal* the landscapes had been 'principally taken in the County of Wicklow, including the Gold, Copper, and Lead Mines; shewing the Machinery and manner of working them' (Fig. 165).[32] 'The most interesting Views' were considered to be those 'taken from the new Military Roads and close Scenes of the Dargle, Seven Churches' or Glendalough. Twelve of the exhibited views were 'proposed for publication' as prints 'to accompany a Tour through that romantic country'.[33]

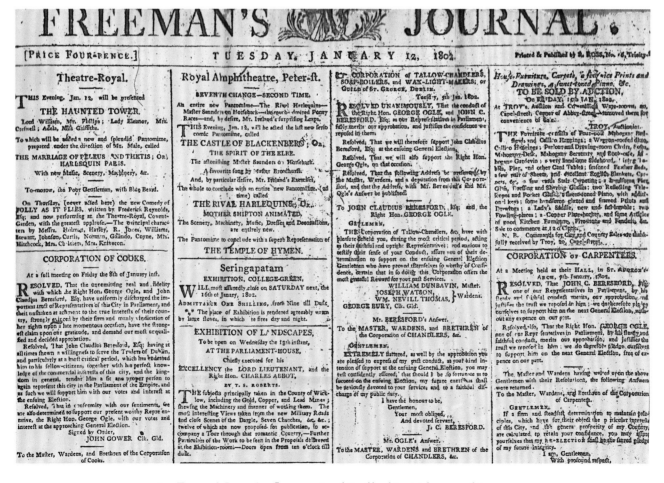

165. *Freeman's Journal*, 12 January 1802. http://archive.irishnewsarchive.com

166. Thomas Sautelle Roberts, 'View in the Valley of Glencree with an officer and the Rt. Hon. Charles Abbot discussing the proposed "Via Militaris"', 1801. Watercolour. Private collection

Thomas Sautelle Roberts was born in Waterford and attended the Dublin Society's Schools, where he learnt to draw. He was initially apprenticed to the architect James Ivory, but inspired perhaps by his older brother's success he chose to become a painter, exhibiting his works in the Society of Artists of Ireland from 1800 onwards. In the 1790s he produced many views of predictable tourist spots, principally castles in Munster (Lismore, Blarney, Dromana and Blackrock). He exhibited views of both British and Irish landscapes in the Royal Academy from 1789 to 1811, and again in 1818, and at the British Institution from 1807 to 1818.[34] One of the earliest views exhibited in the Royal Academy was a 1791 *View of Lord Powerscourt's Park* but his interest did not swing definitively to Wicklow until the nineteenth century. As an exhibition catalogue does not exist for the 1802 Parliament House exhibition, its composition may be hazarded from his known output between 1800 and 1808 and the *Freeman's Journal* advertisement.[35] The whereabouts of many of Thomas Sautelle Roberts's exhibited works are unknown and some of the watercolours probably did not survive the march of time.[36]

THE MILITARY ROADS, COUNTY of WICKLOW.

The Roads and Aurora Camp, appear in the Middle ground — in the Fore ground the Lord Lieutenant and Suit — with the Soldiery and Peasantry employed in blasting, and removeing the huge rocks, so numerous in this romantic Country

167. Thomas Sautelle Roberts, *The Military Roads, County of Wicklow*, T.S. Roberts fecit. S. Alken sculpt., 1804.
Print. British Library, Maps K. Top.55.45.g

The exhibition evidently interspersed military landscapes with picturesque views of the Dargle, the Devil's Glen, Powerscourt and Luggelaw, conservative demesne portraits of Killruddery and its estate town of Bray, and well-crafted views of Dublin from its traditional prospect points. The central body of views was dominated by Wicklow, and only views in or about the military road included named individuals in their titles. *View in the Valley of Glencree* probably depicted the Lord Lieutenant, Lord Hardwicke and Charles Abbot (Fig. 166). *View of the Military Road from the Vicinity of Upper Lough Bray* depicted the Lord Lieutenant (Fig. 167 shows the print made from the watercolour) and *A View of Powerscourt with*

the Golden Spears to the right (the Small and Big Sugar Loaves) and Bray Head beyond, in County Wicklow probably depicted either Charles Abbot or Alexander Taylor (Fig. 168), together forming the principal views 'taken from the military road' that the *Freeman's Journal* so admired. The Glencree views were amongst the first of Wicklow's inner highland fastnesses, depicting landscapes considerably more barren than any of the Powerscourt or Dargle views, which conformed more closely to the quotidian picturesque.

These military views made sure that it was the Lord Lieutenant, Lord Hardwicke, and not a local mountain rebel, who stood beside the waterfall. *View in the Valley of Glencree* is

168. Thomas Sautelle Roberts, 'A View of Powerscourt with the Golden Spears to the right (the Small and Big Sugar Loaves)
and Bray Head beyond, in County Wicklow'. Watercolour. Private collection

a military scouting landscape with all the men on horseback, suggesting that all are of the officer and gentry class (Fig. 166). No workmen or private soldiery appear – this is a surveying party in the early sense of *surveier* or to overlook – they are scoping out the territory before the theodolites, chains, wheelbarrows, gunpowder and pickaxes arrive. Only the small corner of a thatched cottage with a smoking chimney in the middle ground gives some evidence of habitation and scale, together with the figures themselves, and the landscape is essentially unimproved save for one straight-ish section of road on the left bank. The print *The Military Roads*, also set in a sublime highland setting, is a landscape of considerable

military activity (Fig. 167). No longer merely engaged in over-sight, the landscape is now being actively surveyed, inhabited and irrevocably altered. It positions the Lord Lieutenant, direct representative of the Crown, on the new military road as it is blasted and hacked out of the sheer cliffs and precari-ous boulders that line the route. Professional men with imple-ments have arrived and some natives may also be employed, although the white breeches suggest not. A beam of sunlight pierces through heavy clouds to fall on a large rectangular military encampment in the middle ground. In the distance the new straight roads zig-zag heavily over the Dublin moun-tains. Smoke rises now from the gunpowder blasting and mess-house cooking rather than from any cottage fires. The caption to the print that was subsequently made of the watercolour explained its structural composition, while also acting as an able witness to its ideological manoeuvres (Fig. 167):

> The Roads and Aurora Camp, appear in the Middle ground – in the Fore ground the Lord Lieutenant and Suit – with the Soldiery and Peasantry employed in blasting, and removing the huge rocks, so numerous in this romantic Country.

Thomas Sautelle Roberts increased the sublimity of the print by compressing the surrounding landscape into a steeper and more highland geography than that which existed in reality. By following picturesque structure with a fore, middle and rear ground, the correctly composed image diverted attention from the essential act of destruction that it depicted. It was not merely depicting a picturesque landscape, it also showed how it was being destroyed by 'blasting, and removing the huge rocks'. The engineering, wide roads, stone barracks and non-native soldiers that this image recorded effectively undermined Wicklow's dangerously subversive picturesque, one with no infrastructure, buildings or loyal inhabitants.

In *A View of Powerscourt with the Golden Spears to the right (the Small and Big Sugar Loaves) and Bray Head beyond, in County Wicklow* only figures that denote a military presence are included (Fig. 168). One mounted officer (either Charles Abbot or Captain Alexander Taylor), two workmen and a lone kilted Scottish fencible sit, stand or bend on the corner of a road softened by stray boulders and bushes. Otherwise this view is a classic demesne portrait of broadleaf tree belts, clumps, haystacks, boundary walls and inhabited cottages. In the middle ground stands Powerscourt House and to the left the view opens towards the Irish Sea. Yet this spur of the military road was built to connect the large east-coast towns of Bray and Wicklow, and such military camps as Loughlinstown, with the military road, 'giving access with promptitude, & dispatch, to the march of Troops, from the nearest Military Posts, or Quarters, to those places, which had been heretofore the Haunts of Outlaws, Rebels, & Robbers'.[37] It ran along the northern boundary of Lord Powerscourt's estate, a much more gentle and improved landscape than that depicted at Glencree and the confused Highland fencible was removed from another version of this polite view.[38] In altering the staffage

Roberts may have been responding to client preferences, or his collaborator Comerford, who completed many of the miniature figures, may have inserted different figure groupings to suit anticipated market interest.

These incongruous images of displaced Scottish Highlanders in an Irish highland served to highlight rather than align the diverging identities of Ireland and Scotland in the early 1800s. When the road was complete the gentlemen of Wicklow suggested to the government that it should buy 'the waste mountain land on either side of the military road, and settle a colony there of Highland soldiers'. Thinking in particular of Scottish emigrants to America who could perhaps be 'induced to change their course and settle in the Wicklow mountains', the proprietors believed that they 'should soon behold a sturdy race of loyal mountaineers, who would not only greatly improve the appearance of the country, but would strengthen the hands of Government by rendering what has lately been considered the shelter for lawless rebels, the residence of a population, grateful to those who had rescued them from a transatlantic emigration'. The proposal apparently met with a 'cordial reception from Lord Hardwicke' as did everything 'that tended to the improvement of Ireland'. Attempts to purchase the land were made but failed because it was owned by the Church of Ireland. This was 'much to be lamented' and, somewhat optimistically, the Bog Commissioners assessed that 'had it been carried into execution, a great part of the mountain lands would by this time have been reclaimed, at least those along the verge of the military road'.[39] Yet the unrealistic aspects of the proposal must have been evident to even the most inexperienced and naive officials in Dublin Castle. Using the Scots to inspire loyalty in the Irish forced a comparison of both countries and could lead to subversive conclusions. Whereas in Scotland the Gaels had often been successfully transformed from Jacobite rebels to British heroes by the 1780s, in Ireland such a transformation remained elusive. The key ideological hurdles of religion and monarchy remained, particularly in locations where the landscape retained a sectarian structure. As the Ordnance Surveyor Eugene Curry noted, 'the bulk of the tenantry on the Powerscourt estate are Protestants who hold the best part of the lands the Catholics being principally located on the mountain sides, and in the rugged bottoms of Glencree'.[40] Thomas Sautelle Roberts's images blurred Wicklow's political and religious faultlines, but it remained easier to do this in painted images than on the ground.

Néw near Loch Rannoch
√ 83 – 2

169. Paul Sandby, *Surveying Party by Kinloch Rannoch*, 1749. British Library, Maps K.Top.50.83.2

These Irish images of military survey and construction diverge powerfully from Paul Sandby's well-known depictions of surveying parties along Scottish military roads in the late 1740s.[41] In those images the kilted Highlanders stand tall and equal to the English surveyors and genteel noblemen and women (Fig. 169), and together they form polite groupings within successfully negotiated British landscapes of improvement. This happy rapprochement between wild upland landscape, loyal busy Highlanders and the Crown was partly translated into Wicklow, and yet a few key errors were made. Thomas Sautelle Roberts's Wicklow images depict Scottish Highlanders as the hierarchical instructors of a native workforce – mercenaries brought in to tame a foreign landscape and its native populace. Philip Yorke, the Lord Lieutenant and Charles Abbot only converse with Scottish Highlanders in the Wicklow images and never with any natives, who are not trusted with theodolites or surveying chains. The Lord

Lieutenant remained but a proxy for the Crown and his direction of travel in the Wicklow images is typically back to Dublin rather than further into the wilderness (Fig. 167). This did not suggest that he had any inclination to remain in Wicklow, or even holiday there for a few weeks. As with many of the Royal Collection's Irish landscapes, that mostly depict the royal family leaving Ireland in the royal yacht, senior British royals, administrators and officers were in transit, never in situ.

Predictable if accomplished views of the Dargle were hung beside those that actively reversed the rebel position, appropriating Wicklow's romantic landscape visually from the rebel cause. Yet memories of recent and ongoing violent insurgency must have been invoked in the exhibition's visitors, and this may have acted against the counter-revolutionary agenda that Roberts and his patron, the Lord Lieutenant, hoped to advance. Of all the lost views, the most suggestive is *A Rebel*

The Scalp

London Published May 30th 1796 by Thos Macklin, Poets Gallery, Fleet St.

170. John Le Porte [Laporte], 'The Scalp in the County of Wicklow', 1796. British Library, Maps K.Top.55.52.b

Retreat in the Devil's Glen: General Holt is Represented as Appointing his Guards. 'General' Joseph Holt had been captured in 1798, unlike Michael Dwyer who evaded capture until 1803, and, as Tom Bartlett has observed, 'the romantic award of the title "General" to Holt blurred the distinction between public and private men of violence',[42] making it hard to discern where one's loyalties should lie. Moreover 'the emerging romanticist admiration for man in harmony with nature, at one with a wild landscape – not rendered savage by it – fixed on the careers of Holt ("the master of the mountains") and Dwyer ("this

mountain general") and reinterpreted them in keeping with the new aesthetics'.[43] When the 1802 exhibition opened sufficient time had elapsed for the rebel 'General' to have entered into both myth and image. Dwyer's more recent activity, coupled with his lack of a mutable Protestant identity, and subsequent banishment to Van Diemen's Land (Tasmania), must have made his inclusion into such a sequence of views problematic. If the image of General Holt spoke of 'the paradoxical situation of Wicklow – a rebel stronghold, a last frontier, yet located on the outskirts of a capital city', other titles suggest

171. John Laporte, 'The Town of Bray, London: Publish'd March 1 1796 by Thos Macklin, Poets Gallery, Fleet Street'.
British Library, Maps Ktop LIII, 24.a

how 'military red and Scots plaid' might vie with 'Whiteboy white and republican green'.[44]

What did the lost *View of Vinegar Hill*, site of one of the United Irishmen's most resounding defeats, look like? Was a triumphant post-siege or battle analysis like the topographical views and paintings of Drogheda or Derry examined in Chapter 1? Or did it seek to play on the romantic character of a lost revolutionary cause? What of the lost image of *An Irish Hut, Co. Wicklow*, its title reminiscent of Young's '*An Irish Cabbin*' (Fig. 70)? Wicklow's great prospect of 'The Scalp',

where visitors enjoyed a sudden and spectacular view of the Sugarloaf Mountain, took its name from *scailp*, the Irish word for a 'cleft or fissure in rock', and 'a shelter formed therein, or a cave, den or earthen hut' (Fig. 170).[45] And what of the *View from the Commons of Bray*? John Laporte's 1796 view of *The Town of Bray* used the river Dargle to separate the sensible upright estate town on the right, with its Protestant church and large well-appointed buildings, from the cabins and cottages of Bray common on the left (Fig. 171). Common land was not at all common in Ireland, where the seventeenth-century

MEETING of THE WATERS, COUNTY of WICKLOW.

In the distance is seen the Vale of Avondale & Wooden Bridge, to the right on a rising Ground the Seat of Captain Mills, and in the fore Ground a Stone Bridge, with the junction of the Rivers Avon and Avoca.

London Published as the Act directs 1st January, 1804.

172. '*Meeting of the Waters, County of Wicklow*, London: Published as the Act directs; 1st January, 1804, T Sautell Roberts delit. F.C. Lewis fecit'. Print. British Library, Maps K.Top.55.45.e

property transfers of land had ensured that few lands remained in ambiguous or communal ownership. The many acts of enclosure, which had inspired much aggrieved political commentary and considerable landscape theory in England, had little parallel in Ireland, where many property rights had been lost in its seventeenth-century upheavals. Laporte's view and Sautelle Roberts's title appear to knowingly suggest the spatial legacy of sectarian conflict.

Prints derived from the Parliament House exhibition include views of the Military Road, Powerscourt Waterfall, Luggelaw, the Meeting of the Waters, multiple views of the Dargle, and the Gold Mines. No prints exist of the *View of Powerscourt from Glencree*, nor of the many ambiguous titles that are now lost. Even seemingly innocuous images such as *Meeting of the Waters* were not entirely innocent. Located at the confluence of the Avonbeg and Avonmore rivers, the site's eventual renown as a tourist spot, as commemorated in song by Thomas Moore, was only in its infancy (Fig. 172).[46] Sautelle Roberts's image caught the river winding its way to the port of Arklow between the properties of two hardline loyalist mine-owners and the caption to the print betrayed its motivation: 'In the distance is seen the Vale of Avondale and Wooden Bridge to the right on a rising Ground the Seat of Captain Mills and in the fore Ground a Stone Bridge with the junction of the Rivers Avon and Avoca.' Subsequently called Castle Howard, the house on the ridge to the right-hand side was owned by Abraham Mills of Cronebane, the owner of Cronebane Mines and a 'captain of a Yeomanry Corps' who 'was active in the suppression of the 1798 rebellion'. To the left Sautelle Roberts depicted Kingston House, home of Thomas King, a leading member of the Wicklow militia and a local mineralogist.[47] He was so hardline a loyalist in suppressing the rebellion that Lord Cornwallis, who preceded Philip Yorke as Lord Lieutenant of Ireland, found his methods unacceptable.[48] The watercolour was less genteel than its eventual print, which included a well-appointed carriage crossing the Avon. With the house and fort visibly gentrified, the river's picturesque quality was converted into publishing gold while simultaneously reinforcing its political identification as a newly minted loyalist landscape (Fig. 172).

The Wicklow gentry were dedicated followers of improvement in all its forms but most particularly mining with Theophilus 'Monck, Abraham Mills of Cronebane, Thomas King of Kingston (Rathdrum), Turner Camac

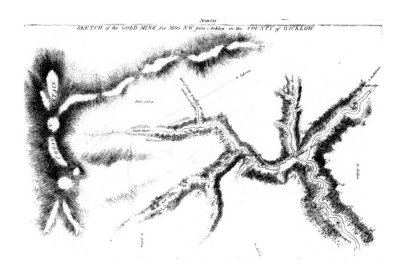

173. Major Alexander Taylor, *Mineralogical Maps of Croaghan Mountain, Co. Wicklow*, 1801, or *Sketch of the Gold Mine five miles N.W. from Arklow in the County of Wicklow*. Engraved by Basire, based on sketches by Major John Brown, Royal Engineers, 1796. British Library, Add. Ms. 32451 F

of Castlemacadam, William Tighe of Rossana and John Blachford of Powerscourt', all members of the Dublin Society's 'Committee of Chemistry and Mineralogy'.[49] A letter written by Abraham Mills from 'Cronebane Copper Mines, near Rathdrum' on 21 November 1795 to Joseph Banks gave 'a mineralogist's account of native gold lately discovered in Ireland' and included 'a map of the area'.[50] It was read out at London's Royal Society and published in the *Dublin Society Transactions* in 1801. In that year Alexander Taylor had also made maps of Croghaun Mountain (Fig. 173). 'In general the mines of East Avoca were owned by British companies, loyal to the Crown, and the mines of West Avoca were owned by Irish companies.'[51] Lying upstream of King's house on the left-hand side of *Meeting of the Waters* (Fig. 172), Croghaun Mountain was one of 'General' Holt's last outposts of rebellion.[52] It was also the origin of an October 1795 gold rush, 'prompted by the discovery of alluvial gold in streams running off' the mountain. The requisite 'royal assent' for a gold mine was granted 'in April 1797 after trials and exploratory surveys by local mineralogists King, Mills and Weaver' but this perceived 'government takeover' had duly 'aroused considerable animosity' and the military camp constructed to subdue the goldmines 'was burned by the Wicklow United Irishmen when the opportunity arose in July 1798.'[53]

Joining the outlawed United Irishmen involved an oath-taking ceremony. Workplaces, particularly mines, where people could congregate without arousing suspicion, were used to enlist new members. This might be accomplished in stages at different locations and Ruan O'Donnell has researched how 'John Tyson of Cronebane was taken to the mines stampyard' where he laid 'his hand on The Book of Common Prayer' and gave an oath 'to keep the secrets of the United Irishmen and not to prosecute them'. The next day Tyson was 'brought to Tigroney Hill' to meet Thomas Brady 'the captain of the local rebel company' and 'chief clerk of the mines'[54] who 'administered the military oath that made him a fully-fledged United Irishman.' Thomas Sautelle Roberts included a *View of the Wicklow Gold Mines* taken at the contentious site of Croghaun Mountain in his exhibition. He could have chosen one of Wicklow's other mines but they did not have the romantic power and threatening overhang of a great mountain, nor the recent memory of revolutionary events. In the print the mines, like the military road, were inhabited by eager and diligent workmen, another instance of a visibly loyal population displacing one known not to be (Fig. 174). The caption explained:

> In the Foreground are several Figures employed in working or buddeling; in the Middle Ground they are seen digging and barrowing the Earth, which contains the particles of Gold; on the first discovery of these Mines pieces of pure Gold were found valued at eighty pounds and upwards, one of which may be seen at the Levarian Museum. The scene closes with Croughan and the adjoining Hills.

When the watercolours were transferred to London for exhibition in the Royal Academy, ignorance of the details of the 1798 rebellion probably made their interpretation less military and more picturesque. Highlanders are after all supposed to reside in highlands, whether in Ireland or in Scotland. But such ignorance was impossible in Dublin in January 1802, where they were first exhibited. Visitors to Parliament House must have interpreted images such as the *View of the Wicklow Gold Mines* for what it was – a calculated visual representation of Wicklow as an imperial military landscape, but one that was also picturesque. The 1802 Parliament House exhibition 'prompted reflections on Sautelle's watercolour style from an anonymous diarist who noted his two distinct manners of painting before concluding, somewhat grudgingly, that his talents were "much

above mediocrity"'.[55] Reviewed by the *Literary Gazette* in the Royal Academy's 1818 annual show, the article singled out 'No. 156. A Waterfall, T.S. Roberts', by noting, 'We are not much acquainted with this artist, but the present is a favourable specimen of his talent.'[56] Roberts's talent for reframing scenes of violent insurrection as polite views was not remarked upon.

Both landscape and personal identity were in flux in the Wicklow uplands. Inhabited by pseudo-generals yet situated so close to Dublin, there the romantic paradigms of wilderness, noble savage and radical rebellion were all prone to revision. Thomas Sautelle Roberts's watercolours of the heartlands of these mountains at Glencree, the Military Road, the Gold Mines, the General Holt view and Vinegar Hill, while seeming loyal, contain too many romantic details of rebellion to be fully convincing of a straightforward counter-revolutionary agenda. Ambiguous and paradoxical, these counter-revolutionary images find the romantic too attractive and the loyal inscriptions attached to the print only serve to further emphasise their contradictions. Eight days after the opening of Thomas Sautelle Roberts's 1802 exhibition in the old Parliament House, the play *The Wicklow Gold Mines* opened at the Theatre Royal, again by 'command of his Excellency the Lord Lieutenant and Countess of Hardwicke'.[57] The play had been first performed in 1795, 'the same year in which the United Irishmen became a secret society', and featured 'a range of stock Irish characters', but also introduced 'a new figure: a violent member of a secret society who is on the side of good, the native Redmond O'Hanlon'.[58] With O'Hanlon positioned in upland Wicklow, his foil was the grouse hunter and Dubliner, Squire Donnybrook, who tried to marry his daughter Helen to the owner of a Wicklow gold mine, the suggestively American Mr Franklin.[59] O'Hanlon and the local people prevent a miscarriage of justice when they bundle Felix, an accused man, into a secret tunnel that leads from a chapel to an abbey ruin so that he can escape over the mountains. In the theatre, the mountain rebel proved more dramatically attractive than any city loyalist.

Geographically unstable, the *The Wicklow Gold Mines'* dialectic between rebel and landlord, mountain and city, eastern seaboard and western wilderness continued to define native and foreign landscapes in Ireland and the association of national and revolutionary identity with romantic mountain strongholds and the western horizon was not easily dislodged. Unlike Scotland, the late date of the 1798 rebellion allowed republican ideals from the French Revolution to attach

GOLD MINES, COUNTY of WICKLOW.

In the Fore-ground are several Figures employed in working or buddeling; in the Middle ground they are seen digging & barrowing the Earth, which contains the particles of Gold; on the first discovery of these Mines, pieces of pure Gold were found valued at eighty pounds and upwards, one of which may be seen at the Levarian Museum. The Scene closes with Croughan and the adjoining Hills.

London Published as the Act directs, 10th May 1804.

174. Thomas Sautelle Roberts, 'Gold Mines, County of Wicklow. T. Sautell Roberts delit. J. Bluck fecit, London: Published as the Act directs, 1804'. Print. British Library, Maps K.Top.55.45.f

175. Francis Jukes, 'Another View of the Salute Battery in the Phoenix Park', 1795. British Library, Maps Ktop LIII 2.m

themselves permanently to 'native' Irish identity. With the religious identity of the majority diverging substantially from the imposed state identity (with the unhelpful imposition of the penal laws), the transformation of native Gaels into British heroes became impossible, with Ireland's picturesque sites rarely, if ever, successfully cast as British. Where it was attempted, such as in Thomas Sautelle Roberts's watercolours, the requirement that the views should be military *and* picturesque led to ambiguous and mixed messages. Who was the hero – the pretend general or the real one? Where were they going – home to Dublin Castle, further into Wicklow or by ship to Van Diemen's Land? Thomas Sautelle Roberts's images did document the close temporal adjacency of the insurrection itself, the infrastructural projects it created and the representational projects it seeded. The dangerously close spatial

'contiguity' of mountain to city is echoed in the alignment of violent military activity and painted propaganda. In Wicklow the government's plans to improve the military road network aligned somewhat too closely with the county's promotion as a picturesque destination. The history, design and representation of Wicklow's military roads reveals a logical line of descent from the military to the tourist viewpoint, and from maps and topographical drawings to landscape views. That such overlaps should occur during the ongoing Irish insurrections of 1800–9 suggests the power of images to both support and simultaneously undermine the established point of view.

Loyal and rebel topographies continued to war in the wake of the rebellion when a constant state of military tension initiated yet more 'map work'[60] of Dublin and its setting by the British Ordnance. Countless new barracks, forts, martello

176. Samuel Brocas, *View of the Phoenix Park, Dublin, Ireland, with two cows grazing in the foreground and military maneuvers taking place in the background. In the distance is the Viceregal Lodge. In the foreground is the Khyber*, October, 1820. National Library of Ireland, PD 4194 TX 1

towers, batteries and magazines were drawn as dark figures against a pink city ground in such maps as Major Fryer's 1813 'Sketch of Dublin and its Environs'.[61] Artists and engravers set out to frame Dublin's expanding military landscape as a series of polite views, depicting the predominantly military buildings from multiple points of view, most of them ungainly and few of them picturesque. Making the military picturesque was difficult and when such views collapsed into the ridiculous they lost any counter-revolutionary effect they hoped to inspire. Even Francis Jukes admitted that one of his two views of the Salute Battery in the Phoenix Park 'exhibit[ed] an irregular and confused appearance', and his scattering about of a few cows hardly made it picturesque (Fig. 175). The six long lines of uniformed infantry men that Samuel Brocas placed behind two large contented cows in his watercolour of the Phoenix Park's Viceregal Lodge did not really improve the scene (Fig. 176).

Counter-revolutionary landscape took many forms, and among the most interesting are the many cartographic board games that were produced from the mid-eighteenth century onwards. Such European board games in the period 1750–1815 sublimated the control of fraught and dangerous landscapes through play.[62] They taught children and adults how to perceive the ruling nation as a single hierarchical structure that should be approached from a particular direction and in the correct frame of mind. *Wallis's tour through the United Kingdom of England, Scotland and Ireland* was published in 1811 as 'a new geographical game comprehending all the cities, principal towns, rivers &c. in the British Empire', not merely those of the British Isles (Fig. 177). Players set off from London and completed a thirty-nine-stop tour of the north of England before moving onto a twenty-seven-stop tour of Scotland (stops 40–66). Ireland was reached via the Isle of Man (stop 67) and toured in a predominantly anti-clockwise direction for forty-four stops (stops 68–111). By far the longest entry was no. 102 for the Giant's Causeway where players stopped for two turns to 'admire the architecture of Nature'. Clonmel, in

WALLIS'S
Tour through the
UNITED KINGDOM
of
England, Scotland and Ireland,
a new Geographical Game,
Comprehending all the
Cities, Principal Towns, Rivers, &c.
in the
BRITISH EMPIRE.

Published 1 July 1811,
by JOHN WALLIS, N.º 13 Skinner Street, Snow Hill, LONDON.

SCALE of MILES.

contrast, 'had been dismantled by Cromwell, who found from the inhabitants more resistance than he expected' while Sligo was 'very ill-built' and Castlebar 'a neat little town, but the country about it' was 'mostly composed of bogs and mountains'. The players then crossed the Irish Sea to Holyhead to begin quite a short tour of Wales (stops 112–28), and a fluid Welsh–English border required two cross-border jumps to visit Chester and Shrewsbury. The English tour began again in Hereford before looping down to Cornwall and up to Lincolnshire in an anti-clockwise direction. Whoever arrived first in London won the game because it was 'universally acknowledged to exceed every other city in Europe, if not in the whole world'.[63] The comparative geography of the British Isles that such tours created firmly reinforced the figure that had resulted from the Act of Union of 1800.

William Darton published *Walker's Tour through Ireland: A New Geographical Pastime* in 1812 (Fig. 178), inspired by the 1809 *Walker's Journey through England and Wales*. The 1809 tour had concluded that Wales in general was 'but a poor place' with no overnight stops recommended for visitors. Bath, despite exceeding 'every town in England for splendor and elegance of buildings', surprisingly required no stopover, while an overnight stop was awarded to Newcastle, Carlisle, Pontefract, Nottingham and Oxford. Two stops were awarded to Scarborough, Leeds, Manchester and Plymouth, and the maximum of four stops was awarded to Portsmouth 'the most considerable haven for men of war, and the most strongly fortified place in England' as well as to Birmingham 'to see Mr. Boulton's extensive manufactory for coining and stamping the penny, and twopenny pieces'. Cardinal Wolsey featured prominently as a historical figure (Ipswich, stop 7 and Leicester, stop 79) and the birthplace of Oliver Cromwell was carefully noted. The *Tour through Ireland* required 'A General Description of Ireland' that set out an abbreviated history and geography of the country, placing particular emphasis on its

native fauna (Fig. 178). A much more leisured pastime than touring England and Wales, Cork's four turns were for 'attentively' considering 'the advantages to nations and individuals by the governments of the world living on terms of peace with each other', while Kildare required 'a stop for four turns, not to see the cruel and disgraceful practice of horse-racing, but to consider how much the late Union of both kingdoms is likely to promote the general happiness of the whole British empire, and to render the inhabitants one vast brotherhood, endeared by the most friendly offices and the mutual ties of interest'.[64] The recent rebellion of 1798, if unacknowledged, must have influenced such meditations.

Some of Darton's other commentary was more ambiguous, such as the strange instruction to 'stop four turns' in Limerick 'to consider how despicable a profession is that of the military'. In Castlebar, 'a shire town, and most considerable in the county of Mayo', players were informed that 'in 1798, the British were here defeated by the French under Humbert', the only direct reference to the rising and a strange one to include. The various conflicting roles and activities that had been adopted by Irishmen in Castlebar, Limerick, Cork and Kildare escaped comment. Mention of French landings presumably added some frisson of excitement to the game, as it had done in Fraser's tour-guide reminiscences of guerrillas at Glencree. In contrast, the English tour's stop at Whitehaven recorded how 'the famous Paul Jones, in the American war' had landed there 'spiked the guns, set fire to two ships in the dock, and damaged many houses', but in notable contrast to any Irish town, Whitehaven's 'vigilant inhabitants soon made him fly'. The board game also passed comment on historical events that were more distant yet still charged. Drogheda (stop 77) had 'suffered so much' since 'Oliver Cromwell took it by storm, and put to the sword the governor, Sir Arthur Aston, and the garrison' and 'the inhabitants likewise' that 'for a long time it remained almost in ruins'. 'Londonderry' (stop 110) had been 'built in the reign of James I by the company of London Adventurers, and surrounded with a strong wall' and had 'made a brave defence against the Irish rebels' in 1641.

Individuals could also take a counter-revolutionary turn. In the rebellion's aftermath Arthur O'Connor was imprisoned in Fort George, Scotland, with many of the other United Irishmen. In May 1801 he asked his brother to apply to the government for him 'to be suffered to emigrate to America'.[65] Unsuccessful in his request he wrote plaintively to Lady Lucy

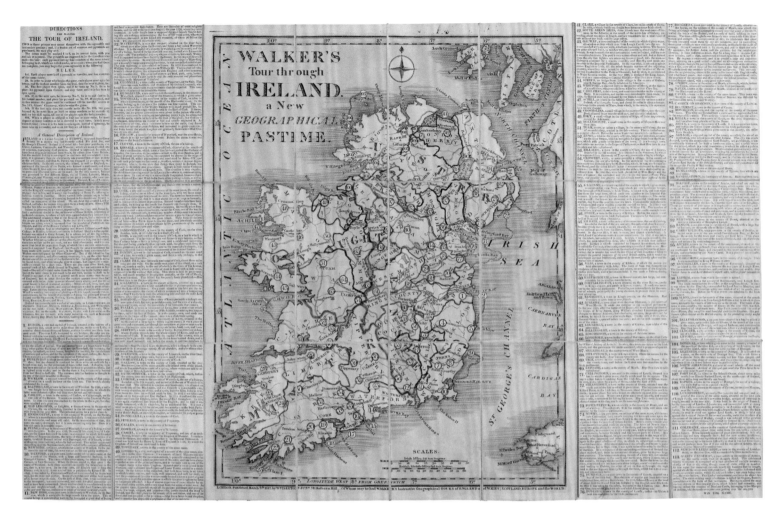

178. *Walker's Tour through Ireland. a New Geographical Pastime*. Published March 9th 1812 by Wm Darton Junr.
58 Holborn Hill. Private collection

FitzGerald that mention 'of the fireside and the green fields' of Kildare was 'like recalling' to his 'recollection very old but long absent friends'.[66] Lucy hoped that he had 'the same recourse' from memory that she enjoyed, 'a pretty garden to work in' with 'some violets'. She was also busy defending Edward's reputation, then fixed in her social circle as 'the great author and contriver of all the mischief and Treason which has already cost so many lives'.[67] But Lucy remained loyal to both her brother's memory and the revolutionary ideals for which he had fought, writing to 'Citizen' Thomas Paine of 'those happy days' in Kildare when she 'dwelt under the humble roof of my beloved Brother Edward' with Paine's portrait ornamenting the chimney. 'As the small social circle drew round the fire their eyes rested on the semblance of the author of the Rights

of Man.'[68] In 'Lady Lucy's address to Irishmen', she was definitively Irish by nationality, as was her brother, an identity that not all of her family would have shared:

Irishmen, Countrymen, it is Ed Fitz[gerald]'s sister who addresses you, it is a Woman but that Woman is his Sister she would therefore die for you as he died. I don't mean to remind you of what he did for you 'twas no more than his duty without ambition he resigned every blessing this world could afford to be of use to you to his country whom he loved better than himself but in this he did not more than his duty; he was a <u>Paddy</u> and no more he desired no other title this was his only ambition; will you ever forget yourselves? Will you forget this title; which it is still in your power to enoble? Will you disgrace it? will you make it the scoff of yr triumphant enemies? while tis still in yr power to raise it beyond others? glory to immortality? … or raise the Paddies to happiness, freedom; glory.[69]

Many of her relatives analysed the rebellion rather differently. A letter from one of them blamed the liars that 'betray themselves into the hands of their enemies' for the 'Phenomena' causing 'rage in the Irish breast' with 'cruelty … added to Lying'. The violent military response to the rebellion, which led to the loss of 30,000 lives, was only 'self defence', which had made 'the English man wary, cautious and shady' and 'thus he keeps the superiority by the common laws of Nature & the clever Paddy ruins his own cause'. In conclusion it was 'evident' that 'Paddy' was 'formed to be Governed'.[70]

In the aftermath of the failed rebellion of 1798, and the Act of Union of 1800, Arthur O'Connor published a series of revolutionary tracts in his newspaper *The Beauties of the Press.* Significantly for the study of revolutionary landscape, these position statements were specific in their viewpoint and entitled: 'Letters from the Mountains. Being a series of Letters from an old Man in the Country to a young Man in Dublin'. Standing on a height outside Dublin, this elevated point of view allowed O'Connor's elderly protagonist Montanus to postulate on the current state and future of Ireland and to advise his younger friend, lost in the spatial chaos of the city centre. O'Connor's letters were inspired by Jean-Jacques Rousseau's 1764 publication *Letters Written from the Mountain*, which was in turn Rousseau's response to the publication of *Letters Written from the Country* by Procurator General Tronchin. Rousseau wrote nine letters from his mountains; O'Connor wrote eleven, couched in the same oratorical style and declamatory tradition as Rousseau's. In these works Rousseau projects his own identity onto a specific environment, that of the mountain, a republican and egalitarian refuge from both the country and the city. O'Connor's appropriation of Rousseau's title and setting translated Switzerland into Ireland, where native mountains began to evoke native freedoms.

On the formation of Great Britain from the three sister kingdoms of England, Scotland and Ireland, Montanus had much to say, writing that 'although Ireland is dignified with the name of independent kingdom, and honored by Great-Britain with the appellation of sister country – a distinction for which … she pays dearly, in the maintenance of a luxurious Court,

and a cumbrous establishment; yet Ireland, in the opinion of many acute observers, is, to all intents and purposes, in a state of provincial dependence'.[71] Montanus also made a figure/ground spatial analogy between Ireland and Great Britain:

> Britain, according to their political arithmetic, is the only integral figure of the British empire; Ireland they consider as a mere cypher, or even on some occasions as a negative quantity, and on these principles they have conducted themselves like an insulated garrison, with difficulty maintaining its station, and supporting itself by inroads and depredations, in a hostile and exhausted country.[72]

If Britain is the figured garrisoned fort on the ground of rural empire, this suggests that the city is likewise the occupied stronghold on the countryside of a colony or imagined independent nation. During the French revolutionary period the mountain, or representations of mountains, had become firmly established as a design typology. As O'Connor's Montanus suggests, Ireland did differ from France in that the capital city, as the military and political centre of a sometime foreign power, had to be undermined for any revolutionary movement to gather momentum. Thus Irish radical gardening culture is more firmly situated in the countryside and the suburb than its corollary in France, and French radical gardening culture had to be carefully manipulated for the Irish situation. Wicklow's position as the free mountain to the repressive foreign capital of Dublin inspired O'Connor's comparison of Dublin with Rousseau's fastness at Neuchâtel in his *Letters Written from the Mountain.*

Arthur O'Connor, unlike Edward FitzGerald, survived the rising of 1798. In its aftermath he was incarcerated in prison in Fort George, Scotland, until 1802 when he was taken to Hamburg under condition of banishment by the British frigate *Ariadne.* He reached Paris later that year, and in 1804 was made a General of France 'with the rights of a citizen of France'[73] by Napoleon. He was introduced by Napoleon's friend the Marquis de Lafayette to Sophie de Condorcet, daughter of the great *philosophe*, whom he married in 1807. They set up home in the Château du Bignon, once the home of Mirabeau, 60 km south of Paris, and so the man from the mountain took up residence on the plain of the Île de France. Carefully drawn plans of his drainage and manuring schemes, his fish ponds and his enclosure of medieval strip farms into large open fields

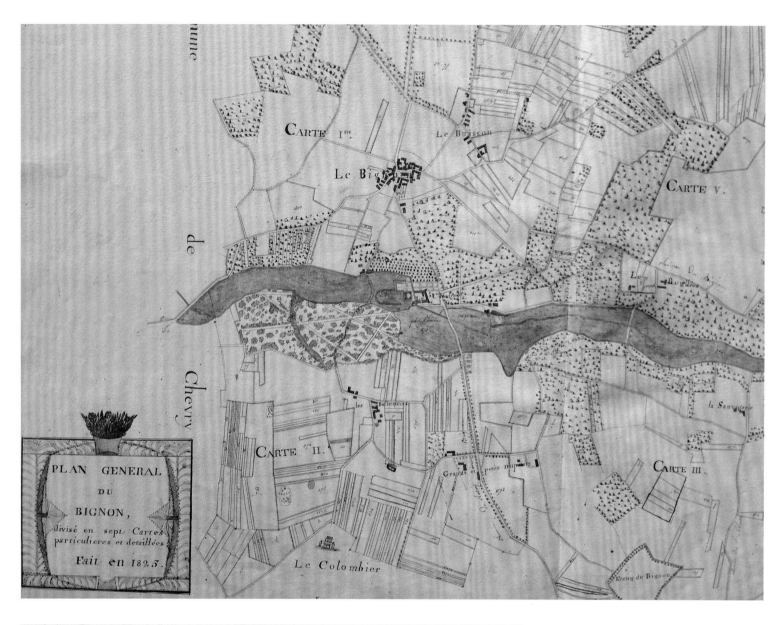

Within the map, the following labels appear:

CARTE I.ᵉ
Le Buisson
Le Bi[gnon]
CARTE V.
Le Rozelle
de
Chevry
la Sauvagerie
CARTE II.
les Bellemains
Grands et petits Dupuis
CARTE III.
PLAN GENERAL
DU
BIGNON,
divisé en sept Cartes
particulieres et detaillées
Fait en 1825.
Le Colombier
Etang du Bignon

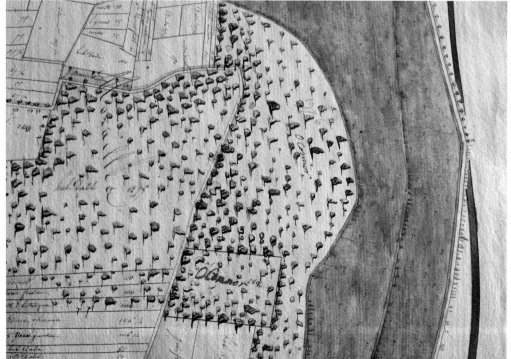

O'Connor

179. *(above) Plan General du Bignon divisé
en sept Cartes particulieres et detaillées, Fait en
1825.* Château du Bignon Mss, Loiret, France

180. *(left) Plan General du Bignon, 1825,
Detail showing O'Connor name.*
Château du Bignon Mss, Loiret, France

depict a nineteenth-century iteration of the aristocratic land-scape tradition his friend Edward FitzGerald had tried so hard to abandon (Fig. 179). A landscape of agricultural improve-ment, it is also a familiar elite estate landscape of parkland, tree-belts, clumps and front and rear lawns of considerable scale (Fig. 180). The title page of the 1832 *Atlas de la Commune du Bignon* suggests the scale and reach of O'Connor's landed property (Fig. 181).

Counter-revolutionary landscape attempted to reverse or eliminate dangerous revolutionary ideas. Yet these could be remarkably tenacious and attractive, particularly the rep-resentation of revolutionary landscapes in paintings, prints, plays or board games. At the broader scale of national identity the spatial legacy of revolution continued to enjoy some long-evity and to perpetuate familiar spatial tropes. Cottages, if not still burning, continue to represent Ireland. Irish identity is still carefully oriented by facing north or south, east or west, city or mountain.

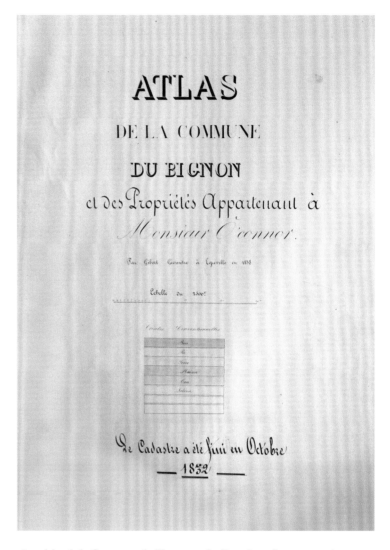

181. *Atlas de la Commune du Bignon at des Propriétés Appartenant à Monsiour O'connor, par Gibert, Géometre a Egreville en 1838, Échelle du 2,500, Le Cadastre a été fini en Octobre 1832*. Château du Bignon Mss, Loiret, France

CONCLUSION

A More Equal Landscape?

Many design currents flowed between Ireland, Great Britain, France, the Caribbean, the United States and the wider Atlantic world in the revolutionary period of 1688–1815. These helped to create various plantation, improving and revolutionary landscapes that warrant detailed transnational analysis as sophisticated artistic constructs. Because the legacy of a framed composition may be very slight or very generic it is sometimes easy to forget its origin as a design, an intention. But eighteenth-century revolutionaries did not forget landscape's power to actively reform space, believing that the landscape expression of revolutionary thoughts and ideals, whether in the farm, cottage, landed estate, suburb, town or nation, could instigate revolution at a profoundly 'ground' level. The vast designed landscapes of the Boyne valley, spun from Cromwell's ruins, a battle obelisk, and Drogheda's polite promontories, although biased towards the victor's viewpoint, together form an impressive aesthetic achievement. They remain more convincingly revolutionary than those of Derry/Londonderry, where the sharp gradient from the city's wall walks to the Bogside beneath exposed a commonwealth riven by sectarianism and producing little spatial liberty. The American plantation landscapes of the Chesapeake Bay, Virginia and Georgia, and the Irish sites of Belcamp House, Mitchelstown and Vernon Mount document a rich reciprocal transfer of revolutionary ideas that was, however, complicated by very different concepts of improvement. What

was to be improved, how and for whom, sometimes aligned across the Atlantic, but often did not.

Mostly originating as villa landscapes, European aristocracies played some part in creating many of the landscapes studied in this book. They took the lifestyle concept of Italian *villegiatura*, and its origin in classical sources, to inform their many and various modulations of the villa into country houses and landscape gardens, suburban enclaves and plantation mansions. Aristocracies have always harnessed setting and lifestyle as powerful tools to maintain their ascendancy, and although these should inspire critical scepticism, they often do not, partly because they mostly create such sophisticated, well-designed and desirable environments.[1] Widespread, familiar and seductive imagery supported their professed design superiority and facilitated its transfer into the collective subconscious, generating awe, aspiration and emulation in the wider population. But if the social and symbolic formation of villa landscapes were to be more precisely deconstructed, particularly its calculated representation in drawings and other images, would this encourage a more equal landscape? The canon of architectural and landscape history is often threaded as a string of such villas, which permits the design principles of hierarchy and order to be readily demonstrated and instances of deliberate subversion remain relatively ignored in the historiography. But countries with colonial or contested pasts are

182. James Barry, *The Phoenix or the Resurrection of Freedom*, 1776. Yale Center for British Art, Paul Mellon Collection, B1977.14.11067

difficult to corral into an agreed canon of buildings and land-scapes, and architectural history's implicit hierarchy of sources, where primacy is mostly awarded to the plan drawing and principal elevation, mostly loses the wider landscape context.

Translating Europe to America and America to Europe ran into many roadblocks along the way, where the landscape type that was being transferred, whether landed estate, landscape garden or picturesque tour, had to be adjusted and modified for the new environment. Many saw freedom and equality writ large in America, an equality born of an extraordinary wealth of land, and a mutable border that could shift and enlarge indefinitely to accommodate any number of people. Free to enjoy individual property and profit, Americans were also relatively free of the fixed landlord and tenant relationship that prevailed in most of Europe. The Irish landscape, in contrast, was a zone of complex land titles, sectarian penal laws, middle men, discoverers and absentees. But other European landscapes were more resolved and aspirational, such as Rousseau's garden of Les Charmettes, where the middle ground of this outer suburban landscape mediated between garden, town and Alps.

Spatial character and identity became conflated with the individual, and the choice of where to live and what landscape to see outside your window affected not only your spatial prospects but those also of any planned revolution. Europeans who followed in Rousseau's footsteps, such as Arthur Young, were influenced by his concepts of spatial equality. They recast Les Charmettes elsewhere for their purposes, considerably aided by French precedents of the 1790s, when spatial hierarchies were subverted and distorted for political intent. Arthur Young's seminal publications suggested that countries, together with their landscapes, could be redesigned to emulate the best examples. Landscape's ability to suggest change in seemingly apolitical ways was key to its widespread adoption as a way of seeing and thinking about the world – from the *montagnards* of the French Legislative Assembly to the farmers of the Chesapeake Bay.

In 1776 the Irish artist James Barry painted an allegory entitled *The Phoenix or the Resurrection of Freedom* where a despondent Europe gazes across the Atlantic at the promised land of the newly independent America (Fig. 182). Father Time strews flowers upon the ruined remains of Athens, Rome and Florence while across the water they rise again in the young republic. Surrounded by American conifers, a farmer ploughs the soil while pastoral soldiers mind their sheep. Collapsing geography into his drawing, Barry suggests that frontiers are not fixed but oscillate depending upon national and political points of view and, optimistic about the United States' future, he indicates that cities, mountains and people could move and reposition themselves in the new world. This complex image by an Irish painter of the late eighteenth century positioned landscape at the core of a republican ideology that restructured nations in their scale, reach and perspective. But the equality of American landscape, that Barry's farm suggested, was poised in a state of immense contradiction as the equality claimed for some was not applied to all. Mount Vernon's landscape design that concealed the problematic plantation and slavery conditions at its edge and Monticello's serpentine walks around a carefully delimited lawn represent entirely American resolutions of the landed estate, where scale and visual reach were carefully constrained so as to lend the young republic a contrived equilibrium. Pierce Butler's plantation landscapes express this essentially conflicted character of the landed estate in the United States – that independent farmers could not create landscapes that evoked the principles of liberty and freedom when some people were forms of property in themselves. Unlike Butler, other Irishmen did not compromise their principles in unfamiliar environments and some may have read the lay of the land particularly well. The Irish revolutionary Archibald Hamilton Rowan, arriving into Philadelphia in 1796, exhibited a commendable moral clarity when he wrote home that he would 'not kill Indians, nor keep slaves'.[2]

Revolution was facilitated by the landscape tour, which, when coupled with the philosophy of improvement acquired a revolutionary impact. The tour's essential character of motion made it easily comparable to time and change, and a changed or changing environment, whether political, social or cultural, is the aim of all revolution. French revolutionaries sought to overturn the spatial structure of France, placing mountains in churches and gardens on forts, and others rewrote the map of Europe and its sequence of key sites and vistas. The introduction of new routes, the reversal of old ones, the upset of ordered and hierarchical destinations and the insistence that some routes were more significant than others, became shaping forces in the consciousness of European men and women,

particularly those who sought to reimagine America in translation. To voyage, to explore, to experience, to move, to travel was innate to America; it had none of the static qualities of Europe, its frontiers were unbounded and unfixed, and it could logically effect change and revolution as a result. As the historian Leo Marx observed in his 1974 lecture 'The American Revolution and the American Landscape', Americans seemed to be 'particularly receptive to the idea that the native landscape has had a specially important part in the formation of our national identity' with landscape 'no mere setting or backdrop, but an active shaping force in the consciousness of men and women'.[3] This book has explored the extent to which that correlation was projected back to Europe in order to engender revolution in the old world. It has tried to identify which European and American sites were invoked to do so, and to what degree comparative travel became a precondition for revolutionary thought. Landscape experience could be profoundly affected by the memory of landscapes experienced in the past, and once travellers had experienced Stowe's political landscape garden, the egalitarian farms of Pennsylvania, the Niagara Falls and the liberties of Lake Geneva, their home landscape also shifted and changed. The landscapes of Chambéry, the Champ des Mars in Paris, Cave Hill outside Belfast, the Curragh and the Wicklow mountains became 'no mere settings or backdrops'[4] but shaping forces in the evolution of nations. Moving from west to east, and from Philadelphia and Virginia to Dublin and Geneva, reversed vistas question the implicit trajectory of much historical narrative.

When landlords or planters landscaped as absentees, often at vast distances from the sites themselves, there were many good reasons why they did. Lord Fitzwilliam could plan for Dublin's redevelopment more effectively from London, while his brother dealt with the locals on the ground. The layers of calculated deception that the Irish penal laws encouraged in closet Catholics created a flat and dampened spatial hierarchy that protected, through its sheer humdrum equality, vulnerable landed assets. Suburbia did generally create a more equal landscape, and Blackrock's Frescati and Lord Fitzwilliam's 'Porter's Lodge' did much to muddy the hierarchy of the landed estate. But Butler's suburban villa residence in Philadelphia also empowered its owner to occlude and repress the violent inequality on which his success was built, and Samuel Vaughan's drawings expose the gap between the image of Mount Vernon as a virtuously republican farm and its reality as a much larger slave plantation. Vaughan's other drawings of his own plantations in Cornwall county, Jamaica, are also relevant for those he made of Mount Vernon's landscape because they reveal what he chose not to depict. Such absent points of view result in strangely contorted and contradictory places, conveying on one hand some ideal combination of use and beauty but on the other a grimly enslaved reality. This dark side of design, where freedom in one sphere of activity led to human bondage in another, remains under-acknowledged, and we continue to cut the narrative frame too close to the pretty picture leaving the more problematic spaces outside. The gap is also revealed in Europe's unseemly pride in instigating emancipation, which forgets that matrilineal chattel slavery and the wider Atlantic plantation system were created by European colonialism for that continent's financial benefit. Absenteeism greatly aided and abetted colonialism's advance by removing the burden of witnessing its lived reality from those whom it benefited most.

Military landscapes, like plantation landscapes, often concealed their notable aesthetic antecedents and inputs. Fortifications, wall walks, embankments and inclines were transferred into the garden by military men throughout the eighteenth century, when their preoccupations with sightlines, surveys and prospect points became very useful in laying out more leisured landscapes. Yet military motives sat uncomfortably with those of the aesthetic, leisured and tourism variety, particularly in Wicklow in the 1790s, and although Ireland's ruling military men enjoyed making tours, for both landscape beauty and strategic oversight, such overlaps, when adopted by rebel forces, could work against them. Michael Dwyer and the pseudo-General Holt had the advantage in Dublin's overhanging mountains while the United Irishmen Edward FitzGerald and Arthur O'Connor knew well how touring could conceal sedition.

Revolution in the eighteenth century was generally initiated and pursued by a fraternity, making it mostly a young man's story. All these revolutionaries, if they survived the awful violence that almost invariably accompanied revolution's latter stages, grew into sober and sensible middle-aged men while those who died young, such as Edward FitzGerald and Wolfe Tone, never had to grow into a compromised middle age. Washington, wise and careful, curated his identity and that of Mount Vernon, until his death. Its landscape has remained, in general, faithful to his wishes, particularly the outlying areas' erasure by suburban housing. Other revolutionaries, such as

Pierce Butler and Arthur O'Connor, trundled on through life, their youthful enthusiasms curdled into conservative nineteenth-century mindsets. Exiled to France in the 1800s, O'Connor enclosed many acres of French soil, while children's board games impressed the 'correct' map of Europe onto immature and malleable minds. Pierce Butler adopted more counter-revolutionary precepts as he grew older, particularly in the aftermath of the Haitian revolution of 1791. His few surviving letters to Roswell King that postdate 1791 record little of his thoughts on the 1798 rebellion, and no letters to Weedon Butler postdate 1797. Butler's Island's reputation, and that of Butler himself, never recovered from the publication of Fanny Kemble's *Journal of a Residence on a Georgian Plantation in 1838–1839*[5] and 'the weeping time' of her husband and Pierce Butler's grandson Pierce Mease Butler's auction of all the Butler slaves at the Savannah racecourse in Georgia on 2–3 March 1859.

The eighteenth-century effort to create egalitarian landscapes free of inherited and entitled privilege was a worthwhile project even if it enjoyed little long-term spatial impact. It continues to resonate in current conceptions of the constituent nations of Ireland and Great Britain, many erstwhile colonies and the wider Atlantic world. The Irish gardens of a middle size that became revolutionary environments are mostly derelict and do not feature as tourist destinations or national sites of significance. Belcamp House and Vernon Mount, Cork, like many of Ireland's most significant designed landscapes, have been destroyed by planning apathy, fire, neglect and, ultimately and ironically, suburban housing. But suburbia, although bearing none of the glory of a *grand projet*, is perhaps the most logical spatial resolution of egalitarian ideals, and Rousseau's balanced suburban garden may yet bear a greater legacy. Other iconic landscapes could try to escape the constraints of a single national identity and move towards more international narratives that acknowledge fully the role of foreign people, ideas and plants in their creation. The calculated appropriation of picturesque landscape, in the aftermath of rebellion and for repressive purposes, makes for an instructive art history that could be more interrogated. Many ephemeral wisps of revolutionary spaces and places remain tentative, unresolved and easy to dismiss or not see at all. But the great revolutionary precepts of liberty, equality, fraternity (now mostly expanded to include sorority) and the pursuit of happiness, ideally for all people regardless of nationality, remain touchstones, not only for politics, but for space.

Notes

INTRODUCTION

1   See Denis Cosgrove and Stephen Daniels (eds), *The Iconography of Landscape* (Cambridge: Cambridge University Press, 1988), p. 1: 'A landscape is a cultural image, a pictorial way of representing, structuring or symbolising surroundings.'

2   W. J. T. Mitchell (ed.), *Landscape and Power* (Chicago: University of Chicago Press, 1994), pp. 1–2.

3   David Dickson, *Old World Colony: Cork and South Munster 1630–1830* (Cork: Cork University Press, 2005).

4   The 1800 census of the United States in 1800 returned a population of 5,308,483, https://www.census.gov/history/www/through_the_decades/fast_facts/1800_fast_facts.html (accessed 6 October 2022). The Irish Central Statistics Office estimates the population of Ireland in 1804 as 5,395,436, https://www.cso.ie/en/census/censusthroughhistory/ (accessed 6 October 2022). Ireland's first successful census of 1821 returned a population of 6,846,949.

5   Dublin was the sixth largest city in Europe in 1800 with a population of 200,000, while New York had a population of 60,515, Philadelphia 41,220 and Boston only 24,937, population figures from US Census of 1800, https://www.census.gov/history/pdf/histstats-colonial-1970.pdf (accessed 10 October 2019).

6   For an early usage see Thomas Blennerhasset's *A Direction for the Plantation of Ireland* (London, 1610) and DIB, 'Thomas Blennerhassett (–1624)' (accessed 13 May 2021).

7   Lorena S. Walsh, *Motives of Honor, Pleasure, and Profit: Plantation Management in the Colonial Chesapeake, 1607–1763* (Chapel Hill: University of North Carolina Press, 2010); Holly Brewer, 'Entailing Aristocracy in Colonial Virginia: "Ancient Feudal Restraints" and Revolutionary Reform', *William and Mary Quarterly*, 3rd series, 54:2 (Apr. 1997); John Michael Vlach, *Back of the Big House: The Architecture of Plantation Slavery* (Chapel Hill and London: University of North Carolina Press, 1993); Dell Upton, 'White and Black Landscapes in Eighteenth-Century Virginia', *Places*, 2:2 (1984), pp. 59–72.

8   See William Smyth, *Map-Making, Landscapes and Memory: A Geography of Colonial and Early Modern Ireland, c.1530–1750* (Cork: Cork University Press, 2006), Chapter 12: 'A Global Context. Ireland and America: England's First Frontiers'.

9   See Vlach, *Back of the Big House*, p. 2 and Louis P. Nelson, *Architecture and Empire in Jamaica* (New Haven and London: Yale University Press, 2016), pp. 54–64.

10 B. W. Higman, *Jamaica Surveyed: Plantation Maps and Plans of the Eighteenth and Nineteenth Centuries* (Barbados, Jamaica, Trinidad and Tobago: University of West Indies Press, 2001), p. 56. See also J. H. Andrews, *Plantation Acres: An Historical Study of the Irish Land Surveyor* (Omagh: Ulster Historical Foundation, 1985); *A Paper Landscape: The Ordnance Survey in Nineteenth-Century Ireland* (Dublin: Four Courts Press, 2002), pp. 9–10.

11 This argument is perhaps most forcibly made in Barbara Wells Sarudy, *Gardens and Gardening in the Chesapeake 1700–1805* (Baltimore and London: Johns Hopkins Press, 1998), Preface. See also Therese O'Malley, 'Landscape Gardening in the Early National Period' in *View and Visions: American Landscape before 1830*, ed. Edward J. Nygren (Washington DC: The Corcoran Gallery of Art, 1986).

12 Dell Upton, 'Architectural History or Landscape History?', *Journal of Architectural Education*, 44:4 (Aug., 1991), pp. 195–9, Peter Martin, *The Pleasure Gardens of Virginia: From Jamestown to Jefferson* (Princeton: Princeton University Press, 1991); Vlach, *Back of the Big House*; Vlach, *The Planter's Prospect: Privilege and Slavery in Plantation Art* (Chapel Hill and London: The University of North Carolina Press, 2002).

13 Edward W. Said, *Culture and Imperialism* (New York: Vintage, 1994); Declan Kiberd, Introduction to *Ulysses* by James Joyce (London: Penguin, 2000).

14 John Barrell, *The Dark Side of the Landscape: The Rural Poor in English Painting, 1730–1840* (Cambridge: Cambridge University Press, 1980); Cosgrove and Daniels (eds), *The Iconography of the Landscape*; Stephen Copley and Peter Garside (eds), *The Politics of the Picturesque: Literature, Landscape and Aesthetics since 1770* (Cambridge: Cambridge University Press, 1994).

15 Malcolm Andrews, *The Search for the Picturesque: Landscape Aesthetics*

and Tourism in Britain, 1760–1800 (Aldershot: Stanford University Press, 1989); Jill H. Casid, *Sowing Empire: Landscape and Colonization* (Minneapolis: University of Minnesota Press, 2005); Kay Dian Kriz, *Slavery, Sugar and the Culture of Refinement* (New Haven and London: Yale University Press, 2008); Geoff Quilley and Kay Dian Kriz (eds), *An Economy of Colour: Visual Culture and the North Atlantic World, 1660–1830* (Manchester: Manchester University Press, 2003); John Bonehill and Geoff Quilley, *Conflicting Visions: War and Visual Culture in Britain and France c.1700–1830* (Abingdon: Routledge, 2005); Tim Barringer, Gillian Forrester and Barbaro Martinez-Ruiz (eds), *Art and Emancipation in Jamaica: Isaac Mendes Belisario and his Worlds* (New Haven: Yale University Press), 2007; Sarah Thomas, *Witnessing Slavery – Art and Travel in the Age of Abolition* (New Haven and London: Yale University Press, 2019).

16 P. Roebuck, 'The Making of an Ulster Great Estate: The Chichesters, Barons of Belfast and Viscounts of Carrickfergus, 1599–1648', *Proceedings of the Royal Irish Academy*, 79C (1979); Andrews, *Plantation Acres*; Higman, *Jamaica Surveyed*; Audrey Horning, *Ireland in the Virginian Sea: Colonialism in the British Atlantic* (Chapel Hill: University of North Carolina Press, 2013).

17 See Peter Burke, *Venice and Amsterdam: A Study of Seventeenth Century Élites* (Cambridge: Polity Press, 1994), Introduction. See also Peter Kolchin, *Unfree Labor: American Slavery and Russian Serfdom* (Cambridge and London: Belknap, Harvard University Press, 1987).

18 Arthur Young, *A Tour in Ireland, 1776–1779* (London: T. Cadell, Strand, and J. Dodsley, 1780); *Travels in France during the Years 1787, 1788, 1789* (London: George Bell and Sons, 1906); *Letters from His Excellency General Washington, to Arthur Young … with a map of his farm* (London: B. M'Millan, 1801).

19 Arthur Young, *Travels in France*, p. 109.

20 See Ann Bermingham, 'The Simple Life: Cottages and Gainsborough's Cottage Doors' in *Land, Nation and Culture, 1740–1840: Thinking the Republic of Taste*, ed. Peter de Bolla, Nigel Leask and David Simpson (Basingstoke and New York: Palgrave Macmillan, 2005), p. 56.

21 Arthur Young to George Washington, 7 January 1786, *The Papers of George Washington Digital Edition*, ed. Theodore J. Crackel (Charlottesville: University of Virginia Press, Rotunda, 2008), canonical url http://rotunda.upress.virginia.edu/founders/GEWN-04-03-02-0425 (accessed 27 March 2013), original source Confederation Series (1 January 1784–23 September 1788), Volume 3 (19 May 1785–31 March 1786).

22 See James S. Ackerman, *The Villa: Form and Ideology of Country Houses* (London: Thames and Hudson, 1990); Bentmann, R. and M. Muller, *The Villa as Hegemonic Architecture* (Humanities Press, 1992).

23 J. C. A. Pocock, *Three British Revolutions, 1641, 1688, 1776* (Princeton: Princeton University Press, 1980), p. 18.

24 Kevin Whelan, *The Fellowship of Freedom: The United Irishmen and 1798* (Companion Volume to the Bicentenary Exhibition by The National Library and The National Museum of Ireland at Collins Barracks, Dublin 1998) (Cork: Cork University Press, 1998), p. 119. In Ireland the bicentennial anniversary of 1798 in 1998 produced a stream of worthy publications, particularly Thomas Bartlett, David Dickson, Dáire Keogh and Kevin Whelan (eds), *1798 : A Bicentenary Perspective* (Dublin: Four Courts Press, 2003).

25 The literature on plantations and enslavement in the United States is vast and growing rapidly. Books that have proved particularly influential for this study include: Lorena S. Walsh, *From Calabar to Carter's Grove: The History of a Virginia Slave Community* (Charlottesville and London: University Press of Virginia, 1997); Peter A. Coclanis, *The Shadow of a Dream: Economic Life and Death in the South Carolina Low Country, 1670–1920* (New York: Oxford University Press, 1989); David Brion Davis, *Inhuman Bondage: The Rise and Fall of Slavery in the New World* (Oxford: Oxford University Press, 2006); Ronald Hoffman, Mechel Sobel and Fredrika J. Teute (eds), *Through a Glass Darkly: Reflections on Personal Identity in Early America* (Chapel Hill and London: University of North Carolina Press, 1997); Richard Dunn, *A Tale of Two Plantations: Slave Life and Labor in Jamaica and Virginia* (Cambridge and London: Harvard University Press, 2014); Rhys Isaac, *Landon Carter's Uneasy Kingdom: Revolution and Rebellion on a Virginia Plantation* (Oxford: Oxford University Press, 2004) and *The Transformation of Virginia 1740–1790* (Williamsburg: University of North Carolina Press, 1982); Mechal Sobel, *The World They Made Together: Black and White Values in Eighteenth-Century Virginia* (Princeton: Princeton University Press, 1989); Philip D. Morgan, *Slave Counterpoint: Black Culture in the Eighteenth-Century Chesapeake and Low Country* (Chapel Hill and London: University of North Carolina Press, 1998).

26 See Janet Polasky's *Revolutions Without Borders: The Call to Liberty in the Atlantic World* (New Haven and London: Yale University Press, 2015), p. 8.

27 See Julius S. Scott's *The Common Wind: Afro-American Currents in the Age of the Haitian Revolution* (London and New York: Verso, 2018); Polasky, *Revolutions Without Borders*.

28 For more general discussion see Crane Brinton, *The Anatomy of Revolution: Towards a Poetics of Experience* (London: Vintage, 1965); A. J. Groth (ed.), *Revolution and Revolutionary Change* (Aldershot: Dartmouth, 1996); David Parker (ed.), *Revolutions and the Revolutionary Tradition in the West, 1560–1991* (Abingdon: Routledge, 2000).

29 R. F. Foster, *Vivid Faces: The Revolutionary Generation in Ireland 1890–1923* (London: Penguin, 2014).

30 Simon Schama, *Landscape and Memory* (London: Vintage, 1996); W. J. T. Mitchell, *Landscape and Power* (Chicago: University of Chicago Press, 1994); Ann Bermingham, *Landscape and Ideology: The English Rustic Tradition, 1740–1860* (Berkeley: University of California Press, 1986); Stephen Daniels, *Fields of Vision: Landscape Imagery and National Identity in England and the United States* (Princeton: Princeton University Press, 1993).

31 Mona Ozouf, *Festivals and the French Revolution* (Cambridge: Harvard University Press, 1988).

32 Lynn Hunt, *Politics, Culture and Class in the French Revolution* (Oakland: University of California Press, 2004).

33 James Leith, *Space and Revolution: Projects for Monuments, Squares and Public Buildings in France 1789–1799* (Montreal: McGill University Press, 1991). See also Simon Schama, *Citizens: A Chronicle of the French*

Revolution (London: Penguin, 1989). For a corrective to the generally negative perception of the French Revolution that pervades much of the English historiography see François Furet, *Interpreting the French Revolution* (Cambridge: Cambridge University Press, 1981).

34   See Antoine Picon, *French Architects and Engineers in the Age of Enlightenment* (Cambridge: Cambridge University Press, 1992), Chapter 10.

35   The concept of making a tour to appreciate landscape predates the eighteenth century. John Evelyn praised the educated traveller over someone who was merely 'making the Tour as they call it' in his 1652 publication *The State of France*. According to the Oxford English Dictionary, one of the first instances of the use of the verb 'tour' comes from the pen of Mary Delany, who prepared 'to tour in the park' with her husband in 1746.

36   Thomas Bartlett (ed.), *Life of Theobald Wolfe Tone, Compiled and Arranged by William Theobald Wolfe Tone* (Dublin: Lilliput, 1998), p. 746: 'Journals' [April 1797].

37   Château du Bignon, Arthur O'Connor's Mss., folio 3, p. 113.

38   See Finola O'Kane, *Landscape Design in Eighteenth-Century Ireland: Mixing Foreign Trees with the Natives* (Cork: Cork University Press, 2004); O'Kane, *Ireland and the Picturesque: Design, Landscape Painting and Tourism in Ireland, 1700–1840* (New Haven and London: Yale University Press, 2013).

CHAPTER ONE

1   Philip D. Curtin, *The Rise and Fall of the Plantation Complex* (Cambridge: Cambridge University Press, 1998), p. 77.

2   B. W. Higman, 'The Sugar Revolution', *Economic History Review*, 53:2 (2000), p. 226.

3   See Louis P. Nelson, *Architecture and Empire in Jamaica* (New Haven and London: Yale University Press, 2016), pp. 54–64; B. W. Higman, *Jamaica Surveyed: Plantation Maps and Plans of the Eighteenth and Nineteenth Centuries* (Barbados, Jamaica, Trinidad and Tobago: University of West Indies Press, 2001), p. 56; William Smyth, *Map-Making, Landscapes and Memory: A Geography of Colonial and Early Modern Ireland, c.1530–1750* (Cork: Cork University Press, 2006): Chapter 12, 'A Global Context. Ireland and America: England's First Frontiers'; John Michael Vlach, *Back of the Big House: The Architecture of Plantation Slavery* (Chapel Hill and London: University of North Carolina Press, 1993), p. 2.

4   OED, 'plantation': *Minutes of Council and General Court of Virginia* (accessed 26 October 2022).

5   Booleying or transhumance is the practice of moving livestock to higher pastures during the summer months. Gavelkind is the practice of dividing an estate equally between offspring. The Norman preference was for primogeniture, where the estate was inherited only by the eldest, typically male, child. An entailed estate was one where there was a legal obligation to follow primogeniture.

6   OED, 'plantation' (accessed 26 October 2022).

7   John Hooker, *The first and second volumes (third volume) of [Holinshed's] Chronicles, comprising … the description and historie of England … Ireland … and … Scotland* (London: Henry Denham, 1587), 2:3, p. 7.

8   Thomas Blennerhasset, *A Direction for the Plantation of Ireland* (London: Ed Allde for John Budge, 1610), B2.

9   Ibid., C2.

10   Ibid., B2: 'What shall we then say? Or to what course shal we betake our selves? Surely by Building of a wel fortified Towne, to be able at any time at an hours warning with five hundred men well armed, to encounter all occasions: neither will that be sufficient, except that be seconded with such another, and that also (if it may be, as easily it may) with a third: so there will be helpe on every side, to defend, and offend: for as in England, of a privy watch be set, many malefactors are apprehended, even amongst their cuppes: so there when the spaces in the Woods be cut out, and the bogges be made somewhat passable, then these newly erected townes intending a reformation, must often times at the first set a vniuersall [universal] great hunt, that a suddaines search may be made in all suspitious places, for the Woolfe and the Wood-kerne, which being secretly and wisely appointed by the governors, they with the helpe of some Irish, well acquainted with the holes and holdes of those offenders, the genreallitie shall search every particular place.'

11   Ibid., A4.

12   Ibid., D3.

13   Higman, *Jamaica Surveyed*, pp. 21–3.

14   For a recent comparative analysis of Virginian and Irish plantation practice see Audrey Horning, *Ireland in the Virginian Sea: Colonialism in the British Atlantic* (Chapel Hill: University of North Carolina Press, 2013), p. 19: 'The seventeenth century … witnessed far greater overlap between colonial efforts in both lands'; p.181: 'The Ulster Plantation was unsuccessful in its aims and incomplete in its execution. At the same time, the settlement of Virginia and the Ulster Plantation and the subsequent history of the north of Ireland are more closely linked and reflective of one another than the sixteenth-century attempts at plantation in Laois and Offaly and in Munster were in any way similar to the unsuccessful English efforts in the New World.'

15   P. Roebuck, 'The Making of an Ulster Great Estate: The Chichesters, Barons of Belfast and Viscounts of Carrickfergus, 1599–1648', *Proceedings of the Royal Irish Academy*, 79C (1979), pp. 11–12.

16   Ibid.

17   ODNB, 'Sir Arthur Chichester' (accessed 3 February 2018): Chichester to Salisbury, November 1610, TNA PRO SP 63/229/135.

18   Roebuck, 'The Making of an Ulster Great Estate', p. 15, Note 64: PRO SP 63/217, 67; calendared in CSPI, 1603–6, p. 326.

19   ODNB, 'Sir Arthur Chichester' (accessed 3 February 2018): Chichester to privy council, 17 Sept 1607, TNA PRO SP 63/222/137.

20   J. H. Andrews, 'The Maps of the Escheated Counties of Ulster, 1609–10', *Proceedings of the Royal Irish Academy: Archaeology, Culture, History, Literature*, 74 (1974), p. 141.

21   Ibid., p. 170. See also J. H. Andrews, 'An Early Map of Inishowen', *Long Room*, 7 (1973), pp. 19–25.

22 Andrews, 'The Maps of the Escheated Counties of Ulster, 1609–10', pp. 140–1, Note 28: Sir John Davies [the Irish Attorney-General] to Salisbury, 24 August 1609.

23 See Alain Corbin, *The Lure of the Sea: The Discovery of the Seaside in the Western World 1750–1840* (London: Penguin, 1994).

24 Roebuck, 'The Making of an Ulster Great Estate', p. 17, Note 70: Brian Bonner, That Audacious Traitor …, Dublin 1975, pp. 218–22.

25 Amy Isabel Young, *Three Hundred Years in Inishowen: Being More Particularly an Account of the Family of Young of Culdaff, With Short Accounts of Many Other Families Connected With Them During That Period* (Belfast: McCaw, Stevenson & Orr, 1929). See also Claire Burke, 'The Architectural Legacy of Sir Arthur Chichester's Plantation of Inishowen', MUBC thesis (University College Dublin, 2017).

26 James Caird, *The Plantation Scheme; or, the West of Ireland as a Field for Investment. [With a map.]* (Edinburgh and London: W. Blackwood & Sons, 1850), see Chapter 6 for the 1801 Wicklow plantation proposal.

27 Peter Benes, *New England Prospect: A Loan Exhibition of Maps at the Currier Gallery of Art* (Manchester, NH: Boston University for the Dublin Seminar for New England Folklife, 1981), p. 81.

28 Martin Bruckner, *The Geographic Revolution in Early America: Maps, Literacy and National Identity* (Chapel Hill: University of North Carolina Press, 2006), p. 23. Bruckner references Sarah S. Hughes, *Surveyors and Statesmen: Land Measuring in Colonial Virginia* (Virginia: Virginia Surveyors Foundation, 1979), p. 48.

29 Dan Hicks, '"Material Improvements": The Archaeology of Estate Landscapes in the British Leeward Islands, 1713–1838' in *Estate Landscapes: Design, Improvement and Power in the Post-Medieval Landscape*, ed. K. Giles and J. Finch (Woodbridge: Bowdell and Brewer, 2008), pp. 205–27.

30 Oxford English Dictionary (Oxford: Oxford University Press, 1998), p. 1897: Triangulation is a surveying term that describes 'the tracing and measurement of a series or network of triangles in order to determine the distances and relative positions of points spread over an area, especially by measuring the length of one side of each triangle and deducing its angles and the length of the other two sides by observation from this baseline.'

31 Higman, *Jamaica Surveyed*, p. 56. See also J. H. Andrews, *A Paper Landscape: The Ordnance Survey in Nineteenth-Century Ireland* (Dublin: Four Courts Press, 2002), pp. 9–10.

32 *Minutes of the Council and General Court of Colonial Virginia, 1622–1632, 1670–1676, with Notes and Excerpts from Original Council and General Court Records, into 1683, Now Lost*, ed. H. R. McIlwaine (Richmond, Virginia: Virginia State Library, 1924), p. 283, https://archive.org (accessed 7 April 2022): 'At a General Court held in James Citty the 21st of November, 1671'.

33 Andrews, *A Paper Landscape*, pp. 9–10.

34 Roger J. P. Kain and Elizabeth Baigent, *The Cadastral Map in the Service of the State* (Chicago: University of Chicago Press, 1992), pp. 257–9.

35 Pierre Clergeot, 'The Origins of the French General Cadastre', FIG (International Federation of Surveyors) Working Week 2003, Paris, France, 13–17 April 2003, pp. 1–17, https://fig.net/resources/proceedings/fig_proceedings/fig_2003/PS_1/PS1_2_Clergeot.pdf (accessed 26 October 2022); Richard Grover, 'Why Does the United Kingdom not have a Cadastre – and Does it Matter', FIG Commission, Annual Meeting 2008, Open Symposium on Environment and Land Administration, Verona, Italy, 11–12 September 2008, https://www.fig.net/resources/proceedings/2008/verona_am_2008_comm7/papers/12_sept/7_2_grover.pdf (accessed 14 May 2020).

36 Kain and Baigent, *The Cadastral Map in the Service of the State*, p. 336.

37 See Trevor Burnard and John Garrigus, *The Plantation Machine: Atlantic Capitalism in French Saint-Domingue and British Jamaica* (Philadelphia: University of Pennsylvania Press, 2016), p. 35. See also James McClellan, *Colonialism and Science: Saint Domingue in the Old Régime* (Chicago: University of Chicago Press, 2010), pp. 18–20.

38 For a discussion of the impact of the different imperial survey and mapping traditions and their impact on landscape design see Finola O'Kane, 'Comparing Imperial Design Strategies; The Franco-Irish Plantations of Saint-Domingue' in *Ireland, Slavery and the Caribbean: Interdisciplinary Perspectives 1700–1830*, ed. Finola O'Kane and Ciaran O'Neill (Manchester: Manchester University Press, 2023).

39 See for example BNF, *Plan de la ville du Cap et de ses environs depuis Limonade jusques et compris la baye de l'Acul pour servir à faire voir les ouvrages projetés pour sa déffense / dressé par ordre de Monsieur de Bellecombe, … gouverneur général de St. Domingue*, 1760, gallica.bnf.fr.

40 Lorena S. Walsh, *Motives of Honor, Pleasure, and Profit: Plantation Management in the Colonial Chesapeake, 1607–1763* (Chapel Hill: University of North Carolina Press, 2010), p. 111.

41 Ibid., p. 142: 'Councillors also registered more than half of black headrights claimed in land patents, the final step in getting a title. (Maryland slave buyers got no additional land for importing Africans, since the Lords Baltimore granted land rights only for transporting persons of British or Irish descent.)'

42 Ibid., p. 251.

43 Trevor Burnard, *Planters, Merchants, and Slaves: Plantation Societies in British America, 1650–1820* (Chicago: University of Chicago Press, 2015), pp. 3–4.

44 Walsh, *Motives of Honor, Pleasure, and Profit*, p. 251.

45 Ibid., p. 251.

46 For a study of the Jamaican plantation map tradition see Higman, *Jamaica Surveyed*.

47 Walsh, *Motives of Honor, Pleasure, and Profit*, p. 245.

48 OED, 'entail' (accessed 26 September 2019).

49 Walsh, *Motives of Honor, Pleasure, and Profit*, p. 401.

50 Holly Brewer, 'Entailing Aristocracy in Colonial Virginia: "Ancient Feudal Restraints" and Revolutionary Reform', *William and Mary Quarterly*, 3rd series, 54:2 (Apr. 1997), p. 311.

51 Brewer, 'Entailing Aristocracy in Colonial Virginia', p. 338.

52 Walsh, *Motives of Honor, Pleasure, and Profit*, p. 629.

53 Brewer, 'Entailing Aristocracy in Colonial Virginia, p. 337.

54 Lord Dunboyne, *When the States were Young: A Remarkable Collection of Letters 1784–1799 Preserved in the British Library as Additional Manuscript 16603* (www.lulu.com, 2006), pp. 80–2, Pierce Butler to Weeden Butler, 18 July 1788.

55 Marquis de Chastellux, *Travels in North America in the Years 1780, 1781, and 1782 by the Marquis de Chastellux … 2 vols* (London: G. G. J. & J. Robinson, 1787), 2, p. 56.

56 Peter Martin, *The Pleasure Gardens of Virginia: From Jamestown to Jefferson* (Princeton: Princeton University Press, 1991), pp. 108–9.

57 Thomas Jefferson, *Notes on the State of Virginia, Edited and with an Introduction by William Peden* (Chapel Hill: University of North Carolina Press, 1982), pp. 134–5: 'Slaves, as well as lands, were entailable during the monarchy: but, by an act of the first republican assembly, all donees in tail, present and future, were vested with the absolute dominion of the entailed subject'.

58 Jefferson, *Notes on the State of Virginia*, p. 137.

59 For an interesting comparison of two maritime, trading and villa-building environments see Peter Burke, *Venice and Amsterdam: A Study of Seventeenth-century Élites* (Cambridge: Polity Press, 1994).

60 James S. Ackerman, *The Villa: Form and Ideology of Country Houses* (London: Thames and Hudson, 1990), p. 12.

61 Ibid., pp. 15–16.

62 Dell Upton, 'White and Black Landscapes in Eighteenth-Century Virginia', *Places*, 2:2 (1984), p. 63.

63 Therese O'Malley, *Keywords in American Landscape Design* (New Haven and London: Yale University Press, 2010), p. 513, Spotswood, Gov. Alexander, 17 August 1710, describing Williamsburg, Va. (1952:227).

64 Sean Connolly, *Religion, Law, and Power: The Making of Protestant Ireland 1660–1760* (Oxford: Oxford University Press, 1992), p. 13.

65 Ibid., p. 15.

66 Walter G. Strickland, *A Dictionary of Irish Artists* (Shannon and New York: Irish University Press and Hacker, 1968 [1913]), p. 113. The Boyne view was 'taken from the only original picture painted on that subject by the celebrated Battle Painter, Mr. Wyke, Rt. Ho. the Earl of Leicester's Collection'.

67 See James Stevens Curl, *The Londonderry Plantation, 1609–1914: The History, Architecture and Planning of the Estates of the City of London and Its Livery Companies in Ulster* (Chichester: Phillimore & Co. Ltd, 1986); James Stevens Curl, *The Honourable the Irish Society and the Plantation of Ulster, 1608–2000* (Chichester: Phillimore & Co. Ltd, 2000); Rolf Loeber, *The Geography and Practice of English Colonisation in Ireland from 1534–1609* (Athlone: Group for the Study of Irish Historic Settlements, 1991).

68 Avril Thomas, *Derry-Londonderry, Irish Historic Towns Atlas No. 15* (Dublin: Royal Irish Academy, 2005), pp. 2–3.

69 Gerald Boate, *Ireland's Natural History* (London: John Wright, 1657), p. 15.

70 Ibid., A3: 'Dedicatory … For whether we reflect upon the first settlement of a plantation, to prosper it, or upon the wealth of a nation that is planted, to increase it this is the head spring of all the native commerce and trading which may be set afoot therein by any way whatsoever.'

71 Toby Barnard, *Improving Ireland? Projectors, Prophets and Profiteers, 1641–1786* (Dublin: Four Courts Press, 2008), p. 20.

72 Boate, *Ireland's Natural History*, A6.

73 *Londonderry Sentinel*, Saturday Morning, 24 December 1949, p. 3: 'In 1760 the Corporation directed that "the several inhabitants of this city who are papists should be given notice to leave this city by tomorrow morning, and in case of refusal that the Mayor should order the Sergeants-at-Mace and Constables to turn them and their effects out of doors".' The quotation is from the Corporation Minutes.

74 See T. G. Fraser, 'The Siege: Its History and Legacy, 1688–1889' in *Derry & Londonderry: History and Society*, ed. G. O'Brien (Dublin: Geography Publications, 1999).

75 See Finola O'Kane, 'Green Lines of Power: The Apprentice Boys' Trees and the Walls of Derry/Londonderry' in *The Politics of Street Trees*, ed. Camilla Allen and Jan Woudstra (Abingdon: Routledge, 2022), pp. 43–54.

76 Strickland, *A Dictionary of Irish Artists*: 'John Brooks … Line Engravings and Etchings by Brooks. … The Obelisk at the Boyne. I. Tudor Pinx. J. Brooks & Crofts scul.* A folio print with lettered references to the localities, and a dedicatory inscription in Latin to the Duke of Dorset, Lord Lieutenant 1731–37. An advertisement in April, 1745, announces the speedy publication by Brooks of "The Obelisk at the Boyne and the adjacent country, with references where the most remarkable actions happened." The only impression of this print met with belongs to Mr. B. R. Balfour of Townley Hall, Drogheda. The only location of this print in --- was at Townley Hall in the possession of Mr. B. R. Balfour, a demesne located immediately west of King William's Glen.'

77 Anne Crookshank and Desmond FitzGerald, the Knight of Glin, *Ireland's Painters* (New Haven and London: Yale University Press, 2002), pp. 73–4.

78 Mary Delany, *The Autobiography and Correspondence of Mary Granville, Mrs. Delany, ed. Lady Llanover …*, 1st series, 3 vols (London: Ricard Bentley, 1861), pp. 134–5: Mrs Delany to Mrs Dewes, Mount Panther, Friday, 25 June 1752.

79 Ibid.

80 Ibid. Delany's religious affiliation is constantly apparent: 'Unluckily it happened to be the Eve of St. John – a great Roman Catholic holiday, and at our return to our inn we were forced to pass by several monstrous bone fires (*actually made of bones*,) and firing of guns and squibs, and by the time we got to our inn, the whole air was impregnated with the vile stench.'

81 J. Wooley (ed.), *Thomas Sheridan and Jonathan Swift, the Intelligencer* (Cambridge: Cambridge University Press, 1992), pp. 87–8.

82 For a description of the war-torn landscape see Rolf Loeber, David Dickson and Alan Smyth, 'Journal of a Tour to Dublin and the Counties of Dublin and Meath in 1699', *Analecta Hibernica*, 43 (2012), pp. 47–67.

83 For a description of the physical survey methods employed in Ireland in this period see J. H. Andrews, *Plantation Acres:*

An Historical Study of the Irish Land Surveyor (Omagh: Ulster Historical Foundation, 1985).

84 For a detailed analysis of the landscape design of Beaulieu, Oldbridge and Dowth see Finola O'Kane, 'Views of Victory: The Landscapes of the Battle of the Boyne' in *Landscapes of Authority in the Modern World*, ed. Stephen Whiteman (Philadelphia: University of Pennsylvania Press, forthcoming).

85 NLI, LO 10203, Extra-illustrated copy of Arthur Young, *A Tour in Ireland; with general observations on the present state of that kingdom: made in the years 1776, 1777, and 1778. and brought down to the end of 1779*, quarto edn (London: printed for T. Cadell, Strand; and J. Dodsley, 1780), p. 149. For all of Young's published and unpublished illustrations see Finola O'Kane, 'Arthur Young's Published and Unpublished Illustrations for "A Tour in Ireland 1776–1779"', *Irish Architectural & Decorative Studies*, 19 (Kinsale: Gandon, 2017), pp. 118–60.

86 See Chandra Mukerji, *Territorial Ambitions and the Gardens of Versailles* (Cambridge: Cambridge University Press, 1997), p. 86. See also Finola O'Kane, 'Military Memory Manoeuvers in Dublin's Phoenix Park 1775–1820' in *Military Landscapes*, ed. A. Tchikine and J. D. Davis (Cambridge: Harvard University Press, 2021), pp. 311–29.

87 Blennerhasset, *A Direction for the Plantation of Ireland*, D3.

88 *Londonderry Sentinel*, Saturday Morning, 24 December 1949, p. 3, Note 8: Corporation Minutes, 22 February 1752.

89 Ibid., Note 9: Corporation Minutes, 20 August 1776. See also Finola O'Kane, 'Green Lines of Power: The Apprentice Boys' Trees and the Walls of Derry/Londonderry' in *The Politics of Street Trees*, ed. Camilla Allen and Jan Woudstra (Abingdon: Routledge, 2022), pp. 43–54.

90 Ibid., Saturday Morning, 24 December 1949, p. 3, Note 10: Corporation Minutes, 14 May 1782.

91 NLI, LO 10203, Extra-illustrated copy of Arthur Young, *A Tour in Ireland*, pp. 97–8.

CHAPTER TWO

1 See Tom Williamson and Liz Bellamy, *Property and Landscape: A Social History of Land Ownership and the English Countryside* (London: George Philip, 1987), Chapters 2 and 4.

2 P. Roebuck, 'The Making of an Ulster Great Estate: The Chichesters, Barons of Belfast and Viscounts of Carrickfergus, 1599–1648', *Proceedings of the Royal Irish Academy*, 79C (1979), pp. 24–5, citing Lawrence Stone, *The Crisis of the Aristocracy, 1568–1641* (Oxford: Clarendon Press, 1965), pp. 303–22.

3 See for example the history of the design of the Carton demesne and its estate in Arnold Horner, 'Carton, Co. Kildare, A Case Study in the Making of an Irish Demesne', *Quarterly Bulletin of the Irish Georgian Society*, 18:2 and 18:3 (Apr.–Sept. 1975), pp. 45–101; Finola O'Kane, *Landscape Design in Eighteenth-Century Ireland: Mixing Foreign Trees with the Natives* (Cork: Cork University Press, 2004), Chapter 3.

4 Arthur Young, *Rural Oeconomy or Essays on the Practical Parts of Husbandry to which is added The Rural Socrates, being the Memoirs of a Country Philosopher* (London: Becket, 1770), pp. 173–7. See also Paul H. Johnstone, 'The Rural Socrates', *Journal of the History of Ideas*, 5:2 (Apr. 1944), pp. 151–75.

5 John Evelyn, *The Miscellaneous Writings of John Evelyn*, ed. William Upgott (London: Henry Colburn New Burlington St, 1825), pp. 45–6: from *The State of France as it stood in the IXth year of this present Monarch, Lewis XIII* (London, 1652), Prefatory Letter: 'But this hee shall never attain unto, till he begin to be somwhat ripened and seasoned in a place; for it is not every man that crosses the Seas, hath been of an Academy, learned a Corranto, and speaks the Language, whom I esteem a Traveller (of which piece most of our English are in these countryes at present) but that he (instead of making the Tour as they call it) or, as a late Embassador of ours facetiously, but sharply reproached, (like a Goose swimms down the River) having mastered the Tongue, frequented the Court, looked into their customes, been present at their pleadings, observed their Military Discipline, contracted acquaintance with their Learned men, studied their Arts, and is familiar with their dispositions, makes this accompt of his time.'

6 Mary Delany, *The Autobiography and Correspondence of Mary Granville, Mrs. Delany, ed. Lady Llanover* …, 3 vols. (London: Ricard Bentley, 1861), 2:3, p. 443: 'The coach is ready for D[r]. D[elany]. and me to tour in the park, and to see my lord's improvements.'

7 See Finola O'Kane, *Ireland and the Picturesque: Design, Landscape Painting and Tourism in Ireland 1700–1840* (New Haven and London: Yale University Press, 2013), Chapter 4.

8 This chapter draws from Finola O'Kane, 'Arthur Young's Study of Landscape Gardens and Parks for his Publication "A Tour in Ireland 1776–1779"', *Journal of Scottish Thought*, 9 (2017), pp. 110–24 and Finola O'Kane, 'The Limits of Brown's Landscape: Translations of the Landscape Garden into Ireland', Capability Brown 300 Year Anniversary Special Issue, *Garden History, Journal of the Garden History Society*, 44:2 (2016).

9 ODNB, 'Arthur Young', G. E. Mingay (accessed 15 July 2015).

10 Arthur Young, *Travels in France during the Years 1787, 1788, 1789* (London: George Bell and Sons, 1906), p. 127: 'The eye discovers them [the Bretons] at first glance to be a people absolutely distinct from the French. Wonderful that they should be found so, with distinct language, manners, dress, &c. after having been settled here 1300 years.'

11 Arthur Young, *The Autobiography of Arthur Young*, ed. M. Betham-Edwards (New York: Augustus M. Kelley, 1967 [1898]), p. 67.

12 Arthur Young, *A Tour in Ireland, 1776–1779*, 2 vols (Shannon: Irish University Press, 1970), 1, p. 65.

13 Finola O'Kane, 'Arthur Young's Published and Unpublished Illustrations for 'A Tour in Ireland 1776–1779', *Irish Architectural and Decorative Studies* (Kinsale: Gandon, 2017), 19, pp. 118–60.

14 NLI, LO 10203, Extra-illustrated copy of Arthur Young, *A Tour in Ireland; with general observations on the present state of that kingdom: made in the years 1776, 1777, and 1778. and brought down to the end of 1779*, quarto edn (London: printed for T. Cadell, Strand; and J. Dodsley, 1780). The NLI catalogue record http://catalogue.nli.ie/Record/vtls000209724 states: 'All the pen and ink views are thought to be by Young himself.'

15   Arthur Young, *A Six Months Tour through the North of England …*, 3 vols (Dublin: P. Wilson, J. Exshaw, H. Saunders, W. Sleater, D. Chamberlaine et al., 1770).

16   Ibid., 1:3, p. 352.

17   Young, *A Tour in Ireland, 1776–1779* (1970), 1, pp. 392–3.

18   Ibid., pp. 284–5: 'I should remark, as I have now left Galway, that that county, from entering it in the road to Tuam to leaving it today, has been, upon the whole, inferior to most of the parts I have travelled in Ireland in point of beauty: there are not mountains of a magnitude to make the view striking. It is perfectly free from woods, and even trees, except about gentlemen's houses, nor has it a variety in its face.'

19   Ibid., p. 352.

20   Ibid., p. 354.

21   Ibid., pp. 31–2.

22   Ibid., p. 21.

23   Ibid., p. 32: 'From this building [Carton's prospect tower] his Grace has another sort of view, not everywhere to be met with; he looks over a great part of 60,000 acres, which lie around him nearly contiguous.'

24   Ibid., pp. 277–8.

25   Ibid., p. 392.

26   Ibid., p. 113: 'This great improver, a title more deserving estimation than that of a great general or a great minister, lives now to overlook a country flourishing only from his exertions. He has made a barren wilderness smile with cultivation, planted it with people, and made those people happy.'

27   For an in-depth discussion of improvement in Ireland see Toby Barnard, *Making the Grand Figure: Lives and Possessions in Ireland, 1641–1770* (New Haven and London: Yale University Press, 2004), Chapter 6; Barnard, *Improving Ireland? Projectors, Prophets and Profiteers 1641–1786* (Dublin: Four Courts Press, 2008).

28   For Lough Erne: Castle Caldwell, Castle Hume, Bellisle. For Killarney notably Muckross House and Kenmare House.

29   William Laffan and Brendan Rooney, *Thomas Roberts 1748–1777: Landscape and Patronage in Eighteenth-Century Ireland* (Tralee and Dublin: Churchill House Press, 2009), p. 73. Richard Wilson's painting of the great woodland demesne of Cassiobury, seat of the Earl of Essex, for his client Sir Lawrence Dundas provides the sole known comparable instance in England.

30   Young, *A Tour in Ireland, 1776–1779* (1970), 1, pp. 213–14.

31   Young published a list of absentees in his *A Tour in Ireland, 1776–1779* but did not estimate what percentage they constituted of the entire landlord class. Terence Dooley estimates absenteeism at 33 per cent in 1800 in his 'Estate Ownership and Management in Nineteenth- and Early Twentieth-Century Ireland' in *Sources for the History of Landed Estates in Ireland* (Dublin: Irish Academic Press, 2000), pp. 3–16.

32   Young, *A Tour in Ireland, 1776–1779* (1970), 1, pp. 189–90: 'There is a great deal of letting lands in the gross to middle men, who re-let it to others; these middle men are called terney begs, or little landlords, which prevail very much at present. These men make a great profit by this practice.'

33   For the difficulties involved in reading the legal structure of Irish eighteenth-century landscape see Finola O'Kane, 'Dublin's Fitzwilliam Estate: A Hidden Landscape of Discovery, Catholic Agency and Egalitarian Suburban Space', *Eighteenth-Century Ireland / Iris an dá chultúr*, 31 (2016), pp. 94–118.

34   George Washington to Arthur Young, 18–21 June 1792, *Founders Online*, https://founders.archives.gov/documents/Washington/05-10-02-0308 (accessed 23 November 2022).

35   George Washington to Arthur Young, Mount Vernon, 4 December 1788, *Founders Online*, https://founders.archives.gov/documents/Washington/05-01-02-0120 (accessed 23 November 2022).

36   T. H. Breen, *Tobacco Culture: The Mentality of the Great Tidewater Planters on the Eve of Revolution* (Princeton: Princeton University Press, 2001), p. xxv.

37   Lorena S. Walsh, *Motives of Honor, Pleasure, and Profit: Plantation Management in the Colonial Chesapeake 1607–1763* (Chapel Hill: University of North Carolina Press, 2010), p. 226.

38   In this chapter the term 'American' will at times be used to describe the thirteen colonies that became the United States in 1776, because of its persistent use in the revolutionary period. For post-1776 material 'United States' will be used in preference to 'America'.

39   John R. Stilgoe, *Common Landscape of America, 1580 to 1845* (New Haven and London: Yale University Press), 1982, p. 65.

40   Anthony S. Parent Jr., *Foul Means: The Formation of a Slave Society in Virginia, 1660–1740* (Chapel Hill: University of North Carolina Press, 2003), p. 1: 'The historian Edmund Morgan "resuscitated American history by placing black slavery and white freedom as its central paradox".' See Edmund S. Morgan, 'Slavery and Freedom: The American Paradox', *Journal of American History*, 59 (1972) and Morgan, *American Slavery, American Freedom: The Ordeal of Colonial Virginia* (New York: W. W. Norton, 1975). This chapter seeks to explore the design implications of this paradoxical condition on the American landed estate.

41   Susan Myra Kingsbury (ed.), *Records of the Virginia Company*, 3:4 (Washington: United States Government Printing Office, 1906–33), p. 15.

42   Charles C. Wall, 'Notes on the Early History of Mount Vernon', *William and Mary Quarterly*, 2:2 (1945), p. 179.

43   Dennis J. Pogue, 'Mount Vernon: Transformation of an Eighteenth-Century Plantation System' in *Historical Archaeology of the Chesapeake*, ed. Paul A. Shackel and Barbara Little (Washington DC: Smithsonian, 1994), p. 104.

44   'Washington's Map of Mount Vernon', *Huntington Library Quarterly*, 17:2 (Feb. 1954), p. 1.

45   The area was later itemised in a 1859 map: W. Gillingham, *Map of George Washington's Land at Mount Vernon Fairfax Coy Virginia. As it was & As it is laid down from old Maps made by G. Washington, and from actual surveys by W. Gillingham*, lithograph by E. Sachse & Co., Sun Iron Building Baltimore, MD. 'The content of the entire tract of land is about 7600 acres.'

46   Pogue, 'Mount Vernon: Transformation of', p. 103.

47   George Washington to George William Fairfax, 30 June 1785, Mount Vernon, *Founders Online*, https://founders.archives.gov/documents/Washington/04-03-02-0080 (accessed 18 November 2022).

48   Ibid.

49   Appleton P. C. Griffin, *A Catalogue of the Washington Collection in the Boston Athenaeum* (Cambridge, MA: The Boston Athenaeum, 1897), p. 231. Both volumes also contain his bookplate.

50   To George Washington from Arthur Young, 7 January 1786, *Founders Online*, https://founders.archives.gov/documents/Washington/04-03-02-0425: 'Your expression concerning manure being the [f]irst transmutation towards gold, is good, and shews that you may be as great a farmer as a general. The culture of those plants that support cattle you will probably find the true means of improvement, & amongst those, turneps, cabbages and potatoes all very important' (accessed 18 November 2022).

51   George Washington to Arthur Young, 6 August 1786, *Founders Online*, https://founders.archives.gov/documents/Washington/04-04-02-0185 (accessed 18 November 2022).

52   From George Washington to Arthur Young, 15 November 1786, *Founders Online*, https://founders.archives.gov/documents/Washington/04-04-02-0330 (accessed 24 November 2022).

53   To George Washington from Arthur Young, 1 February 1787, *Founders Online*, https://founders.archives.gov/documents/Washington/04-05-02-0004 (accessed 18 November 2022).

54   Arthur Young (ed.), *The Annals of Agriculture and Other Useful Arts* (Bury St Edmunds: Arthur Young, 1791), 16, pp. 149–51, https://babel.hathitrust.org/cgi/pt?id=hvd.32044083427740;view=1up;seq=159;size=50 (accessed 22 February 2018). No plate is contained within this Harvard University copy.

55   To George Washington from Arthur Young, 1 February 1787, *Founders Online*.

56   George Washington to Arthur Young, 1 November 1787, *Founders Online*, https://founders.archives.gov/documents/Washington/04-05-02-0372 (accessed 18 November 2022).

57   To George Washington from Arthur Young, 1 July 1788, *Founders Online*, https://founders.archives.gov/documents/Washington/04-06-02-0329 (accessed 18 November 2022). For an example of such published letters see Michel Guillaume Jean de Crèvecœur, *Letters from an American Farmer* (London: Thomas Davies, 1782).

58   George Washington to Arthur Young, 4 December 1788, *Founders Online*, https://founders.archives.gov/documents/Washington/05-01-02-0120 (accessed 18 November 2022).

59   George Washington to Arthur Young, 5 December 1791, *Founders Online*, https://founders.archives.gov/documents/Washington/05-09-02-0153 (accessed 18 November 2022).

60   George Washington to Arthur Young, 1 November 1787, *Founders Online*, https://founders.archives.gov/documents/Washington/04-05-02-0372 (accessed 18 November 2022).

61   To George Washington from Arthur Young, 18 January 1792, *Founders Online*, https://founders.archives.gov/documents/Washington/05-09-02-0280: 'Be so obliging Sir as to inform me what the rate of labour is that can be commanded (by paying for it) in quantity, both by free hands & by slaves. At present I see no reason to calculate it less than 100 per cent higher than England, and the general information I have ay various times had from other persons seems to confirm the idea: No wonder while every man by going over the Mountains can have land for himself' (accessed 18 November 2022).

62   George Washington to Arthur Young, 18–21 June 1792, *Founders Online*, https://founders.archives.gov/documents/Washington/05-10-02-0308 (accessed 18 November 2022).

63   To George Washington from Richard Peters, 20 June 1792, *Founders Online*, https://founders.archives.gov/documents/Washington/05-10-02-0320 (accessed 18 November 2022).

64   George Washington to Arthur Young, 18–21 June 1792, *Founders Online*, https://founders.archives.gov/documents/Washington/05-10-02-0308 (accessed 18 November 2022).

65   George Washington to Arthur Young, 2 December 1792, *Founders Online*, https://founders.archives.gov/documents/Washington/05-11-02-0274: 'No Negros under twelve years of age are taxed—nor are any under Sixteen subjected to the payment of County, or Parish levies. Horses, at present, are the only species of Stock, in that State, which pays a tax. Carriages were, when I left Virginia, and I believe still are, subject to a tax by the Wheel' (accessed 18 November 2022).

66   To George Washington from Arthur Young, 17 January 1793, *Founders Online*, https://founders.archives.gov/documents/Washington/05-12-02-0008 (accessed 18 November 2022).

67   George Washington to Arthur Young, 1 September 1793, *Founders Online*, https://founders.archives.gov/documents/Washington/05-14-02-0005 (accessed 18 November 2022).

68   To George Washington from Richard Peters, 20 June 1793, *Founders Online*, https://founders.archives.gov/documents/Washington/05-13-02-0084#GEWN-05-13-02-0084-fn-0001: The remarks were contained in an 'undated enclosure titled "Observations on an Extract of a Letter dated 17. January 1793 from Arthur Young Esqr to The President"' (accessed 18 November 2022).

69   George Washington to Arthur Young, 12 December 1793, *Founders Online*, https://founders.archives.gov/documents/Washington/05-14-02-0337 (accessed 18 November 2022). What exactly Washington was concerned about is difficult to interpret: 'At the time it was written [previous letter of GW to AY, 1 September 1793] the thoughts which I am now about to disclose to you were not even in embryo; and whether, in the opinion of others, there be impropriety, or not, in communicating the object which has given birth to them, is not for me to decide. My own mind reproaches me with none, but if yours should view the subject differently, burn this letter and the draught which accompanies it, and the whole matter will be consigned to oblivion.'

70   George Washington to Arthur Young, 12 December 1793, Philadelphia, *Founders Online*. https://founders.archives.gov/documents/Washington/05-14-02-0337 (accessed 18 November 2022).

71   Ibid.

72   Young, *The Autobiography of Arthur Young*, p. 191: 'October 21 [1791], A Letter today from general Washington– Gracious! from the representative of the Majesty of America, all written in his own hand. Also one from the Marquis de la Fayette desiring my assistance to get him a bailiff that understands English ornamental gardening; for both he gives fifty louis a year– this is a French idea to unite what was never united, and, when gained, rewards it with the wages of a common labourer.'

73   George Washington to Arthur Young, 12 December 1793, Philadelphia, *Founders Online*, https://founders.archives.gov/documents/

Washington/05-14-02-0337 (accessed 18 November 2022).

74 Holly Brewer, 'Entailing Aristocracy in Colonial Virginia: "Ancient Feudal Restraints" and Revolutionary Reform', *William and Mary Quarterly*, 3rd series, 54:2 (Apr., 1997), pp. 337–8. See also Lorena S. Walsh, 'Land, Landlord, and Leaseholder: Estate Management and Tenant Fortunes in Southern Maryland, 1642–1820', *Agricultural History*, 59:3 (Jul., 1985), pp. 373–96.

75 Ibid., p. 337: The claim that land was 'cheap and easily available', which Brewer contests, was made in Bernard Bailyn, 'Politics and Social Structure in Virginia' in *Seventeenth-Century America: Essays in Colonial History*, ed. James Morton Smith (Chapel Hill: University of North Carolina Press, 1959), p. 108.

76 Brewer, 'Entailing Aristocracy in Colonial Virginia', p. 337: Note 104 citing James H. Merrell, *The Indians' New World Catawbas and their Neighbors from European Contact through the Era of Removal* (Chapel Hill: University of North Carolina Press, 1989).

77 George Washington to Arthur Young, 12 December 1793, Philadelphia, *Founders Online*, https://founders.archives.gov/documents/Washington/05-14-02-0337 (accessed 18 November 2022).

78 Young, *A Tour in Ireland, 1776–1779* (1970), 1, p. 343: 'From there I reached Sir John Coulthurst's at Knightsbridge [Ardtully House, Co. Kenmare], who has a very extensive estate here, 7,000 acres of which are mountain and bog. I was unfortunate in not having seen Sir John's seat, near Corke, for there he is at work upon 1,000 acres of mountain, and making great improvements.'

79 Benjamin Henry Latrobe, *The Journal of Latrobe, being the Notes and Sketches of an Architect, Naturalist and Traveler in the United States from 1796 to 1820* (New York: D. Apleton & Co., 1905), p. 51.

80 Young, *A Tour in Ireland, 1776–1779* (1970), 1, p. 94.

81 J. P. Brissot de Warville, *New Travels in the United States of America Performed in 1788* (Dublin: P. Byrne, A. Grueber, W. McKenzie et. al., 1792), pp. 428–9: 'The General came home in the evening, fatigued with having been to lay out a new road in some part of his plantations. You have often heard of him compared to Cincinnatus: the comparison is doubtless just. This celebrated General is nothing more at present than a good farmer, considerably occupied in the care of his farm and the improvement of cultivation. He has lately built a barn one hundred feet in length and considerably more in breadth, destined to receive the productions of his farm, and to shelter his cattle, horses, asses, and mules. It is built on a plan sent him by that famous English farmer Arthur Young. But the General has much improved the plan … His three hundred negroes are distributed in different log houses, in different parts of his plantation, which in this neighbourhood consists of ten thousand acres.'

82 BL, Add. Ms. 35126, Arthur Young Correspondence, vol. 1, no. 171: 'London Feb. 26. 1777, Memorandum of the purport of a conversation with Lord Kingsborough and Mr Danby upon Mr. Young's going to Ireland agent to his Lordship'.

83 George Washington to Arthur Young, 1 November 1787, *The Papers of George Washington Digital Edition*, ed. Theodore J. Crackel (Charlottesville: University of Virginia Press, Rotunda, 2008): 'I am now preparing materials to build a Barn precisely agreeable to your plan, which I think an excellent one.' Editor's Note referring to

84 Young's (ANNALS, 16:150–51): 'Although GW built his new barn of brick, he did not do it on the recommendation of Arthur Young.'

84 Young, *A Tour in Ireland, 1776–1779* (1970), 1, pp. 320–2.

85 See David Buisseret, *Rural Images: The Estate Plan in the Old and New Worlds. A Cartographic Exhibit at The Newberry Library on the Occasion of the Ninth Series of Kenneth Nebenzahl Jr., Lectures in the History of Cartography* (Chicago: The Newberry Library, 1988) and Martin Bruckner, *The Geographic Revolution in Early America: Maps, Literacy and National Identity* (Chapel Hill: University of North Carolina, 2006), p. 23.

86 Buisseret, *Rural Images*, pp. 1–2.

87 Bruckner, *The Geographic Revolution in Early America*, p. 25.

88 George Washington to Anthony Whitting, 11 November 1792, *Founders Online*, https://founders.archives.gov/documents/Washington/05-11-02-0206 (accessed 18 November 2022).

89 Ibid.

90 George Washington to William Pearce, 23 December 1793, *Founders Online*, https://founders.archives.gov/documents/Washington/05-14-02-0377 (accessed 23 November, 2022).

91 George Washington to Arthur Young, 12 December 1793, *Founders Online*, https://founders.archives.gov/documents/Washington/05-14-02-0337 (accessed 18 November 2022).

92 Joseph Manca, *George Washington's Eye: Landscape, Architecture and Design at Mount Vernon* (Baltimore: Johns Hopkins University Press, 2012), p. 84: Manca is summarising the conclusions of many other American garden historians for many other American estates.

93 This argument is perhaps most forcibly made in Barbara Wells Sarudy, *Gardens and Gardening in the Chesapeake, 1700–1805* (Baltimore and London: Johns Hopkins Press, 1998), Preface.

94 To George Washington from Arthur Young, London, 2 June 1794, *Founders Online*, https://founders.archives.gov/documents/Washington/05-16-02-0146 (accessed 18 November 2022).

95 Jean B. Lee (ed.), *Experiencing Mount Vernon: Eyewitness Accounts, 1784–1865* (Charlottesville and London: University of Virginia Press, 2006), pp. 67–8: 'Louis-Philippe, 1797, future King of France: 'The general owns ten thousand acres of land around Mount Vernon. Hardly half of it is under cultivation. There are about 400 blacks scattered among the different farms. These unfortunates reproduce freely and their number is increasing. I have been thinking that to accomplish their emancipation gradually and without upheaval it might be possible to grant them first a status in mortmain [Note 2: Inalienable status] by depriving their owners of the right to sell them.'

96 George Washington to Arthur Young, 9 November 1794, Philadelphia, *Founders Online*, https://founders.archives.gov/documents/Washington/05-17-02-0108 (accessed 18 November 2022).

97 Ibid.

98 To George Washington, from Tobias Lear, 26–30 January 1794, *Founders Online*, https://founders.archives.gov/documents/Washington/05-15-02-0095: 'He is about 5 feet 10 inches high – rather thin – an interesting countenance, aquiline nose & good eye; his conversation is animated and he handles his subject with dexterity; but many who know him well consider him rather as a theorist on the subject of farming – and even say that he never made half the

experiments of which he has published the result – and his own farm is said to be one of the most slovenly in the part of the Country where he lives: It is however acknowledged by All, that he has done very great good to the cause of agriculture, by his writings and perseverence. In his political opinions it is said there has been a change since the commencement of the war with France – and some are so ill-natured as to impute it to the 500£ which he receives as Secy to the Board of Agriculture – Certain it is that he is now as high a monarchist as any in Britain' (accessed 18 November 2022).

CHAPTER THREE

1   For these meetings see Dixon Wecter, 'Benjamin Franklin and an Irish "Enthusiast"', *Huntington Library Quarterly*, 4 (1941), pp. 205–34.

2   James Kelly, *Sir Edward Newenham, MP, 1734–1814: Defender of the Protestant Constitution* (Dublin: Four Courts Press, 2004), p. 17.

3   George Washington to Edward Newenham, 10 June 1784, *Founders Online*, https://founders.archives.gov/documents/ Washington/04-01-02-0302 (accessed 21 November 2022).

4   Kelly, *Sir Edward Newenham*, pp. 190–1: Newenham entered 'negotiations in 1781 with John Wilmot to rent an additional 14 acres over and above the 45 he already had on a long lease, and to pay three guineas per acre for an additional 66 acres when the current lifetime or forty-year lease had expired'.

5   To Benjamin Franklin from Edward Newenham, Belcamp, 29 September 1784, *Founders Online*, https://founders.archives.gov/ documents/Franklin/01-43-02-0106 (accessed 21 November 2022).

6   George Washington to Edward Newenham, 10 June 1784, *Founders Online*, https://founders.archives.gov/documents/ Washington/04-01-02-0302 (accessed 21 November 2022).

7   Ibid.

8   To Benjamin Franklin from Sir Edward Newenham [9 October 1784], *Founders Online*, National Archives, https://founders.archives.gov/ documents/Franklin/01-43-02-0106 (accessed 21 November 2022).

9   George Washington to Edward Newenham, Mount Vernon, 25 November 1785, *Founders Online*, https://founders.archives.gov/ documents/Washington/04-03-02-0346 (accessed 21 November 2022).

10 George Washington to Edward Newenham, Mount Vernon, 10 June 1786, *Founders Online*, https://founders.archives.gov/documents/ Washington/04-04-02-0106: 'I little expected when I wrote you last, that Tharpe was to be the principal workman in the ornamental parts of my new room. I had not, at that time, even heard of his arrival in this country; but having engaged one Rawlins of Baltimore in Maryland (lately from England) to finish it, I found when he had brought his men and tools here, that Tharpe had been contracted with and was the person on whom Rawlins depended for the execution of the plan on which we had, two or three months before, agreed. To this man I objected 'till it became evident that it must be him, or no work; there being no other, Rawlins said, competent to the undertaking. This being the case, and the inconvenience of laying another year out of the room being great, I consented to try him on condition that Rawlins, who I believe has left off work, himself should superintend it closely.

Tharpe has been here now, more than six weeks, and hitherto has demeaned himself soberly and well' (accessed 21 November 2022).

11 See Joseph Manca, *George Washington's Eye: Landscape, Architecture and Design at Mount Vernon* (Baltimore: Johns Hopkins University Press, 2012), pp. 22–3.

12 Kelly, *Sir Edward Newenham*, p. 191; see Newenham to Franklin, 29 September 1784, 9 October 1784, 11 January 1786, *Founders Online*.

13 To George Washington from Edward Newenham, 10 October 1789, *Founders Online*, https://founders.archives.gov/documents/ Washington/05-04-02-0107 (accessed 21 November 2022). This was General Benedict Arnold who had betrayed the Continental army to the British in 1780.

14 George Washington to Edward Newenham, Mount Vernon, 25 November 1785, *Founders Online*, 'I have never seen more than one picture of Genl. Green, and that a mezzotinto print, sent to me a few days ago only, by the publisher a Mr. Brown at No. 10 George Yard, Lombard street, London; taken it is said from a painting done at Philada.'

15 To George Washington from Edward Newenham, 22 December 1791, *Founders Online*, https://founders.archives.gov/documents/ Washington/05-09-02-0193 (accessed 21 November 2022).

16 See Ruth Johnstone, 'Lady Louisa Conolly's Print Room at Castletown' in *Castletown: Decorative Arts* (Dublin: Office of Public Works, 2011), pp. 67–77.

17 George Washington to Edward Newenham, 20 April 1787, *Founders Online*, https://founders.archives.gov/documents/ Washington/04-05-02-0142 (accessed 21 November 2022). In his excellent book *The Pleasure Gardens of Virginia: From Jamestown to Jefferson* (Princeton: Princeton University Press, 1991) Peter Martin mistakenly located 'Bell Champ' in England (p. 144), leading many to underestimate the connections between the historic landscape at Belcamp and Mount Vernon in Virginia.

18 To Benjamin Franklin from Sir Edward Newenham [9 October 1784], *Founders Online*.

19 Ibid.

20 Edward Newenham to Benjamin Franklin, Belcamp, 29 September 1784, *Founders Online*, https://founders.archives.gov/documents/ Franklin/01-43-02-0095 (accessed 21 November 2022).

21 To Benjamin Franklin from Edward Newenham, 12 August 1786, *Founders Online*, https://franklinpapers.org/framedVolumes, 'Unpub. 1786-87' (accessed 20 February 2023). These Alpine firs produced the 'finest deal in Europe' for building but it was 'not much used, as the expence … in bringing the timber over' the Alps was so great.

22 To Benjamin Franklin from Edward Newenham, 25 August 1787, *Founders Online*, https://franklinpapers.org/framedVolumes, 'Unpub. 1787-88' (accessed 20 February 2023).

23 To Benjamin Franklin from Edward Newenham, 1 March 1787, *Founders Online*, https://franklinpapers.org/framedVolumes, 'Unpub. 1786-87' (accessed 20 February 2023).

24 To Benjamin Franklin from Edward Newenham, 25 August 1787, *Founders Online*: Kirwan had improved his land by 'burning the Surface, then laying about 80 car Load of Limestone Gravel Spread on the Surface, ploughing it Gently' and then the next spring planting

potatoes under a 'very little dung'. The following year it would 'bear wheat, oats, Rope or flax, and if kept properly drained' would not 'require any Manure for 3 or 4 years' when another layer of limestone gravel would be required.

25   Ibid.

26   To George Washington from William Persse, 11 October 1788, *Founders Online*, https://founders.archives.gov/documents/ Washington/05-01-02-0031: 'Plant the goosberries in a rich deep soyle; put a good Deal of roten Dung into Each hole before you plant them keep them open in the Midle, dont allow to many Branches on a Tree, & the fruit will be very Large & fine, I have them as Large as Wallnuts, give them a North Aspect & as Little sun as you Can, but not the shade of Trees, I fear your Climate is to hot' (accessed 21 November 2022).

27   Hugh Young to George Washington, 16 February 1789, *Founders Online*, https://founders.archives.gov/documents/ Washington/05-01-02-0231 (accessed 21 November 2022).

28   To Benjamin Franklin from Edward Newenham, 25 August 1787, *Founders Online*.

29   See Finola O'Kane, 'A Cabin and not a Cottage – The Architectural Embodiment of the Irish Nation' in *Ireland in the European Eye*, ed. B. Migge and G. Hofter (Dublin: The Royal Irish Academy, 2019), pp. 259–83.

30   BL, Add. Ms. 35127, Arthur Young Correspondence, vol. 1, no. 304, Arthur Young to anon.

31   Ann Bermingham 'The Simple Life: Cottages and Gainsborough's Cottage Doors' in *Land, Nation and Culture, 1740–1840: Thinking the Republic of Taste*, ed. Peter de Bolla, Nigel Leask and David Simpson (Basingstoke and New York: Palgrave Macmillan, 2005), p. 56. See John Barrell, *The Dark Side of the Landscape: The Rural Poor in English Painting, 1730–1840* (Cambridge: Cambridge University Press, 1980).

32   Bermingham, 'The Simple Life: Cottages and Gainsborough's Cottage Doors', p. 56.

33   George Washington to Edward Newenham, Mount Vernon, 29 August 1788, *Founders Online*, https://founders.archives.gov/ documents/Washington/04-06-02-0436 (accessed 20 February 2023).

34   George Washington to Edward Newenham, Mount Vernon, 2 March 1789, *Founders Online*, https://founders.archives.gov/documents/ Washington/05-01-02-0265 (accessed 21 November 2022).

35   To George Washington from Edward Newenham, 22 December 1791, *Founders Online*, https://founders.archives.gov/documents/ Washington/05-09-02-0193 (accessed 21 November 2022).

36   Ibid.

37   To Benjamin Franklin from Edward Newenham, 1787?, *Founders Online*, https://franklinpapers.org/framedVolumes, 'Unpub. 1787-88' (accessed 20 February 2023).

38   To George Washington from Edward Newenham, 9 January 1792, *Founders Online*, https://founders.archives.gov/documents/ Washington/05-09-02-0247 (accessed 21 November 2022). For further letters on the Catholic threat posed to Protestant property see Edward Newenham to George Washington, 9 January 1792, 12 February 1792, 29 September 1792.

39   George Washington to Edward Newenham, Philadelphia, 20 October

40   Ibid.

41   To George Washington from Edward Newenham, 12 February 1792, *Founders Online*, https://founders.archives.gov/documents/ Washington/05-09-02-0335 (accessed 21 November 2022). Janet Livingston Montgomery was the widow of the patriot General Richard Montgomery.

42   Kelly, *Sir Edward Newenham*, p. 261.

43   Ibid., p. 266.

44   To George Washington from Edward Newenham, *c.*3 November 1794, *Founders Online*, https://founders.archives.gov/documents/ Washington/05-17-02-0093 (accessed 21 November 2022).

45   George Washington to Edward Newenham, 6 August 1797, *Founders Online*, https://founders.archives.gov/documents/ Washington/06-01-02-0248 (accessed 21 November 2022). This is Washington's final letter.

46   To George Washington from Edward Newenham, 30 October 1797, *Founders Online*, https://founders.archives.gov/documents/ Washington/06-01-02-0394 (accessed 21 November 2022). This is Newenham's final letter.

47   To Benjamin Franklin from Edward Newenham, 1787?, *Founders Online*, https://franklinpapers.org/framedVolumes. jsp?vol=45&page=277 (accessed 21 November 2022).

48   T. W. Moody, R. B. McDowell and C. J. Woods (eds), *The Writings of Wolfe Tone 1763–98*, 3 vols (Oxford: Oxford University Press, 2001), 2, p. 1: 'Theobald Wolfe Tone, Philadelphia, to Thomas Russell, Belfast, 7 August 1795'.

49   Jean-Jacques Rousseau, *Émile* (London: Everyman, 1995), p. 160.

50   See Finola O'Kane, *Ireland and the Picturesque: Design, Landscape Painting and Tourism in Ireland 1700–1840* (New Haven and London: Yale University Press, 2013), Chapter 4.

51   Arthur Young, *A Tour in Ireland, 1776–1779*, 2 vols (Shannon: Irish University Press, 1970), 1, p. 79.

52   John R. Stilgoe, *Common Landscape of America, 1580 to 1845* (New Haven and London: Yale University Press, 1982), p. 70: 'Planters typically concerned themselves with building roads from their plantations to the nearest shipping wharf, which they often sited at the edge of their holdings. Most roads ran at right angles to the estuaries and rivers, then, and most followed ridges rather than crossing valleys, because householders "rolled" tobacco to the wharves, despite its being brutal work.'

53   Isaac Weld, *Travels through the States of North America, and the Provinces of Upper and Lower Canada, during the years 1795, 1796, and 1797* (London: John Stockdale, 1799), vol. 1, p. 49.

54   The two lodges which now flank the Mount Vernon gate on the Alexandria road were built by Washington's heir, Bushrod Washington.

55   Benjamin Henry Latrobe, *The Journal of Latrobe, being the Notes and Sketches of an Architect, Naturalist and Traveler in the United States from 1796 to 1820* (New York: D. Appleton & Co., 1905), p. 51. See also Edward C. Carter II, John C. Van Horne and Charles E. Brownell (eds), *Latrobe's View of America, 1795–1820, Selections from the Watercolors and Sketches* (New Haven and London: Yale University Press, 1985).

56 Jean B. Lee (ed.), *Experiencing Mount Vernon: Eyewitness Accounts, 1784–1865* (Charlottesville and London: University of Virginia Press, 2006), pp. 26–7: 'Robert Hunter 1785'.

57 Weld, *Travels through the States of North America*, pp. 51–2.

58 Lee, *Experiencing Mount Vernon*, p. 48: 'Samuel Powel, 1787'.

59 Latrobe, *The Journal of Latrobe*, p. 52.

60 Lee, *Experiencing Mount Vernon*, p. 70: 1798, Julian Ursyn Niemcewicz.

61 For a detailed analysis of the sectional constraints posed by adapting seventeenth-century Irish houses to the ideals of Brown's compositional style see Finola O'Kane, 'The Limits of Brown's Landscape: Translations of the Landscape Garden into Ireland', Capability Brown 300 Year Anniversary Special Issue, *Garden History, Journal of the Garden History Society*, 44:2 (2016).

62 Joseph Jackson Howard (ed.), *Miscellanea genealogica et heraldica*, 2nd series, vol. 4 (London: Hamilton Adams, 1892), p. 86: 'Vaughan. The following notes are from a small book which for a couple of generations served as a diary and note-book for the Vaughan family of Ballyboe, in county Tipperary, and London, etc … On the fly-leaf: "Ben Vaughan His Book July 8, 1698. There is many good Recepts and other things in this book."'

63 Manca, *George Washington's Eye*, p. 173.

64 C. L. Vaughan-Arbuckle, 'A Tipperary Farmer and Waterford Tradesman of Two Centuries Ago from Materials Furnished by Capt. C. L. Vaughan-Arbuckle', *Journal of the Waterford and South-East of Ireland Archaeological Society* (1st quarter, Jan. to Mar. 1902), pp. 80–9, http://snap.waterfordcoco.ie/collections/ejournals/100583/100583.pdf (accessed 30 November 2018).

65 Howard, *Miscellanea genealogica et heraldica*, p. 87.

66 Ibid.: 'Son Samll left Waterford to go to his brother Wm in London June 9, 1733, got to Bristole ye 14 and to London ye 19 of ye same month.'

67 Ibid.: 'Son Samll was bound an apprentice to Mether Corr, mercht, Oct. 2, 1736, for five years, went with his master to Jamaica Octr 15, 1736.'

68 UCL, *Legacies of British Slaveownership*: Samuel Vaughan, https://www.ucl.ac.uk/lbs/person/view/2146643669 (accessed 19 October 2018).

69 Andrew Hamilton, 'Benjamin Vaughan on Commerce and International Harmony in the Eighteenth Century' in *Sociability and Cosmopolitanism: Social Bonds on the Fringes of the Enlightenment World*, ed. Scott Breuniger and David Burrow (Abingdon: Routledge, 2016), pp. 103–4.

70 MVLA, Ms-4996, Samuel Vaughan's Diary, 1787, p. 57: 1. Mansion House; 2. Kitchen & Servant Hall; 3. Store house &c.; 4. Smoak house; 5. Wash house; 6. Coach house; 7. Double do. & Stables; 8. Barn & Carpenters shop; 9. Lodgings for white Servants; 10. Taylor & Shoemakers shop; 11. -----; 12. [Sp]inning House; 13. Blacksmiths shop; 14. house for Families; 15. Hot house; 16. Kitchen Gardens; 17. Neccessaries; 18. Spring house; 19. Lawn; 20. for Manure; 21. School; 22.

71 Samuel Vaughan, 1787 presentation plan of Mount Vernon, DI_1309-1_W-1434, MVLA (Fig. 76) : a. The Mansion House; b. Smiths shop; c. White Servants appartments; d. Kitchen; e. Repository for Dung; f. Spinning House; g. -; h. Shoemaker & Taylors' appartments; i. Store House &c.; k.Smoak House; l. Wash House; m&n Coach Houses; n. Quarters for Families; o.o.o Stables; p.p.p Necessaries; q. Green House; r.r. Cow Houses; s. Barn & Carpenters shop; t. School Room; u. Summer House; w. Dairy; x.x. Kitchen Gardens.

72 Manca, *George Washington's Eye*, pp. 93–5.

73 Dennis J. Pogue, 'Mount Vernon: Transformation of an Eighteenth-Century Plantation System' in *Historical Archaeology of the Chesapeake*, ed. Paul A. Shackel and Barbara Little (Washington DC: Smithsonian, 1994), p. 108.

74 MVLA, Ms-4996, Samuel Vaughan's Diary, 1787, p. 56: 'In good years he [Washington] raises 10,000 bushels of wheat a like quantity of corn besides oats, barley, rye buckwheat peas potatoes &c. breeds horses cattle mules & has 700 sheep, plants no tobacco. Has an excellent great mill on a creek supplied by various springs collected in a run of two miles, flower & c. shiped on craft in the creek very near the River, has a fishery & a ferry. The General has 200 mouths to feed, & makes most part of the wollen cloathing & a considerable quantity of linnen made at home. The General seldom goes out but on public business, always making experiments the farms neat, kept perfectly clean & in precise orders, keeps an excellent table, & is indisputably the best, if not the only good farmer in the state.'

75 Lee, *Experiencing Mount Vernon*, pp. 26–7: Robert Hunter, 1785.

76 *'A Map of General Washington's farm of Mount Vernon from a transmitted drawing by the General 1793'* in *Letters from His Excellency general Washington, to Arthur Young …'*, London, 1801, The Library of Congress overlaid with Samuel Vaughan, *Sketch Plan of Mount Vernon*, August, 1787, Mount Vernon Ladies' Association.

77 See also Robert Clark, 'The Absent Landscape of America's Eighteenth Century' in *Views of American Landscapes*, ed. Mick Gidley and Robert Lawson (Cambridge: Cambridge University Press, 1989), pp. 81–99.

78 Marquis de Chastellux, *Travels in North America in the Years 1780, 1781, and 1782*, 2 vols (London: G. G. J. & J. Robinson, London, 1787), 2, p. 42.

79 Dumbarton Oaks Research Library, Humphry Repton, *Observations by H. Repton for the Improvement of Shrublands*, 1789: '1. General Remarks on the Situation: The House which stands upon the highest Ground in the Park, is not placed in the best Situation that might have been chosen, from the unfortunate Mistake so often made in not distinguishing between an extensive Prospect and a pleasing Landscape. The former can only be had from an Eminence, the latter must seldom be expected there because in proportion as we are lifted above the Tops of the Trees we lose the advantage of a foreground which is essential to a good Composition.'

80 Merrill D. Peterson, *Visitors to Monticello* (Charlottesville: University of Virginia Press, 1989), pp. 22–3: 1796, Duc de la Rochefoucauld-Liancourt. He continued 'but in the back part the prospect is soon interrupted by a mountain more elevated than that on which the house is seated.'

81 Ibid., Duc de la Rochefoucauld-Liancourt.

82 See Manca, *George Washington's Eye*, for a detailed analysis of the landscape around the house and for some of its wider landscape concerns. The various views are reproduced in Chapter 6.

83   For Jefferson's plantation practices see Robert C. Baron (ed.), *The Garden and Farm Books of Thomas Jefferson* (Golden, CO: Fulcrum, 1987) and Barbara J. Heath, *Hidden Lives: The Archaeology of Slave Life at Thomas Jefferson's Poplar Forest* (Charlottesville: University of Virginia Press, 1999).

84   Three views of roads make up the five estate portraits of Mulberry that Coram produced. These are reproduced in Angela D. Mack and Stephen G. Hoffus (eds), *Landscape of Slavery: The Plantation in American Art* (Columbia: University of South Carolina Press, 2008).

85   To George Washington from Edward Newenham, 31 August 1795, *Founders Online*, https://founders.archives.gov/documents/Washington/05-18-02-0407: 'This Letter will be personaly presented to your Excellency by Isaac Weld Esqr., Son of an old & truly respectable Friend of Mine, now in a high Department in the Irish Revenu; This young Gentleman, of an Amiable Character & Virtuous Character, is <going> a Tour of pleasure & Curiosity to Visit your Happy Country; his father & Grandfather were *warm friends* to the *Liberties* of America, & of the most Independent Spirit—they always supported my Election for the County of Dublin' (accessed 21 November 2022).

86   Weld, *Travels through the States of North America*, Preface, A2.

87   Kelly, *Sir Edward Newenham*, p. 271, Note 13: Newenham to Pelham, 27 October 1797 (NA Rebellion Papers, 620/33/35). Note 14 states: 'Other than the remnant of his 1782 trip to France now in the National Archives of Canada, none of these accounts are known to survive.'

88   Weld, *Travels through the States of North America*, p. 3.

89   To James Madison from Richard Peters, 1 June 1801, *Founders Online*, National Archives, https://founders.archives.gov/documents/Madison/02-01-02-0328: '… such Kind of Itineraries. There are many Truths; some unpleasant, & others encouraging. There are also many Errors & among them general Conclusions drawn from partial Premises—the Mistake of all Travellers … A silly Book written by one Weld & one more so by Liancourt have done us much Mischeif in Europe, in Point of Character. I knew both these Book Makers; & neither is qualified to do Justice to any Subject.'

90   ODNB, 'Isaac Weld' (accessed 4 July 2019).

91   Weld, *Travels through the States of North America*, p. 83.

92   Ibid., p. 141.

93   Ibid., pp. 84.

94   Ibid., Preface, pp. iv–v: 'If it shall appear to anyone, that he has spoken with too much asperity of American men and American manners, the Author begs that such language may not be ascribed to hasty prejudice, and a blind partiality for everything that is European. He crossed the Atlantic strongly prepossessed in favour of the people and the country, which he was about to visit; and if he returned with sentiments of a different tendency, they resulted solely from a cool and dispassionate observation of what chance presented to his view when abroad.'

95   Isaac Weld, *Illustrations of the Scenery of Killarney and the Surrounding Country by Isaac Weld Esq. M.R.I.A. Author of Travels in North America* (London: Longman, Hurst et al., 1812), p. 149.

96   Weld, *Travels through the States of North America*, p. 134.

97   Ibid., p. 168.

98   Ibid., p. 175.

99   Ibid., p. 53.

100   *Dublin University Magazine*, 49 (Jan.–Jun. 1857), p. 74, https://babel.hathitrust.org/cgi/pt?id=njp.32101064302399&view=1up&seq=82 (accessed 4 July 2019).

101   Hamilton, 'Benjamin Vaughan on Commerce and International Harmony in the Eighteenth Century', pp. 103–4.

102   John H. Sheppard, *Reminiscences of the Vaughan Family and More Particularly of Benjamin Vaughan, LLD* (Boston: David Clapp & Son, 1865), p. 34: 'This was compiled by Dr. Vaughan, and printed in Hallowell by Peter Edes, in 1800–8vo. pp. 227, including preface and appendix … The account of the Farmer, except the artificial name, Kliyogg, is the life of James Gouyer, a native of Wermetschweil, in the parish of Uster, Canton of Zurich. He was called the 'Rural Socrates', and died in 1785, … Nine years after his death, Dr. Vaughan visited Switzerland, and saw many who knew him', https://babel.hathitrust.org/cgi/pt?id=hvd.32044089923338;view=1up;seq=7 (accessed 19 October 2018).

103   Arthur Young, *Rural Oeconomy or Essays on the Practical Parts of Husbandry to which is added The Rural Socrates, being the Memoirs of a Country Philosopher* (London: Becket, 1770).

104   This chapter was inspired by my own first visit to Mount Vernon on Presidents' Day, 2013, when I attempted to project my own experience of eighteenth-century Irish, British, French, Italian and European landscapes onto that quintessential Virginian territory (and in that order).

105   Therese O'Malley, 'Landscape Gardening in the Early National Period' in *View and Visions: American Landscape before 1830*, ed. Edward J. Nygren (Washington DC: The Corcoran Gallery of Art, 1986), p. 133.

CHAPTER FOUR

1   Jean-Jacques Rousseau, *Les Confessions de Jean-Jacques Rousseau*, Book 15, in *Collection complète des oeuvres* (Geneva: 1780–9), 10, p. 229, édition en ligne www.rousseauonline.ch version du 7 octobre 2012, https://www.rousseauonline.ch/pdf/rousseauonline-0075.pdf (accessed 22 October 2019).

2   Ibid., Book 15, p. 234: 'La réflexion jointe à l'usage donne des idées nettes & alors on trouve des méthodes abrégées dont l'invention flatte l'amour-propre, dont la justesse satisfait l'esprit & qui font faire avec plaisir un travail ingrat par lui-même.'

3   OED: 'cadastre' (accessed 12 August 2019), see also 'cadastral survey n. (a) (strictly) a survey of lands for the purposes of a cadastre; (b) (loosely) a survey on a scale sufficiently large to show accurately the extent and measurement of every field and other plot of land.'

4   Rousseau, *Les Confessions*, Book 15, pp. 234–5: 'Le lavis des mappes de nos géometres m'avoit aussi rendu le goût du dessin. J'achetai des couleurs & je me mis à faire des fleurs & des paysages. C'est dommage que je me sois trouvé peu de talent pour cet art; l'inclination y étoit toute entière.'

5   Ibid., Book 15, pp. 229–30. This chapter has been informed by the first volume of Maurice Jean-Jacques Cranston's three-volume biography

The Early Life and Work of Jean-Jacques Rousseau 1712–1754 (Chicago: University of Chicago Press, 1982).

6   Ibid., Book 15, p. 237.

7   Ibid., Book 15, p. 296: 'Le jardin du faubourg n'étoit pas proprement à la campagne, entouré de maisons & d'autres jardins, il n'avoit point les attraits d'une retraite champêtre.'

8   Ibid., Book 15, p. 297: 'Cherchons quelque réduit assez loin de la ville pour vivre en paix & assez près pour y revenir toutes les fois qu'il sera nécessaire.'

9   Ibid., Book 15, p. 297: 'mais retirée & solitaire comme si l'on étoit à cent lieues'.

10   Ibid., Book 15, p. 297: 'Entre deux coteaux assez élevés est un petit vallon nord & sud au fond duquel coule une rigole entre des cailloux & des arbres. Le long de ce vallon à mi-côte sont quelques maisons éparses fort agréables pour quiconque aime un asyle un peu sauvage & retiré.'

11   Ibid., Book 15, p. 297: 'Après avoir essayé deux ou trois fois de ces maisons, nous choisîmes enfin la plus jolie, appartenant à un gentilhomme qui étoit au service, appellé M. *Noiret*. La maison étoit très-logeable …'

12   Ibid., Book 15, p. 298: 'Ce séjour est celui du bonheur & de l'innocence. Si nous ne les trouvons pas ici l'un avec l'autre, il ne les faut chercher nulle part.'

13   Ibid., Book 15, p. 315.

14   Ibid., Book 15, p. 315: 'Je revenois en me promenant, par un assez grand tour, occupé à considérer avec intérêt & volupté les objets champêtres dont j'étois environné, les seuls dont l'oeil & le coeur ne se lassent jamais.'

15   Ibid., Book 16, p. 299: 'Ici commence le court bonheur de ma vie; ici viennent les paisibles, mais rapides momens qui m'ont donné le droit de dire que j'ai vecu.'

16   Ibid., Book 16, p. 231: 'Tel étoit mon train de vie aux Charmettes quand je n'étois occupé d'aucuns soins champêtres; car ils avoient toujours la préférence & dans ce qui n'excédoit pas mes forces, je travaillois comme un paysan. mais il est vrai que mon extrême foiblesse ne me laissoit gueres alors sur cet article que le mérite de la bonne volonté. D'ailleurs, je voulois faire à la fois deux ouvrages & par cette raison je n'en faisois bien aucun.'

17   Ibid., Book 16, p. 326: 'Des dîners faits sur l' Montagnole, des soupés sous le berceau, la récolte des fruits, les vendanges, les veillées à teiller avec nos gens, tout cela faisoit pour nous autant de fêtes auxquelles Maman prenoit le même plaisir que moi. Des promenades plus solitaires avoient un charme plus grand encore, parce que le coeur s'épanchoit plus en liberté.'

18   Ibid., Book 17, p. 10: 'Je me suis laissé, dans ma premiere partie, partant à regret pour Paris, déposant mon coeur aux Charmettes, y fondant mon dernier château en Espagne, projetant d'y rapporter un jour aux pieds de maman, rendue à elle-même, les trésors que j'aurois acquis & comptant sur mon système de musique comme sur une fortune assurée.'

19   William Gilpin, *Essays on Picturesque Beauty* (London: R. Blamire, 1794), p. 43: 'The spiry pinnacles of the mountain, and the castle-like arrangement of the rock, give no peculiar pleasure to the picturesque eye … The Giant's causeway in Ireland may strike it as a novelty; but the lake of Killarney attracts its attention. It would range with supreme delight among the sweet vales of Switzerland; but would view only with a transient glance, the Glaciers of Savoy.' See also Marjorie Hope Nicolson, *Mountain Gloom and Mountain Glory: The Development of the Aesthetics of the Infinite* (Seattle and London: University of Washington Press, 1997).

20   For an earlier exposition see Finola O'Kane, 'Route Reversal: The Design Consequences of Travelling in Contrary Motion in Eighteenth-Century Europe', *Studies in the History of Gardens and Designed Landscapes: An International Quarterly*, 35:4 (2015), pp. 156–65.

21   Arthur Young, *Travels in France during the Years 1787, 1788, 1789* (London: George Bell and Sons, 1906), p. 87.

22   In particular René Girardin's, *An Essay on Landscape and a Tour to Ermenonville* (London: J. Dodsley, 1982).

23   BL, Add. Ms. 35126, Arthur Young Correspondence, vol. 1, no. 304.

24   Young, *Travels in France*, p. 279.

25   Ibid., p. 84.

26   Ibid., p. 280.

27   Ibid., p. 134: It was also a prescient work: 'The American revolution has laid the foundation of another in France, if the government does not take care of itself.'

28   Arthur Young, *A Tour in Ireland; with general observations on the present state of that kingdom: made in the years 1776, 1777, and 1778. And brought down to the end of 1779*, quarto edn (London: printed for T. Cadell, Strand; and J. Dodsley, 1780).

29   Young, *Travels in France*, p. 26.

30   Ibid., p. 28.

31   Ibid., p. 109.

32   For the Duc de la Rochefoucauld's own landscape see Gabriel Wick, *Paysage des Lumières: le jardin anglais du château de La Roche-Guyon* (Paris: Artlys, 2014).

33   Young, *Travels in France*, p. 74.

34   Ibid., p. 21.

35   Ibid., p. 22.

36   Ibid., p. 34.

37   Ibid., pp. 34–5.

38   For the contemporary efforts to restructure France see Alan Forrest and Peter Jones (eds), *Reshaping France: Town, Country and Region during the French Revolution* (Manchester: Manchester University Press, 1991).

39   Young, *Travels in France*, p. 84.

40   Ibid., pp. 65–6: 'As it was formerly in most parts of Europe; it seems to have resulted from a feudal arrangement, that the Grand Seigneur might keep his slaves the nearer to his call.' Young's definition of slavery became more precise over time.

41   Ibid., p. 56.

42   Ibid., p. 90.

43   Ibid., p. 58.

44   Ibid., p. 61.

45   Ibid., p. 54.

46   Georges Weulersse, *Le mouvement physiocratique en France (de 1756 à 1770)*, 2 vols (Paris: Félix Alcan, 1910), 2, pp. 151–2.

47   See Susan Taylor-Leduc, 'Luxury in the Garden: La Nouvelle Héloise Considered', *Studies in the History of Gardens and Designed Landscapes:*

An International Quarterly, 19:1 (1999), p. 75.

48 BL, Add. Ms. 35127, Arthur Young Correspondence, vol. 1, no. 304, Arthur Young to anon.

49 See Dora Wiebenson, *The Picturesque Garden in France* (Princeton: Princeton University Press, 1978) and John Dixon Hunt, *The Picturesque Garden in Europe* (London: Thames and Hudson, 2004).

50 BL, Add. Ms. 35127, Arthur Young Correspondence, vol. 1, no. 304: Arthur Young to anon.

51 The contradictory principles of Marie Antoinette's Hameau have been explored by Jill H. Casid, *Sowing Empire: Landscape and Colonization* (Minneapolis and London: University of Minnesota Press, 2005), pp. 158–9.

52 BL, Add. Ms. 35127, Arthur Young Correspondence, vol. 2, 1790–7, Paris, 10 January 1790: Arthur Young to Mary Young: 'Here is going on the most wonderful revolution the world ever saw: I was in the Tuileries today & met the Queen in one party, the King in another, & the Dauphin in a third. they are all close & strict prisoners … All hats however are off in their presence – the general opinion is that things will be arranged, & as soon as they have finished with the constitution that the [royal] family will be at large.'

53 Jean-Jacques Rousseau, *The Social Contract* (Ware: Wordsworth, 1998), p. 93.

54 Mona Ozouf, *Festivals and the French Revolution* (Cambridge: Harvard University Press, 1988), p. 5.

55 Lynn Hunt, *Politics, Culture, and Class in the French Revolution* (Oakland: University of California Press, 2004), p. 13.

56 Ibid., p. 14.

57 Ibid., p. 3.

58 James A. Leith, *Space and Revolution: Projects for Monuments, Squares and Public Buildings in France 1789–1799* (Montreal: McGill University Press, 1991), p. 222: Note 47 citing Jean Silvestre de Sacy, *Alexandre-Théodore Brongniart. Sa Vie. Son Oeuvre* (Paris: Librarie Plon, 1940), p. 97.

59 Ozouf, *Festivals and the French Revolution*, pp. 134–5: 'Mathieu's "What is a mountain, if not an eternal protest against Equality?"'.

60 The scale and conviction of this history was uncovered by James A. Leith in his *Space and Revolution: Projects for Monuments, Squares and Public Buildings in France 1789–1799* (Montreal: McGill University Press, 1991).

61 Jean-Jacques Rousseau, *Émile* (London: Everyman, 1995).

62 Mary Delany, *Letters from Georgian Ireland: The Correspondence of Mary Delany, 1731–68*, Angélique Day (ed.) (Belfast: Friar's Bush, 1991), p. 286.

63 Le Château du Bignon, Arthur O'Connor's Mss., folio 2, p. 2.

64 NLI, Ms. 35,011, Lord Edward Fitzgerald's letter-book: 21 April 1780, Lord Edward Fitzgerald to his mother Emily, Duchess of Leinster. This letter-book was acquired by the NLI in 1999. Its original letters contain passages that were excised by Thomas Moore when he published many extracts from the letters in *The Life and Death of Lord Edward Fitzgerald*, 2 vols (London: Longman, Rees, Orme, Brown, Green, 1732). The letter-book has been used in preference to Thomas Moore's book, which nevertheless still contains passages from letters that are now lost.

65 NLI, Ms. 35,011, Lord Edward Fitzgerald's letter-book: 17 June 1780,

66 Ibid., St Lucia, 4 February 1783, Lord Edward Fitzgerald to his mother Emily, Duchess of Leinster.

67 Ibid., St Lucia, 3 March 1783, Lord Edward Fitzgerald to Emily, Duchess of Leinster.

68 Ibid., Castletown [Co. Kildare], 9 October, Lord Edward to Emily, Duchess of Leinster.

69 Ibid., Jersey, St Helier, 31 July 1786, Lord Edward Fitzgerald to Emily, Duchess of Leinster.

70 Moore, *The Life and Death of Lord Edward Fitzgerald*, 1, p. 39.

71 NLI, Ms. 35,011, Lord Edward Fitzgerald's letter-book: 7 August 1787, Granada, Lord Edward Fitzgerald to Emily, Duchess of Leinster.

72 Ibid., Cadiz, 2 July, 1787, Lord Edward Fitzgerald to Emily. He had 'not quite determined which Women' were 'best', but the Spanish men were 'much superior to the Portug[u]ese'.

73 Ibid., Granada, 7 August 1787, Lord Edward Fitzgerald to Emily.

74 Ibid.

75 Ibid., Gibraltar, May 1787, Lord Edward Fitzgerald to Emily.

76 Ibid.

77 Ibid., Granada, 7 August 1787, Lord Edward Fitzgerald to Emily.

78 Ibid., Cadiz, 2 July 1787, Lord Edward Fitzgerald to Emily.

79 Ibid., St John's, New Brunswick, 18 July 1788, Lord Edward Fitzgerald to Emily. See also Daniel Gahan, '"Journey after My Own Heart": Lord Edward Fitzgerald in America, 1788–90', *New Hibernia Review/Iris Éireannach Nua*, 8:2 (Summer 2004), pp. 85–105.

80 NLI, Ms. 35,011, Lord Edward Fitzgerald's letter-book: Halifax, 24 June 1788, Lord Edward Fitzgerald to Emily, Duchess of Leinster.

81 Ibid., St John's, New Brunswick, 18 July 1788, Edward Fitzgerald to Emily. See also Harry Liebersohn, *Aristocratic Encounters: European Travelers and North American Indians* (Cambridge: Cambridge University Press, 1998).

82 NLI, Ms. 35,011, Lord Edward Fitzgerald's letter-book: St John's, New Brunswick, 18 July 1788, Edward Fitzgerald to Emily.

83 NLI, Ms. 35,008: Quebec, 22 May 1789, Hamilton Moore to the Duke of Leinster.

84 Ibid., They had 'steered by Compass and so well as to enter the River St Lawrence, within a league of Quebec, in a direct line from Frederickstown'.

85 NLI, Ms. 35,011, Lord Edward Fitzgerald's letter-book: Fort Erie, 1 June 1789, Lord Edward Fitzgerald to Emily, Duchess of Leinster.

86 Moore, *The Life and Death of Lord Edward Fitzgerald*, 1, p. 145.

87 Ibid., p. 147: Detroit, 20 June 1789, Lord Edward to Emily.

88 Moore, *The Life and Death of Lord Edward Fitzgerald*, 1, p. 148.

89 NLI, Ms. 35,008: Hamilton Moore to Duke of L, Quebec, 22 May 1789. The folder also contains a letter of Lord Cornwallis dated 11 August 1798 with the covering note of: 'Lord E. as the great author and contriver of all the mischief and Treason which has already cost so many lives.'

90 Moore, *The Life and Death of Lord Edward Fitzgerald*, 1, p. 157.

91 Ibid., 1, p. 172.

92 Mathieu Ferradou, '"Adresse des Anglais, des Ecossais et des Irlandais résidans et domiciliés à Paris" to the Convention, presented on 25 November 1792, Archives Nationales, Pierrefitte-sur-Seine', *Annales*

historiques de la révolution Francaise, 382, Oct.–Dec. 2015, pp. 123–43, https://journals.openedition.org/ahrf/13560 (accessed 3 September 2019).

93   Moore, *The Life and Death of Lord Edward Fitzgerald*, 1, p. 173.

94   Jane Hayter Hames, *Arthur O'Connor: United Irishman* (Cork: Collins Press, 2001), p. 13.

95   Le Château du Bignon, Arthur O'Connor's Mss., folio 3: Autobiography, p. 77.

96   Ibid., folio 3, Autobiography, pp. 86–7: O'Connor cites 'the Rev. doctor Playfair[?] quoted by Mr. McCulloch in his statistics of the British Empire'.

97   Ibid., folio 3, Autobiography, p. 98.

98   Ibid., folio 3, Autobiography, p. 99.

99   Ibid., folio 3, Autobiography, p. 102.

100   Ibid., folio 3, Autobiography, pp. 105–6.

101   Ibid., folio 3, Autobiography, p. 110.

102   Ibid., folio 3, Autobiography, p. 112.

103   Ibid., folio 3, Autobiography, p. 113.

104   Ibid., folio 3, Autobiography, pp. 113–14

105   The OED defines the word as 'A shared table for diners at a hotel, restaurant, tavern, etc., at which a set menu is served at a stated time', dating its usage in English from 1617 (accessed 4 September 2019).

106   Le Château du Bignon, Arthur O'Connor's Mss., folio 3, Autobiography, p. 115: He also explained that 'this was done away in 1803 when le Pays de Vaux became an independent Canton'.

107   Ibid., folio 3, Autobiography, p. 143: Burke replied, 'You put me a question which is most disagreeable for me to answer but I can refuse you nothing. You know that since my disagreement with Charles Fox [Edward FitzGerald's first cousin] I never rise to speak in the House that Sheridan does not fling a dagger in my side but truth obliges me to say that Challam, Fox, Townsend, Barré, Pitt they do me the honor to class me as the best, we are all but children to Sheridan.'

108   Ibid., folio 3, Autobiography, p. 115.

109   Ibid., folio 3, Autobiography, p. 152. The estate 'had been mortgaged to my Grand Father for more than it was worth but by the indolence of my father he suffered it to be entangled with conditions which rendered the recovery of the mortgage a most difficult affair, my brothers and I had shares in it, and to render the payment practicable I purchased all the shares and in a short time I became sole possessor of the whole estate'.

110   Ibid., folio 3, Autobiography, p. 152.

111   *Hibernian Magazine*, 1783.

112   For Frescati's pedagogical landscape see Finola O'Kane, *Landscape Design in Eighteenth-Century Ireland: Mixing Foreign Trees with the Natives* (Cork: Cork University Press, 2004), Chapter 4.

113   NLI, Ms. 35,004, f. 2, 1 March 1993, Duchess of Leinster and William Ogilvie to Lady Sophia Fitzgerald.

114   NLI, Ms. 35,011, Lord Edward Fitzgerald's letter-book, 27 April 1794, Lord Edward Fitzgerald to his mother Emily.

115   Ibid., Kildare, 19 July 1794.

116   Ibid., 23 June 1794, Lord Edward Fitzgerald to his mother Emily.

117   Lena Boylan, 'Kildare Lodge. Lord Edward Fitzgerald's House', *Journal of the County Kildare Archaeological Society*, 16:1 (1977–8), pp. 26–35.

118   NLI, Ms. 35,011, Lord Edward Fitzgerald's letter-book, 23 June 1794, Lord Edward Fitzgerald to his mother.

119   Ibid., Kildare, 11 July 1794, Lord Edward Fitzgerald to Sophy.

120   Ibid., Kildare, 19 July 1794, Lord Edward Fitzgerald to his mother Emily.

121   Ibid., March 2st[sic] 1794, Lord Edward Fitzgerald to his mother.

122   See O'Kane, *Landscape Design in Eighteenth-Century Ireland*, p. 160.

123   NLI, Leinster Mss., Ms. 35,005, Letters to Lady Lucy Fitzgerald (1771–1851), f. 13, 14 February 1797, Arthur O'Connor to Lady Lucy Fitzgerald.

124   Ibid., f. 3: undated, Haley St, Tuesday, an unidentified sister to Lady Lucy.

125   Ibid., f. 3, undated, unidentified sister to Lady Lucy Fitzgerald.

126   See Paul Weber, *On the Road to Rebellion: The United Irishmen and Hamburg 1796–1803* (Dublin: Four Courts Press, 1997), Chapter 1. For a general history of the United Irishmen's French connections see Marianne Elliott, *Partners in Revolution: The United Irishmen and France* (New Haven and London: Yale University Press, 1990).

127   Hames, *Arthur O'Connor: United Irishman*, p. 113.

128   NLI, Ms. 35,011, Lord Edward Fitzgerald's letter-book, 29 July 1796, Lord Edward Fitzgerald to his mother Emily.

129   Ibid.

130   Gerard Campbell, *Edward and Pamela Fitzgerald, Being Some Account of their Lives. Compiled from the Letters of those who knew them* (London: E. Arnold, 1904), p. 108: Edward to Emily, 29 July 1796.

131   Le Château du Bignon, Arthur O'Connor's Mss., folios 1–5, Autobiography: The autobiography must be considered skeptically as a document that remembers events in hindsight and is probably affected by memory loss, nostalgia and self-congratulation.

132   Le Château du Bignon, Arthur O'Connor's Mss., folio 5, p. 210.

133   Ibid., folio 5, p. 211.

134   Ibid., folio 5, p. 246.

135   Ibid., folio 5, p. 212.

136   Ibid.

137   Ibid., folio 5, p. 246.

138   Campbell, *Edward and Pamela Fitzgerald*, p. 108: Edward to Emily, 29 July 1796.

139   Le Château du Bignon, Arthur O'Connor's Mss., folio 5, p. 247.

140   Ibid., folio 5, p. 252.

141   Ibid., folio 5, p. 257.

142   Arthur O'Connor, *The State of Ireland* (Dublin: Lilliput, 1988), p. 62.

143   Ibid., p. 32.

144   See in particular Arthur Young's letters in BL, Add. Ms. 35127, Arthur Young Correspondence, vol. 2.

145   Moore, *The Life and Death of Lord Edward Fitzgerald*, 2, p. 41.

CHAPTER FIVE

1   *Butler Plantation Papers: The Papers of Pierce Butler (1744–1822) and Successors from the Historical Society of Pennsylvania*, Adam Matthew Publications, 1997, Microfilm Reel 3, 'Plantation Managers' Correspondence: Roswell King, 1803–14', 3 January 1813, Roswell King, Butler's Island to Pierce Butler.

2   George Washington to Arthur Young, 12 December 1793, *Founders Online*, https://founders.archives.gov/documents/ Washington/05-14-02-0337 (accessed 24 November 2022).

3   See David A. Wilson, *United Irishmen, United States: Immigrant Radicals in the Early Republic* (Ithaca and London: Cornell University Press, 1998).

4   For Philadelphia's radical gardening culture see Michael Durey, 'Thomas Paine's Apostles: Radical Emigrés and the Triumph of Jeffersonian Republicanism', *William and Mary Quarterly*, 3rd series, 44:4 (Oct. 1987), pp. 661–88; Joseph Ewan, 'Bernard M'Mahon (c.1775–1816), Pioneer Philadelphia Nurseryman, and his American Gardener's Calendar', *Journal of the Society for the Bibliography of Natural History*, 3, pt 7 (Oct. 1960); Andrea Wulf, *Founding Gardeners: The Revolutionary Generation, Nature, and the Shaping of the American Nation* (New York: Vintage, 2011); Allen Lacy, 'Bernard M'Mahon's Declaration of Independence' in *Farther Afield: A Gardener's Excursions* (New York: Farar, Straus and Giroux, 1986); Sarah Pattee Stetson, 'American Garden Books, Transplanted and Native, Before 1807', *William and Mary Quarterly*, 3rd series, 3:3 (Jul. 1946), pp. 343–69.

5   Thomas Bartlett (ed.), *Life of Theobald Wolfe Tone, Compiled and Arranged by William Theobald Wolfe Tone* (Dublin: Lilliput, 1998), p. 365: from 'Petition of the Catholics of Ireland, January 2, 1793'.

6   Bernard M'Mahon, *The American Gardener's Calendar; adapted to the climates and seasons of the United States containing a complete account of all the work necessary to be done in the kitchen garden, fruit garden, orchard, vineyard, pleasure-ground, flower-garden, green-house, hot-house and forcing frames … also General as well as minute instructions, for laying out, or erecting, each and every of the above departments, according to modern taste and the most approved plans; the ornamental planting of pleasure grounds, in the ancient and modern stile* (Philadelphia: Graves, 1806).

7   Bernard McMahon to Thomas Jefferson, 2 April 1807, *Founders Online*, https://founders.archives.gov/documents/Jefferson/03-02-02-0063 (accessed 24 November 2022): 'I do myself the pleasure of sending you per Mr. Duane who intends leaving this City for Washington tomorrow, 90 plants of the white Antwerp Raspberry, cut to the proper lengths for planting; and 8 plants of the true red Alpine Strawberry, being all I could procure of these kinds at present.'

8   Theobald Wolfe Tone, *Life of Theobald Wolfe Tone … written by himself, and continued by his son; with his political writings, fragments of his diary, his mission to France: with a complete diary of his negotiations to procure the aid of the French and Batavian Republic, for the liberation of Ireland; of the expeditions of Bantry bay, the Texel, and of that wherein he fell. Narrative of his trial, defence before the court martial, and death. Ed. by his son, William Theobald Wolfe Tone; with a brief account of his own education and campaigns under the Emperor Napoleon* (Washington: Gales & Seaton, 1826), p. 128.

9   Ibid.

10   Ibid.

11   T. W. Moody, R. B. McDowell and C. J. Woods (eds), *The Writings of Wolfe Tone 1763–98*, 3 vols (Oxford: Oxford University Press, 2001), 2, p. 1: Theobald Wolfe Tone, Philadelphia, to Thomas Russell, Belfast, 7 August 1795.

12   Bartlett, *Life of Theobald Wolfe Tone*, p. 745.

13   William H. Drummond (ed.), *The Autobiography of Archibald Hamilton Rowan* (Shannon: Irish Academic Press, 1972), p. 296.

14   Moody, McDowell and Woods, *The Writings of Wolfe Tone 1763–98*, 2, p. 12: 'Theobald Wolfe Tone, Philadelphia, to Thomas Russell, Belfast, 1 Sept. 1795'.

15   Ibid., 2, p. 338: Autobiography (1792, 1795–6), *c*.28 September 1796. Marianne Elliott notes in *Wolfe Tone* (Liverpool: Liverpool University Press, 2012, p. 440), Note 12: 'Rowan's *Autobiography*, 273–314, contains a very full account of his residence in America. Tone's description resembles so closely much of what Rowan says that Tone may have been influenced by Rowan's opinions.'

16   Moody, McDowell and Woods, *The Writings of Wolfe Tone 1763–98*, 2, p. 338: Autobiography (1792, 1795–6), *c*.28 September 1796.

17   Ibid., 2, p. 30: 'Theobald Wolfe Tone, Philadelphia, to Thomas Russell, Belfast, Sept. 1st, 1795'.

18   Drummond, *The Autobiography of Archibald Hamilton Rowan*, p. 291: Note: 'Major Butler made him a generous offer of 2,000 acres of unsettled land, on such terms as few, if any, who wished for a permanent residence in America, would not accept with avidity.'

19   Ibid., pp. 299–300.

20   Ibid., p. 298.

21   Terry W. Lipscomb (ed.), *The Letters of Pierce Butler 1790–1794: Nation Building and Enterprise in the New American Republic* (Columbia: University of South Carolina Press, 2007), pp. 203–4: Pierce Butler to John Rea, 2 November 1792.

22   Ibid., p. 44: Pierce Butler to Roger Saunders, 24 May 1790.

23   Ibid., pp. 145–6: 'Pierce Butler to John Rea (in Letterkenny Co. Donegal), 18 November 1791.

24   Paddy Butler, Lord Dunboyne (ed.), *When the States were Young: A Remarkable Collection of Letters 1784–1799 Preserved in the British Library as Additional Manuscript 16603* (www.lulu.com, 2006), pp. 80–2: Pierce Butler to Weeden Butler, 18 July 1788.

25   Ibid., p. 125: Pierce Butler to Weeden Butler, 22 May 1790.

26   Ibid., p. 156: Pierce Butler to Weeden Butler, 19 November 1791.

27   Moody, McDowell and Woods, *The Writings of Wolfe Tone 1763–98*, 2, p. 30: 'Theobald Wolfe Tone, Philadelphia, to Thomas Russell, Belfast, Sept. 1st, 1795'.

28   Ibid., 2, p. 30: 'Theobald Wolfe Tone, Philadelphia, to Thomas Russell, Belfast, 25 October, 1795'.

29   Ibid.

30   See Malcolm Bell, *Major Butler's Legacy: Five Generations of a Slaveholding Family* (Athens: University of Georgia Press, 1987) and Theresa A. Singleton, 'The Archaeology of Afro-American Slavery in Coastal Georgia: A Regional Perception of Slave Household and Community Patterns', PhD thesis (University of Florida, 1980). See also Nini Rodgers, *Ireland, Slavery and Anti-Slavery: 1612–1865* (London: Palgrave Macmillan, 2007), pp. 215–19.

31   Dunboyne, *When the States were Young*, p. 19.

32   The house was burnt down in 1917.

33   Lipscomb, *The Letters of Pierce Butler 1790–1794*, p. 37: Note 3.

34   See Toby Barnard, *Improving Ireland? Projectors, Prophets and Profiteers 1641–1786* (Dublin: Four Courts Press, 2008), p. 16.

35   For the Carroll family's history see: Charles Carroll, *Dear Papa, dear*

Charley: the peregrinations of a revolutionary aristocrat, as told by Charles Carroll of Carrollton and his father, Charles Carroll of Annapolis, with sundry observations on bastardy, child-rearing, romance, matrimony, commerce, tobacco (Williamsburg: Omohundro Institute, 2001); Ronald Hoffman, *Princes of Ireland, Planters of Maryland: A Carroll Saga, 1500–1782* (Chapel Hill and London: University of North Carolina Press, 2002); Rodgers, *Ireland, Slavery and Anti-Slavery*, pp. 198–207; and Ann C. Van Devanter, *'Anywhere So Long As There Be Freedom', Charles Carroll of Carrollton, His Family & His Maryland* (Baltimore: The Baltimore Museum of Art, 1975).

36 James Carroll, 'James Carroll Daybook (1714–21)', Special Collections Division, Georgetown University Library, Washington, DC, folders 160–1, Oversize Box 1: Item 160, p. 108.

37 Charles M. Flanagan, 'The Sweets of Independence: A Reading of the "James Carroll Daybook, 1714–21"', PhD thesis (University of Maryland, 2005).

38 Lipscomb, *The Letters of Pierce Butler 1790–1794*, p. 118: Pierce Butler to William Cope, 7 September 1791.

39 Ibid., p. 60: Pierce Butler to Roger Saunders, 26 August 1790.

40 Ibid., p. 65: Pierce Butler to Roger Saunders, 6 September 1790.

41 The map (Figure 136) is a copy 'from a survey taken the 19th April 1759 by Nathaniel Bradwell' and of a 'plan of a tract of land or Plantation containing 1002 acres on Ashley River, on the east side'. The map may depict land 'belonging to Major Butler's Estate' which is annotated twice on the drawing but one of these is crossed out.

42 See also Burnette Vanstory, *Georgia's Land of the Golden Isles* (Athens: University of Georgia Press, 1981).

43 Bell, *Major Butler's Legacy*, p. 107.

44 For the low country landscape history of the Carolinas and Georgia see: William B. Lees, 'The Historical Development of Limerick Plantation, a Tidewater Rice Plantation in Berkeley County, South Carolina, 1683–1945', *South Carolina Historical Magazine*, 82:1 (Jan. 1981), pp. 44–62; S. Max Edelson, *Plantation Enterprise in Colonial South Carolina* (Cambridge: Harvard University Press, 2011); S. B. Hilliard, 'Antebellum Tidewater Rice Culture in South Carolina and Georgia' in *European Settlement and Development in North America: Essays on Geographical Change in Honour and Memory of Andrew Hill Clark*, ed. J. R. Gibson (Toronto: University of Toronto Press, 1978); David Doar, 'Rice and Rice Planting in the South Carolina Low Country' in *Contributions from the Charleston Museum*, vol. 8, ed. E. Milby Burton (Charleston: Charleston Museum, 1936).

45 Note in pencil on hand-drawn map of Little St Simons Island (Figure 141), partially in watercolours, from a survey done by Hopkins and Parker in 1790 (oversize), 1797; St Simon's Island: '600 Ac[re]s Oak land; 300 d[itt]o pine; 400 [acres] Myrtle & ponds; 750 Ac[re]s best marsh for Cotton; 2000 Ac[re]s feeding marsh; 2150 D[itt]o Soft marsh= 6200 Acres total amount; 19 April 1805'.

46 Dunboyne, *When the States were Young*, pp. 49–50: Pierce Butler to Weedon Butler, 30 August 1785.

47 *Butler Plantation Papers*, Reel 1: PB letterbook 1790–1794, 2 December 1793, Pierce Butler to Joseph Nutt. See also Bell, *Major Butler's Legacy*, p. 122, Note 17.

48 Lipscomb, *The Letters of Pierce Butler 1790–1794*, p. 62: Pierce Butler to Roger Saunders, 2 September 1790.

49 Ibid., pp. 142–3: Pierce Butler to James la Motte, 30 October 1791.

50 Ibid., p. 172: Pierce Butler to James Seagrove, 7 August 1792.

51 Ibid., p.173: Pierce Butler to Roger Parker Saunders, 9 August 1792.

52 Ibid., p. 183: Pierce Butler to Roger Saunders, 8 September 1792.

53 Ibid., pp. 261–2: Pierce Butler to Jeremiah Wadsworth, 10 October 1793.

54 Ibid., p. 252: Pierce Butler to Nathaniel Hall (a cotton planter on Great Exuma Island in the Bahamas). 16 September 1793. Whitney's gin machine was 'much superior' to the machines Butler had bought in Philadelphia and he had 36 of them at work by 1793 when he planned to expand the cotton fields to 1,200 acres.

55 Ibid., p. 280: Pierce Butler to Messrs Simpson & Davisson (London merchants), 26 November 1793.

56 Ibid., p. 264: Pierce Butler to Thomas Young, 28 October 1793.

57 *Butler Plantation Papers*, Reel 3, Plantation Managers' Correspondence, Box 2: Roswell King to Pierce Butler, 19 August 1803.

58 Lipscomb, *The Letters of Pierce Butler 1790–1794*, p. 308. Butler had already mortgaged 'his 1,700 acre Hampton Point plantation on the Altamaha River, and the 1,500 acre Butlers Island' to James Ladson, planter and future lieutenant governor of South Carolina in 1792.

59 Ibid., p. 280: Pierce Butler to Messrs Simpson & Davisson (London merchants), 26 November 1793.

60 *Butler Plantation Papers*, Reel 3, Box 2, folders 10–26: Roswell King to Pierce Butler, 'Hampton 8th July, 1803'.

61 Lipscomb, *The Letters of Pierce Butler 1790–1794*, p. 315: Pierce Butler to Joseph Eve (cotton gin designer), 25 March 1794.

62 Ibid., p. 316: Pierce Butler to Thomas Young, 25 March 1794.

63 Ibid., p. 306: Pierce Butler to Archibald Brown (South Carolina merchant and Cooper River planter), 14 February 1794.

64 See for example: *Butler Plantation Papers*, Reel 3: Roswell King to Pierce Butler, 16 August 1806: 'Bram has been in the hospital these four days past with a violent vomiting but in some better Old Sacky and Tann? are also in the hospitals. Ned I have given over he cannot live long he has a violent cough & is in a deep confusion and as the Balsium? of L? does his no good I cannot know what will. Nelly has not spirit enough to live I do not know what to do for her, she is little as no better than she was 2 month ago she has no cough, no fever, nor no complaint I can see, the complaints of weakness she has made out this some time past in the Cart; every morning or two, she now says she is not able. I believe Obey? has got hold of her, I think she wants Sarah; both that has been 7 years in bed that C? Sarah I look at with a great deal of impatience; to think she can eat her allowance regular, say more than 90lb of corn since she walked one step. Nelly has been in the hospital for better than 18 month. I with Dr Mease knew her lingering state; I thought he might prescribe some thing for her; It is a great loss to lo[se] so valluable a woman as she has been or may still be.'

65 Ibid., Reel 3: Roswell King, Hampton Plantation, Georgia, to Pierce Butler, 2 June 1804: 'As for Experiment Ditchers for the present I must let Morris have his way – all them … next to Hampton River most the Creeks are in great danger of breaking … As to strengthening the Canal it must be done but as for the machines wanting an unreasonable quantity of water to work for its magnitude I do not think so.'

66   Ibid., Reel 11: 'Statement of Planting for the year 1803'.

67   Ibid., Reel 3, Roswell King, Butler's Island to Pierce Butler, 24 January 1813: 'On the subject of the Rice Island Crop you calculate one fourth Cotton, if it is only on acct of care to the Negroes, it is of no moment for I had rather plant an acre of Rice than Cotton; the method we plant Rice it is about as healthy as Cotton.'

68   Ibid., Reel 3, Roswell King, Hampton to Pierce Butler, 11 July 1813: 'But as long as we have new land to clear, we have no time (or it is not profittable) to level land.'

69   Ibid., Reel 3, Roswell King, Tide Island to Pierce Butler, 11 February 1804.

70   Ibid., Reel 3, Roswell King, Butler's Island to Pierce Butler, 18 October 1806.

71   For an analysis of Lixnaw, Co. Kerry, an Irish designed landscape that used plant rotation to improve the soil, see Finola O'Kane, *Ireland and the Picturesque: Design, Landscape Painting and Tourism in Ireland 1700–1840* (New Haven and London: Yale University Press, 2013), Chapter 2.

72   For a description of the Marquis of Sligo's elaborate attempts to make and use manure on the mountains of Co. Mayo see Arthur Young, *A Tour in Ireland, 1776–1779*, 2 vols (Shannon: Irish University Press, 1970), 1, pp. 250–7.

73   *Butler Plantation Papers*, Reel 3, Roswell King, Tide Island to Pierce Butler, 3 March 1804.

74   Ibid., Reel 3, Roswell King, Hampton to Pierce Butler, 17 September 1803.

75   Ibid., Reel 3, Roswell King, Tide Island to Pierce Butler, 3 March 1804.

76   Ibid., Reel 3, Roswell King, Hampton, to Pierce Butler, 27 August 1808.

77   Ibid., Reel 3, Roswell King, Tide Island to Pierce Butler, 30 March 1804: 'I have had the Ditchers 3 days helping plant Rice, the weak hands will go to planting Cotton – all the rest, Ditchers & Carpenters must put the new Ground in order for planting as soon as possible.'

78   Lipscomb, *The Letters of Pierce Butler 1790–1794*, p. 316: Pierce Butler to Thomas Young, 25 March 1794: 'On my Tide Island I mean twenty workers to remain constantly ditching.'

79   *Butler Plantation Papers*, Reel 3, Roswell King, Hampton to Pierce Butler, 1 February 1813.

80   Ibid., Reel 3, Roswell King, Hampton to Pierce Butler, 13 May 1803.

81   Ibid., Reel 3, Roswell King, Hampton to Pierce Butler, 21 February 1813.

82   Ibid., Reel 3, Roswell King to Pierce Butler, 19 August 1803.

83   Ibid., Reel 3, Roswell King, Hampton to Pierce Butler, 13 August 1808: If they had 'rotted' he would fix on 'some other plan to pack them' and send them 'this time to Savannah'.

84   Ibid., Reel 3, Roswell King, Hampton to Pierce Butler, 22 November 1806.

85   Ibid., Reel 3, Roswell King, Hampton to Pierce Butler, 11 July 1813.

86   Ibid., Reel 3, Roswell King, Hampton to Pierce Butler, 12 May 1804.

87   Ibid., Reel 3, Roswell King, Butler's Island to Pierce Butler, 27 December 1812.

88   Ibid., Reel 3, Roswell King, Butler's Island to Pierce Butler, 27 December 1812. In 1812 they were 6 feet 6 inches high and 28 feet wide at the base.

89   Ibid., Reel 3, Roswell King, Hampton to Pierce Butler, 15 November 1812.

90   See Bell, *Major Butler's Legacy*, p. 114: Aaron Burr (in hiding at Hampton plantation after his duel with Andrew Hamilton) to his daughter Theodosia Burr, Hampton Plantation, Tide Island, Georgia, 6 September 1804.

91   *Butler Plantation Papers*, Reel 3, Roswell King, Tide Island to Pierce Butler, 2 June 1804.

92   Ibid., Reel 3, Roswell King, Tide Island to Pierce Butler, 22 October 1803.

93   Ibid., Reel 3, Roswell King, Hampton to Pierce Butler, 24 June 1803.

94   Ibid., Reel 3, Roswell King, Tide Island to Pierce Butler, 2 June 1804.

95   Ibid., Reel 3, Roswell King, Butler's Island to Pierce Butler, 18 October 1806.

96   Ibid., Reel 3, Roswell King, Hampton to Pierce Butler, 3 September 1808.

97   John Michael Vlach, *Back of the Big House: The Architecture of Plantation Slavery* (Chapel Hill and London: University of North Carolina Press, 1993).

98   *Butler Plantation Papers*, Reel 3, Roswell King, Tide Island to Pierce Butler, 30 March 1804: 'As for the well at Experiment nothing certain as yet, we have got down 60ft & find some of most all kinds of sea shell Limstone Rock & other Stone &c – but what is most Extraordinary for the last 37 ft has been sand stone & shells without hard Earthe.'

99   See Michael S. Sheehan and Lauren B. Sickels-Taves, 'Vernacular Building Materials and the Factors Conditioning their Use: Tabby, A Case Study', *Material Culture*, 34:2 (Fall 2002), pp. 16–28.

100 *Butler Plantation Papers*, Reel 3, Roswell King, Hampton to Pierce Butler, 29 July 1808.

101 Lipscomb, *The Letters of Pierce Butler 1790–1794*, p. 54: Pierce Butler to Mrs. Fitzgerald [PB's niece Dorothea married Charles Lionel Fitzgerald of Co. Mayo], NY, July the 24th, 1790: 'The apple trees shall be sent to you the moment the season will admit of taking them out of ground.'

102 *Butler Plantation Papers*, Reel 3, Roswell King, Butler's Island to Pierce Butler, 27 December 1812.

103 Ibid., Reel 3, Roswell King, Hampton to Pierce Butler, 24 June 1803.

104 Ibid., Reel 3, Roswell King, Butler's Island to Pierce Butler, 14 March 1807.

105 Ibid., Reel 3, Roswell King to Pierce Butler, 27 August 1808.

106 Ibid., Reel 3, Roswell King, Hampton to Pierce Butler, 11 July 1813.

107 Ibid., Reel 3, Roswell King, Butler's Island to Pierce Butler, 20 September 1813.

108 Ibid., Reel 3, Roswell King, Hampton to Pierce Butler, 8 October 1813.

109 Ibid., Reel 3, Roswell King, Hampton to Pierce Butler, 25 May 1811.

110 See Trevor Burnard, *Planters, Merchants, and Slaves: Plantation Societies in British America, 1650–1820* (Chicago: University of Chicago Press, 2015), p. 169.

111 Dunboyne, *When the States were Young*, p. 120: Pierce Butler, New York to Weedon Butler, Chelsea, 27 February 1790. For the general eighteenth-century perception of West Indian planters see Kay Dian Kriz, *Slavery, Sugar and the Culture of Refinement* (New Haven and London: Yale University Press, 2008).

112 *Butler Plantation Papers*, Reel 3, Roswell King, Hampton to Pierce Butler, 8 July 1803.

113 Ibid., Reel 3, Roswell King, Hampton to Pierce Butler, 27 June 1813: 'In looking over your last letter, I perceive you think my purchase of Blanketts was on an extravagant principle, when so little wanted, or could have reasonably been done without. It strikes me you think if I had the sole management of your estate I would make a Jamaica estate of it. For my own defence I must say, I take a pride in thinking I can manage negroes better than most people in my Neibourhood, <u>and at less expence</u>.'

114 Ibid., Reel 3, Roswell King, Butler's Island to Pierce Butler, 27 December 1812.

115 Ibid., Reel 3, Roswell King, Hampton to Pierce Butler, 27 June 1813.

116 Ibid., Reel 3, Roswell King, Hampton to Pierce Butler, 22 August 1813.

117 Ibid., Reel 3, Roswell King, Hampton to Pierce Butler, 27 August 1815.

118 Ibid., Reel 3, Roswell King, Butler's Island to Pierce Butler, 19 November 1815.

119 Ibid., Reel 3, Roswell King, Hampton to Pierce Butler, 22 November 1806.

120 Ibid., Reel 3, Roswell King, Hampton to Pierce Butler, 29 November 1806.

121 Ibid., Reel 3, Roswell King, Hampton to Pierce Butler, 21 August 1808.

122 Ibid., Reel 3, Roswell King, Hampton to Pierce Butler, 4 March 1809.

123 Ibid., Reel 3, Roswell King, Hampton to Pierce Butler, 4 May 1811.

124 Ibid., Reel 3, Roswell King, Hampton to Pierce Butler, 25 May 1811.

125 Ibid., Reel 3, Roswell King, Hampton to Pierce Butler, 1 August 1813.

126 Ibid., Reel 3, Roswell King, Tide Island to Pierce Butler, 3 March 1804: 'Nothing would give me more satisfaction or pleasure than to know how to do everything to your wishes.'

127 Ibid., Reel 3, Roswell King, Tide Island to Pierce Butler, 3 March 1804.

128 Ibid., Reel 3, Roswell King, Hampton to Pierce Butler, 16 July 1806.

129 Ibid., Reel 3, Roswell King, Hampton to Pierce Butler, 4 March 1809. The letter continued with: 'you know I have allways wanted a gang of about 25 Ditchers for proffit'.

130 Ibid., Reel 3, Roswell King, Tide Island to Pierce Butler, 30 March 1804: 'There is but few of the new Negroes taken Wives as yet Sambo says it is hardly time for them they must shew a disposition to plant a little for themselves &c. first, the new Negroes are fat & likely to behave very well.'

131 Ibid., Reel 3, Roswell King, Hampton to Pierce Butler, 19 July 1806.

132 Ibid., Reel 3, Roswell King, Hampton to Pierce Butler, 13 July 1806: 'Frank, the little whipping he got, did, in my judgement as you 500 $ worth of good: for now he hears something to me, the Gins work well & the roller seldom break.'

133 Ibid., Reel 3, Roswell King, Hampton to Pierce Butler, 25 May 1811.

134 Ibid., Reel 3, Roswell King, Hampton to Pierce Butler, 1 August 1813.

135 Ibid., Reel 3, Roswell King, Hampton to Pierce Butler, 21 June 1812.

136 Ibid., Reel 3, Roswell King, Hampton to Pierce Butler, 21 June 1812.

137 Ibid., Reel 3, Roswell King, Hampton to Pierce Butler, 23 May 1813.

138 Ibid., Reel 3, Roswell King, Butler's Island, to Pierce Butler, 3 January 1813.

139 Ibid., Reel 3, Roswell King, Hampton to Pierce Butler, 22 August 1813.

140 Ibid., Reel 1, Pierce Butler Letterbooks, vol. 2, 12 July 1794 – 2 February 1822, p. 147: Philadelphia, 21 January 1813, Pierce Butler to Roswell King.

141 Ibid., Reel 3, Roswell King, Butler's Island, 28 March 1813, to Pierce Butler.

142 Ibid., Reel 3, Roswell King, Hampton, 1 August 1813, to Pierce Butler.

143 Ibid., Reel 3, Roswell King, Tide Island to Pierce Butler, 30 March 1804: 'God never? gave Negroes that presence of mind to take care of their tools & do their work well enough to make white men happy; tho they are very usefull but it wants a hard-hearted man to manage them.'

144 Ibid., Reel 3, Roswell King, Butler's Island to Pierce Butler, 1 June 1813.

145 James S. Ackerman, *The Villa: Form and Ideology of Country Houses* (London: Thames and Hudson, 1990), pp. 15–16.

146 *Butler Plantation Papers*, Reel 3, Roswell King, Hampton to Pierce Butler, 23 September 1808: 'On Sunday last Messrs T Spalding P Hopkins & Gignilliar met at Darien as Commissioners for Barrington Road – they decreed that you pay 6$ for each Negro … 276$ … I informed the board that I did not expect to be so pointedly heated contrary to the custom of the country heretofore.'

147 Ibid., Reel 3, Roswell King, Hampton to Pierce Butler, 17 September 1808.

148 Ibid., Reel 3, Roswell King, Hampton to Pierce Butler, 22 November 1806.

149 Ibid., Reel 3, Roswell King, Hampton to Pierce Butler, 23 September 1808: 'The planters on St Simons and vicinity of Darien' had 'formed a coalition to prosecute all dealers with Negroes (which I have been after for 6 years past) we have fifteen such of 30$ each now defending at Darien.'

150 Ibid., Reel 3, Roswell King, Hampton to Pierce Butler, 16 May 1810.

151 Ibid., Reel 3, Catherine King, Hampton to Pierce Butler, 7 January 1815.

152 Ibid., Reel 3, Roswell King, Hampton to Pierce Butler, 12 July 1818.

153 Ibid., Reel 3, Roswell King, Hampton, to Pierce Butler, 12 July 1818: 'I find near Savannah the swamp plantations do not gain in value by the Increase of the Town. The same may be expected from this, when Darien becomes a town of note, which will soon be the case.'

154 See O'Kane, *Ireland and the Picturesque*, Chapter 4.

155 *Butler Plantation Papers*, Reel 3, Roswell King, Tide Island to Pierce Butler, 30 March 1804.

156 Ibid., Reel 3, Roswell King, Hampton to Pierce Butler, 5 August 1809.

CHAPTER SIX

1 Arthur Young, *A Tour in Ireland, 1776–1779*, 2 vols (Shannon: Irish University Press, 1970), 2, p. 117.

2 Ibid., 2, p. 114: 'Section XIV, Absentees'.

3 Ibid., 2, pp. 116–17.

4 Louis Cullen, John Shovlin and Thomas M. Truxes (eds), *The Bordeaux-Dublin Letters 1757: Correspondence of an Irish Community Abroad* (Oxford: Oxford University Press, 2013), p. 38.

5 See Kristen Block and Jenny Shaw, 'Subjects without an Empire: The Irish in the Early Modern Caribbean', *Past and Present*, 210:1 (2011), pp. 33–60.

6 See Young, *A Tour in Ireland*, p. 114 and A. P. W. Malcomson, 'Absenteeism in Eighteenth-Century Ireland', *Irish Economic and Social History*, 1 (1974), pp. 13–35. For a comparative analysis of rates of absenteeism across Great Britain at the end of the long eighteenth century see Nick Draper, '"Dependent on Precarious Subsistences": Ireland's Slave-Owners at the Time of Emancipation', *Britain and the World*, 6:2 (Sept. 2013), pp. 220–42.

7 Gauvin Alexander Bailey, *Architecture and Urbanism in the French Atlantic Empire: State, Church, and Society, 1604–1830* (Toronto: McGill University Press, 2018), p. 36.

8 Jonathan Jeffrey Wright, *An Ulster Slave Owner in the Revolutionary Atlantic: The Life and Letters of John Black* (Dublin: Four Courts Press, 2018), p. 117.

9 Ibid., p. 110.

10 For the collapse of such oppositions in colonial contexts see Finola O'Kane, 'Moving Landscapes to Saint-Domingue, Jamaica and Ireland: Plantation Design, National Identity and the Colonial Picturesque', *Huntington Library Quarterly*, 84:3 (2022), pp. 561–88.

11 See Bell, Malcolm, *Major Butler's Legacy: Five Generations of a Slaveholding Family* (Athens: University of Georgia Press, 1987) and Theresa A. Singleton, 'The Archaeology of Afro-American Slavery in Coastal Georgia: A Regional Perception of Slave Household and Community Patterns', PhD thesis (University of Florida, 1980).

12 See Finola O'Kane, *William Ashford's Mount Merrion: The Absent Point of View* (Fenit, Co. Kerry: Churchill House Press, 2012), and Finola O'Kane, 'An Absentee Family's Suburban Demesne: The Making of Mount Merrion, Co. Dublin' in *The Irish Country House*, ed. Terry Dooley (Dublin: Four Courts Press, 2011).

13 NAI, Fitzwilliam Mss. 2011/3/1: Jonathan Barker, 'A Book of Maps and References to the Estate of the Right Honourable Richard Lord Viscount FitzWilliam', 1762, p. 59: The total computed for the entire estate is '2700 Irish acres, 39 perches' or '4373 English acres, 3 rods and 31 perches'.

14 This section draws substantially from the longer analysis contained in Finola O'Kane, 'Dublin's Fitzwilliam Estate: A Hidden Landscape of Discovery, Catholic Agency and Egalitarian Suburban Space', *Eighteenth-Century Ireland / Iris an dá chultúr*, 31 (2016), pp. 94–118.

15 NAI, Ms. 97/46 /1/2/5/75, Richard Mathew to Viscount Fitzwilliam, 7 February 1749.

16 T. P. O'Neill, 'Discoverers and Discoveries: The Penal Laws and Dublin Property', *Dublin Historical Record*, 37 (1983–4), p. 4. See also Karen Harvey, *The Bellews of Mounts Bellew* (Dublin: Four Courts Press, 1998), Chapter 2.

17 Harvey, *The Bellews of Mounts Bellew*, p. 53.

18 NAI, Ms. 97/46/1/2/5/66, Richard Mathew to Viscount Fitzwilliam, 1 July 1749.

19 NAI, Ms. 97/46/1/2/1/6, Richard Mathew to Lord Fitzwilliam, 18 October 1735.

20 NAI, Ms. 97/46/1/2/1/5, Richard Mathew to Viscount Fitzwilliam 2 August 1735.

21 NAI, Ms. 97/46/1/2/3/10, Richard Mathew to Lord Fitzwilliam, 14 September 1738. John Fitzgibbon, a lawyer, when giving advice relating to a discoverable lease on the Owenstown part of the estate, noted that Fitzwilliam had the 'power to make leases thereof for three lives or 21 years' (Ms. 97/46/1/2/6/18). I have not been able to discover why twenty-one years rather than the penal laws' general limit of thirty-one years appears to have been obligatory on the Fitzwilliam estate.

22 NAI, Ms. 97/46/1/2/3/10, Richard Mathew, Dublin to Lord Fitzwilliam, 14 September 1738.

23 NAI, Ms. 97/46/1/2/3/11, Richard Mathew, Dublin to Lord Fitzwilliam. Dublin, 21 November 1738. This is a problematic letter to interpret and the actual lease that resulted from the discussion is unknown. The relevant point here that the land's management and subsequent appearance seem to have been planned in order to manipulate an onlooker's perception of the length of lease and connected strategies of improvement.

24 NAI, Ms. 97/46 /1 /2/5/60, Richard Mathew to Viscount Fitzwilliam, 16 February 1748[49].

25 NAI, Ms. 97/46/1/2/7/72, William Fitzwilliam to Viscount Fitzwilliam, 10 February 1756.

26 NAI, Ms. 97/46 /1 /2/6/76, John Enraght to Viscount Fitzwilliam, 28 March 1772.

27 NAI, Ms. 97/46/1/2/7/153, William Fitzwilliam, Dublin to Viscount Fitzwilliam, 26 March 1763.

28 NAI, Ms. 7/46/1/2/7/25, William Fitzwilliam to Viscount Fitzwilliam, 23 October 1753.

29 NAI, Ms. 97/46/1/2/7/13, William Fitzwilliam to Viscount Fitzwilliam, 21 April 1753.

30 NAI, Ms. 97/46/1/2/7/13, William Fitzwilliam to Viscount Fitzwilliam, 31 May 1753.

31 NAI, Ms. 97/46 /1 /2/5/46, Richard Mathew to Lord Fitzwilliam, 27 August 1747.

32 NAI, Ms. 97/46/1/2/8/13, Bryan Fagan to the Rt Hon. Richard Lord Viscount Fitzwilliam, 22 February 1757.

33 NAI, Ms. 97/46 /1 /2/7/102, Richard Mathew to the Rt Hon. the Lord Viscount Fitzwilliam, 28 May 1757.

34 For the Leinster and Fitzwilliam antagonism regarding the square's development see Finola O'Kane, '"Bargains in View"; The Fitzwilliam Family's Development of Merrion Square, Dublin' in *The Eighteenth-Century Dublin Townhouse*, ed. Christine Casey (Dublin: Four Courts Press, 2010).

35 NAI, Ms. 97/46/1/2/7/109, William Fitzwilliam to Viscount Fitzwilliam, Dublin, 10 May 1758.

36 NAI, Ms. 97/46/1/2/8/30, William Fitzwilliam to Viscount Fitzwilliam, 3 April 1760.

37 NAI, Ms. 97/46/1/2/7/65, William Fitzwilliam, Dublin, to his brother the Rt. Hon. Viscount Fitzwilliam, Jermyn St, St James, 25 October 1755.

38 *Proceedings of the United Irishmen of Dublin* (Philadelphia: Thomas Stephens, of No. 57, South Second Street, by Jacob Johnson, & Co., 1795).

39 *Butler Plantation Papers: The Papers of Pierce Butler (1744–1822) and Successors from the Historical Society of Pennsylvania*, Adam Matthew Publications, 1997, Microfilm Reel 3, 'Plantation Managers' Correspondence', Roswell King, Hampton, to Pierce Butler Hampton,

4 May 1811: 'The List of Negroes January 1st 1811 … Total 632'.

40   Maurice J. Bric, *Ireland, Philadelphia and the Re-invention of America, 1760–1800* (Dublin: Four Courts Press, 2008), pp. 217–18, 'However, it is clear that Butler's support of Rowan had been influenced by ancestral nostalgia rather than political ideology and there is no evidence that Butler supported the United Irish cause in America.' I would argue that he did work softly in the United Irishmen's interest and that this support was influenced by political ideology rather than any ancestral nostalgia.

41   Paddy Butler, Lord Dunboyne (ed.), *When the States were Young: A Remarkable Collection of Letters 1784–1799 Preserved in the British Library as Additional Manuscript 16603* (www.lulu.com, 2006), p. 214, Pierce Butler to Weeden Butler, 1 September 1794.

42   Lipscomb, Terry W. (ed.), *The Letters of Pierce Butler 1790–1794: Nation Building and Enterprise in the New American Republic* (Columbia, University of South Carolina Press, 2007), pp. 145–6, Pierce Butler, Philadelphia, to John Rea, Esquire (Letterkenny, Co. Donegal), 18 November 1791.

43   *Proceedings of the United Irishmen of Dublin*, p. 4.

44   Terry W. Lipscomb (ed.), *The Letters of Pierce Butler 1790–1794*, p. 187: Pierce Butler, Philadelphia, to the Reverend Mr Frost (assistant minister of St Philip's Episcopal church in Charleston), 14 September 1792: 'I have no knowledge of any Appointment from the Episcopal Convention in So Carolina; and Your Letter gave me the first and only information that the wish'd me to attend at the General Episcopal Convention. It is my inclination to comply with every desire of so very respectable a part of my fellow Citizens. … did my health permitt me to travel to York.'

45   Lipscomb, *The Letters of Pierce Butler 1790–1794*, p. 2, Pierce Butler, New York, to the Revd Mr Smith, 3 January 1790.

46   Dunboyne, *When the States were Young*, p. 158, Pierce Butler to his son, Tom, 19 November 1791: 'I have had a small vault made for the body and placed a marble tombstone thereon. It is contiguous to my pew in the church. On the wall within the church and near the pew may the monument [to Pierce Butler's wife Polly née Middleton] be placed.'

47   Dunboyne, *When the States were Young*, pp. 115–16, Pierce Butler to Weedon Butler, 3 November 1789.

48   Lipscomb, *The Letters of Pierce Butler 1790–1794*, p. 80, Pierce Butler, New York to Doctor Peter Spence, Kensington near London, 20 November, 1790.

49   Dunboyne, *When the States were Young*, pp. 76–7, Pierce Butler to Weeden Butler, 5 May 1788.

50   Ibid., p. 214, Pierce Butler to Weeden Butler, 1 September 1794.

51   Ibid., pp. 80–2, Pierce Butler to Weeden Butler, 18 July 1788.

52   Lipscomb, *The Letters of Pierce Butler 1790–1794*, p. 55, Pierce Butler, New York, to George Mason, 25 July 1790.

53   Dunboyne, *When the States were Young*, p. 154, Pierce Butler to Weeden Butler, 12 November 1791: 'I said in a former letter that I would give you my opinion of Paine's pamphlet. I think it contains much truth (though nothing new) placed in a strong and expressive point of view. But the language is in many places more than inelegant. It is vulgar and ingrammatic.'

54   Ibid., p. 105, Pierce Butler to Weeden Butler, 23 September 1789.

55   Lipscomb, *The Letters of Pierce Butler 1790–1794*, p. 92, Pierce Butler to General Jackson, Philadelphia, 24 January 1791.

56   Ibid., p. 187, Pierce Butler, Philadelphia, to Colonel Anderson, 18 September 1792.

57   Ibid., p. 211, Pierce Butler, Philadelphia, to Peter Freneau Esqr., 22 November 1792.

58   Ibid., pp. 170–1, Pierce Butler, Philadelphia, to Sir John Myngies, 5 August 1792.

59   Ibid., p. 201, Pierce Butler, Philadelphia, to Robert Shuttleworth Esqr., 27 October 1792.

60   Lipscomb, *The Letters of Pierce Butler 1790–1794*, p. 86, Pierce Butler, Philadelphia to Mrs Beaver, 9 January 1791.

61   Ibid., p. 80, Pierce Butler, New York, to Doctor Peter Spence, Kensington near London, 20 November 1790.

62   Ibid., p. 82, Pierce Butler, New York to his mother Lady Henrietta Butler, widow of Sir Richard Butler, Pierce Butler's father, 28 November 1790.

63   The career of George Washington and other eminent Americans had also followed this pattern.

64   Dunboyne, *When the States were Young*, p. 153, Pierce Butler to Weedon Butler, 12 November 1791.

65   Lipscomb, *The Letters of Pierce Butler 1790–1794*, p. 246, Pierce Butler, Philadelphia, to W. T. Franklin Esqr., 11 August 1793.

66   Ibid., p. 128, Pierce Butler, Philadelphia, to Daniel Bourdeux Esqr., 25 September 1791.

67   Ibid., p. 170, Pierce Butler, Philadelphia, to Sir John Myngies [Bart. London], 5 August 1792.

68   Ibid., p. 131, Pierce Butler, Philadelphia, to John Houstoun, 28 September 1791.

69   Ibid., p. 278, Pierce Butler, Philadelphia, to W. T. Franklin Esqr., 22 November 1793.

70   Ibid., p. 293, Pierce Butler, Philadelphia, to W. T. Franklin Esqr., 22 January 1794: 'It is true the Platt appears broken yet you will observe that there is not one inch or corner of the Land but what may be got to without going thro' the land of any other person.'

71   Ibid., p. 306, Pierce Butler, Philadelphia, to Archibald Brown Esqr. (South Carolina merchant & Cooper river planter), 14 February 1794.

72   Dunboyne, *When the States were Young*, p. 191, Sarah Butler to her brother Thomas, 15 April 1793.

73   Theresa A. Singleton, 'The Archaeology of Afro-American Slavery in Coastal Georgia: A Regional Perception of Slave Household and Community Patterns', PhD thesis (University of Florida), 1980, p. 59: 'The degree of absenteeism, however, apparently varied along the rice coast … In the Altamaha Basin, rice planters spent a major portion of the year on their rice estates and moved to nearby pineland retreats or barrier island plantations for the summer months. Often they commuted each day to keep a watchful eye on the progress of the crop and other management problems … The Butlers were the only exception to this rule. They were never full-time residents of Georgia. Because they were generally absent from their Georgian estate, the overseers regularly corresponded with them.'

74   *Butler Plantation Papers*, Reel 3, Roswell King to Pierce Butler, Philadelphia, 5 November 1803: 'Jacob has got the Barn at Settlement

No. 2 almost done (& a fine one it is) & has put up two Negro Houses in No. 3.'

75   Ibid., Reel 3, Roswell King, Hampton Plantation, Georgia, to Pierce Butler, Philadelphia, 8 July 1803.

76   Ibid., Reel 3, Roswell King, Hampton Plantation, Georgia, to Pierce Butler, 10 December 1803.

77   Ibid., Reel 3, Roswell King, Hampton Plantation, Georgia, to Pierce Butler, 12 May 1804.

78   Lipscomb, *The Letters of Pierce Butler 1790–1794*, pp. 99–100, Pierce Butler, Philadelphia, to John Leckey Esqr., 11 February 1792.

79   Dunboyne, *When the States were Young*, p. 209, Sarah Butler to her brother Thomas, 25 August 1794.

80   Rev. S. F. Hotchkin, *The York Road, Old and New* (Philadelphia: Binder and Kelly, 1892), p. 57, https://archive.org (accessed 18 October 2021).

81   Hotchkin, *The York Road, Old and New*, p. 60.

82   Jeffrey A. Cohen, 'Place, Time, and Architecture: Materialized Memory and the Moment of Latrobe's Waln House' in *Classical Splendor: Painted Furniture for a Grand Philadelphia House*, ed. Alexandra Alevizatos Kirtley and Peggy A. Olley (New Haven and London: Yale University Press, 2016), p. 21.

83   Lipscomb, *The Letters of Pierce Butler 1790–1794*, p. 172, Pierce Butler, Philadelphia, to James Seagrove, 7 August 1792.

84   *Butler Plantation Papers*, Reel 3, Roswell King, Tide Island, to Pierce Butler, 28 April 1804.

85   Ibid., Reel 3, Roswell King, Hampton, to Pierce Butler, 13 June 1813: 'There will be eight doors, say four of them will want locks and the other fastnings. there will be eight windows of 18 lights each. Glass 11 by 8– say 144 panes but on acct of breakage I would suppose 200 panes would not be too much– 100ft is 163 panes that may do.'

86   Ibid., Reel 3, Roswell King, Hampton, to Pierce Butler, 13 June 1813.

87   Ibid., Reel 3, Roswell King, Hampton, to Pierce Butler, 20 June 1813.

88   Ibid., Reel 3, Roswell King, Hampton, to Pierce Butler, 3 October 1813.

89   Lipscomb, *The Letters of Pierce Butler 1790–1794*, p. 99, Pierce Butler, Philadelphia, to John Leckey Esqr. (Ballykealey, Ireland, Quaker), 11 February 1791.

90   See ibid., p. 132, Pierce Butler to John Houstoun, 28 September 1791 and pp. 265–6, Pierce Butler to Thomas Young, 28 October 1793.

91   Ibid., p. 265, Pierce Butler to Thomas Young Esqr, Pennsylvania, 28 October 1793.

92   Ibid., p. 271, Pierce Butler, Pennsylvania, to John Bee Holmes Esqr. (Charleston lawyer), 5 November 1793: 'I am very well persuaded, that if Our State Legislature do not pass some laws to prevent the impor-tation of Negroes from the West Indies, and if in their power from the Northern States, Our property in Carolina is held by a slender tye. I would include Virginia Negroes among the proscribed if it can be done, for they are strongly tinctured.'

93   See Maurice Bric, *Ireland, Philadelphia and the Re-invention of America, 1760–1800*, pp. 264–5.

94   Lipscomb, *The Letters of Pierce Butler 1790–1794*, p. 312, Pierce Butler, Philadelphia, to John Allston Esqr., 25 March 1794.

95   Dunboyne, *When the States were Young*, p. 98, Pierce Butler to Weedon Butler, New York, 21 June 1789.

96   Ibid., p. 146, Pierce Butler to Weedon Butler, 14 June 1791.

97   Ibid., p. 169, Pierce Butler to Weedon Butler, 12 April 1792.

98   Ibid., p. 55, Pierce Butler to Weedon Butler, 30 November 1786.

99   Ibid., p. 194, Pierce Butler to Weedon Butler, 23 June 1793.

100 Ibid., p. 182, Pierce Butler to Weedon Butler, 19 November 1792.

101 NAI, Ms. 97/46/1/2/7/102, William Fitzwilliam to the Rt Hon. the Lord Viscount Fitzwilliam, 28 May 1757.

102 NAI, Ms. 97/46/1/2/7/152, William Fitzwilliam to the Rt Hon. the Lord Viscount Fitzwilliam, 17 March 1763.

103 NAI, Ms. 97/46/1/2/7/154, William Fitzwilliam to the Rt Hon. the Lord Viscount Fitzwilliam, 13 April 1763.

104 Dunboyne, *When the States were Young*, p. 192, Sarah Butler to her brother Tom, 15 April 1793.

105 Ibid., p. 209, Sarah Butler to her brother Tom, 25 August 1794.

106 Ibid., pp. 209–11, Sarah Butler to her brother Tom, 25 August 1794.

107 Ibid., p. 201, Pierce Butler to Weeden Butler, 8 November 1793.

108 Ibid., p. 223, Tom Butler to Weeden Butler, 1795 (supposedly September).

109 NAI, Ms. 97/46/1/2/7/64, William Fitzwilliam to Viscount Fitzwilliam, 21 October 1765.

110 Dell Upton, 'White and Black Landscapes in Eighteenth-Century Virginia', *Places*, 2:2 (1984), p. 63.

111 See Finola O'Kane, 'What's in a Name? The Connected Histories of Belfield, Co. Dublin and Belfield, St. Mary's, Jamaica' in *Making Belfield: Space and Place at UCD*, ed. F. O'Kane and E. Rowley (Dublin: University College Dublin Press, 2020), pp. 150–61.

112 For exceptions see Susanne Seymour, Stephen Daniels and Charles Watkins, 'Estate and Empire: Sir George Cornwall's Management of Moccas, Herefordshire and La Taste, Grenada, 1771–1819', *Journal of Historical Geography*, 24:3 (1998), pp. 313–51, and Jonathan Finch, 'Three Men in a Boat: Biographies and Narrative in the Historic Landscape', *Landscape Research*, 33:5 (Oct. 2008), pp. 511–30.

CHAPTER SEVEN

1   Paddy Butler, Lord Dunboyne (ed.), *When the States were Young: A Remarkable Collection of Letters 1784–1799 Preserved in the British Library as Additional Manuscript 16603* (www.lulu.com, 2006), p. 130, Pierce Butler, New York, to Weedon Butler, Chelsea, 1 September 1790.

2   This chapter draws on the following essays: Finola O'Kane, 'The Military Roads of County Wicklow', 2017, website article, https://www.bl.uk/picturing-places/articles (accessed 6 April 2017); Finola O'Kane and Mary-Ann Constantine, 'Strategies of the Picturesque: Romantic-Era Tours of Wales and Ireland' in *Old Ways and New Roads: Travels in Scotland, c. 1720–1830*, ed. N. Leask, J. Bonehill and A. Dulau (Edinburgh: Birlinn, 2021), pp. 194–211; Finola O'Kane, 'Ireland – A New Geographical Pastime?' in Art Institute of Chicago exhibition catalogue, *Ireland: Crossroads of Art and Design, 1690–1840*, ed. William Laffan and Christopher Monkhouse (New Haven and London: Yale University Press, 2015).

3   Ruan O'Donnell, *The Rebellion in Wicklow 1798* (Dublin: Irish Academic Press, 1998), p. 12. For Co. Kildare see Liam Chambers, *Rebellion in Kildare 1790–1803* (Dublin: Four Courts Press, 1998).

4   Ruan O'Donnell, *The Rebellion in Wicklow*, p. 106.

5   C. J. Woods, *Travellers as Source Material for Irish Historians* (Dublin: Four Courts Press, 2009), p. 131: 'from Kohn "Travels in Ireland" 1844'.

6   O'Donnell, *The Rebellion in Wicklow 1798*, p. 12.

7   NAI, O.P. (Official Papers) 293/1(2), 'Reason for making the new Military Road in the County of Wicklow submitted to His Excellency Major Cornwallis by the Royal Proprietors of that County, Feb. 1800', from Peter J. O'Keeffe, *Alexander Taylor's Roadworks in Ireland, 1780–1827* (Dublin: Institute of Asphalt Technology, Irish Branch, 1996), p. 31.

8   NAI, O.P. (Official Papers) 293/1(4), n.d. from O'Keeffe, *Alexander Taylor's Roadworks in Ireland, 1780–1827*, pp. 112–13: 'It is important insofar as it is the only document summarising Taylor's own view of events.'

9   DIB, 'Alexander Taylor' (accessed 4 February 2016).

10 George Taylor and Andrew Skinner, *Maps of the Roads of Ireland, Surveyed 1777* (London: G. Nicol, Strand; I. Murray, Fleet-Street; Dublin: W. Wilson, No. 6 Dame Street, 1778) and George Taylor and Andrew Skinner, *A Map of the County of Louth* (London: Engraved by G. Terry, Paternoster Row, Cheapside, 1777).

11 TNA PRO 30/9/172, Dublin, 22 August 1801, Alexander Taylor, Letter to the administration.

12 See Finola O'Kane, *Ireland and the Picturesque: Design, Landscape Painting and Tourism in Ireland 1700–1840* (New Haven and London: Yale University Press, 2013), Chapter 3.

13 See N. Leask, J. Bonehill and A. Dulau (eds), *Old Ways and New Roads: Travels in Scotland, c.1720–1830* (Edinburgh: Birlinn, 2021), pp. 1–7; Nigel Leask, *Stepping Westward, Writing the Highland Tour c.1720 –1830* (Oxford: Oxford University Press, 2020).

14 Glin Castle transcription, 'Tour to Scotland & Ireland in the Years 1776 1777 … and 1801 etc. to the Honble Mrs Yorke (widow of the Hon. Charles Yorke), Charles & Philip Yorke to their mother', 1781 and C. J. Woods (ed.), *Charles Abbot's Tour through Ireland and North Wales in 1792* (Dublin: Edmund Burke Books, 2019).

15 Felicity Myrone, 'The Monarch of the Plain: Paul Sandby and Topography' in *Paul Sandby: Picturing Britain*, ed. John Bonehill and Stephen Daniels, exhibition catalogue (London: Royal Academy of Arts, 2009), p. 57.

16 Ibid.

17 TNA PRO 30/9/172: Clerk's transcript of letter from Alexander Taylor to Lieut. Colonel Littlehales, Dublin, 22 August 1801.

18 Ibid.

19 O'Keeffe, *Alexander Taylor's Roadworks in Ireland, 1780–1827*, p. 106, Appendix 1 Taylor's Report of 10 February 1802: 'Upon the first 10 Miles there are 86 Small Bridges, Sewers and Water pavements required, some of which upon the larges? Soxams? are finished and Materials prepared for others.'

20 O'Keeffe, *Alexander Taylor's Roadworks in Ireland, 1780–1827*.

21 Ibid., p. 61: Note 59 refers to 'The Fourth Report of the Commissioners Appointed to enquire into the Nature and Extent of the Several Bogs in Ireland and the practicality of draining them, H.C. 1813–14 (131), VI. Second Part, No. 11.'

22 Ibid., p. 61.

23 Robert Fraser, *General View of the Agriculture and Mineralogy, Present State and Circumstances of the County Wicklow* (Dublin: Fraisberry & Campbell, 1801), p. 7.

24 O'Keeffe, *Alexander Taylor's Roadworks in Ireland, 1780–1827*, p. 61.

25 Glin Castle, 'Tour to Scotland & Ireland in the Years 1776 1777 … and 1801', Dublin, 30 August 1781.

26 Ibid., Dublin, 13 September 1781.

27 Woods, *Charles Abbot's Tour through Ireland and North Wales in 1792*, 'Thursday Sept[embe]r 27th [1792]'.

28 Charles Abbot (ed.), *The Diary and Correspondence of Charles Abbot, Lord Colchester*, 3 vols (London: J. Murray, 1861), I, p. 276: These probably resulted in Major Alexander Taylor, *Mineralogical maps of Croaghan Mountain, Co. Wicklow*, 1801, The British Library, Add. Ms. 32451 F.

29 Fraser, *General View of … Wicklow*.

30 Ibid., p. 29: An asterisked note explained: '*It has been found since, that twenty armed rebels were concealed in a cave within a quarter of a mile, where we had pitched our tents, during the whole time of our continuance on this mountain.'

31 G. N. Wright, *A Guide to the County of Wicklow* (London: Baldwin, Cradock & Joy, 1822), p. 96.

32 *Freeman's Journal*, 12 January 1802, http://archive.irishnewsarchive.com (accessed 6 December 2013).

33 Ibid.

34 Nicola Figgis (ed.), *Art and Architecture of Ireland, Volume 2: Painting* (New Haven and London: Yale University Press, 2015), pp. 433–5: William Laffan, 'Thomas Sautelle Roberts'.

35 Dates taken from dates of exhibition provided in Walter G. Strickland, *A Dictionary of Irish Artists*, 2 vols (Dublin and London: Maunsell and Co., 1913) and William Laffan, 'Thomas Sautelle Roberts' in Figgis, *Art and Architecture of Ireland, Volume 2: Painting*, pp. 433–5. Where the image was not exhibited the date is given from its subsequent engraving. Views postdating the January 1802 exhibition, where their completion may predate their transfer to London for exhibition at the Royal Academy by a few years, are also listed: *View of Dublin from the Phoenix Park. Ex. Dublin, 1800; Powerscourt Waterfall. Ex. Dublin, 1802; View of the House of Lords and adjacent buildings, taken from the south side of Carlisle Bridge. Ex. Dublin, 1802; Killiney Bay. Engraved in aquatint by W. Pickett, 1802; View near Powerscourt, with a portrait of Captain Taylor of the Engineers by J. Comerford. Ex. Dublin, 1802; View in the Valley of Glencree, with portrait of the Earl of Hardwicke, Lord Lieutenant, by J. Comerford. Ex. Dublin, 1802; View of the Gold Mines, Co. Wicklow. R.A., 1803. Ex. Dublin, 1802. [engraved in aquatint by J. Bluck, 1804.]; The Lake of Luggelaw. [Engraved in aquatint by F. C. Lewis, 1803]; View of Kilruddery. R.A., 1803; View of Vinegar Hill. R.A., 1803; An Irish Hut, Co. Wicklow. R.A., 1803; View near the town of Bray. R.A., 1803; View from the Commons of Bray. R.A., 1803; The Dargle. R.A., 1803; View near Thomastown, Co. Kilkenny. Engraved in aquatint by Tomkins, 1803; Group of Irish Cabbins, [R.A.?] 1804; The Meeting of the Waters. Engraved in aquatint by S. Aiken. 1804[?]; Military Roads, Co. Wicklow. Engraved in aquatint by S. Aiken. 1804[?]; The Commons of Bray, R.A., 1804; View at the back of Lord Powerscourt's Demesne. R.A., 1804; A View in the Dargle. R.A. 1805; View of the Devil's Glen, Co. Wicklow.*

R.A., 1805; Castle of Oldcourt, Co. Wicklow. Engraved in aquatint by Sutherland, 1805; A View of the New Four Courts and remains of Coal Quay Bridge. Ex. Dublin, 1804, R.A. 1805; St. Patrick's Cathedral. R.A., 1805; A Rebel Retreat in the Devil's Glen; General Holt is represented as appointing his evening guards. R.A., 1806; A View in the Dargle. R.A. 1806; View taken from the Earl of Meath's Park, R.A., 1806; Bray Head. R.A., 1806; The Town of Howth, with part of Dublin Bay. R.A., 1806; A View of College Green and Westmoreland Street, part of Sackville Street and Carlisle Bridge, from near the Provost's House, Grafton Street. R.A., 1806; A View in the Dargle. R.A. 1808; Sugar Loaf Hill. B.I., 1808; A View in the Dargle. R.A. 1811; The Castle, Dublin. Ex. Dublin, 1815; A View in the Dargle. R.A. 1818; The New Post Office, Sackville Street. Engraved in aquatint by R. Havell, 1818.

36   The watercolours have been used to illustrate this chapter where possible.

37   TNA PRO 30/9/172: Dublin, 22 August 1801, Clerk's transcript of letter from Alexander Taylor to Lieut Colonel Littlehalls.

38   The watercolour view with a gentleman directing workmen wearing no kilts was sold as 'Watercolour "View from Glencree towards Powerscourt and the Great and Little Sugar Loafs", 48.2cm × 66.5cm' in the Gorry Gallery, Molesworth Street, Dublin, Sale Catalogue 24 June – 8 July 2009.

39   O'Keeffe, *Alexander Taylor's Roadworks in Ireland, 1780 –1827*, pp. 61–2: O'Keeffe transcribes a substantial section of the 'The Fourth Report of the Commissioners Appointed to enquire into the Nature and Extent of the Several Bogs in Ireland and the practicality of draining them', H.C. 1813–14 (131), VI. Second Part, No. 11.

40   O'Donnell, *The Rebellion in Wicklow 1798*, p. 15.

41   See Stephen Daniels and John Bonehill, 'Designs on the Landscape: Paul and Thomas Sandby in North Britain', *Oxford Art Journal*, 40:2 (Aug. 2017). For the visual construction of Great Britain see Paul Sandby, *A Collection of One Hundred and Fifty Select Views, in England, Wales, Scotland and Ireland* (London: John Boydell, 1780) and *The Virtuosi's Museum* (London: G. Kearsly, 1778–81).

42   Thomas Bartlett, '"Masters of the Mountains": The Insurgent Careers of Joseph Holt and Michael Dwyer' in *Wicklow History & Society*, ed. Ken Hannigan & William Nolan (Dublin: Geography Publications, 1994), p. 393: 'Furthermore the study of banditry has focussed attention on the fudging of the distinction between private men of violence (bandits) and public men of violence (soldiers): state sanction – a fluid shifting concept on the frontier or in a colonial situation – made all the difference.'

43   Ibid., p. 380.

44   Ibid.

45   Niall Ó Dónaill, *Foclóir Gaeilge-Béarla* (Dublin: Oifig an tSoláthair: Foilseacháin Rialtais, 1977): 'scailp'.

46   See John Barrell, 'The Meeting of the Waters', *Critical Quarterly*, 60:1 (Apr. 2018).

47   For Thomas King's role as High Sheriff and in the local yeomanry and for his loyalist connections with Edward Newenham see Louis Cullen, 'Politics and Rebellion: Wicklow in the 1790s' in *Wicklow History & Society*, ed. Ken Hannigan and William Nolan (Dublin: Geography Publications, 1994), pp. 429–30.

48   Ruan O'Donnell, *Aftermath: Post-Rebellion Insurgency in Wicklow 1799–1803* (Dublin: Irish Academic Press, 2000), p. 67.

49   O'Donnell, *The Rebellion in Wicklow 1798*, p. 20: Note 46.

50   Abraham Mills, 'A Mineralogist Account of Native Gold Lately Discovered in Ireland. In a Letter from Abraham Mills, Esq. to Sir Joseph Banks, Bart. KBPRS', *Dublin Society Transactions*, 2 (1801), pp. 454–63; 'Second Report on the Goldmines in the County of Wicklow', *Dublin Society Transactions*, 3 (1802), pp. 81–7.

51   Martin Critchley (ed.), *Exploring the Mining Heritage of County Wicklow* (Wicklow: Wicklow County Council, 2008), p. 10.

52   O'Donnell, *The Rebellion in Wicklow 1798*, p. 305: Miles Byrne's associate Nick Murphy of Monaseed had 'sent word from Dublin to Holt's group at Croghan on 26 August [1798]'.

53   O'Donnell, *The Rebellion in Wicklow 1798*, p. 30.

54   Ibid., pp. 50–1.

55   William Laffan, 'Thomas Sautelle Roberts' in Figgis, *Art and Architecture of Ireland, Volume 2: Painting*, p. 434: Laffan cites RIA Ms. 24 K 14; pp. 113–14, 25 January 1802.

56   *Literary Gazette*, 1818, p. 394, from H. Miles, D. H. Solkin and G. Smith (n.d.) *Reviews of Genre Painting* [Information files] C41, File 1818, The Paul Mellon Centre, London.

57   *Freeman's Journal*, 21 January 1802, https://www.irishnewsarchive.com (accessed 6 December 2013). 'Theatre-Royal. Command of his Excellency the Lord Lieutenant and Countess of Hardwicke, This Evening, Jan. 21, will be presented THE CATLE SPECTRE … To which will be added THE WICKLOW GOLD MINES, Felix, Mr. Walker; Billy O'Rourke, Mr. Stewart's Helen, Mrs. Courtney.'

58   Christopher Morash, *A History of Irish Theatre 1601–2000* (Cambridge: Cambridge University Press, 2002), p. 74.

59   O'Keeffe, John, *The Wicklow Gold Mines or, the Lads from the Hills, A Comic Opera, in Two Acts, as Performed at the Theatre-Royal, Crow-Street* (Dublin: John Whitworth, 1814).

60   See Myrone, 'The Monarch of the Plain', p. 57.

61   TNA, MPHH 1/579/1-2, 'Major Fyers's Map, 1813': 'No. 1 Sketch of Dublin and its Environs shewing in yellow, the proposed Sites of the intended Ordnance Establishments, referred to in M. General Frye's report, 17th June, 1813'.

62   See Megan Norcia, 'Puzzling Empire: Early Puzzles and Dissected Maps as Imperial Heuristics', *Children's Literature*, 37 (2009), pp. 1–32; Paul Elliot and Stephen Daniels, '"No Study So Agreeable to the Youthful Mind": Geographical Education in the Georgian Grammar School', *History of Education*, 39:1 (2010), pp. 15–33; Jane Dove, 'Geographical Board Games: Promoting Tourism and Travel in Georgian England and Wales', *Journal of Tourism History*, 8:1 (2016), pp. 1–18.

63   *Wallis's tour through the United Kingdom of England, Scotland and Ireland, a new geographical game, comprehending all the cities, principal towns, rivers &c. in the British Empire*, Norman B. Leventhal Map Center Collection, Boston Public Library: Instructions, p. 24.

64   *Walker's Journey through England and Wales, a New Pastime* (London: W. & T. Darton, 1809).

65   NLI, Leinster Mss., Ms. 35,005, Letters to Lady Lucy Fitzgerald (1771–1851), f. 11, 29 May 1801, Fort George, Arthur O'Connor to Lady Lucy Fitzgerald.

66 Ibid., f. 11, 24 April 1802, Arthur O'Connor to Lady Lucy Fitzgerald.

67 Lord Cornwallis letter inserted into NLI, Ms. 35,008.

68 NLI, Leinster Mss., Ms. 35,005, f. 14, undated (c.1801). Lady Lucy Fitzgerald to Tom Paine.

69 Ibid., f. 14, undated. 'Lady Lucy's address to Irishmen.'

70 Ibid., f. 3, undated, probably Lady Sarah Napier to Lucy Fitzgerald: An 'unknown cause did not produce this Phenomena? is it not because Lyars betray themselves into the hands of their ennemies who cannot respect of? therefore all that them? this naturally causes rage in the Irish breast & --- follows – thus cruelty is added to Lying; self defence makes the English man wary cautious and shady. thus he keeps the superiority by the common laws of Nature & the clever Paddy ruins his own cause – It is evident he is formed to be Governed.'

71 Arthur O'Connor, *The Beauties of the Press, with an Appendix* (London, 1800), p. 28.

72 O'Connor, *The Beauties of the Press*, p. 30.

73 Jane Hayter Hames, *Arthur O'Connor: United Irishman* (Cork: Collins Press, 2001), p. 227.

CONCLUSION

1   For a recent exploration of how European aristocracies maintained and maintain a seductive ascendancy and particularly their manipulation of memory see Stephen Malinowski, *Nazis and Nobles: The History of a Misalliance* (Oxford: Oxford University Press, 2020): Chapter 1, 'Defining Nobility'.

2   William H. Drummond (ed.), *The Autobiography of Archibald Hamilton Rowan* (Shannon: Irish University Press, 1972), p. 291.

3   Leo Marx, 'The American Revolution and the American Landscape', delivered in Cabell Hall, the University of Virginia, Charlottesville, Virginia, 27 March 1974, Widener Library, Harvard University, p. 4.

4   Ibid.

5   Fanny Kemble, *Journal of a Residence on a Georgian Plantation in 1838–1839* (Athens: University of Georgia Press, 1984).

Bibliography

Manuscript Sources

BRITISH LIBRARY
Arthur Young Correspondence, BL Add. Ms. 35126
The King's Topographical Collection: Prints and Drawings of Ireland
Major Alexander Taylor, 'Mineralogical maps of Croaghan Mountain,
  Co. Wicklow', 1801, BL Add. Ms. 32451 F

CHÂTEAU DU BIGNON, LOIRET, FRANCE
Arthur O'Connor Mss.
Estate Maps

DUMBARTON OAKS RESEARCH LIBRARY
Humphry Repton, *Observations by H. Repton for the Improvement of
  Shrublands*, 1789

**GEORGE J. MITCHELL DEPARTMENT OF SPECIAL COLLECTIONS
& ARCHIVES, BOWDOIN COLLEGE LIBRARY, BRUNSWICK, MAINE**
Samuel Vaughan Folio

GEORGETOWN UNIVERSITY LIBRARY
James Carroll, 'James Carroll Daybook (1714-21)', Special Collections
  Division, Georgetown University Library, Washington, DC. Folder
  160–1, Oversize Box 1: Item 160

GLIN CASTLE
The Knight of Glin's transcript of 'Tour to Scotland & Ireland in the
  Years 1776 1777 … and 1801 etc. to the Honble Mrs Yorke' (widow of
  the Hon. Charles Yorke)

HISTORICAL SOCIETY PENNSYLVANIA
*Butler Plantation Papers: The Papers of Pierce Butler (1744-1822) and
  Successors.* These are available on microfilm in 13 rolls as: *Butler
  Plantation Papers: The Papers of Pierce Butler (1744–1822) and
  Successors from the Historical Society of Pennsylvania*, Adam Matthew
  Publications, 1997

MOUNT VERNON LADIES' ASSOCIATION
The Vaughan Journal, 1787 June 18–September 4, MS-4996, MVLA
*Wallis's tour through the United Kingdom of England, Scotland and Ireland,
  a new geographical game, comprehending all the cities, principal towns,
  rivers &c. in the British Empire*, Norman B. Leventhal Map Center
  Collection, Boston Public Library

NATIONAL ARCHIVES OF GREAT BRITAIN
Charles Abbot, 'A Tour through Ireland N[orth] Wales, 1792', transcribed
  by C. J. Woods, TNA PRO 30/9/23
Maps and Rebellion Mss., TNA PRO 30-9-172

NATIONAL ARCHIVES OF IRELAND
Fitzwilliam Mss.
Pembroke Mss.

NATIONAL LIBRARY OF IRELAND
Arthur Young's own extra-illustrated copy of *A Tour in Ireland; with
  general observations on the present state of that kingdom: made in the
  years 1776, 1777, and 1778. and brought down to the end of 1779*, quarto
  edn (London, printed for T. Cadell, Strand; and J. Dodsley), 1780,
  NLI, LO 10203
Fitzgerald Mss.
Lord Edward Fitzgerald's letter-book, Ms. 35,011
Joly Collection of Prints and Drawings
Leinster Papers (Ms. 606–635, Brit. Mus. Add. Mss. 30,990 P. 743,
  Ms. 13,828, Ms. 16,156, Ms. 18,862, 19,689–19,693)
Westport Mss.
William Lawrence Collection

PAUL MELLON CENTRE, LONDON
H. Miles, D. H. Solkin and G. Smith (n.d.), *Reviews of Genre
  Painting* [Information files]. C41, File 1818

WIDENER LIBRARY, HARVARD UNIVERSITY

Leo Marx, 'The American Revolution and the American landscape', delivered in Cabell Hall, University of Virginia, Charlottesville, Virginia, 27 March 1974

Digitised Collections

Founders Online, https://founders.archives.gov/documents
Freeman's Journal, 18 January 1802, http://archive.irishnewsarchive.com
Londonderry Sentinel, https://www.britishnewspaperarchive.co.uk
The Papers of Benjamin Franklin, http://franklinpapers.org
The Papers of George Washington Digital Edition, ed. Theodore J. Crackel. Charlottesville: University of Virginia Press, Rotunda, 2008, https://rotunda.upress.virginia.edu/founders/GEWN.html

Website Source

University College London, *Legacies of British Slaveownership* website

Newspapers

Dublin University Magazine
Hibernian Magazine, Or, Compendium of Entertaining Knowledge, 1783–11

Databases

American National Biography Online, https://www.anb.org
Dictionary of Irish Biography, https://www.dib.ie
Oxford Dictionary of National Biography, https://www.oxforddnb.com
Oxford English Dictionary, https://www.oed.com

Contemporary Printed Sources

Abbot, Charles (ed.), *The Diary and Correspondence of Charles Abbot, Lord Colchester*, 3 vols. London: J. Murray, 1861

Baron, Robert C. (ed.), *The Garden and Farm Books of Thomas Jefferson*. Golden, CO: Fulcrum, 1987

Blennerhasset, Thomas, *A Direction for the Plantation of Ireland*. London: Ed Allde for John Budge, 1610

Boate, Gerald, *Ireland's Natural History*. London: John Wright, 1657

Brissot de Warville, J. P., *New Travels in the United States of America Performed in 1788*. Dublin: P. Byrne, A. Grueber, W. McKenzie et. al., 1792

Caird, James, *The Plantation Scheme; or, the West of Ireland as a Field for Investment. [With a Map.]*. Edinburgh and London: W. Blackwood & Sons, 1850

Campbell, Gerard, *Edward and Pamela Fitzgerald, Being Some Account of their Lives. Compiled from the Letters of those who knew them*. London: E. Arnold, 1904

Carroll, Charles, *Dear Papa, dear Charley: the peregrinations of a revolutionary aristocrat, as told by Charles Carroll of Carrollton and his father, Charles Carroll of Annapolis, with sundry observations on bastardy, child-rearing, romance, matrimony, commerce, tobacco*. Williamsburg: Omohundro Institute, 2001

Carter, Edward C. II, John C. Van Horne and Charles E. Brownell (eds), *Latrobe's View of America, 1795–1820, Selections from the Watercolors and Sketches*. New Haven and London: Yale University Press, 1985

de Chastellux, Marquis, *Travels in North America in the Years 1780, 1781, and 1782*, 2 vols. London: G. G. J. & J. Robinson, 1787

de Crèvecœur, Michel Guillaume Jean, *Letters from an American Farmer*. London: Thomas Davies, 1782

Delany, Mary, *The Autobiography and Correspondence of Mary Granville, Mrs. Delany, ed. Lady Llanover*, 1st series, 3 vols. London: Ricard Bentley, 1861

—, *Letters from Georgian Ireland: The Correspondence of Mary Delany, 1731–68*, ed. Angélique Day. Belfast: Friar's Bush, 1991

Drummond, William H. (ed.), *The Autobiography of Archibald Hamilton Rowan*. Shannon: Irish University Press, 1972

Dublin University Magazine, 49 (Jan.–Jun. 1857)

Dunboyne, Lord, Paddy Butler (ed.), *When the States were Young: A Remarkable Collection of Letters 1784–1799 Preserved in the British Library as Additional Manuscript 16603*. www.lulu.com, 2006

Evelyn, John, *The Miscellaneous Writings of John Evelyn*, ed. William Upgott. London: Henry Colburn New Burlington St, 1825

—, *The State of France as it stood in the IXth year of this present Monarch, Lewis XIII*. London, 1652

Fitzgerald, Brian, ed., *Correspondence of Emily, Duchess of Leinster*, 3 vols. Dublin: Irish Manuscripts Commission, 1949–67

Fraser, Robert, *General View of the Agriculture and Mineralogy, Present State and Circumstances of the County Wicklow*. Dublin: Fraisberry & Campbell, 1801

Gillingham, W., *Map of George Washington's Land at Mount Vernon Fairfax Coy Virginia. As it was & As it is laid down from old Maps made by G. Washington, and from actual surveys by W. Gillingham*, lithograph by E. Sachse & Co. Sun Iron Building Baltimore, MD, 1859

Gilpin, William, *Essays on Picturesque Beauty*. London: R. Blamire, 1794

Girardin, René, *An Essay on Landscape and a Tour to Ermenonville*. London: J. Dodsley, 1982

Griffin, Appleton P. C., *A Catalogue of the Washington Collection in the Boston Athenaeum*. Cambridge, MA: The Boston Athenaeum, 1897

Hooker, John, *The first and second volumes (third volume) of [Holinshed's] Chronicles, comprising … the description and historie of England … Ireland … and … Scotland*. London: Henry Denham, 1587

Hotchkin, Rev., S. F., *The York Road, Old and New*. Philadelphia: Binder and Kelly, 1892

Howard, Joseph Jackson (ed.), *Miscellanea genealogica et heraldica*, 2nd series, vol. 4. London: Hamilton Adams, 1892

Jefferson, Thomas, *Notes on the State of Virginia, Edited and with an Introduction by William Peden*. Chapel Hill: University of North Carolina Press, 1982

Kemble, Fanny, *Journal of a Residence on a Georgian Plantation in 1838–1839*. Athens: University of Georgia Press, 1984

Kingsbury, Susan Myra (ed.), *Records of the Virginia Company*, 4 vols. Washington: United States Government Printing Office, 1906–33

de Laborde, Jean-Benjamin, *Tableaux topographiques, pittoresques, physiques, historiques, moraux, politiques, littéraires, de la Suisse*. Paris: Née & Masquelier & Ruault, 1780–8

Latrobe, Benjamin Henry, *The Journal of Latrobe, being the Notes and Sketches of an Architect, Naturalist and Traveler in the United States from 1796 to 1820*. New York: D. Appleton & Co., 1905

Lee, Jean B. (ed.), *Experiencing Mount Vernon: Eyewitness Accounts, 1784–1865*. Charlottesville and London: University of Virginia Press, 2006

Lipscomb, Terry W. (ed.), *The Letters of Pierce Butler 1790–1794: Nation Building and Enterprise in the New American Republic*. Columbia: University of South Carolina Press, 2007

Merrell, James H., *The Indians' New World Catawbas and their Neighbors from European Contact through the Era of Removal*. Chapel Hill: University of North Carolina Press, 1989

Mills, Abraham, 'A Mineralogist Account of Native Gold Lately Discovered in Ireland. In a Letter from Abraham Mills, Esq. to Sir Joseph Banks, Bart. KBPRS', *Dublin Society Transactions*, 2 (1801), pp. 454–63

—, 'Second Report on the Goldmines in the County of Wicklow', *Dublin Society Transactions*, 3 (1802), pp. 81–7

Minutes of the Council and General Court of Colonial Virginia, 1622–1632, 1670–1676, with notes and Excerpts from Original Council and General Court Records, into 1683, Now Lost, ed. H. R. McIlwaine. Richmond, VA: Virginia State Library, 1924

M'Mahon, Bernard, *The American Gardener's Calendar*. Philadelphia: Graves, 1806

Moody, T. W., R. B. McDowell and C. J. Woods (eds), *The Writings of Wolfe Tone 1763–98*, 3 vols. Oxford: Oxford University Press, 2001

Moore, Thomas, *The Life and Death of Lord Edward Fitzgerald*, 2 vols. London: Longman, Rees, Orme, Brown, Green, 1732

O'Connor, Arthur, *The Beauties of the Press, with an Appendix*. London, 1800

—, *The State of Ireland*, ed. James Livesey. Dublin: Lilliput, 1988

O'Keeffe, John, *The Wicklow Gold Mines or, the Lads from the Hills, A Comic Opera, in Two Acts, as Performed at the Theatre-Royal, Crow-Street*. Dublin: John Whitworth, 1814

Peterson, Merrill D., *Visitors to Monticello*. Charlottesville: University of Virginia Press, 1989

Proceedings of the United Irishmen of Dublin. Philadelphia: Thomas Stephens, of No. 57, South Second Street, by Jacob Johnson, & Co., 1795

Rousseau, Jean-Jacques, *Les Confessions de Jean-Jacques Rousseau*, Books 15, 16 and 17, *Collection complète des oeuvres*, Geneva, 1780–9, vol. 10, édition en ligne www.rousseauonline.ch version du 7 octobre 2012, https://www.rousseauonline.ch/pdf/rousseauonline-0075.pdf (accessed 22 October 2019)

—, *Émile*. London: Everyman, 1995

—, *Letter to Beaumont, Letters Written from the Mountain and Related Writings, The Collected Writings of Rousseau*, vol. 9, ed. Christopher Kelly and Eve Grace. Dartmouth: University Press of New England, 2001

—, *Reveries of the Solitary Walker*. London: Penguin, 1979

—, *The Social Contract*. Ware: Wordsworth, 1998

—, *The Social Contract and Discourses*. London: Everyman, 1993

Sandby, Paul, *A Collection of One Hundred and Fifty Select Views, in England, Wales, Scotland and Ireland*. London: John Boydell, 1780

—, *The Virtuosi's Museum*. London: G. Kearsly, 1778–81

Taylor, George, and Andrew Skinner, *A Map of the County of Louth*. London: Engraved by G. Terry, Paternoster Row, Cheapside, 1777

—, *Maps of the Roads of Ireland, Surveyed 1777*. London: G. Nicol, Strand; I. Murray, Fleet-Street; Dublin: W. Wilson, No. 6 Dame Street, 1778

Tone, Theobald Wolfe, *Life of Theobald Wolfe Tone … written by himself, and continued by his son; with his political writings, fragments of his diary, his mission to France: with a complete diary of his negotiations to procure the aid of the French and Batavian Republic, for the liberation of Ireland; of the expeditions of Bantry bay, the Texel, and of that wherein he fell. Narrative of his trial, defence before the court martial, and death. Ed. by his son, William Theobald Wolfe Tone; with a brief account of his own education and campaigns under the Emperor Napoleon* (Washington: Gales & Seaton, 1826)

Walker's Journey through England and Wales, a New Pastime. London: W. & T. Darton, 1809

Weld, Isaac, *Illustrations of the Scenery of Killarney and the Surrounding Country by Isaac Weld Esq. M.R.I.A. Author of Travels in North America*, London: Longman, Hurst et al., 1812

— *Travels through the States of North America, and the Provinces of Upper and Lower Canada, during the years 1795, 1796, and 1797*. 2 vols. London: John Stockdale, 1799

Weulersse, Georges, *Le mouvement physiocratique en France (de 1756 à 1770)*, 2 vols. Paris: Félix Alcan, 1910

Woods, C. J., *Travellers as Source Material for Irish Historians*, Dublin: Four Courts Press, 2009

—, (ed.) *Charles Abbot's Tour through Ireland and North Wales in 1792*. Dublin: Edmund Burke Books, 2019

Wooley, J. (ed.), *Thomas Sheridan and Jonathan Swift, the Intelligencer*. Cambridge: Cambridge University Press, 1992

Wright, G. N. (ed.), *The Annals of Agriculture and Other Useful Arts*, 46 vols. Bury St Edmunds: Arthur Young, 1784–1815

—, *A Guide to the County of Wicklow*, London: Baldwin, Cradock & Joy, 1822

Young, Arthur, *The Autobiography of Arthur Young*, ed. M. Betham-Edwards. New York: Augustus M. Kelley, 1967 [1898]

—, *Letters from His Excellency General Washington, to Arthur Young, Esq. F.R.S. containing an account of his husbandry, with a map of his farm, his opinions on various questions in agriculture, and many particulars of the rural economy of the United States*. London: B. M'Millan, 1801

—, *Rural Oeconomy or Essays on the Practical Parts of Husbandry to which is added The Rural Socrates, being the Memoirs of a Country Philosopher*, London: Becket, 1770

—, *A Six Months Tour through the North of England …*, 3 vols, Dublin: P. Wilson, J. Exshaw, H. Saunders, W. Sleater, D. Chamberlaine et. al., 1770

—, *A Tour in Ireland, 1776–1779*, 2 vols. Shannon: Irish University Press, 1970

—, *Travels in France during the Years 1787, 1788, 1789*. London: George Bell and Sons, 1906

Secondary Sources

Ackerman, James S., *The Villa: Form and Ideology of Country Houses*. London: Thames and Hudson, 1990

Andrews, J. H., 'An Early Map of Inishowen', *Long Room, Bulletin of the Friends of Trinity College, Dublin*, 7 (1973), pp. 19–25

—, 'The Maps of the Escheated Counties of Ulster, 1609–10', *Proceedings of the Royal Irish Academy: Archaeology, Culture, History, Literature*, 74 (1974)

—, *A Paper Landscape: The Ordnance Survey in Nineteenth-Century Ireland*. Dublin: Four Courts Press, 2002

—, *Plantation Acres: An Historical Study of the Irish Land Surveyor*. Omagh: Ulster Historical Foundation, 1985

Andrews, Malcolm, *The Search for the Picturesque: Landscape Aesthetics and Tourism in Britain, 1760–1800*. Aldershot: Stanford University Press, 1989

Bailey, Gauvin Alexander, *Architecture and Urbanism in the French Atlantic Empire: State, Church, and Society, 1604–1830*. Toronto: McGill University Press, 2018

Bailyn, Bernard, 'Politics and Social Structure in Virginia' in *Seventeenth-Century America: Essays in Colonial History*, ed. James Morton Smith. Chapel Hill: University of North Carolina Press, 1959

Barnard, Toby, *Improving Ireland? Projectors, Prophets and Profiteers 1641–1786*. Dublin: Four Courts Press, 2008

—, *Making the Grand Figure: Lives and Possessions in Ireland, 1641–1770*. New Haven and London: Yale University Press, 2004

Barrell, John, *The Dark Side of the Landscape: The Rural Poor in English Painting, 1730–1840*. Cambridge: Cambridge University Press, 1980

—, 'The Meeting of the Waters', *Critical Quarterly*, 60:1 (Apr. 2018)

Barringer, Tim, Gillian Forrester and Barbaro Martinez-Ruiz (eds), *Art and Emancipation in Jamaica: Isaac Mendes Belisario and his Worlds*. New Haven: Yale University Press, 2007

Bartlett, Thomas (ed.), *Life of Theobald Wolfe Tone, Compiled and Arranged by William Theobald Wolfe Tone*. Dublin: Lilliput, 1998

—, '"Masters of the Mountains": The Insurgent Careers of Joseph Holt and Michael Dwyer' in *Wicklow History & Society*, ed. Ken Hannigan and William Nolan. Dublin: Geography Publications, 1994, pp. 379–410

—, and David Dickson, Dáire Keogh and Kevin Whelan (eds), *1798: A Bicentenary Perspective*. Dublin: Four Courts Press, 2003

Bell, Malcolm, *Major Butler's Legacy: Five Generations of a Slaveholding Family*. Athens: University of Georgia Press, 1987

Bentmann, R., and M. Muller, *The Villa as Hegemonic Architecture*. Atlantic Highlands, New Jersey, and London: Humanities Press, 1992

Bermingham, Ann, *Landscape and Ideology: The English Rustic Tradition, 1740–1860*. Berkeley: University of California Press, 1986

—, 'The Simple Life: Cottages and Gainsborough's Cottage Doors' in *Land, Nation and Culture, 1740–1840: Thinking the Republic of Taste*, ed. Peter de Bolla, Nigel Leask and David Simpson. Basingstoke and New York: Palgrave Macmillan, 2005

Block, Kristen, and Jenny Shaw, 'Subjects without an Empire: The Irish in the Early Modern Caribbean', *Past and Present*, 210:1 (2011), pp. 33–60

de Bolla, Peter, Nigel Leask and David Simpson (eds), *Land, Nation and Culture, 1740–1840: Thinking the Republic of Taste*. Basingstoke and New York: Palgrave Macmillan, 2005

Bonehill, John, and Geoff Quilley, *Conflicting Visions: War and Visual Culture in Britain and France c. 1700–1830*. Abingdon: Routledge, 2005

Boylan, Lena, 'Kildare Lodge. Lord Edward Fitzgerald's House', *Journal of the County Kildare Archaeological Society*, 16:1 (1977–8), pp. 26–35

Breen, T. H., *Tobacco Culture: The Mentality of the Great Tidewater Planters on the Eve of Revolution*. Princeton: Princeton University Press, 2001

Brewer, Holly, 'Entailing Aristocracy in Colonial Virginia: "Ancient Feudal Restraints" and Revolutionary Reform', *William and Mary Quarterly*, 3rd series, 54:2 (Apr. 1997)

Bric, Maurice J., *Ireland, Philadelphia and the Re-invention of America, 1760–1800*. Dublin: Four Courts Press, 2008

Brinton, Crane, *The Anatomy of Revolution: Towards a Poetics of Experience*. London: Vintage, 1965

Bruckner, Martin, *The Geographic Revolution in Early America: Maps, Literacy and National Identity*. Chapel Hill: University of North Carolina Press, 2006

Burke, Peter, *Venice and Amsterdam: A Study of Seventeenth-century Élites*. Cambridge: Polity Press, 1994

Burnard, Trevor, *Planters, Merchants, and Slaves: Plantation Societies in British America, 1650–1820*. Chicago: University of Chicago Press, 2015

—, and John Garrigus, *The Plantation Machine: Atlantic Capitalism in French Saint-Domingue and British Jamaica*. Philadelphia: University of Pennsylvania Press, 2016

Casid, Jill H., *Sowing Empire: Landscape and Colonization*. Minneapolis and London: University of Minnesota Press, 2005

Chambers, Liam, *Rebellion in Kildare 1790–1803*. Dublin: Four Courts Press, 1998

Clark, Robert, 'The Absent Landscape of America's Eighteenth Century' in *Views of American Landscapes*, ed. Mick Gidley and Robert Lawson. Cambridge: Cambridge University Press, 1989

Clergeot, Pierre, 'The Origins of the French General Cadastre', FIG (International Federation of Surveyors) Working Week 2003, Paris, France, 13–17 April 2003, pp. 1–17, https://www.fig.net/resources/proceedings/fig_proceedings/fig_2003/PS_1/PS1_2_Clergeot.pdf (accessed 26 October 2022)

Coclanis, Peter A., *The Shadow of a Dream: Economic Life and Death in the South Carolina Low Country, 1670–1920*. New York: Oxford University Press, 1989

Cohen, Jeffrey A., 'Place, Time, and Architecture: Materialized Memory and the Moment of Latrobe's Waln House' in *Classical Splendor: Painted Furniture for a Grand Philadelphia House*, ed. Alexandra Alevizatos Kirtley and Peggy A. Olley. New Haven and London: Yale University Press, 2016, pp. 14–35

Colley, Linda, *Britons: Forging the Nation 1707–1837*. London: Pimlico, 2003

Connolly, Sean, *Religion, Law, and Power: The Making of Protestant Ireland 1660–1760*. Oxford: Oxford University Press, 1992

Copley, Stephen, and Peter Garside (eds), *The Politics of the Picturesque: Literature, Landscape and Aesthetics since 1770*. Cambridge: Cambridge University Press, 1994

Corbin, Alain, *The Lure of the Sea: The Discovery of the Seaside in the Western World 1750–1840*. London: Penguin, 1994

Cosgrove, Denis, and Stephen Daniels (eds), *The Iconography of Landscape*. Cambridge: Cambridge University Press, 1988

Cranston, Maurice Jean-Jacques, *The Early Life and Work of Jean-Jacques Rousseau 1712–1754*. Chicago: University of Chicago Press, 1982

Critchley, Martin (ed.), *Exploring the Mining Heritage of County Wicklow*. Wicklow: Wicklow County Council, 2008

Crookshank, Anne, and Desmond FitzGerald, the Knight of Glin, *Ireland's Painters*. New Haven and London: Yale University Press, 2002

Cullen, Louis, 'Politics and Rebellion: Wicklow in the 1790s' in *Wicklow History & Society*, ed. Ken Hannigan and William Nolan. Dublin: Geography Publications, 1994, pp. 429–30

—, John Shovlin and Thomas M. Truxes (eds), *The Bordeaux-Dublin Letters 1757: Correspondence of an Irish Community Abroad*. Oxford: Oxford University Press, 2013

Curl, James Stevens, *The Honourable the Irish Society and the Plantation of Ulster, 1608–2000*. Chichester: Phillimore & Co. Ltd, 2000

—, *The Londonderry Plantation, 1609–1914: The History, Architecture and Planning of the Estates of the City of London and Its Livery Companies in Ulster*. Chichester: Phillimore & Co. Ltd, 1986

Curtin, Philip D., *The Rise and Fall of the Plantation Complex*. Cambridge: Cambridge University Press, 1998

Daniels, Stephen, *Fields of Vision: Landscape Imagery and National Identity in England and the United States*. Princeton: Princeton University Press, 1993

—, and John Bonehill, 'Designs on the Landscape: Paul and Thomas Sandby in North Britain', *Oxford Art Journal*, 40:2 (Aug. 2017), pp. 223–48

Davis, David Brion, *Inhuman Bondage: The Rise and Fall of Slavery in the New World*, Oxford: Oxford University Press, 2006

Dickson, David, *Old World Colony: Cork and South Munster 1630–1830*. Cork: Cork University Press, 2005

Doar, David, 'Rice and Rice Planting in the South Carolina Low Country' in *Contributions from the Charleston Museum*, vol. 8, ed. E. Milby Burton. Charleston: Charleston Museum, 1936

Dooley, Terence, *Sources for the History of Landed Estates in Ireland*. Dublin: Irish Academic Press, 2000

Dove, Jane, 'Geographical Board Games: Promoting Tourism and Travel in Georgian England and Wales', *Journal of Tourism History*, 8:1 (2016), pp. 1–18

Draper, Nick, '"Dependent on Precarious Subsistences": Ireland's Slave-Owners at the Time of Emancipation', *Britain and the World*, 6:2 (Sept. 2013), pp. 220–42

Dunn, Richard, *A Tale of Two Plantations: Slave Life and Labor in Jamaica and Virginia*. Cambridge and London: Harvard University Press, 2014

Durey, Michael, 'Thomas Paine's Apostles: Radical Emigrés and the Triumph of Jeffersonian Republicanism', *William and Mary Quarterly*, 3rd series, 44:4 (Oct. 1987), pp. 661–88

Edelson, S. Max, *Plantation Enterprise in Colonial South Carolina*. Cambridge: Harvard University Press, 2011

Elliot, Paul, and Stephen Daniels, '"No Study So Agreeable to the Youthful Mind": Geographical Education in the Georgian Grammar School', *History of Education*, 39:1 (2010), pp. 15–33

Elliott, Marianne, *Partners in Revolution: The United Irishmen and France*. New Haven and London: Yale University Press, 1990

—, *Wolfe Tone*. Liverpool: Liverpool University Press, 2012

Ewan, Joseph, 'Bernard M'Mahon (c.1775–1816), Pioneer Philadelphia Nurseryman, and his American Gardener's Calendar', *Journal of the Society for the Bibliography of Natural History*, 3, pt 7 (Oct. 1960)

Ferradou, Mathieu, '"Adresse des Anglais, des Ecossais et des Irlandais résidans et domiciliés à Paris" to the Convention, presented on 25 November 1792, Archives Nationales, Pierrefitte-sur-Seine', *Annales historiques de la révolution Francaise*, 382 (Oct.–Dec. 2015), pp. 123–43, https://journals.openedition.org/ahrf/13560 (accessed 3 September 2019)

Finch, Jonathan, 'Three Men in a Boat: Biographies and Narrative in the Historic Landscape', *Landscape Research*, 33:5 (Oct. 2008), pp. 511–30

Finch, J. C., 'A Transatlantic Dialogue: The Estate Landscape in Britain, the Caribbean, and North America in the Eighteenth Century', *Huntington Library Quarterly*, 84:3 (Autumn 2021), pp. 491–515

Forrest, Alan, and Peter Jones (eds), *Reshaping France: Town, Country and Region during the French Revolution*. Manchester: Manchester University Press, 1991

Foster, R. F., *Vivid Faces: The Revolutionary Generation in Ireland 1890–1923*. London: Penguin, 2014

Fraser, T. G., 'The Siege: Its History and Legacy, 1688–1889' in *Derry and Londonderry: History and Society*, ed. G. O'Brien. Dublin: Geography Publications, 1999

Furet, François, *Interpreting the French Revolution*. Cambridge: Cambridge University Press, 1981

Gahan, Daniel, '"Journey after My Own Heart": Lord Edward Fitzgerald in America, 1788–90', *New Hibernia Review/Iris Éireannach Nua*, 8:2 (Summer 2004), pp. 85–105

Genovese, Eugene G., *Roll, Jordan Roll: The World the Slaves Made*. New York: Pantheon Books, 1974

Groth, A. J. (ed.), *Revolution and Revolutionary Change*. Aldershot: Dartmouth, 1996

Grover, Richard, 'Why Does the United Kingdom not have a Cadastre – and Does it Matter', FIG Commission, Annual Meeting 2008, Open Symposium on Environment and Land Administration, Verona, Italy, 11–12 September 2008, https://www.fig.net/resources/proceedings/2008/verona_am_2008_comm7/papers/12_sept/7_2_grover.pdf (accessed 14 May 2020)

Hames, Jane Hayter, *Arthur O'Connor: United Irishman*. Cork: Collins Press, 2001

Hamilton, Andrew, 'Benjamin Vaughan on Commerce and International Harmony in the Eighteenth Century' in *Sociability and Cosmopolitanism: Social Bonds on the Fringes of the Enlightenment World*, ed. Scott Breuniger and David Burrow. Abingdon: Routledge, 2016, pp. 101–20

Harvey, Karen, *The Bellews of Mounts Bellew*. Dublin: Four Courts Press, 1998

Heath, Barbara J., *Hidden Lives: The Archaeology of Slave Life at Thomas Jefferson's Poplar Forest*. Charlottesville: University of Virginia Press, 1999

Hicks, Dan, '"Material Improvements": The Archaeology of Estate Landscapes in the British Leeward Islands, 1713–1838' in *Estate Landscapes: Design, Improvement and Power in the Post-Medieval Landscape*, ed. Jonathan Finch and Kate Giles. Woodbridge: Boydell and Brewer, 2008

Higman, B. W., *Jamaica Surveyed: Plantation Maps and Plans of the Eighteenth and Nineteenth Centuries*. Barbados, Jamaica, Trinidad and Tobago: University of West Indies Press, 2001

—, 'The Sugar Revolution', *Economic History Review*, 53:2 (2000), pp. 213–36

Hilliard, S. B., 'Antebellum Tidewater Rice Culture in South Carolina and Georgia' in *European Settlement and Development in North America: Essays on Geographical Change in Honour and Memory of Andrew Hill Clark*, ed. J. R. Gibson. Toronto: University of Toronto Press, 1978

Hoffman, Ronald, *Princes of Ireland, Planters of Maryland: A Carroll Saga, 1500–1782*. Chapel Hill and London: University of North Carolina Press, 2002

—, Mechel Sobel and Fredrika J. Teute (eds), *Through a Glass Darkly: Reflections on Personal Identity in Early America*. Chapel Hill and London: University of North Carolina Press, 1997

Horner, Arnold, 'Carton, Co. Kildare, A Case Study in the Making of an Irish Demesne', *Quarterly Bulletin of the Irish Georgian Society*, 18:2 and 18:3 (Apr.–Sept. 1975), pp. 45–101

Horning, Audrey, *Ireland in the Virginian Sea: Colonialism in the British Atlantic*. Chapel Hill: University of North Carolina Press, 2013

Hughes, Sarah S., *Surveyors and Statesmen: Land Measuring in Colonial Virginia*. Virginia: Virginia Surveyors Foundation, 1979

Hunt, John Dixon, *The Picturesque Garden in Europe*. London: Thames and Hudson, 2004

Hunt, Lynn, *Politics, Culture, and Class in the French Revolution*. Oakland: University of California Press, 2004

Isaac, Rhys, *Landon Carter's Uneasy Kingdom: Revolution and Rebellion on a Virginia Plantation*. Oxford: Oxford University Press, 2004

—, *The Transformation of Virginia 1740–1790*. Williamsburg: University of North Carolina Press, 1982

Johnston, E. B., *Visitors' Guide to Mount Vernon*. Washington DC: Gibson Brothers, 1892

Johnstone, Paul H., 'The Rural Socrates', *Journal of the History of Ideas*, 5:2 (Apr. 1944)

Johnstone, Ruth, 'Lady Louisa Conolly's Print Room at Castletown' in *Castletown: Decorative Arts*. Dublin: Office of Public Works, 2011, pp. 67–77

Kain, Roger J. P., and Elizabeth Baigent, *The Cadastral Map in the Service of the State*. Chicago: Chicago University Press, 1992

Kelly, James, *Sir Edward Newenham, MP, 1734–1814: Defender of the Protestant Constitution*. Dublin: Four Courts Press, 2004

Kiberd, Declan, Introduction to *Ulysses* by James Joyce. London: Penguin, 2000

Kolchin, Peter, *Unfree Labor: American Slavery and Russian Serfdom*. Cambridge and London: Belknap, Harvard University Press, 1987

Kriz, Kay Dian, *Slavery, Sugar and the Culture of Refinement*. New Haven and London: Yale University Press, 2008

Lacy, Allen, 'Bernard M'Mahon's Declaration of Independence' in *Farther Afield: A Gardener's Excursions*. New York: Farar, Straus and Giroux, 1986

Laffan, William, 'Thomas Sautelle Roberts' in *Art and Architecture of Ireland, Volume 2: Painting*, ed. Nicola Figgis. New Haven and London: Yale University Press, 2015, pp. 433–5

Laffan, William, and Brendan Rooney, *Thomas Roberts 1748–1777: Landscape and Patronage in Eighteenth-Century Ireland*. Tralee and Dublin: Churchill House Press, 2009

Leask, Nigel, *Stepping Westward, Writing the Highland Tour c.1720–1830*. Oxford: Oxford University Press, 2020

—, and David Simpson (eds), *Land, Nation and Culture, 1740–1840: Thinking the Republic of Taste*. Hampshire and New York: Palgrave Macmillan, 2005

Leask, N., J. Bonehill and A. Dulau (eds), *Old Ways and New Roads: Travels in Scotland, c.1720–1830*. Edinburgh: Birlinn, 2021

Lees, William B., 'The Historical Development of Limerick Plantation, a Tidewater Rice Plantation in Berkeley County, South Carolina, 1683–1945', *South Carolina Historical Magazine*, 82:1 (Jan. 1981), pp. 44–62

Leith, James A., *Space and Revolution: Projects for Monuments, Squares and Public Buildings in France 1789–1799*. Montreal: McGill University Press, 1991

Liebersohn, Harry, *Aristocratic Encounters: European Travelers and North American Indians*. Cambridge: Cambridge University Press, 1998

Loeber, Rolf, *The Geography and Practice of English Colonisation in Ireland from 1534–1609*, Athlone: Group for the Study of Irish Historic Settlements, 1991

—, David Dickson and Alan Smyth, 'Journal of a Tour to Dublin and the Counties of Dublin and Meath in 1699', *Analecta Hibernica*, 43 (2012), pp. 47–67

Lucey, Conor, 'Owen Biddle and Philadelphia's Real Estate Market, 1798–1806', *Journal of the Society of Architectural Historians*, 75:1 (2016), pp. 25–47

Mack, Angela D., and Stephen G. Hoffus (eds), *Landscape of Slavery: The Plantation in American Art*. Columbia: University of South Carolina Press, 2008

Malcomson, A. P. W., 'Absenteeism in Eighteenth-Century Ireland', *Irish Economic and Social History*, 1 (1974), pp. 13–35

Malinowski, Stephen, *Nazis and Nobles: The History of a Misalliance*. Oxford: Oxford University Press, 2020

Manca, Joseph, *George Washington's Eye: Landscape, Architecture and Design at Mount Vernon*. Baltimore: Johns Hopkins University Press, 2012

Martin, Peter, *The Pleasure Gardens of Virginia: From Jamestown to Jefferson*. Princeton: Princeton University Press, 1991

McClellan, James, *Colonialism and Science: Saint Domingue in the Old Régime*. Chicago: University of Chicago Press, 2010

Mitchell, W. J. T., *Landscape and Power*. Chicago: University of Chicago Press, 1994

Morash, Christopher, *A History of Irish Theatre 1601–2000*. Cambridge: Cambridge University Press, 2002

Morgan, Edmund S., *American Slavery, American Freedom: The Ordeal of Colonial Virginia*. New York: W.W. Norton, 1975

—, 'Slavery and Freedom: The American Paradox', *Journal of American History*, 59:1 (Jun., 1972), pp. 5–29

Morgan, Philip D., *Slave Counterpoint: Black Culture in the Eighteenth-Century Chesapeake and Low Country*. Chapel Hill and London: University of North Carolina Press, 1998

Morley, Vincent, *Irish Opinion and the American Revolution, 1760–1783*. Cambridge: Cambridge University Press, 2002

Mukerji, Chandra, *Territorial Ambitions and the Gardens of Versailles*. Cambridge: Cambridge University Press, 1997

Nelson, Louis P., *Architecture and Empire in Jamaica*. New Haven and London: Yale University Press, 2016

Nicolson, Marjorie Hope, *Mountain Gloom and Mountain Glory: The Development of the Aesthetics of the Infinite*. Seattle and London: University of Washington Press, 1997

Norcia, Megan, 'Puzzling Empire: Early Puzzles and Dissected Maps as Imperial Heuristics', *Children's Literature*, 37 (2009), pp. 1–32

Ó Dónaill, Niall, *Foclóir Gaeilge-Béarla*. Dublin: Oifig an tSoláthair: Foilseacháin Rialtais, 1977

O'Donnell, Ruan, *The Rebellion in Wicklow 1798*. Dublin: Irish Academic Press, 1998

—, *Aftermath: Post-Rebellion Insurgency in Wicklow 1799–1803*. Dublin: Irish Academic Press, 2000

O'Kane, Finola, 'An Absentee Family's Suburban Demesne: The Making of Mount Merrion, Co. Dublin' in *The Irish Country House*, ed. Terry Dooley. Dublin: Four Courts Press, 2011

—, 'Arthur Young's Published and Unpublished Illustrations for "A Tour in Ireland 1776–1779"', *Irish Architectural and Decorative Studies*, 19. Kinsale: Gandon, 2017, pp. 118–60

—, 'Arthur Young's Study of Landscape Gardens and Parks for his Publication "A Tour in Ireland 1776–1779"', *Journal of Scottish Thought*, 9 (2017), pp. 110–24

—, '"Bargains in View": The Fitzwilliam Family's Development of Merrion Square, Dublin' in *The Eighteenth-Century Dublin Townhouse*, ed. Christine Casey. Dublin: Four Courts Press, 2010

—, 'A Cabin and not a Cottage – The Architectural Embodiment of the Irish Nation' in *Ireland in the European Eye*, ed. B. Migge and G. Hofter. Dublin: The Royal Irish Academy, 2019, pp. 259–83

—, 'Dublin's Fitzwilliam Estate: A Hidden Landscape of Discovery, Catholic Agency and Egalitarian Suburban Space', *Eighteenth-Century Ireland / Iris an dá chultúr*, 31 (2016), pp. 94–118

—, 'Green Lines of Power: The Apprentice Boys' Trees and the Walls of Derry/Londonderry' in *The Politics of Street Trees*, ed. Camilla Allen and Jan Woudstra. Abingdon: Routledge, 2022, pp. 43–54

—, *Ireland and the Picturesque: Design, Landscape Painting and Tourism in Ireland 1700–1840*. New Haven and London: Yale University Press, 2013

—, 'The Irish-Jamaican Plantation of Kelly's Pen, St. Dorothy's Parish, Jamaica and the Rare 1749 Inventory of its Slaves, Stock and Household Goods', *Caribbean Quarterly*, vol. 64. Barbados, Jamaica, Trinidad and Tobago: University of the West Indies Press, 2018

—, *Landscape Design in Eighteenth-Century Ireland: Mixing Foreign Trees with the Natives*. Cork: Cork University Press, 2004

—, 'The Limits of Brown's Landscape: Translations of the Landscape Garden into Ireland', Capability Brown 300 Year Anniversary Special Issue, *Garden History, Journal of the Garden History Society*, 44:2 (2016)

—, 'Military Memory Manoeuvers in Dublin's Phoenix Park 1775–1820' in *Military Landscapes*, ed. A. Tchikine and J. D. Davis. Cambridge: Harvard University Press, 2021, pp. 311–29

—, 'The Military Roads of County Wicklow', 2017, https://www.bl.uk/picturing-places/articles (accessed 6 April 2017)

—, 'Moving Landscapes to Saint-Domingue, Jamaica and Ireland: Plantation Design, National Identity and the Colonial Picturesque', *Huntington Library Quarterly*, 84:3 (2022), pp. 561–88

—, 'Route Reversal: The Design Consequences of Travelling in Contrary Motion in Eighteenth-Century Europe', *Studies in the History of Gardens and Designed Landscapes: An International Quarterly*, 35:4 (2015), pp. 156–65

—, 'Spatial Subversion in Eighteenth-Century Dublin: The Suburban Design Practices of the Fitzwilliam Estate', *Built Environment*, 41:4 (2015), pp. 463–76

—, 'Views of Victory: The Landscapes of the Battle of the Boyne' in *Landscapes of Authority in the Modern World*, ed. Stephen Whiteman. Philadelphia: University of Pennsylvania Press (forthcoming)

—, 'What's in a Name? The Connected Histories of Belfield, Co. Dublin and Belfield, St. Mary's, Jamaica' in *Making Belfield: Space and Place at UCD*, ed. F. O'Kane and E. Rowley. Dublin: University College Dublin Press, 2020, pp. 150–61

—, *William Ashford's Mount Merrion: The Absent Point of View*. Fenit, Co. Kerry: Churchill House Press, 2012

—, and Mary-Ann Constantine, 'Strategies of the Picturesque: Romantic-Era Tours of Wales and Ireland' in *Old Ways and New Roads: Travels in Scotland, c. 1720–1830*, ed. N. Leask, J. Bonehill and A. Dulau. Edinburgh: Birlinn, 2021

—, and Ciaran O'Neill (eds), *Ireland, Slavery and the Caribbean: Interdisciplinary Perspectives 1700–1830*. Manchester: Manchester University Press, 2023

O'Keeffe, Peter J., *Alexander Taylor's Roadworks in Ireland, 1780–1827*. Dublin: Institute of Asphalt Technology, Irish Branch, 1996

O'Malley, Therese, *Keywords in American Landscape Design*. New Haven and London: Yale University Press, 2010

—, 'Landscape Gardening in the Early National Period' in *View and Visions: American Landscape before 1830*, ed. Edward J. Nygren. Washington DC: The Corcoran Gallery of Art, 1986

O'Neill, T. P., 'Discoverers and Discoveries: The Penal Laws and Dublin Property', *Dublin Historical Record*, 37 (1983–4), pp. 2–13

Ozouf, Mona, *Festivals and the French Revolution*. Cambridge: Harvard University Press, 1988

Parent, Anthony S. Jr., *Foul Means: The Formation of a Slave Society in Virginia, 1660–1740*. Chapel Hill: University of North Carolina Press, 2003

Parker, David (ed.), *Revolutions and the Revolutionary Tradition in the West, 1560–1991*. Abingdon: Routledge, 2000

Peterson, Merrill D., *Visitors to Monticello*. Charlottesville: University of Virginia Press, 1989

Picon, Antoine, *French Architects and Engineers in the Age of Enlightenment*. Cambridge: Cambridge University Press, 1992

Pocock, J. C. A., *Three British Revolutions, 1641, 1688, 1776*. Princeton: Princeton University Press, 1980

Pogue, Dennis J., 'Mount Vernon: Transformation of an Eighteenth-Century Plantation System' in *Historical Archaeology of the Chesapeake*, ed. Paul A. Shackel and Barbara Little. Washington DC: Smithsonian, 1994

Polasky, Janet, *Revolutions Without Borders, The Call to Liberty in the Atlantic World*. New Haven and London: Yale University Press, 2015

Quilley, Geoff, and Kay Dian Kriz (eds), *An Economy of Colour: Visual Culture and the North Atlantic World, 1660–1830*. Manchester: Manchester University Press, 2003

Rhys, Isaac, *Landon Carter's Uneasy Kingdom: Revolution and Rebellion on a Virginia Plantation*. Oxford: Oxford University Press, 2004

—, *The Transformation of Virginia 1740–1790*. Williamsburg: University of North Carolina Press, 1982

Rodgers, Nini, *Ireland, Slavery and Anti-Slavery: 1612–1865*. London: Palgrave Macmillan, 2007

Roebuck, P., 'The Making of an Ulster Great Estate: The Chichesters, Barons of Belfast and Viscounts of Carrickfergus, 1599–1648', *Proceedings of the Royal Irish Academy*, 79C (1979)

Said, Edward W., *Culture and Imperialism*. New York: Vintage, 1994

Sarudy, Barbara Wells, *Gardens and Gardening in the Chesapeake, 1700–1805*. Baltimore and London: Johns Hopkins Press, 1998

Schama, Simon, *Landscape and Memory*. London: Vintage, 1996

—, *Citizens: A Chronicle of the French Revolution*. London: Penguin, 1989

Scott, Julius S., *The Common Wind: Afro-American Currents in the Age of the Haitian Revolution*. London and New York: Verso, 2018

Seymour, Susanne, Stephen Daniels and Charles Watkins, 'Estate and Empire: Sir George Cornwall's Management of Moccas, Herefordshire and La Taste, Grenada, 1771–1819', *Journal of Historical Geography*, 24:3 (1998), pp. 313–51

Sheehan, Michael S., and Lauren B. Sickels-Taves, 'Vernacular Building Materials and the Factors Conditioning their Use: Tabby, A Case Study', *Material Culture*, 34:2 (Fall 2002), pp. 16–28

Sheppard, John H., *Reminiscences of the Vaughan Family and More Particularly of Benjamin Vaughan, LLD*. Boston: David Clapp & Son, 1865

Smyth, William, *Map-Making, Landscapes and Memory: A Geography of Colonial and Early Modern Ireland, c.1530–1750*. Cork: Cork University Press, 2006

Sobel, Mechal, *The World They Made Together: Black and White Values in Eighteenth-Century Virginia*. Princeton: Princeton University Press, 1989

Stetson, Sarah Pattee, 'American Garden Books, Transplanted and Native, Before 1807', *William and Mary Quarterly*, 3rd series, 3:3 (Jul. 1946), pp. 343–69

Stilgoe, John R., *Common Landscape of America, 1580 to 1845*. New Haven and London: Yale University Press, 1982

Stone, Lawrence, *The Crisis of the Aristocracy, 1568–1641*. Oxford: Clarendon Press, 1965

Strickland, Walter G., *A Dictionary of Irish Artists*, 2 vols. Shannon and New York: Irish University Press and Hacker, 1968 [Dublin and London: Maunsell and Co., 1913]

Taylor-Leduc, Susan, 'Luxury in the Garden: La Nouvelle Héloïse Considered', *Studies in the History of Gardens and Designed Landscapes: An International Quarterly*, 19:1 (1999)

Thomas, Avril, *Derry-Londonderry, Irish Historic Towns Atlas No. 15*. Dublin: Royal Irish Academy, 2005

Thomas, Sarah, *Witnessing Slavery – Art and Travel in the Age of Abolition*. New Haven and London: Yale University Press, 2019

Upton, Dell, 'White and Black Landscapes in Eighteenth-Century Virginia', *Places*, 2:2 (1984), pp. 59–72

—, 'Architectural History or Landscape History?', *Journal of Architectural Education*, 44:4 (Aug., 1991), pp. 195–9

VanHuss, Laura Kilcer (ed.), *Charting the Plantation Landscape from Natchez to New Orleans*. Baton Rouge: Louisiana State University Press, 2021

Vanstory, Burnette, *Georgia's Land of the Golden Isles*. Athens: University of Georgia Press, 1981

Vaughan-Arbuckle, C. L., 'A Tipperary Farmer and Waterford Tradesman of Two Centuries Ago from Materials Furnished by Capt. C. L. Vaughan-Arbuckle', *Journal of the Waterford and South-East of Ireland Archaeological Society* (1st quarter, Jan. to Mar. 1902), pp. 80–9

Vlach, John Michael, *Back of the Big House: The Architecture of Plantation Slavery*. Chapel Hill and London: University of North Carolina Press, 1993

—, *The Planter's Prospect: Privilege and Slavery in Plantation Art*. Chapel Hill and London: The University of North Carolina Press, 2002

Wall, Charles C., 'Notes on the Early History of Mount Vernon', *William and Mary Quarterly*, 2:2, 1945, pp. 173–90

Walsh, Lorena S., *From Calabar to Carter's Grove: The History of a Virginia Slave Community*. Charlottesville and London: University Press of Virginia, 1997

—, 'Land, Landlord, and Leaseholder: Estate Management and Tenant Fortunes in Southern Maryland, 1642–1820', *Agricultural History*, 59:3 (Jul., 1985), pp. 373–96

—, *Motives of Honor, Pleasure, and Profit: Plantation Management in the Colonial Chesapeake, 1607–1763*. Chapel Hill: University of North Carolina Press, 2010

'Washington's Map of Mount Vernon', *Huntingdon Library Quarterly*, 17:2 (Feb. 1954)

Weber, Paul, *On The Road to Rebellion: The United Irishmen and Hamburg 1796–1803*. Dublin: Four Courts Press, 1997

Wecter, Dixon, 'Benjamin Franklin and an Irish "Enthusiast"', *Huntington Library Quarterly*, 4 (1941), pp. 205–34

Wells, Camille, 'The Eighteenth-Century Landscape', *Northern Neck of Virginia Historical Magazine*, 37 (1987)

Whelan, Kevin, *The Fellowship of Freedom: The United Irishmen and 1798* (Companion Volume to the Bicentenary Exhibition by The National Library and The National Museum of Ireland at Collins Barracks, Dublin 1998). Cork: Cork University Press, 1998

Wick, Gabriel, *Paysage des Lumières: le jardin anglais du château de La Roche-Guyon*. Paris: Artlys, 2014

Wiebenson, Dora, *The Picturesque Garden in France*. Princeton: Princeton University Press, 1978

Williamson, Tom, and Liz Bellamy, *Property and Landscape: A Social History of Land Ownership and the English Countryside*. London: George Philip, 1987

Wilson, David A., *United Irishmen, United States: Immigrant Radicals in the Early Republic*. Ithaca and London: Cornell University Press, 1998

Wright, Jonathan Jeffrey, *An Ulster Slave Owner in the Revolutionary Atlantic: The Life and Letters of John Black*. Dublin: Four Courts Press, 2018

Wulf, Andrea, *Founding Gardeners: The Revolutionary Generation, Nature, and the Shaping of the American Nation*. New York: Vintage, 2011

Young, Amy Isabel, *Three Hundred Years in Inishowen: Being More Particularly an Account of the Family of Young of Culdaff, With Short Accounts of Many Other Families Connected With Them During That Period*. Belfast: McCaw, Stevenson & Orr, 1929

Unpublished Theses

Burke, Claire, 'The Architectural Legacy of Sir Arthur Chichester's Plantation of Inishowen'. MUBC thesis, University College Dublin, 2017

Flanagan, Charles M., 'The Sweets of Independence: A Reading of the "James Carroll Daybook, 1714–21"'. PhD thesis, University of Maryland, 2005

Mather, Laura, 'The Life and Networks of Pamela Fitzgerald, 1773-1831'. MA thesis, University of Limerick, 2017

Singleton, Theresa A., 'The Archaeology of Afro-American Slavery in Coastal Georgia: A Regional Perception of Slave Household and Community Patterns'. PhD thesis, University of Florida, 1980

Exhibition Catalogues

Adamson, Jeremy Elwell, *Niagara, Two Centuries of Changing Attitudes, 1697–1901*, The Corcoran Gallery of Art, Washington DC, 1985

Benes, Peter, *New England Prospect: A Loan Exhibition of Maps at the Currier Gallery of Art*. Manchester, NH: Boston University for the Dublin Seminar for New England Folklife, 1981

Bonehill, John, and Stephen Daniels (eds), *Paul Sandby: Picturing Britain*, London: Royal Academy of Arts, 2010

Buisseret, David, *Rural Images: The Estate Plan in the Old and New Worlds. A Cartographic Exhibit at The Newberry Library on the Occasion of the Ninth Series of Kenneth Nebenzahl Jr., Lectures in the History of Cartography*. Chicago: The Newberry Library, 1988

Elder, William Voss III, 'The Carroll House in Annapolis and Doughoregan Manor' in *'Anywhere So Long As There Be Freedom', Charles Carroll of Carrollton, His Family & His Maryland*, ed. Ann C. Van Devanter. Baltimore: The Baltimore Museum of Art, 1975

Laffan, William, and Christopher Monkhouse (eds), *Ireland: Crossroads of Art and Design, 1690–1840*. New Haven and London: The Art Institute of Chicago and Yale University Press

Myrone, Felicity, 'The Monarch of the Plain: Paul Sandby and Topography' in *Paul Sandby: Picturing Britain*, ed. John Bonehill and Stephen Daniels. London: Royal Academy of Arts, 2009

O'Kane, Finola, 'Ireland – A New Geographical Pastime?' in Art Institute of Chicago, *Ireland: Crossroads of Art and Design, 1690–1840*, ed. William Laffan and Chistopher Monkhouse. New Haven and London: Yale University Press, 2015

Van Devanter, Ann C., *'Anywhere So Long As There Be Freedom', Charles Carroll of Carrollton, His Family & His Maryland*. Baltimore: The Baltimore Museum of Art, 1975

Index